AUTONOMY IN EDUCATION

Yearbook of the European Association for Education Law and Policy

Volume 3

The titles published in this series are listed at the end of this volume.

Autonomy in Education

Yearbook of the European Association for Educational Law and Policy

Edited by

Walter Berka,
Jan De Groof

and

Hilde Penneman

This publication is sponsored by

S.A. PHILIP MORRIS BELGIUM N.V.

This book is published with the support of the Austrian Government

KLUWER LAW INTERNATIONAL
THE HAGUE / LONDON / BOSTON

A C.I.P. Catalogue record for this book is available from the Library of Congress.

ISSN 1387-2664
ISBN 90-411-1311-8

Published by Kluwer Law International,
P.O. Box 85889, 2508 CN The Hague, The Netherlands.

Sold and distributed in North, Central and South America
by Kluwer Law International,
675 Massachusetts Avenue, Cambridge MA 02139, U.S.A.

In all other countries, sold and distributed
by Kluwer Law International, Distribution Centre,
P.O. Box 322, 3300 AH Dordrecht, The Netherlands.

Printed on acid-free paper

Table of Contents

APPROACH OF ISSUES

COUNTRY REPORTS

JAN DE GROOF

Preface

1. Most international reports on education refer to the push towards greater autonomy as one of the three main trends in every modern educational policy, alongside quality assurance and quality evaluation techniques and the need to devote attention to special – and often disadvantaged – target groups.

It is, however, difficult to derive a unified concept of 'autonomy' from the comparative indicators which are published on a regular basis, and it has emerged that there are significant differences depending on the specific area and the administrative organization of education in the country in question.[1] It does not even seem to be a contradiction for the increasing delegation of authority to the local education level to be associated with increasing powers being taken by the central authority – as, for example in relation to steering educational processes, defining the national curriculum framework, or in cases where there is output control by the government.

Autonomy is, in that case, considered to be the best precondition for an effective response to changing needs in terms of knowledge, skills and qualifications.[2] The OCDE *Reviews of National Policies for Education* have also been referring to the ever-present option of decentralizing administrative responsibilities and increased school autonomy since the early 1980s. With regard to higher education, independence should even be one of the key characteristics of the administration and policy of a university or college.[3]

The degree of autonomy therefore seems to have a direct influence on key

[1] e.g. the European Commission booklet *Key data on education in the European Union 1997* (16 ** areas of school decisions during the year 1995–1996) and, of course OCDE, *Education at a Glance – 1998.*

[2] e.g. by the White Paper on Education and Training: *Teaching and Learning – Towards the Learning Society.*

[3] De Groof, J., Neave, G. and Svec, J., *Democracy and Governance in Higher Education, 'Legislating for Higher Education in Europe'*, Council of Europe, Kluwer Law International, Strasbourg–Den Haag, 1998.

Walter Berka, Jan de Groof and Hilde Penneman (eds.), Autonomy in Education, ix–xiv.

aspects of the administration and functioning of a school, including the method used for quality assessment and particularly the contribution which self-evaluation by the school[4] makes on decision-making procedures and participation structures.[5]

In many cases it is assumed that there is also a direct correlation between the extent of decentralization and flexibility – a concept which seems to have become much more important in recent years. Hence, the aforementioned White Paper on Education and Training *Teaching and Learning* stated that 'Experience has shown that the most decentralised systems are also the most flexible, are the quickest to adapt and hence have the greatest propensity to develop new forms of social partnership'. It remains to be demonstrated to what extent this statement will prove to be true – also in the context of education law. Useful comparative research could be set up to look at the flexibility of regulation in educational affairs in Europe.

2. Autonomy ought to be considered in its various applications. Autonomy for school boards is all realized through management, administrative mechanisms, management of personnel and pedagogical options.

Certainly, the first and traditional interpretation of autonomy through the freedom of education, especially the freedom of *establishment* acquired a different tonality as soon as planning and finance measures became an inevitable part of government care for education.

This freedom is, first and foremost, invoked as a modern ground for (partial) rights for school boards *vis-à-vis* the government, rather than as an independent demand for new institutions and/or departments *vis-à-vis* the government.

At the same time, it is curious that *freedom of conviction* is not always equally recognizable. For this, various reasons may be given. One of them is the changed profile of the denominational school, as well as for example of 'socio-cultural Christianity', which replaced 'church Catholicism' in the Sixties.

Although the identity of the confessional school is changing – also in the light of the vision of the church on this[6] – each free school can in principle autonomously determine its identity, and impose this on the pupil and parent who have preference for and confidence in that school.

And, although the criteria for admission/rejection of pupils should be treated with the utmost care, it nevertheless can be concluded that very few cases are known in which enrolment has been refused because of the apparent resistance

4 European Commission, *Evaluating quality in school education. A European pilot project. Final Report*, June 1999.

5 Eurydice, *School Autonomy and Europe. Consultative Councils and other Forms of Social Participation in the European Union.*

6 In this respect, see our contribution over 30 years *Gravissimum Educationis Momentum.*

of the person involved to conform in one way or another or to refrain from a hostile attitude towards the ideology of the project.

However, at issue is also the autonomy of the public school with regard to *conviction.*

In our other contributions we have tried to show that the freedom of *organization* of teaching – which covers educational freedom – is neither unlimited, nor free from threats.

It also remains the cornerstone in current educational law cases and will certainly lead to new case law if no consensus is reached between the organizing bodies and government.

In the first place, there is the problem of financing – traditionally the first source of confrontation between State and organizing bodies, especially as regards the non-official education.

However, it is also unnecessary to repeat that the freedom of organization of teaching was not always emphatically aimed at. One example of this – somewhat less risky – is the history of curriculum policy. Although pre-eminently one of the core issues of educational freedom, this autonomy was apparently only reluctantly nurtured to shape the educational individuality of a school, organizing body or school network.[7]

3. Autonomy of administration also requires *competence,* the ability for autonomous administration.

It is gratifying to state that – gradually and by both the civil authorities and the school governing boards themselves – great care of this is taken. It is now likewise necessary that the organizing bodies pay similar attention to this and that they consider drawing up a 'progress report' – so far as each is concerned.

May we add to this a concern and an in perspective relativization?

Such competence also implies being familiar with the diversity of legal rules on education (including social and civil law) and with case law on educational matters. Many disasters in personnel matters, for instance, or *mismanagement* may be avoided. Education law ranks as an inseparable part of education administration and policy at *micro-*, *meso-* and *macro* level. 'Perhaps there is an even greater danger if the legislation is regarded as "belonging" to someone else'[8].

Teacher training courses, refresher courses, and postgraduate courses should start to pay much more attention to this than up to now.

Recently the ability for *self-regulation* as part of independent administration

[7] Cf. the corresponding chapter in De Groof, J., *De overheid en het gesubsidieerd onderwijs (Government and grant-aided education),* Brussels, 1985.

[8] Whalley, G., in *Education and the Law,* 1993, nr. 1, p. 6.

was also described.[9] However, the literature nevertheless puts this in perspective somewhat.

4. Administrative autonomy also requires that one is conscious of each other's responsibility in the educational process and activities.

There is a tendency in the literature to search for factors which separate the partners, rather than for those that bind them. An atmosphere of hostility is then suspected between the school, on the one hand, and parents, teachers, pupils, courts, and government, on the other hand – where only partnership and co-responsibility are acceptable, although the mutual rights and obligations must be regularly defined.

The school governing board, in constant association with the teachers, must in all respects comply with its *duty of responsibility*. It should explain its own education project, should, in consultation, make choices for its teaching activities and school organization, and give explanations in respect of the mutual relations, both formal and informal, between the various groups involved in the school organization.

The rules are essentially based on the responsibility of the parents. In our opinion, this makes it *necessary* that they participate, if possible, in the organization of a school (through representatives in the organizing body), that they cooperate in designing and defining the educational project and the school curriculum, and agree with the pedagogical options and the school rules.

On the other hand, the parents and pupils who put themselves into the care of *that* school, should also have respect for the objectives which have been endorsed.

Therefore, in a recent dispute, a Belgian court rightly agreed with the *school* in its refusal to enrol a pupil if the parents refused to sign the school rules, and another court rightly agreed with the *parents* and reversed the decision to remove a pupil, since the procedure of consultation with the parents had not been followed – although it concerned a pupil who was blamed for ' inciting his fellow pupils against the director and the mathematics teacher!'[10].

Even more pressing than before, how can the task for the school authorities be formulated, to make the school and its project more *recognizable*, to make the integration of parents and pupils in developing the educational project

9 See, for example, the publications from the 'Schoordijk Institute – Centre for legislative issues', Eijlander, Ph., *et al.*, *Overheid en zelfregulering. Alibi voor vrijblijvendheid of prikkel tot actie? (Government and self-regulation. Excuse for non-commitment or inaction?)*, Zwolle, 1993.

10 It will be useful to keep up with the anthology of case law – also in regard to the school-teacher-pupil relationship. In a recent judgment the Council of State proclaims: 'Every teacher must be capable of teaching. The fact, that a teacher is appointed in a school in which the pupils are allegedly more unruly than in others, cannot be considered a disadvantage and it can be redressed'.

more tangible, and to do everything possible to force mutual commitment? The school as *community*.

5. In connection with this, there are several questions which may be raised on the autonomy of the school with regard to its core, its specificity, both for educational institutions with a private statute and for schools with a public statute.

Perhaps a legal and comparative study into this area will be organized in future.

The question for the near future unmistakably remains to what extent the regulations either *support* or *threaten* the autonomy of the school.

It is asking what are the key tasks of government and what is the status of school autonomy.[11] It is also a question of education law. When the national authorities prescribed a minimum lesson curriculum, even though the grant-aided sector of education still only partially pursued its own curriculum policy, the objection was soon raised that this constituted an infringement of the autonomy of the teaching institutions. Inspection and verification were always under discussion.

Furthermore, the debate about autonomy will, in the future, never die down. This applies, intellectually, at least, elsewhere in Europe to the debate about the balance between outdated centralism and giving up authority completely, which in a short time would lead to overlap and proliferation.

It is recommended that scientists measure the present and intended balance and the task of the community in this matter.

Responsibility makes freedom possible.

6. It was decided at an earlier stage by the European Education Law and Policy Association (ELA) to set up a study during the Austrian Presidency of the European Union to look at how legislatures are responding to this trend towards greater responsibility, decentralization and autonomy. In other words, how the Member States of the European Union have made efforts to apply the principle of subsidiarity themselves. Six years after the publication of the first ELA book,[12] we are therefore proud to be able to present this book on *Autonomy*.

Right at the outset we must pay tribute to the team of legal experts led by Dean and ELA Board Member Prof. Dr Walter Berka, who organized the

[11] Cf. our contribution 'Onderwijs en regelgeving. Enkele notities', (*Education and legislation. Some notes*) *T.O.R.B.*, 1996–1997, nr. 4 and 'Omtrent de pedagogische vrijheid. Enkele juridische en beleidsmatige beschouwingen', (*About educational freedom. Some legal and policy observations*) *Nova et Vetera*, 1995–1996, nr. 1–2.

[12] De Groof, J. (ed.), *Subsidiarity and Education. Aspects of comparative Education Law*, Leuven 1994.

annual conference in Salzburg in a 'pioneering' marriage of content and style, and who also contributed towards the creation of this book.

All policy thinking in educational affairs will, in the long term, fail unless the required consequences in terms of reforms of educational management and pedagogy are not also accepted *in legislation.*

A special vote of thanks therefore goes to the leading officials from the authorized Federal Ministries, including Sigurd Höllinger, Director General Higher Education (Federal Ministry for Science and Transport) and Dr Elsa Hackl, who were able to combine a high level of responsibility in Austria and a clear international interest and experience, which are also clearly present in this book. For the members of ELA they are certainly, to use the words of the Federal Minister for Science and Transport, Dr Caspar Einem, in the introduction to his book *In Anderer Augen. Die Staaten der Europäischen Union in der österreichischen Literatur,*[13] our 'fellow countrymen'.

[13] Published by M. Gruber, M. Müller and H.A. Niederle, Wiener Verlag, 1998.

General Framework

WALTER BERKA

The Legal and Philosophical Meaning of Autonomy in Education

I.

If we consider the meaning of 'autonomy' one might be tempted to think of a passage in Aldous Huxley's novel *Eyeless in Gaza*. There, Huxley considers the meaning of 'freedom': 'Freedom's a marvellous name. That's why you're so anxious to make use of it. You think that, if you call imprisonment true freedom, people will be attracted to the prison. And the worst of it is you're quite right' (A. Huxley, *Eyeless in Gaza*, London 1955, 123). Freedom has – and Huxley makes this quite clear – a strong emotive undertone, which enables the speaker to use this notion in the way of a persuasive definition. If you want someone to do something, you just have to make clear to him that his freedom lies in doing precisely this thing. Isn't that true for autonomy? Doesn't autonomy also open the possibility to use it in the way of a persuasive definition? Can't autonomy also be a seductive word which can lead to ends which are not always laid open by its protagonists? These are some of the questions I want to deal with in my short presentation.

As a starting point, I will begin with the following observation: like the term freedom, the notion of autonomy can be a focus of collective and individual hopes and aspirations. It is connected with values that are highly esteemed in our society. Self-determination, self-responsibility, command over one's own affairs are some of these values. On the other side, autonomy can be used as a camouflage for different and sometimes selfish interests. It can be a strategy mobilized by those who try to slip away from external control and accountability, even if this is a legitimate power of control like those that are is exercized by a parliament or a responsible government. Used as a loose slogan, autonomy can therefore give rise to suspicion. This is especially true for legal reasoning. For lawyers, autonomy is anything but a well-tailored legal concept although it is used as a term in modern administrative law.

Walter Berka, Jan de Groof and Hilde Penneman (eds.), Autonomy in Education, 3–10.

What are the reasons that we hold autonomy in such high esteem even though it is a rather vague and uncertain term? And how can we tackle this uncertainty? I guess that it has something to do with the fact that autonomy is a kind of wanderer between two different worlds – the world of philosophy in general and education theory in particular, and the legal world.

II.

Taken literally autonomy seems to be bear a clear meaning. It derives from ancient Greek and means 'self-legislation' in the sense of self-administration or self-government. In modern European thinking at the end of the 16th century, it was a legal and political context in which this word was originally used. What is even more interesting is the fact that the first use of the word placed a disparaging meaning on it. In a pamphlet written by Franciscus Burgcardus, which was the first German text in which the word was used, autonomy served as a kind of 'killer-phrase'. It stood for the unlawful desire of Protestants to obtain freedom of religion and freedom of conscience. In this context, therefore, autonomy was associated with individualistic arbitrariness and the illegitimate wish of people to escape from the sphere of a lawful order. As we can see, there is a shadow of ambivalence that falls on autonomy from its very first use in modern history.

Some decades later in the legal texts of the 17th and 18th centuries, autonomy had become a common phrase. It stood for the capacity of the individual to govern his own affairs by contract. Furthermore, autonomy referred to the legal power of local communities to enact autonomous regulations, which were called 'statutes' to mark the difference to legal acts of the sovereign. With the rise of the modern state, autonomous powers became suspect and at the end of the 19th century, many legal authors opposed the notion of autonomy, which seemed to them out of date and a remnant of the Dark Ages. The modern nation state of the 19th century left little room for autonomous powers beside the State, be it in the field of political, cultural or educational institutions.

Autonomy would be used subsequently in civil law to refer to the treaty-making power of private individuals (*Privatautonomie*). Further, it played a certain role in the terminology of international law in connection with the rights of self-determination of peoples. In public law, it was replaced in many legal cultures by the notion of self-administration, which is, for instance, the common phrase for the autonomous powers of local communities in German-speaking countries. What we can observe is, at least in these countries, a replacement of autonomy, which was considered more or less as a political phrase, by the notion of self-administration, which seemed to be more apt to be used in formal and legal contexts.

Having made these first observations on the legal meaning of autonomy, I will now move from the statute books to the chalkboards, that is from the field of jurisprudence to the field of philosophy and the theoretical playgrounds of the educationalists. Of course, we have to come back to legal considerations and we will have to deal with the modern concept of autonomy again. But the following detour might help us to understand some of the difficulties that confront us when we speak about autonomy.

III.

After Immanuel Kant had declared the autonomy of the human will as the supreme principle of morality, autonomy gained a new significance. It became one of the cornerstones of philosophy and could be used as the foundation stone of various social sciences, for instance, of ethics, psychology or religion. In all these connections, autonomy could be supplied with quite distinct and varied meanings. It was this very broad philosophical usage that made autonomy become a notion at one's disposal, an empty jar that could be filled with different spirits. Also, the educationalists could not resist the temptation of this phrase and they put the concept of autonomy at the centre of their reasoning.

Of course, the basic relation between autonomy and education seems to be quite clear. If autonomy of a person is a good thing *per se*, a person's self-determination must be the ultimate goal of education. Considering this aim, different conclusions are possible.

First, education as a social science has to be autonomous by itself. Therefore, the notion of autonomy was the banner under which educationalists tried to emancipate their science from the guardianship of religion and philosophy. *Autonomie der Pädagogik*, which means autonomy of education theory, became a common phrase in German educational writing, for instance. Furthermore, autonomy of educational theory also meant that this science should not fall under the sway of other social forces, like politics, economy or the churches. Autonomy was therefore the *raison d'être* for education theory as a rather new social science, which had to fight for its place in the scientific community. If we consider this fact, we ought not to wonder that autonomy became one of the favourite subjects of educational theory.

Secondly, autonomy served not only as a foundation for educational theory as a science. If a person's self-determination is the final goal of education, the education process itself must be self-regulative. As Eduard Spranger put it in 1928: 'Learning and education will only be successful if teachers and students come together in freedom and the schools themselves are free.' In this respect, autonomy seems to be an essential prerequisite for education, associated with the principle of pedagogical or academic freedom and deduced from specific conditions of the teaching process.

If we were to take a closer look into educational theory, we could find very different theories using this concept of autonomy. There is the traditional theory of 'personality education' (*Persönlichkeitspädagogik*), which puts the individual personality in the centre of its theory. Alternative models like the so-called *Reformpädagogik* tried to remodel educational institutions under aspects of pedagogical freedom and democracy. And we would find, of course, many modern theoretical approaches trying to improve education by means of granting more autonomy. One of the most influential is the discourse theory by Jürgen Habermas. Habermas has shown that education is grounded in autonomous structures of communication, which have to be respected in the educational process.

On the other hand, there were and still are some educational theories that would call into question the concept of autonomy of education. If the aim of education is founded in prefixed values, for instance religious or moral values, there is indeed no room left for educational autonomy, which would endanger the realization of these values. Again, autonomy shrouds itself in ambivalence.

I will not linger long on these various educational theories. More important is the fact that even those theories that put autonomy in the centre of their reasoning would only speak about a 'relative autonomy': That means, that they have to admit that the educational system does not exist within a vacuum. Instead, it is exposed to various social influences. The State as well as different social forces, such as the economic or the political systems or the churches influences schools or institutions of higher education, thus making them more or less subject to heteronomous laws. If therefore, autonomy of education can probably only be a relative autonomy, its limits become necessarily open and fluid.

IV.

Let me come to the point. In philosophy in general and in educational theory in particular, the concept of autonomy is not a fixed concept. On the contrary, it is an ambiguous and ambivalent notion. Educationalists are not to be blamed therefore, because ambiguity and ambivalence are necessarily linked with this word, which refers to a multilateral relation. It is a multilateral relation, because we speak about autonomy when a certain subject, be it an individual person or an organization, claims self-regulation and freedom *vis-à-vis* another determinative power. Take this formal structure of a multilateral relation and you can use autonomy for each and every claim that is directed to freedom, emancipation or independence. In this sense, autonomy is rather more a programme than an analytical notion. It is this ambiguity that makes the concept of autonomy one to be freely disposed to very different purposes, as a political parole, a vogue expression or an ideological camouflage.

If we consider ambiguity and ambivalence as inherent elements of the notion of autonomy, it is not surprising that lawyers have their troubles with this notion. At this point, I can take up my former thread. As I have said, in legal thinking, at least in German-speaking and some other countries, autonomy was considered more or less as a political phrase and in many contexts replaced by the more formal notion of self-administration. But autonomy seems to be a persistent word. As we all know, autonomy of education, meaning autonomy of schools or autonomy of institutions of higher education, has gained a high significance in education policy within the last two decades. That means whether we as lawyers like it or not, the notion of autonomy has returned from the realm of philosophy to the legal world, either as a political reform concept or as a legal notion. May I give you an example from Austrian developments? In legal thinking in Austria, autonomy was until recently nearly an outcast. This had something to do with the positivistic and formal approach which was, in the legacy of Hans Kelsens 'Pure theory of Law', a prominent feature of the Austrian legal tradition. Nowadays, many statutes like the University Organisation Act from 1993 or the Act on *Fachhochschul-* (Poly-Technical) Courses use the phrase autonomy in different relations and the notion of autonomy has gained certain legal consequences. The concept of autonomy also spilled over from higher education into the field of primary and secondary education, as the Austrian country report at this conference demonstrates. One can doubt whether the notion of autonomy is correctly used in all of these statutes. But, be that as it may, there is no doubt that autonomy has re-entered the realm of the Austrian law, like the Prodigal Son of the Bible.

So, what could be the consequences if we consider on the one hand ambiguity and ambivalence as inherent elements of the notion of autonomy but have to grapple with it on the other hand because it is a legal notion? I guess we have to mobilize some virtues of lawyers, first of all the ability to distinguish. We must make clear what we are speaking about when we are using the word autonomy. Therefore, I would like to give you some examples of what I think could be useful distinctions for the purpose of this conference.

V.

As I have already said, autonomy implies a certain *vis-à-vis*, which means a determinative power as the counterpart of the claim for self-regulation. In the concept of autonomy, this could be any counterpart, but when we use the notion in a legal context we should make quite clear which counterpart is meant.

As Figure 1 shows, it could be the State, the political system, economic forces or other social powers like cultural institutions that serve as counterparts. As we know, in the European tradition of education, the struggle for autonomy was often connected with the emancipation of education from the supervisory power of the Church. In this fight, the State was an ally of the education

Figure 1:

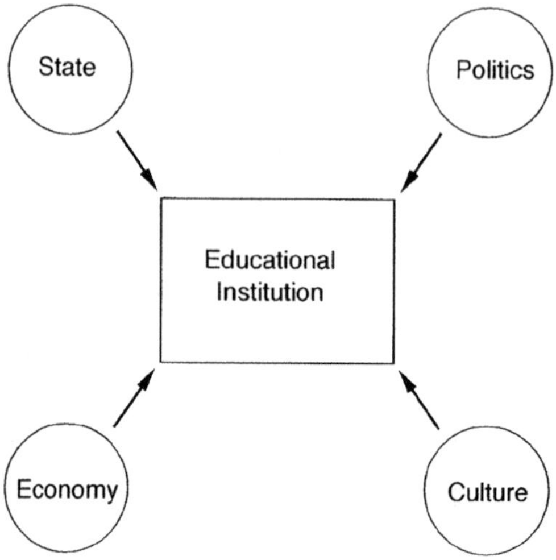

"Counterparts" of Autonomy

system, a fact which inevitably increased the influence of the State in many cases when the influence of the Church was driven back. Therefore, we have to consider that a claim for autonomy might be successful but can lead to new forms of dependency. It is, therefore, quite clear that autonomy of schools in terms of reducing the influence of governmental control can increase the influence of the economic system, which means more market control. This might be intended or not, but we have to consider such consequences when we are speaking about autonomy. And we have to give autonomy a precise setting. It must be made clear to whom autonomy should be granted and within which limits, for what purpose and who is the respective counterpart.

In most legal contexts autonomy will, therefore, and probably should be restricted to the relationship between an educational system or an educational institution on one side and the State on the other, as Figure 2 shows.

But even if we concentrate on one relationship, that of State–educational institution, it might again be necessary to take a closer look (Figure 3).

Because most schools or universities are complex organizations, we will find a certain organizational pattern within them, which can also give rise to the question of autonomy. Autonomy can, therefore, amount to certain spheres of independence within a given organization, for instance, if there are independent bodies like a teacher's conference, or if we think of the concept of pedagogical freedom or the liberty of scientific teaching. Taking this into account, we have to further distinguish between external autonomy and internal autonomy and between organizational autonomy and the autonomy of individual persons.

Figure 2:

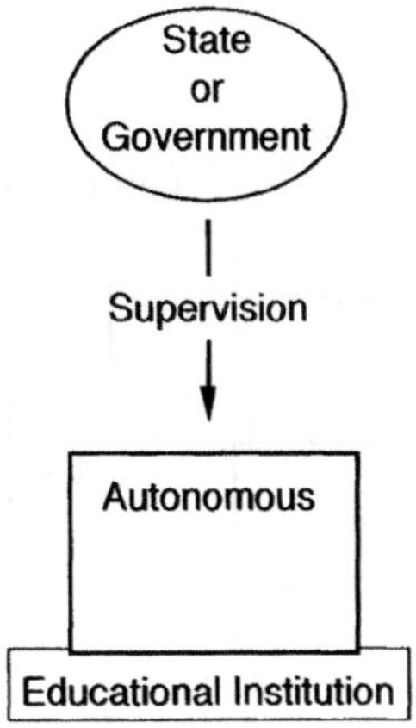

Figure 3:

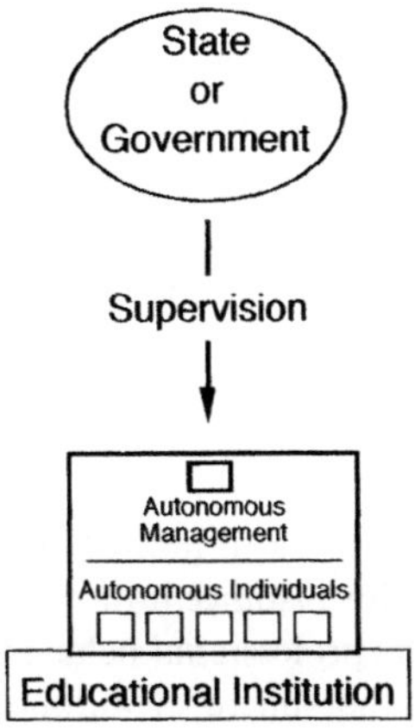

Misunderstandings will easily occur if we fail to distinguish properly between autonomy of organizations and individual autonomy. In modern society, education takes place in organizations where different persons try to achieve common aims and shared values. If we state or claim that autonomy should be granted to this organization, it is not yet decided who will be the bearer of decision-making power. It could be a single person, let's say the head of a school where a strict hierarchical organization leaves little room for pedagogical liberty of the teachers. In this case, education would be autonomous

Figure 4:

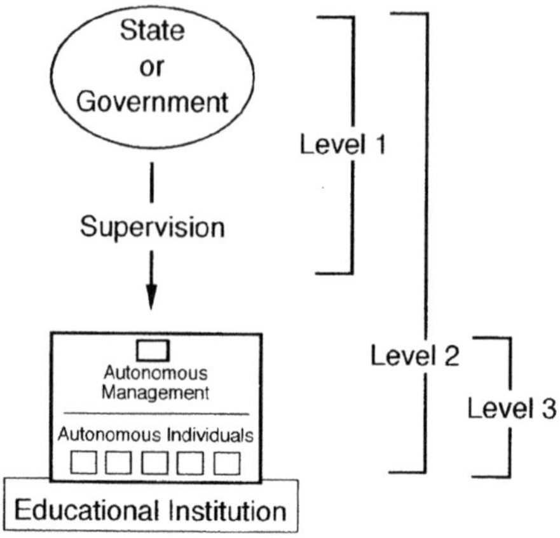

but within very authoritarian structures. On the other side, if all decision-making power were granted to the individual teachers, who could independently decide all questions of education, it would also be autonomy in education but within a quite different setting. I believe that most issues of autonomy in education have something to do with proper balancing of autonomy within a given organization and we will have to consider the various tasks that are concerned.

Figure 4 tries to demonstrate that even in the simple relationship State–educational institution we might have to distinguish between at least three different levels of autonomy.

Level 1 stands for the relationship of the State or the government to the institution, let's say the range of supervisory powers of the government over a university. Level 2 depicts the issue of individual autonomy against the State or government, which means for instance how much control the State or public authorities can exercise on the professional behaviour of a teacher or professor. Finally, Level 3 deals with the sphere of autonomy that is granted to self-governing bodies and individuals within the organization and in relation to each other. It is my impression that nowadays Level 3 seems to cause most problems of autonomy. At this level we are most likely to encounter conflicts between institutional and personal autonomy.

Well, I think that is all I will to say at the moment. I don't want to give the mistaken impression that I intended to clarify the issue of autonomy exhaustively. What I wanted to discuss, just for the sake of a little more clarity, was that autonomy could sometimes be an intriguing concept, and why. I guess this conference will prove this thesis.

CHARLES L. GLENN

The Concept of Educational Autonomy

What does it mean to say that schools or universities are 'autonomous', or are not autonomous? In either case, is it desirable? Is there a tension between the autonomy of educational institutions and that of those who teach within them? Should it be a goal of public policy to increase, or to limit, educational autonomy, however we understand it? What policy mechanisms would serve to make schools or universities more genuinely autonomous or, if that is undesirable, to impose an outside discipline upon them?

Like most policy questions which are posed in terms of simple choices, these are really far from simple, nor can the answer to any of them be unambiguous. My task at the start of our conference is not to suggest norms for educational autonomy – indeed, that would be well beyond my capability – but to 'unpack' the concept in the interest of a fruitful discussion from the perspective of our various national experiences and our individual interests.

What does it mean to say that schools or universities are 'autonomous', or are not?

Strictly speaking, very few educational institutions are autonomous, that is, a law unto themselves. By the very nature of their mission, they must answer to demands from the wider society. Elite independent schools in the United States, for example, can largely ignore government, but they cannot ignore the expectations of the élite universities for which they prepare their students. There are, indeed, a handful of 'progressive' schools around the world which disavow all vocational and academic objectives in the name of a pedagogical theory which places exclusive reliance upon the flowering of the child's own inner gifts, but even these schools must rely upon a 'market' of parents attracted to such a vision of education. Even they, and every other educational institution, are in some sense creatures and servants of their society.

In more common usage, the autonomy of an educational institution is a function of whether its owner or governing board can make all significant

Walter Berka, Jan de Groof and Hilde Penneman (eds.), Autonomy in Education, 11–20.

decisions about employment, admission of students, curriculum, and budget ... both coming in and going out.

Let's start with money. A school which relies upon tuition paid by parents – as do non-public schools in the United States – has a significant basis for autonomy from government, though this is by no means unlimited. We say that public funding always has strings attached to it, but government can choose to attach strings even in the absence of funding. For example, a privately-funded school may be required to meet certain government standards in order for its pupils to qualify as meeting a mandatory school attendance law, or a privately-funded university may be required to do so in order to grant degrees permitting its graduates to practise certain professions. Lack of public funding does not always translate into lack of government regulation.

On the other hand, public funding – especially if it is essentially guaranteed – increases the autonomy of schools and universities *vis-à-vis* their 'customers': parents and students. I teach in a non-public university which derives almost its entire income from tuition; my colleagues in European universities might be surprised at how much of my attention is devoted to strategies for attracting applications. I can testify that functioning in a free market is a constant reminder of the importance of offering programs which satisfy real needs of students.

Funding, then, is not the decisive consideration in describing the autonomy enjoyed by an educational institution. This is of course even more the case in Europe than it is in the United States, where a fairly clear line can be drawn between public schools and colleges, which are government-funded, and non-public schools and universities, which (at least in principle) are not. In most European countries – Italy is one exception – government funds its own schools and schools which are independently-owned on essentially the same basis, and regulates them both alike.

The extent to which an educational institution is government-regulated, then, is another important dimension of autonomy, though in this case there is a continuum of autonomy without the sharp distinction between those which are publicly-funded and those which are not. Every educational institution, almost without exception in the OECD nations, is regulated to some extent. As already noted, enforcement of mandatory school attendance laws requires some degree of government determination that attendance at a particular school meets the requirement. Even 'home schooling', a rapidly-growing phenomenon in the United States, takes place within a context of government oversight, and the jurisprudence over its reach and specificity is growing just as rapidly.

Regulation is too complex and touches upon too many dimensions for me to review, but the continuum can be described as reaching from the minimal specification of health and safety requirements (American universities, for example, must report on incidents of crime on their campuses, which in turn impacts upon their ability to attract students) to detailed specification of who may be hired as teachers and administrators.

Employment decisions could be called 'the canary in the coal mine' of educational autonomy: the extent to which the boards or administrators of schools or universities can make these decisions is an excellent indication of whether they are truly autonomous. Our ELA colleague Andries Postma points out, in his splendid handbook of Dutch education law, the dilemma created by a law adopted in 1994 forbidding discrimination in employment on the basis of race, sex, and other characteristics including homosexuality and marital status; this seems to prevent a faith-based school from not hiring a teacher who is gay or an unwed mother, even if the school is the agent of a group of families who believe strongly in traditional sexual morality. On the other hand, the law makes an exception for the right of non-public schools to make demands that are essential to carrying out their mission, provided that these demands are not based upon making distinctions on the basis of race, sex ... homosexuality or marital status.[1] Similarly, American federal law allows distinctively religious institutions to take religion into account in hiring, though not when the position in question is publicly-funded (as are, of course, teachers in Dutch non-public schools). Political scientist Stephen Monsma points out that 'if the teachers or other staff of a nonprofit agency cannot be hired on the basis of their faith commitments, the religious character of that nonprofit would be destroyed.'[2] The importance of allowing such 'discrimination' in the interest of the First Amendment right to the free exercise of religion has been recognized by Congress and by the Supreme Court *in principle*, though its application in practice has by no means always protected faith-based organizations sufficiently. Sexual orientation is not (yet) a 'protected category' in American federal law, though it is in some states; no doubt we will be seeing litigation in this area, and it may affect profoundly the character of schools and universities which have sought to resist evolving societal norms which they regard as contrary to their fundamental mission.

Of course, employment decisions are not the only dimension of school or university life which can exhibit more or less autonomy of independent decision-making, but they may well be the most crucial. No attempt will be made here, however, to catalog, much less discuss, the other ways in which educational institutions may possess a real autonomy, or lack it.

One more comment is appropriate under this heading, however. While public and non-public schools or universities may be subject to generally comparable levels of government regulation and oversight, there is nevertheless a crucial difference between being accountable to government and actually

1 Andries Postma, *Handboek van het Nederlandse Onderwijsrecht* (Handbook of Dutch Educational Law), Zwolle: W.E.J. Tjeenk Willink, 1995, 131, 147–48.

2 Stephen V. Monsma, *When Sacred and Secular Mix*, Rowman & Littlefield, 1996, 126.

belonging to government. While it is true that non-profit voluntary organizations which derive their support from government must inevitably bureaucratize their own operations to some extent,[3] they nevertheless retain a relative freedom of action which may be decisive, both practically and psychologically. Even the most burdensome regulation cannot erase all of the advantages which flow from managerial autonomy.

IN WHAT WAYS IS IT *DESIRABLE* FOR SCHOOLS OR UNIVERSITIES TO BE AUTONOMOUS?

Educational institutions which are a 'law unto themselves' (the literal meaning of *autonomous*) are more likely to be characterized by agreement among all participants about their mission and the spirit in which it is to be carried out. Studies on school effectiveness in the United States show that clarity of mission makes an important contribution to positive results. Some scholars have argued that 'the most important prerequisite for the emergence of effective school characteristics is school autonomy, especially from external bureaucratic influence' and that 'America's existing system of public education inhibits the emergence of effective organizations. This occurs, most fundamentally, because its institutions of democratic control function naturally to limit and undermine school autonomy.'[4]

The conclusion that clarity of mission is very important finds support from effective schools research in The Netherlands (Marwijk Kooy-von Baumhauer, 1984), in Britain (Mortimore, Sammons, Stoll, Lewis and Ecob, 1988; National Commission on Education, 1996), and in France (Ballion, 1991).

Autonomous schools and universities may also be more responsive to those they serve, who in some sense function as 'customers' in a marketplace rather than as clients of a bureaucratic monopoly. When market dynamics are introduced into systems of which the constituent parts enjoy little autonomy, experience suggests that the effect tends to be to hierarchize the alternative providers (enabling those in the upper ranks to be more selective) rather than to promote the sort of diversity which serves the interests of a diverse population.[5]

Autonomous educational institutions are also less subject to political interference, and it is for this reason that university faculty, in particular, have long sought to increase their individual and collective autonomy.

[3] Adriaansens, H.P.M. and A.C. Zijderveld, *Vrijwillig initiatief en de verzorgingsstaat* (Voluntary initiative and the Welfare State), Deventer: Van Loghum Slaterus, 1981, 87.

[4] John E. Chubb and Terry M. Moe, *Politics, Markets and America's Schools*, Washington: The Brookings Institution, 1990, 23.

[5] Donald Hirsch, *School: a Matter of Choice*, Paris: Organisation for Economic Co-operation and Development, 1994, 51.

In what ways is it *not* desirable for schools or universities to be autonomous?

As so often in policy questions, there is a reverse side to a positive statement. The autonomy of universities or schools, for example, may result in their faculty being *less* autonomous individually, as we will see below.

Institutional autonomy and insulation from politics may also make schools and universities less accountable to the needs of the wider society. When faculty recoil from 'political' considerations, they forget that democratic systems are inherently and necessarily political; man is, as Aristotle pointed out, a political animal. How universities, in particular, become more actively engaged in finding solutions to society's problems while claiming immunity from political direction is one of the conundrums which ELA might well consider.

Autonomy of educational institutions also implies that they will be free to express different educational cultures and seek to form their pupils or students in different ways. This has distinct advantages in societies which are increasingly diverse and accepting and funding autonomous schools has been essential to resolution of the 'culture wars' which raged around schooling in Europe (*lutte scolaire*, *schoolstrijd*, *Kulturkampf*, and so forth) and which continue to rage in the United States, where we have not yet accepted that public education may be structurally pluralistic. But there is a potential down side to this as well.

E pluribus unum is the motto which you will find on the American dollar bill: 'from many, one'.[6] *From many, one*, is an apt summary of the project which every country in the world faces to a greater or a lesser extent, and which most look to their educational systems to address. I have argued elsewhere that this challenge, the threat of '*deux jeunesses*', and not literacy, was the primary motivation of those who created national or state education systems in the 19th century.[7] The challenge is all the greater in free societies. A society with a democratic political system and legal protections for individual and group activities must find ways to accommodate and set to common purposes the diverse energies and loyalties, the conflicting interests and worldviews, of a population that, in most cases, can no longer simply be thought of as 'a people'. The acids of modernity have done their work.

The challenge for policy is to allow for diversity among schools, even providing support for schools which are created by minority communities in the process of assimilation, while ensuring that the common elements throughout the educational system are sufficiently coherent and compelling that schools

6 Not, as Vice President Al Gore famously mis-spoke, 'from one, many', though opponents of multi-culturalism insist that he was expressing the real tendency of our educational system.

7 Charles L. Glenn, *The Myth of the Common School*, University of Massachusetts Press, 1988.

which are very different, working apart, can nevertheless arrive at common educational goals. The Netherlands, with its support for Muslim and Hindu schools, is perhaps the furthest along in this social experiment. Some encouragement can be taken from the historical experience of the United States, where the millions of immigrant children who have attended Catholic and, to some extent, Protestant or Jewish schools have turned out to be just as patriotic and civically-engaged as the graduates of public schools.[8]

Another problem associated with autonomy of schools and universities is that injustices may occur in their treatment of pupils/students or (as we will see below) of teachers. Autonomy in admission or disciplinary decisions plays an important part in an institution's ability to preserve its distinctive character, but also is subject to abuse. In enacting legislation for 'charter' schools – autonomous public schools – in the United States, legislators have tended to err on the side of caution in limiting the ability of these schools to select their pupils. They have done so because of the strong American tradition of civil rights protections, deriving from the equally strong tradition of racial and other discrimination. Those designing charter school policies have been unwilling to risk the scandals which would follow if it turned out that schools were selecting pupils on the basis of race, national origin, sex, religion, or handicap. As a result, they have often insisted that admission to over-subscribed charter schools be on a random basis, preventing these schools from selecting pupils from families which strongly support the mission of the school.

Is there a tension between the autonomy of educational institutions and that of teachers?

Teachers may feel that their individual rights are better protected in schools or universities which have limited autonomy; thus, for example, the powerful teachers' union in Mexico has resisted measures to increase the autonomy of individual schools. Teachers in many countries prefer to engage in collective bargaining or in political measures at the highest possible level to increase their pay and their control over working conditions.

By the same token, those education reformers and administrators who believe strongly that schools should have a distinctive character, or who are committed to protecting the religious mission of a school, usually seek to increase their capacity – through control over hiring and through supervision – to ensure that all of the staff of the school share the same vision. This is the source of the apparent paradox that, in American public 'schools of choice'

[8] Charles L. Glenn, 'Minority Schools on Purpose', in *Changing Populations, Changing Schools: 94th Yearbook of the National Society for the Study of Education*, Part II, edited by Erwin Flaxman and A. Harry Passow, Chicago: National Society for the Study of Education, 1995.

such as magnet and charter schools, the teachers have less freedom to shut their classroom doors and ignore everyone else than they commonly do in ordinary public schools.

As ELA members know, this question has been litigated in most – perhaps in all – of our countries, and questions of how to reconcile the *caractère propre*, the *carácter propio*, the *identiteit* of schools with the rights and interests of teachers is frequently on the policy agenda. To take a single example, in Spain publicly-funded non-state schools must comply with government requirements as to materials and programs, the methods that must be employed, the levels to reach for graduates, and the means of evaluation of graduates. There has been considerable controversy over whether these requirements trespass upon the right of those operating non-state schools 'to define their distinctive character and to ensure effectively that this is carried out as necessary in the educational process.'[9] This 'distinctive character' (*carácter propio*) is significant since it may form the basis for selecting particular teachers and for insisting that teachers not undermine the mission of the school; for example, a teacher mocking Catholic doctrine would be dismissible from a Catholic school, though he or she could not be dismissed for refusing to endorse such doctrine contrary to conscience. (But a school's distinctive character must be consistent with Spain's constitutional principles of 'liberty, equality, justice, pluralism.')

The issue of the autonomy of non-state schools was brought before Spain's Constitutional Court, which ruled that the government could set standards but should do so with careful respect to the constitutional guarantee of educational freedom. While non-state schools were required to 'conform to the minimums set by the public authorities with respect to the content of the various subjects, the number of hours of instruction, etc.,' they were free to do so in a way that gave expression to the educational concepts on the basis of which the school had been established.[10] A later ruling of the Court confirmed that teachers could be required to conform their teaching to the distinctive character of the school, and found unconstitutional a provision of Spain's comprehensive education law that gave the authorities scope to rule on the appropriateness of this distinctive character.[11]

Nor is the right of school managers to insist that teachers conform to the school's mission necessarily an infringement upon the freedom of teachers, in at least one significant sense. After all, as José Luis Martínez Lopez-Muñiz has perceptively noted, teachers should have the right to work in a school which

[9] Francesc Riu i Rovira de Villar, *'Todos tienen el derecho a la educación'*, Madrid: Consejo General de la Educación Catolica, 1988, 53.

[10] Ruling of the *Tribunal Constitucional* on 13 February 13 1981, reprinted by Riu i Rovira de Villar, 107.

[11] Ruling of the *Tribunal Constitucional* on 27 June 1985, reprinted by Riu i Rovira de Villar, 134–137.

reflects their own convictions, and they are deprived of this right if no school can consistently reflect *any* convictions. There is indeed evidence that teachers are more contented and have more sense of control over their teaching in schools marked by a shared sense of mission. An American government study found that 71.4 per cent of the teachers in small (less than 150 students) private schools agreed that 'colleagues share beliefs and values about central mission of school', compared with 26.2 per cent in large (over 750 pupils) public schools.[12] It comes as no surprise that the first groups were considerably more satisfied with their jobs, despite much lower pay than teachers in public schools.

The same considerations apply, but rather differently, in universities. The academic freedom of university professors is a more formidable barrier to efforts to insist upon the distinctive character of an institution, and the hundreds of American universities which were established on religious grounds have in most (though by no means all) cases abandoned the effort to maintain that character in their instructional program.[13]

Should it be a goal of public policy to increase, or to limit, educational autonomy?

Both! Reducing the procedural requirements placed upon schools and universities would be desirable in many cases. Many of these requirements have grown up because of the natural tendency of government bureaucrats to regulate broadly – in relation, for example, to purchasing or hiring procedures – to prevent the possibility of embarrassment in cases of malfeasance which may occur only very seldom. It is a common feature of bureaucratic existence to act defensively, since one failure weighs more heavily than many successes. Too-extensive efforts to prevent failure can have the effect of preventing success, of those whose initiative and responsiveness are essential to success have their hands tied by procedural requirements.

Education today needs, as perhaps never before, a willingness to respond quickly to new demands. Both schools and universities are facing the challenge of educating young people who are more diverse in their goals and their abilities than ever before, and as we raise the effective school-leaving age (President Clinton and others have spoken of higher education as a universal entitlement!), this challenge will become all the more difficult to meet. We need entrepreneurial school and university leaders, and teachers who are willing to

[12] Susan P. Choy, *Public and Private Schools: How Do They Differ?* Washington: National Center for Education Statistics (NCES 97–983), 1997, 21.

[13] Three important studies of this phenomenon are: George M. Marsden, *The Soul of the American University*, Oxford University Press, 1994; Philip Gleason, *Contending with Modernity*, Oxford University Press, 1995; and James T. Burtchaell, *The Dying of the Light*, Eerdmans, 1998.

examine and to change their own practices. Nothing will prevent attracting such individuals into education, and retaining them, so much as to tie their hands with procedural safeguards based upon mistrust of their judgement.

But having said that, it is equally important that we become clearer about the common goals of education. In this respect, the United States is seeking to benefit from the experience of a number of European educational systems. The achievement gap between high-scoring and low-scoring schools in the United States is substantially larger than that in other industrialized societies with many immigrant children in their schools but a common curriculum for all schools. The gap (though smaller than in the United States) is larger for those European countries like The Netherlands and England with loose requirements than it is for countries like France with a more prescriptive curriculum. E.D. Hirsch, Jr has argued convincingly that this is in large part the result of the incoherence of our educational standards.[14] Poor children are especially at the mercy of schooling which fails to provide them with knowledge and skills which middle-class children acquire in part at home.

Government should also have an effective system in place to intervene on behalf of groups of pupils or individuals who are discriminated against or for whom the educational system does not function to their advantage. The trade-off for doing away with procedural requirements should be transparency on the part of schools and universities and aggressive advocacy on behalf of those for whom the system is not working well.

Concluding remarks: the Welfare State and the Civil Society

There is a fundamental difference between *decentralization* within the institutional structures of the Welfare State, and true *subsidiarity* which places primarily responsibility for 'the human care of human beings' upon Civil Society institutions, with government playing a watchdog role on behalf of the vulnerable, and subsidizing services through its ability to raise and distribute revenue from the entire society. Either decentralization or subsidiarity could be characterized as measures promoting 'autonomy', but the advantages of the first are limited to the greater efficiency which decentralization may bring, while promoting subsidiarity is intended to change the *nature* of the services provided.

Civil Society institutions (such as schools which are controlled by independent boards) are able to have a more powerful effect in shaping character and giving direction to lives than can institutions which must comply with bureaucratic rationality. The movement toward greater autonomy of educational institutions in most of the countries represented in ELA should be understood

[14] E.D. Hirsch, Jr, *The Schools We Need ... and Why We Don't Have Them*, New York: Doubleday, 1996.

as an attempt to preserve the gains of the Welfare State while drawing upon the energies and the freely-chosen commitments characteristic of the associations of Civil Society. Their significance goes beyond efficiency to address the heart of the educational enterprise.[15]

[15] This point is discussed extensively, drawing upon European and American developments, in Charles L. Glenn, *The Ambiguous Embrace: Government's Relationship with Schools and Social Agencies*, 1999.

ROGER STANDAERT

Deregulation Versus Regulation: A European Perspective

The following presentation, originating from a European perspective, is restricted to compulsory education. The problem of higher, university or non-university level is completely different because the government has a different responsibility towards adults.

The problem of deregulation in education is at this moment on top of the agenda in almost all European countries. The case is however that, when almost everybody is in favour of deregulation, the interpretation strongly varies depending on the different contexts of the countries. Yet deregulation occurs in various gradations of intensity. Discussions in several countries make clear that there is not a ONE-dimensional idea of deregulation but that there are different ways to realize it depending on the context of the country.

It often concerns various sub-aspects that can be deregulated or not.

Often a distinction must be made in policy levels on which rules are delegated. It concerns levels that can more or less be situated on a geographical scale: central level, province or state, district, village, school group(complex), local school. We may refer to this as territorial deregulation. Deregulation in this sense overlaps strongly with the idea of decentralization.

Releasing rules, essentially means that lower levels and local schools get more autonomy. Deregulation, decentralization and local autonomy form a cluster of notions that are closely related.

Comparing the degree of deregulation in various countries of Europe is NOT possible without differentiating the uni-dimension of the notion into compound dimensions and sub-aspects. We can indeed deregulate or decentralize a tenfold of aspects or leave them to the autonomy of local schools. The first thing to be done is creating a framework in which the variously possible policy aspects can be situated. Keeping this model in mind, we can work out which aspects in which country can be deregulated. This method allows us to draw up profiles of deregulation or decentralization.

In the INES-indicators that are followed by the OECD a three-dimensional frame is developed by which one departs from the dimensions 'level', 'domain' and 'mode'.

Walter Berka, Jan de Groof and Hilde Penneman (eds.), Autonomy in Education, 21–27.

In most recent studies, 'level' is distinguished on six sorts of levels: central government, state government, provincial/regional government,sub-regional or inter-municipal government, local authorities or governments, school-school board or committee.

In a lot of countries this territorial dimension results in a rather pseudo-deregulation. When a central state transfers central rules to a state of the federation, we do not create a real deregulation, but something that is often called 'deconcentration'. The rules stay as they are, but it is on a lower level in the hierarchy that they are controlled and eventually also defined.

Next to the territorial dimension of the policy-making bodies, there is still the area of competence-dimension, in other words the functional dimension. In the same study a distinction is made between four domains that can be deregulated: the pedagogical-didactical domain, human resources, planning and structures (curriculum, career structures in the educational system) and financial/resource matters.

We prefer a greater refinement in five areas of control:

1. the pedagogical-didactical area: methods, in service-training, grouping of pupils, assistance of pupils;
2. the structures of the education system: career structures, timetables; subjects, planning of the study-branches (study-disciplines).
3. the curriculum and its assessment: curriculum, core curriculum, examination structures at the end of study or during the study, monitoring systems for performance, occupational profiles;
4. the human resources: the recruitment and dismissal of teachers, conditions of employment, competence certificates, duration of the working week, staff policy, participation mechanisms; and
5. financial and material matters and budget: salaries, fees, sponsoring, working costs, lump sum, merit pay, premiums, school buildings, transport of pupils.

The OECD study also distinguishes a third dimension, namely the 'mode' of deregulation, the level of autonomy as : decisions in full autonomy, decisions in consultation with other levels and decisions following the higher framework.

Profound research is necessary to make meaningful comparisons. Studies must differentiate between the areas that are examined, as well as the levels on which autonomy takes form. The interaction between territorial decentralization within and between different policy-making bodies on the one hand, and functional decentralization in areas (domains) of control on the other, offers as a result a contrasting picture as to the degree and form of deregulation. This variety finds its roots in the particular historical and cultural traditions of the respective countries and people.

Looking for trends in deregulation in Europe, little consistent research is available. The already mentioned pioneering studies of the OECD give a picture of the relative number of decisions taken in local schools as opposed to decisions on more central levels. This happened by measures classified in six areas.

In a thorough comparative study of 26 economically important countries, dealing with common demands and diversity Charles Glenn (Boston University) comes to the following conclusion: the government will almost always pursue a central policy in three domains.

1. the subjects that have to be taught, together with the number of (teaching) hours (course hours) for each, at every level of the educational programme;
2. a system of school inspection; and
3. a system of central examinations at the end of secondary education, with important consequences for the future of the pupil.

Obviously this is a rather universal hard-core of central impact.

Looking at Europe, we find variants for the first domain in which optional subjects are also allowed for a certain limited part of the programme. We also note that the time to be spent is no longer defined in hours per week, but globally per year, or per two or three years.

Concerning school inspection, we find that Denmark and Greece do not have school inspection.

As regards central exams, only few countries do not have them: Belgium and a number of states in Germany.

The OECD-studies referred to above show – among other things – a picture of the number of decisions that are taken in terms of percentage on local level. These decisions were classified in four categories: organization of instruction, personnel management, planning and structures and resource allocations and use.

For the organization of instruction, the following items have been selected:

- bodies determining the school attended;
- decisions affecting school careers;
- instruction time;
- choice of textbooks;
- grouping pupils;
- assistance to pupils;
- teaching methods; and
- assessment of pupils' regular work.

For personnel management:

- hiring and dismissal of principal, teachers and other persons in non-teaching posts;

- duties and conditions of service of principal and teaching staff;
- fixing of salary scales; and
- influence on the careers of principals and teachers.

For planning and structures:

- creation or closure of schools;
- creation or abolition of a grade level;
- designing programmes of study;
- selection of subjects taught in the local school;
- definition of course content;
- setting of qualifying examinations for a certificate or diploma; and
- credentialling.

For resource allocation and use:– allocations to the school for staff;
- allocations for capital expenditure; and
- use of resources for staff, capital expenditure and operating expenditure.

The indicators were calculated to give equal importance to each of the four domains. Each domain contributes 25 per cent to the results of the indicators.

Table 1: Distribution of decisions at school level for public lower secondary education 1998 (shown as percentages)

Greece	23
Portugal	24
Belgium	26
France	29
Italy	33
Spain	41
Austria	24
Ireland	54
Germany	38
Denmark	32
Netherlands	76
England	62
Sweden	66
Scotland	40
Finland	36

(Source: CERI, 1998, p. 299).

After the data have been corrected by comparing the decisions taken on the municipality level, which is still a rather local level, it would appear that the Scandinavian countries are very decentralized.

Another necessary correction is the relative weight and importance of every domain. The attribution of 25 per cent for each of the four categories may be called arbitrary. This is a fine example illustrating that quantitative measurement can only constitute an initial approach.

The importance attached to every category is linked to traditions relating to values and attitudes that colour in different ways the relative importance of every domain.

Within the categories, we also get inequalities in appreciation and impact e.g. on school careers, pupil orientation, selection mechanisms, etc. Bodies determining which school is to be attended is a factor with apparently less impact than 'decisions affecting school careers', which in its turn outweighs the choice of textbooks.

When taking note of these deregulation items in a concrete manner, we will always find diverse variants that cannot be interpreted in isolation.

Let's take for example the item 'assistance to pupils'. Is assistance provided by the usual teachers, by special personnel, by which sort of special personnel, by non-subject orientated teachers and so on? Depending on the interpretation and realization, it might be better to situate the item on a higher or lower level of the hierarchy.

When operating with specialized personnel, the allocation may more easily be situated on a local authority or government level, being the second differentiated level. An interesting amendment however, is the use of the criterium 'mode'.

All of these considerations do not alter the fact that the research method reveals certain, though rough tendencies. Yet it is still meaningful to concentrate the analysis on very specific items within each category, with the intention to apply to them 'level-indication' or 'mode-interpretation', to make them more transparent and significant.

It seems, as was expected, that the decisions about the organization of instructions are predominantly taken at school level. The interpretation, however, is not always taken for granted. An example may illustrate this.

The decisions about the school attended by students are taken at a central level in Portugal and France, and at school level in Greece, Austria, Italy, England and The Netherlands. Scotland, Finland and Sweden are placed on the second level. Whether the decision is taken on the indicated level in consultation or within a framework, on the one hand or with full autonomy on the other hand is noted on each occasion. When we compare the local situations in this case with the criterion 'full autonomy', only three countries out of ten will remain: Belgium, Ireland and Germany.

To take another example, in the category 'planning and structures', the item 'setting of examinations for a diploma' is placed on the central level in Portugal, Austria, Italy, France, Denmark, Ireland, Scotland, Finland, England, The Netherlands and Sweden. Belgium is not set on the intermediate level, neither is Germany. Spain is not indicated, for unknown reasons.

Here too we find the distinction between 'full autonomy' or 'within a framework'. The question remains, whether all possible variants are covered. In Germany there are clear differences depending on the states. In most states the exams are local, however not in Baden-Württemberg and Bavaria, for example.

The situation in The Netherlands is also a variation: only half of the evaluation of the pupils is based on central exams, the other half is based on evaluation in the local school.

Belgium is placed on the intermediate level, which means the existing 'network of schools' (pillars), but they are not involved in certificating.

These examples will suffice to prove the difficulty in describing and comparing the degree and form of deregulation in the different countries of Europe.

Credible research is underway. At a more developed stage the configurations of the different items will be dealt with, by an even more qualitative and analytical method aiming at precise statements on the matter.

Nevertheless the main problem remains (and will be) to decide on the value of deregulation itself, which is a rather philosophical matter. In other words, which aspects of deregulation are interesting and which are not? To answer such questions I think we need a kind of framework with a more normative structure. This framework or different modules of framework has to be based on clear criteria. For instance, to what extent do pupils in the actual class or school profit from an initiative to deregulate?

Results must always be interpreted in the historical and cultural context of every country. Last, but not least, highly skilled competence and profound knowledge will be required of the bodies which observe the items of each country.

Literature

Administration et Education. La décentralisation six ans après. Actes du XIVe colloque. 1992, n° 55, 3ème trimestre, 172 pp. Thematic issue.

Administration et Education. Problématique de la décentralisation. 1992, 2ème trimestre, 110 pp. Thematic issue.

Australian Education Union, *Partnerships in education reform.* International diologue – OECD countries. Melbourne, AEU, 1994, 49 pp.

CERI, *Education at a glance OECD indicators 1998.* Paris, OECD-publications 1998, 432 pp.

CERI, *Education at a glance. OECD indicators 1992.* Paris, OECD-publications, 1992, 148 pp.

CERI, *Education at a glance. OECD-indicators. Indicators of education systems.* Paris, OECD-publications, 1995, 373 pp.

European Commission, *Kerncijfers op onderwijsgebied in de Europese Unie.* Luxembourg, Office for official publications, 1995, 109 pp. (Also in English, French).

EURYDICE, *Administrative and financial responsibilities for education and training in the European Community.* Brussels, Eurydice, 1993, 23 pp.

Glenn, C., Common standards and educational diversity. – In: J. De Groof (ed.), *Subsidiarity and educations.* Leuven – Amersfoort, Acco, 1994, 835–413.

Karsten, S., Scheerens, J. and Van Wieringen, A.M.L., *Deregulering en decentralisatie in het onderwijs.* Twente, Uitgeverij Universiteit, Twente 1998, 35 pp.

Liket, Th., Van Marwijk-Kooy, Liesbeth and Van Bruggen, J., *Report of the conference on autonomy and central legislation in education.* Enschede, Foundation for Curriculum Development – Nederlands Forum voor Onderwijsmanagement, 1985, 121 pp.

Solomon, J. (ed.), *Trends in the evaluation of education systems: school (self-) evaluation and decentralization.* (European Network of Policy Makers for the Evaluation of Education Systems). Athens, Hellenic Ministry of Education, 1998, 135 pp.

Standaert, R., Technical rationality in education management: a survey covering England, France and Germany. *European Journal of Education,* 1993 (28), No. 2, 159–176.

HILDE PENNEMAN

Autonomy in Education: Review of the Country Reports

This overview is the result of a comparison between the country reports which you will find further in this publication. The country reports consist of the answers to a questionnaire provided by an expert in education law. This questionnaire was composed by Professor Dr W. Berka of the Austrian host country in collaboration with the ELA Board.

1. Constitutional legal basis

1.1. *Is autonomy of the educational system or of some of its parts constitutionally guaranteed?*

At school level (i.e. primary and secondary education level), it is noticeable that in most countries the education system enjoys a certain degree of autonomy. One of the explanations therefor is that the State has to take into account the freedom of choice between various religious and non-religious schools. In other words, this 'autonomy' is the expression of the principle of 'freedom of education' and 'the right to maintain and run private religious schools', and is apparent from the bodies entrusted with running schools. Private schools are run by genuinely private bodies, and are governed by civil law. State schools are generally run, not directly by the State, but by a state organ, whether or not an autonomous state organ.

There is one notable exception, namely France. In France the autonomy of the school system is not guaranteed. The State itself is considered to be responsible for the education system, and the State is constitutionally obliged to organize this system.

The Irish constitution merely states that 'The family is the primary and natural educator of the child'. In Belgium the word 'autonomy' appears only in Art. 24 § 2 of the Constitution. This provision creates the possibility of organizing autonomous Community education. The Belgian Constitution indirectly guarantees that free education and education organized by the local authorities may act with relative autonomy in relation to the government.

Walter Berka, Jan de Groof and Hilde Penneman (eds.), Autonomy in Education, 29–40.

1.2. *Does the constitution guarantee the teacher's educational freedom or the liberty of scientific teaching (academic freedom)?*

It is clear that individual schoolteachers' pedagogical freedom is not constitutionally guaranteed in all countries. Moreover, even in countries where the individual teacher's freedom is guaranteed, a number of restrictions are imposed by law.

For example in The Netherlands, an individual teacher loses their right to provide education according to their views as soon as they are employed by a school. In Denmark, parents and guardians may make their own arrangements for their children's education, but the output has to be equivalent to the general school standard. In Spain, the individual teacher's pedagogical freedom is protected in so far as this freedom is compared to the freedom of expression. However, it seems unlikely that this should not be subject to any restrictions. It is, for example, hard to believe that a teacher employed by a Catholic school should not have to conform to this religious view.

Academic freedom is constitutionally guaranteed in The Netherlands, Germany, France, Austria and Spain. Other countries give no constitutional guarantees in this respect, although some have a strong tradition of academic freedom.

1.3. *The underlying notion of autonomy*

In no country is the constitutionally guaranteed educational autonomy at primary and secondary level absolute. Schools can never be entirely independent from the State. In both The Netherlands and in Belgium, the constitutionally guaranteed freedom consists of three components: first, the freedom to found a school; secondly, freedom of direction; and, thirdly, freedom of organization. In Ireland, autonomy is guaranteed by the principle that the family is recognized as the primary and natural educator. However, the constitution adds that this is subject to the State's right as guardian of the common good.

1.4. *Are there strict legal bases and describe these*

In countries where school autonomy is not constitutionally guaranteed, it is contained in other legislation. Thus, for example, in Austria, where school autonomy has been gradually introduced since 1993 through ordinary legislation.

In countries where school autonomy is constitutionally guaranteed, it is worked out, and limited or made subject to rules, through legislation. The same is true for universities' autonomy.

2. Autonomy of educational institutions

2.1. *Is autonomy granted with respect to the organization of educational institutions? Are schools or universities vested with a legal personality of their own? Do schools or universities have individual constitutions of their own (basic statutes, basic charters)? Are these autonomously set up by the educational institutions or conferred on them by the State or government?*

As regards legal personality and the founding Acts of the various types of education institutions, this must be examined separately for each type of institution in the various countries.

In Belgium, for example, subsidized private schools (so-called 'free schools') are governed by non-profit associations (VZW/ASBL). These are private law legal persons. State schools, on the other hand, are governed by the autonomous council for community education (the ARGO).

In The Netherlands, private schools are managed by foundations or associations and most public schools are run by a municipal executive or a committee of governors. Neither in Germany nor in Portugal do schools have individual legal personality, being instead a part of the administrative system of the State. In Austria as in Belgium and The Netherlands, schools themselves do not have legal personality but the governing bodies do. These bodies must submit annual accounts to the education authorities.

Some categories of private school have a foundational statute which must be submitted to the Education Ministry. For example, in Denmark private institutions are often subject to approval by the Ministry of Education. For state schools there is a statutory framework within which the municipality must set out a school constitution. In France, schools do not enjoy statutory autonomy; their organization is determined by the government and is equal for all institutions. In England and Wales every maintained school has a so-called governing body which is a body corporate under English Law. In Ireland primary schools have an informal structure, whilst secondary schools have minimal organizational provision. In Spain state education institutions are those owned by a public authority. Private education institutions are owned by an individual or by a legal entity, and the form of ownership must figure in the Ministry of Education and Culture's public register of institutions.

In France, Germany, Portugal, Denmark and Belgium, universities enjoy organizational autonomy and legal personality, although their basic statutes must be in accordance with the statutory framework. In Austria universities have legal personality and they are entitled to adopt and amend basic rules, but these are subject to the approval of the Austrian Minister for Science and Traffic.

In Ireland new universities are established by Act of Parliament. In Spain public universities have their own status as public entities, as a public service, with their own legal title and capital independent of the State and other public entities. Private universities are recognized by Act of the national or autonomous regional parliament.

2.2. *How independently can they determine the recruitment of their personnel, etc.?*

In many countries a clear distinction is drawn between the manner in which subsidized private schools and public schools may employ staff. The main question which arises is the following. A number of reports state that subsidized private schools are free to employ staff. However, it is not altogether clear what degree of freedom is meant and what rules are imposed by the authorities.

In Belgium the recruitment in public schools and private subsidized schools is subject to various Acts on the status of school staff. A private subsidized school is free to choose its staff but has to respect statutory rules concerning certain degrees and certificates, priority and tenure. Tenure as a civil servant is subject to approval by the Ministry of Education. The appointment of teachers in private schools is a contractual matter governed by civil law. In state schools, on the other hand, the appointment of a teacher is a unilateral administrative decision.

In Austria the situation is the following: teachers in private schools are employed on the basis of a contract with the institution which maintains the school. In state schools, teachers are appointed by means of a contract between the teacher and a public body. There are no exams. In The Netherlands the Government has the right to examine the competence and moral integrity of teachers.

In France each appointment of a teacher constitutes an administrative decision. There is no difference between private subsidized schools and state schools Likewise in Germany schools do not have any right to participate in recruitment of their staff. In Belgium, the government subsidizes a number of teachers determined on the basis of the number of pupils. In Spain and Portugal teachers are recruited in a selection process under the auspices of the national educational authorities.

For universities there are various procedures. In Germany there is a mixed system. The Higher Education Institute draws up a list of three candidates, from which the ministry normally selects the candidate ranked highest in this list. In Denmark teachers are appointed by the Ministry of Education on the basis of recommendations by a review board. In Austria the state budget specifies the maximum number of posts at each level. In Belgium, the Non-university Higher Education Centres Act contains a fixed maximal proportion of some functions. There is also a financial limitation: the cost for staff cannot exceed 80% of the rate of the global subsidy.

The Portuguese and Spanish arrangements are similar. In these countries public universities have examining committees which organize competitive exams. Private universities in Spain and Portugal have their own procedures which take into account some basis requirements concerning academic qualifications. In Sweden, anyone who has applied but not been awarded the position has the right to appeal the appointment decision to the Higher Education Appellate Board.

2.3. *Are schools or universities entitled to choose freely among applicants with necessary qualifications?*

Here again a difference must be drawn between state and non-state schools. The latter enjoy more freedom, but have to take into account the employment protection legislation. Moreover in some countries, such as Belgium, a priority system exists. This means that teachers with more seniority have a better position. For state schools, it is generally a public body which organizes competitive examinations.

2.4. Is autonomy granted with respect to the fulfilment of the educational objective? Can schools or universities independently organise their curricula,?

As regards the curricula, it is noticeable that all countries provide for standardized curricula at primary and secondary level.

The question is to what extent they may depart from the standards. Although some deviation is apparently permitted, it appears that the individual school's margin is rather limited.

In both The Netherlands and Belgium, the fulfilment of the educational objective is achieved by means of qualitative or quantitative standards. The Primary Education Targets describe the level of knowledge, understanding and skills which pupils should have attained in each subject when they leave primary school. Attainment targets have also been established for the basic secondary education subjects. These provide a description of minimum qualities in the areas of knowledge, understanding and skills. A similar arrangement exists in Denmark, known as the Central Knowledge and Proficiency areas (CKP).

In France the school curricula in secondary education are largely determined by legislation which applies not only to public schools but also to non-state schools placed under an association contract with the State. However, a list of all matters in which secondary schools may act freely and autonomously is fixed by Decree. This list includes the organization of the setting up of classes and the rules for the distribution of pupils, the use to be made of the subsidies, the school timetables and the organization of school life.

Universities enjoy much greater freedom with regard to the curriculum than primary and secondary schools. We may conclude that, in general, the effective achievement of legal autonomy depends on the staff and financial resources available. We may distinguish a variation in autonomy depending on the statuary provisions or the necessary approval by the State.

In Austria the universities' autonomy is governed by the University Studies Act which sets out the principles for the structure and the contents of study schemes. In the Flemish Community of Belgium, the Non-University Higher Education Centres Act and the University Act describe the global study structure and the study fields, and fix the educational competence of each institution.

In Spain, the government must approve the general guidelines for any syllabus which leads to an official qualification. Such approval is granted upon recommendation by the Universities Council. In Portugal universities are autonomous as regards their educational objectives. They are free to create, modify and terminate study programmes. In England and Wales there is no legal regulation of curricular content or aims at university level.

2.5. *Can schools decide autonomously on the number of students?*

In almost all countries, governments may directly or indirectly exercise an influence on the number of students.

In France the number of pupils in primary education is fixed by the mayor of the municipality. For secondary education the decentralized state authorities decide on the geographical allocation of students.

In Germany the number of pupils per class is determined by the Ministry of Education. In Ireland there are recommended maximum and minimum numbers for a class. In Denmark the Public Schools Act sets certain limits, i.e. a maximum number of pupils per class. In Belgium the number of pupils per class is not explicitly laid down. The number of pupils per class depends on the number of teachers, and the number of funded teachers depends on time equivalents calculated in relation to the total number of pupils in the school. Only the Swedish report mentions that there are no regulations about the number of pupils per class.

Various systems exist to determine the number of university students.

In The Netherlands there are central entry systems. In France entry selection is prohibited except in medicine and certain technical subjects. Likewise in Belgium, there are no entry exams, except in medicine and engineering

Germany operates *numerus clausus* and *numerus fixus* systems, in which higher educational institutions are not free to determine the number of students.

In Portugal universities decide autonomously on the number of students per class. However, they have to observe the prescribed staff/student ratio limits.

2.5. *Autonomy of resources: Are schools/universities free to determine the raising and expenditure of financial resources? Do they have facilities to raise money through sponsoring or through other means, etc.? Are they allowed to charge tuition fees?*

State and subsidized schools receive their money from the State (salaries) and from the local community. Sometimes there is a relationship between the number of pupils and the money they receive.

Tuition fees are prohibited for so long as education remains compulsory.

Financial contributions may be raised for the non-education part of all full-time education subjects, up to a certain maximum.

Sponsoring is allowed in all schools. These have the right to raise money via sponsoring but such revenue should preferably be used for educational aims.

As regards state funding the universities and/or the non-university higher education centres receive a lump-sum, but the salaries are already fixed by law and often paid direct by the state. In Austria 98% of the financial resources of Austrian universities are covered by the state budget but the real level of financial autonomy depends on the restrictions which may be imposed on the use of state subsidies.

Besides the subsidies received from the State, universities may raise finances by other means. In general universities are free to use income from donations and services as they see fit.

At university level tuition fees are not allowed in Austria, Sweden, Ireland, Denmark and Germany. In France the registration fee is fixed by the Minister for Education.

However, in view of the state subsidies, additional charges may be imposed on students. In England, Wales and Belgium tuition fees are allowed. In the latter country the amount of the tuition fee is fairly low.

2.6. *Autonomy of organization for schools?*

In nearly all countries education legislation interferes with the internal organization of both state and non-state schools. This reflects government attempts to rationalize the structure of the education system. The political organs of the local authorities determine how their schools will be managed. Non-state schools have more freedom but they are obliged to have participation organs in which parents and teachers are represented.

Universities are free to determine their internal organization, subject to the obligation to establish various types of boards, allowing a broad representation of interest groups. In Spain, for example the election process and powers of the bodies are determined in the university basic charter, which must comply with the minimum requirements imposed by the University Reform Act.

2.7. *Are schools or universities entitled to defend their autonomous sphere by legal means against the state or government? Do schools have the legal capacity to appeal against acts of a supervisory authority?*

Judicial action against the government is only possible if education is organized by a body which is independent from the central government. Where schools have no right of action, this is usually because they are so closely connected to the authorities that they are part of the authority itself.

In general, schools may defend their autonomous sphere by challenging a decision in an administrative court.

In The Netherlands, for example, the school and the university are legal persons which may defend their autonomy sphere against the minister or the inspectorate in an administrative court. In France, decisions are subject to appeal before an administrative judge. In Belgium, a legislative act which is in breach of the rights and freedoms with regard to education or the principle of equality can be annulled by the Constitutional Court. If a government Act is unlawful, any interested party, including a school board or the competent organ of the Community Education may request the Council of State to suspend and annul it. The law may also organize an administrative procedure. Sometimes this procedure has to be followed before an appeal to the Council of State is admissible.

Austrian universities have the right to lodge a complaint with the Austrian Supreme Administrative Court against the final supervisory decision.

In England and Wales it would in principle be possible to defend any unlawful interference in the governance or conduct of a school by a Local Education Authority or the Secretary of State by way of an Application for Judicial Review in the High Court. Recently, the conduct by the Office of Standards in Education (OFSTED) of school inspections has given rise to considerable dissatisfaction on the part of individual school governing bodies, and it is possible to envisage a legal challenge by way of Judicial Review in this context. A significant recent development in this context has been the appointment of an Adjudicator to adjudicate over such disputes between school governing bodies and OFSTED.

In Ireland the process of Judicial Review of administrative acts is available to schools and teachers. In Denmark any educational institution defined as a self-governing body will be regarded as a legal person distinct from the State, and accordingly may defend its legal sphere against the State.

In Spain, direct-grant schools have recourse to a complaints procedure, conducted before a conciliation committee. If no agreement can be reached, the matter may be submitted to the courts.

In Germany schools do not have the right to appeal against decisions of the Ministry of Science. In Austria the same is true. Schools have no legal capacity to appeal against measures taken by the supervisory authority. In Spain and in Portugal state schools do not have the power to contest decisions.

3. Individual autonomy

3.1. *How much latitude of discretion is granted to teachers/professors in educational matters (content of education and methodological decisions)?*

In principle, schools enjoy less autonomy than universities in pedagogical matters.This is due to the principle of academic freedom. Teachers are mostly considered as members of a pedagogical team, which reduces their freedom. This team works out a pedagogical project and a local school policy. The teacher's margin to act autonomously is rather limited. In fact, this autonomy is limited to actual decisions, such as teaching method, punishment and the assessment of pupils.

For universities, even more than for non-university institutions, academic freedom is considered axiomatic. In most countries the professor may determine the content of the course, the teaching method and the principles for assessment. However there is a tendency towards less freedom through the introduction of quality assessment and educational plans and new methods.

At Austrian universities, persons qualified for scientific teaching enjoy full discretion as regards the content and methods of their teaching. This rule applies only to universities, not to other higher-education institutions.

3.2. *Is the head of a school (university) or any of its bodies entitled to issue instructions in professional matters to the teaching staff?*

The general tendency is for the school headteacher to have pedagogical and administrative responsibility, including the power to give instructions to the teaching staff.

In France, for example, the idea of pedagogical autonomy is strongly rooted among teachers and their unions, despite the recent tendency towards granting the headteacher or inspectorate more pedagogical power.

In Belgium new legislation governs the relationship between the headteacher and the teachers. The headteacher has to work out a function description for each teacher. This description sets out the teacher's tasks. Once every three years teachers are assessed on the basis of their function description. The manner in which teachers fulfil their tasks and exercise their pedagogical autonomy may thus be monitored.

For universities the relationship between professors and the head of the institutes is more decentralized at faculty or departmental level.

3.3. *Do teachers/professors participate in the universities' or schools' self-governing bodies?*

In nearly all European countries, schools are required to set up a participation council. Sometimes the school itself, the city or town council, and even pupils are represented in this body. Only in Ireland do teachers not yet have a self-governing body.

In universities, the academic staff is included in the different bodies. The terminology varies from country to country and even from university to university. However, the basic principles appear to be the same in all cases.

In France, for example, universities' organs are firstly, the administrative council; secondly, the scientific committee; and thirdly, the committee on study and university life. The administrative council is the most important organ since it takes policy decisions, votes on the university budget, decides on the allocation of posts and approves agreements and conventions signed by the vice-chancellor. All three bodies (the administrative council, the scientific committee and the committee on study and university life) are made up of representatives elected from the teaching body, research workers, students and management, technical, manual and administrative staff as well as representatives from outside the university.

4. Consequences of autonomy

4.1. *If educational institutions can act autonomously, how are general aims or values like quality and unity of the education guaranteed?*

In Belgium and The Netherlands, quality and unity of education are guaranteed by attainment targets. Likewise in Denmark, the Central Knowledge and Proficiency areas form a tool to ensure unity.

In Austria the unity of education is guaranteed by curricula based on the School Organisation Act. These are binding, although schools may focus on specific priorities within the curriculum.

The education inspection has the most important task in order to guarantee the unity of education. The inspection may take different forms and may be organized at different levels.

In Belgium a distinction should be drawn between the assessment of schools and teacher guidance. The assessment is aimed at the functioning of a school and the achievement of targets; guidance, on the other hand, is targeted at the individual teacher.

In Germany there are new systems of monitoring and quality assessment which try to combine internal and external evaluation. The level of quality control in this new system should be a 'school-programme' in which schools have to describe their aims and goals in advance.

In France the unity of the system is guaranteed by inspection teams at national, regional and local level. At national level there are two kind of inspection teams: the General Inspectorate of National Education charged with the inspection of pedagogical matters, and the General Inspectorate of the Administration of National Education for administrative and financial matters.

In England and Wales the key mechanism for quality assurance in schools is the periodic inspection of the school by OFSTED (Office of Standards in Education).

In Ireland unity is guaranteed by inspections at primary level and by examinations at secondary level.

In Spain schools are assessed by the civil service of the respective central and autonomous community, with the aid of the State Education Council.

For universities and non-university higher education centres, special bodies exist to guarantee the unity and the non-university quality of the education.

In France, the universities' activities are monitored by a National Assessment Committee. This consists of 17 members, elected by a scientific committee, the Conseil d'Etat and the Cour des Comptes.

In Germany systems of quality control are organized with a view to respecting the principle of academic freedom. In Denmark the Centre for Quality Assurance and Assessment of Higher Education has to contribute to quality ensuring the higher education programmes.

In Spain co-ordination is carried out by the Minister of Education and Culture of the Autonomous Community. The regional Autonomous Community exercises political control; at state level this supervision is exercised by the Spanish parliament. In Austria there are two instruments to guarantee the achievement of general aims or values such as quality and unity of education at universities. The first is cooperation between the Austrian universities, and the second lies in the supervisory function of the Minister of Science and Traffic. Other significant organs are the Curatorium of Universities and the Conference of Rectors, both with advisory powers.

4.2. *Is autonomy linked with a supervisory power?*

Supervisory power is necessary, but the obligations and monitoring should not affect autonomy by going further than is necessary to achieve their purpose in the public interest, and in order to guarantee the quality and equality of education at the level concerned.

School autonomy has been developed and refined but has been paralleled by significant supervisory and monitoring trends. External inspection teams have the power to issue 'warning notices' to schools, where concern exists over the quality of educational provision. In Austria, for example the inspection may issue instructions to individual teachers and governing bodies.

In England and Wales the Secretary of State has important powers of intervention at individual school level and may ultimately direct the closure of a school which is severely failing. He also has a significant role to play in approving, modifying or rejecting education development plans drawn up by the Local Education Authorities. Besides the Secretary of State, OFSTED remains a central feature of process of monitoring and control. In Spain there is likewise a central inspection institution, the National Quality Assessment Institute in which the education administrations are involved. In Portugal, Education Inspection Services are to be noted.

At university level, more and more inspections are taking place both at internal and external level.

To The Netherlands and Belgium visitation committees exist. These must draw up a report on the functioning of each university. In Portugal new external audits are compulsory and the reports must be sent to the Ministry of Education.

4.4. *If there are recent trends in your country with respect to autonomy of educational institutions: is there a tendency towards enlargement of autonomy or towards more government control? Why is this so? (examples)*

In most countries, a tendency towards more autonomy is noticeable. School boards are made more responsible and in particular have gained autonomy in the field of financial matters.

In Belgium there is the principle of lump-sum financing. Schools receive a budget, which they are free to use as they wish, provided it is for educational purposes.

On the other hand we observe that pedagogical autonomy appears to be decreasing. The State imposes numerous requirements with regard to the aims of education, the output to be achieved and the duty to cooperate with other school boards.

In Spain, where schools have always enjoyed less autonomy, there appears to be a tendency (albeit in its early phases) towards greater freedom. Likewise in France, the principles of subsidiarity and autonomy are becoming established in the organization of the administrative system.

The Austrian report mentions that 'decentralising decision making power' is a better reflection of reality than 'autonomy for schools'. Because of the power of superior administrative units to overrule decisions, it is not appropriate to talk about autonomy in connection with schools.

Despite the general tendency towards more autonomy, certain shifts in the opposite direction may be observed.

In England and Wales there is a major centralizing policy. A significant expansion of external and centralized control is underway from the level of the central department down through the Local Education Authority to the level of each individual school. Likewise in Ireland and Denmark there is a clear tendency towards less autonomy.

For universities there is a tendency towards more autonomy. Autonomy has been recognized as a means of strengthening the responsibility and accountability of universities, to activate the innovative potential and to reduce a counter-productive bureaucracy. The quality of the fulfilment of the tasks of universities can be improved by strengthening university autonomy.

HILDE PENNEMAN

Synoptic Review of the Country Reports

1. Constitutional legal basis

1.1. Is autonomy of the educational system or of some of its parts constitutionally guaranteed?

The Netherlands	The autonomy of the educational system is guaranteed by Article 23 of the Dutch Constitution. Public (-authority) schools are generally governed by an organ of the state. Private schools are run by corporate bodies under civil law and enjoy autonomy–freedom of education. Article 23 of the Constitution is concerned with primary and secondary education. Many principles of Article 23 of the Constitution also apply to other sectors like secondary education, vocational training and higher education.
Belgium	Article 24 of the Constitution, which deals with the rights and liberties with regard to education, does not guarantee autonomy 'as such'.
France	L'autonomie du système éducatif n'est pas garaneste constitutionnellement. Au contraire: l'Etat est le responsable du système éducatif et à l'obligation d'organiser un enseignement public, laïque et gratuit.
Germany	By constitution schools are not autonomous. Therefore teachers in the school have no constitutional right of freedom in teaching. Autonomy of Higher Education Institutions is a part of Article 5 § 3 of the German Federal Constitution, the Basic Law.

Walter Berka, Jan de Groof and Hilde Penneman (eds.), Autonomy in Education, 41–91.

Austria	For schools there is not a constitutional guarantee of academic freedom but the constitution does guarantees the freedom to maintain and run private schools and the right to education. Since 1993 the autonomy of universities in Austria is constitutionallyguaranteed by Article 2 paragraph 2 of the Austrian Act on the Organisation of Universities. Until then the autonomy of universities was considered to be an emanation of the freedom of science.
England and Wales	There is no written constitution.
Ireland	Yes. The family is recognized as the primary and natural educator of the child, which is subject to the State's right as guardian of the common good. Every religious denomination has the right to maintain and manage its own educational institutions.
Denmark	Article 76 Constitution: 'All children of school age shall be entitled to free instruction in primary schools. Parents or guardians making their own arrangements for their children or wards to receive instruction equivalent to the general primary school standard shall not be obliged to have their children or wards taught in a publicly provided school.' Education offered after compulsory education is not covered by the Constitution.
Sweden	There are no guarantees in the Constitution.
Spain	The principle of autonomy is guaranteed in the Constitution Freedom of Education means that there cannot be a State monopoly in education. The Constitution also guarantees to individuals and corporations the freedom to establish educational centres. The Constitution recognizes: university autonomy is 'in the terms established by law'.
Portugal	No. The autonomy of Universities is legally granted by the Constitution.

1.2. Does the constitution guarantee teacher's educational freedom or the liberty of scientific teaching (academic freedom)?

The Netherlands	Article 23 § 2 of the Constitution (freedom of education) contains the right of the individual to teach. (This right

	is given up when he/she accepts an appointment at a school.) The school board becomes the subject of the right (the freedom of education). Academic freedom is constituted by Article 23 of the Constitution. The teacher at a university also has to accept the authority of the board.
Belgium	The Constitution does not actually guarantee any form of academic freedom or freedom to teach.
France	Le Conseil Constitutionnel fait de l'indépendance des professeurs de l'enseignement supérieur un principe fondamental reconnu par les lois de la République, qui a donc valeur constitutionnelle. Préciser les contours du principe (voire rapport). Le fait de prévoir par voie réglementaire l'organisation de procédures d'évaluation des enseignements supérieurs « faisant notamment appel à l'appréciation des étudiants » ne porte pas atteinte au principe, dans la meseure où cela ne comporte aucune incidence sur les prérogatives ou la carrière des enseignants.
Germany	No. The constitutional right of academic freedom and autonomy of the single researcher is primarily directed towards persons who are involved in scientific research and teaching.
Austria	No. The schoolteacher is subject to the directions of the public administration. The liberty of scientific teaching is constitutionally guaranteed by the Basic Law 1867. The liberty does not relate to teachers/professors at institutes and classes of the non-university sector of higher education. They educate on the basis of scientific views and findings. Universities educate by science.
England and Wales	No constitutional guarantees.
Ireland	No. There is a tradition to respect it within certain parameters.
Denmark	Parents or guardians can make their own arrangements for instruction but the output has to be equivalent to the general primary school standard'. In the constitution there are no requirements for standards of academic freedom.

Sweden	No.
Spain	There is educational freedom for each teacher, whatever their teaching level comparable with the right of freedom of expression. The right to academic freedom is protected by the Constitution.
Portugal	No. Academic freedom is not mentioned in the Constitution.

1.3. If autonomy is constitutionally granted: which notion of autonomy underlies the constitution?

The Netherlands	The autonomy is not absolute. Schools can never be entirely independent from the State. The freedom of education consists of three rights: the right to found a school, freedom of direction, freedom of organization.
Belgium	Article 24 § 1 of the Constitution establishes the 'freedom of education'. Freedom of education means that everyone has the right to organize education and to establish educational institutions without any interference, not even preventive measures, by the government.
France	No answer.
Germany	No. The old German idea: university is a community of persons who do research and teaching. Freedom of scientific research is important for the single researcher and also for the development of the society.
Austria	Autonomy is not embodied in the Constitution. Autonomy is granted by the constitutional provision of the Austrian Act on the Organization of Universities 1993. It means the right to decide independently those public affairs which are linked to the picture of universities and scientific research. The autonomy of institutes and classes of the non-university sector of higher education in Austria is part of social autonomy and means the practice of social freedom.
England and Wales	No constitutional guarantees.
Ireland	Family and parental autonomy as family is recognized as the primary and natural educator.

Denmark	To ensure the principle of free choice of school types, the State provides subsidies amounting to 80% of the costs for various types of private schools to ensure their organizational independence.
Sweden	–
Spain	– University autonomy is a basic constitutional concept for the configuration of the regular legal system governing universities.
Portugal	– Framework Law on the Autonomy of Public Universities 1988. Universities have statutory, financial, administrative, scientific and pedagogic autonomy.

1.4. Are there strict legal bases and describe it

The Netherlands	The freedoms of the Constitution are further developed in the Acts for Education. The freedom of scientific teaching is protected by the Higher Education Act.
Belgium	Yes, ARGO Act of 1988 and the Act of Community Education of 1998.
France	Dans l'enseignement primaire public, il n'y a pas d'établissement au sens strict du terme. Les écoles ne disposent donc ni de la personnalité juridique, ni de l'autonomie financière; elles ne constituent que de services non personnalisés assurant un service public d'Etat et fonctionnant dans des locaux propriétés communales. Elles n'ont pas de budget propre et leur administration matérielle incombe à la commune. Le directeur d'école appartient au même corps que les autres enseignants et il a surtout des compétences de coordination et d'animation. L'enseignement secondaire public est au contraire traditionnellement assuré par des établissements publics. Le collèges et lycées publics constituent des établissements publics locaux d'enseignement (E.P.L.E.), rattachés aux départements (collèges) ou aux régions (lycées). C'est donc de la loi que les collèges et les lycées tirent leur

caractère d'établissements publics, et donc l'existence de leur personnalité juridique et de leur autonomie financière ; ils ont en particulier un conseil d'administration élu et un budget propre voté par ce conseil.
Dans l'enseignement supérieur, une nouvelle catégorie d'établissement public, l'établissement public à caractère scientifique, culturel et professionnel (E.P.S.C.P.). Toutes les universités sont des E.P.S.C.P.; en revanche, tous les E.P.S.C.P. ne sont pas des universités. Et par ailleurs, il existe des établissement d'enseignement supérieur qui ne sont pas des E.P.S.C.P.

Germany	– In fields closely connected with scientific research the professors must have the majority in the deciding committees. Therefore in the Framework Law of the Federal State in Germany on Higher Education regulations are set which had to be accepted by the Länder and incorporated into their Laws on Higher Education.
Austria	School autonomy is not embodied in Constitutional law. It has gradually been introduced since 1993 and is based upon ordinary legislation. State responsibility for schools and the right to found private schools are also developed in other Acts. The legal basis of the autonomy of universities in Austria is shaped by the Austrian Act on the Organisation of Universities 1993, which has been supplemented concerning studies at Austrian Universities by the Austrian Act on Studies at Universities. The Act on the Organisation of Universities defines duties of Austrian universities, statutes and other organizational elements. The Austrian Act on Studies at Universities forms the legal framework for studies, courses, students' rights and duties, admission, rules of exams etc. The legal basis for institutes and classes of the non-university sector of Higher Education is continued in the Austrian Act on Classes of the Non-University Sector of Higher Education. The Act defines the holders of such classes and the purposes and principles of the classes.
England and Wales	Education Act 1996; School Inspection Act on school inspections and quality control in schools; Education Act 1997; School Standards and Framework Act 1998.

The Higher Education Act 1998 provided for the establishment of General Teaching Councils for England and Wales with wide-ranging functions relating to the school-teaching profession, for professional qualifications specifically for the headteachers of schools, and new arrangements for financial support for students and for the payment of fees at institutions of further and higher education.

Ireland –

Denmark The restrictions of academic freedom are set out in ordinary acts.

Sweden Swedish Education Act: Each individual municipality is free to decide how its schools should be run.
Higher Education Act: Methods shall be freely developed.

Spain Freedom of creation of educational centres is also regulated by ongoing legislation: the freedom to establish a particular ideology or nature, the right of the owner to manage the centre as they see fit, the possibility of public funding of private centres.

Portugal –

No, there are no strict legal bases, so the government and Parliament can regulate the way autonomy is put into practice.

2. Autonomy of educational institutions

2.1. Is autonomy granted with respect to the organization of educational institutions? Are schools or universities vested with a legal personality of their own? Have schools or universities individual constitutions of their own (basic statutes, basic charters)? Are these autonomously set up by the educational institutions or conferred onto them by the state or government?

The Netherlands The freedom of private schools and other educational institutions is constrained by funding conditions. Private schools are governed by foundations of associations. These legal persons have their base in the Civil Law Code book. Most public primary and secondary schools are run by a municipal executive or a committee of governors. Since 1996 public schools can also be governed by a foundation indirectly related to the municipality.

The public institutions for higher education are administered by public legal persons which are regulated in the Higher Education Act.

Belgium

Free education: the Primary Education Act set up an organizing body or school board as a condition for subsidies. Almost all bodies have adopted the form of a VZW (non-profit association). The Act on Community Education of 1998 redrew the whole structure of Community education. The Act created a new body: the Community education. This body has legal personality in public law. The schools which are organized by the provinces and the municipalities do not have legal personality.
Legal personality in private law is a subsidy condition for the free non-university higher education centres. The free non university higher education centres are all organized like a non-profit association (cf. Hogenscholen Act)
The autonomous non-university higher education centres each have legal personality and their own school board. Universities are recognized by law in the University Act. They all have legal personality.

France

Même s'ils disposent aussi de la personnalité juridique, les établissements secondaires n'ont pas cette autonomie statutaire et leur organisation est déterminée par décret donc par décisions du gouvernement, générale, commune à tous les établissements.
Les E.P.S.C.P. bénéficient de l'autonomie statutaire; ils ont donc le pouvoir de déterminer 'leur statuts et leurs structures internes conformément aux dispositions de la loi'. D'autre part, la désignation de leurs organes résulte exclusivement du principe de l'élection; en particulier, le président de l'E.P.S.C.P. est élu librement par les conseils qui existent au sein de l'établissement. Pour le reste, les E.P.S.C.P. répondent au régime juridique général des établissements publics (personnalité juridique et autonomie financière).
Seules les universités ont l'autonomie statutaire qui leur permet de s'organiser librement et de voter leurs propres statuts. Encore faut-il rappeler que cette autonomie ne peut s'exercer que dans le cadre de la loi votée par le Parlement.

Germany

Schools are legal institutions but they do not have a legal personality. They are still organized as a part of the administrative system of the State.
Higher Educational Institutions have a legal personality; they are corporations following the rules of public law. They have the right to organize their own internal affairs. The procedures and rights are described in basic statutes but within the legal framework set by the Law on Higher Education.

Austria

Schools are not vested with a legal personality of their own but considered as dependent units. A legal personality may be established at school level according to Article 128c of the School Organisation Act. Bodies with a legal personality are obliged to produce an annual account which must be submitted to the educational authorities. Money obtained from sponsoring or advertizing activities is retained by the school.
Austrian school law does not provide for charters in which the schools may decide on their internal structure. Only some categories of private schools take decisions regarding their internal structure by means of a statute which has to be submitted to the Minister of Education and Cultural Affairs for approval.
The organs which represent a university (rector, dean, senate etc.) are prescribed by law. The organizational autonomy of universities centres on the autonomous election of the central monocratic university organs. Universities are considered to be institutions of the Federal State of Austria. They are federal offices. They are vested with a limited personality under private law but are now recognized as legal persons under public law by judicial decree. Universities are entitled to adopt foundational statutes. These statutes are adopted and amended autonomously, but subject to the approval of the Austrian Minister of Science and Traffic.
The holders of classes and institutes of the non-university sector in higher education may be legal persons under public law as well as under private law. The Act on classes of the Non-university Sector in Higher Education only contains a few provisions with reference to the internal structure of the respective institutions. All the other legal structural prerequisites follow from the gene-

ral law applicable depending on the legal corporation, etc. Those Classes must be formally recognized by the Council of the Non-university Sector in Higher Education. The decisions on recognition need the approval of the Minster of Science and Traffic. The autonomous right to adopt statutes of their own follows from the law ruling the organization of the respective holder.

England and Wales — School Standard and Framework Act 1998. Every maintained school is required to have a governing body, which is a body corporate in English law.
Universities fall into two main categories: (a) those founded before the Further and Higher Education Act 1992, which are generally governed in accordance with a Royal Charter; and (b) those founded since the enactment of the 1992 Act, whose governance is provided for in that Act. The majority of those in category (b) are former 'Polytechnics'.

Ireland — Primary Education: primary schools were not established by statute but as a result of an educational experiment. This informal structure has continued until today. The education Bill 1997 proposes to establish a statutory framework for first- and second-level education.
Secondary Education: minimum statutory provision made in the Intermediate Education Act.
The Vocational Education Act provides a statutory basis for the vocational schools and community colleges.
Universities: Trinity College, or the University of Dublin, was established by Queen Elizabeth 1 in 1592.
Maynooth College was established by Act of Parliament.
Newer universities are grounded in statutes by University Acts.
The Universities Act 1997 reconstitutes the three colleges of the national University of Ireland as full universities; provides for the updating of the universities' governing structures and redefines the relationship between the State and the universities.

Denmark — Two groups of institutions: Basic institutions provide publicly approved tuition and education in accordance with the respective laws. Alternative institutions are not established with the view of fulfilling a public obligation. They enjoy greater autonomy.

An educational institution may well be vested with a legal personality of its own. As for private self-governing institutions, the statutes are often subject to approval by the Ministry of Education.

Non-public schools: their approval by the Ministry of Education is quite closely regulated.

Public schools: the law provides a legal framework, within which the municipality must set out a statute.

Youth education: the system is flexible and designed to meet the individual needs of a large variety of students.

Higher education: at university level the universities are administered by a Framework Act and their individual statutes. The system is based on extensive self-government. At non-university level a majority of institutions are self-governing, private, state-financed institutions; the others are state institutions or county institutions. They all have a board and a rector. The appointments of rector and institutional staff are made by the Ministry of Education. Short-cycle higher education is governed by a ministerial framework.

Sweden

The board of the school in each municipality has a legal personality. Each independent school approved by the National Agency for Education has a legal personality.

State universities are regulated by the Higher Education Act. Non-state universities have a wider autonomy and are only subject to the Higher Education Act to a limited degree.

Spain

State educational institutions are those owned by a public authority.

They are under the control of local government. They are bound by constitutional guarantee and the guarantee of ideological neutrality. Direct-grant educational establishments are under private ownership and are individual legal entities which have signed an educational accord establishing rights and obligations on both sides.

Private educational institutions are owned by either an individual or legal entity and the type of ownership must be recorded in the Ministry of Education and Culture's public register of institutions.

Public universities have their make-up defined in the University Reform Act and in their own statutes as Public Entities, Corporations or Institutions, as a public service,

with their own legal title and capital, independent of the State and other public entities.
Private Universities and Catholic Church Universities are recognized by Act of National or autonomous Parliament. Their statutes were approved by the owner and the university community is involved in their drafting.

Portugal

Schools have a private budget and are regulated internally. Schools do not have legal personality.
Public universities are vested with a legal personality and free to organize themselves under the general broad framework defined by the legislation. They are free to approve their own statutes.

2.2. How independently can they determine the recruitment of their personnel, etc.?

The Netherlands

Private schools and institutions have the right of appointment of teachers (cf. Article 33 § 6 Dutch Constitution). This also includes the appointment of school managers and non-teaching staff. Private denominational schools can ask their employees to make a commitment towards the religious principles of the school. Recruitment of personnel is an autonomous competence but several Education Acts require that teachers have certain degrees and certificates concerning competence and conduct. Government has the right to examine the competence and moral integrity of teachers. Government has taken measures to cut down on expenditure for unemployed teachers.

Belgium

Free education: free educational institutions have the right to recruit their personnel. Once recruited, the relationship between the personnel and the school board of a free institution is regulated by private contract. The personnel of the Community education and the official subsidized education are civil servants under a specific statute. The personnel of the institutions of the local authorities are appointed by the Executive College. This recruitment has to be ratified by the Provincial or Municipal Council. In the new system, the personnel or the Community education will be recruited by the head of the school.

The Non-university Higher Education Act contains rules on maximum numbers for teaching staff, on job specifications and there is a fixed maximum proportion of some functions. There is also a financial limitation. The University Act ensures a broad range of autonomy. The salary scales of the teaching staff of all universities are fixed by the government, but Education Act X gives more options for the university board to vary between several scales according to the merits and reputation of the teaching staff.

France

Aucune institution d'enseignement, à quelque niveau que ce soit, n'a le pouvoir de déterminer le nombre des emplois de personnels titulaires (enseignants ou non enseignants) dont elle peut disposer. Ses dotations en la matière sont déterminées par le ministère central à partir du budget voté par le Parlement.

Pour les autres ordres d'enseignement (primaire et secondaire), toutes les nominations de personnels résultent d'une décision individuelle des autorités de l'Etat.

En revanche, les Universités peuvent engager sur leurs budgets propres des personnels vacataires ou contractuels dont elles ont la maîtrise du recrutement. Les textes leur fixent cependant certaines limites en matière de recrutement d'enseignants.

Quant au choix des personnes, il y a des distinctions à opérer. Le principe général, dans l'enseignement supérieur, est le principe du choix du personnel enseignant par des conseils internes regroupant des représentants du grade au moins égal au personnel recruté. Absolu en matière de mutation, ce principe peut connaître des atténuations en matière de première nomination, des personnels reçus à un concours de recrutement pouvant être affectés à un établissement universitaire par décision du ministère central.

Germany

Schools do not have any right of participation in recruiting their personnel.

The recruitment of scientific personnel is a 'mixed' system. The Higher Educational Institution produces a list of three persons who fulfil the conditions imposed by the Higher Educational Institute. The Ministry will normally choose the first name on the list, but can also refuse the whole list. The State has the right of final selection because it is the employer of civil servants.

Austria

Schools are dependent institutions and cannot act as employers. A contract has to be concluded with the body (Federation, provinces or local communities for public schools, for private schools an institution) which maintains the school. For teachers holding a public law appointment there is an appointment procedure which consists of three sets of proposals referred to the Minister of Education by a committee composed of parents' and teachers' representatives and vested at provincial level. The same procedure does not exist in connection with compulsory schooling.

The majority of the personnel of the Austrian Universities are employed by the Federal State of Austria. (cf. programme of posts in the state budget). The organs are entitled to make a proposal. Only within the programme of posts is the university free to decide. Decisions on posts for university professors can be taken, subject to the right of veto by the Minister of Science and Traffic. The decision of which person to actually choose falls within the autonomy of the universities, taking into account the qualifications mentioned in the Act on the Organisation of Universities.

The holders of classes or institutes are free to determine the recruitment of their personnel as well as to choose between applicants with the necessary qualifications. (For exceptions to these requirements, see the report.) They are only bound by general labour law.

England and Wales

The staffing of schools in the maintained sector, and the staffing of foundation, voluntary aided and foundation special schools is now governed by the School Standards and Framework Act 1998. There is detailed provision for the appointment, discipline, suspension and dismissal of teachers (including headteachers). Within this highly prescriptive framework, however, school governing bodies do enjoy a significant element of autonomy and discretion in the process of appointing teaching and other staff.

Ireland

Yes.

Denmark

Non-public schools are free to determine the recruitment of their personnel.

For public schools the municipality has freedom to

choose within the boundaries of the Act on Public Schools. Recruitment is one of the powers that cannot be delegated to the school.
Youth education: the board of the school hires teachers with certain requirements in vocational schools, or the county council has competence to hire upon recommendations of the headteacher in private and public gymnasium and higher preparatory examination schools.
Higher education: rules regarding the awarding of doctoral degrees, appointment of professors and academic staff are covered by ministerial orders. A review board lays the recommendations before the ministry.

Sweden

Independent schools are free to recruit their personnel. Public schools are subject to the regulations regarding qualifications in the Educational Act.
Higher Education Act: For professors there are regulations on scientific and pedagogical skills. There is the right of appeal to the Appellate Board of Higher Education.
Independent Universities and University Colleges are free to recruit their personnel and there is no right of appeal.

Spain

Non-university teachers in State Education Institutes have civil servant status. Access to the non-university state teaching service is by competitive examination under the auspices of the competent educational authorities. In direct-grant schools the selection of non-university teaching staff is governed by principles appearing in Article 60 of the Regulatory Right to Education Act. In private schools the selection of teaching staff is free, the only requirement being that the applicant possesses the qualifications required by the legislation in force.
In public universities the teaching staff are regulated by the University Reform Act. There are competitive examinations and examining Committees.
The selection of teaching staff for private universities is governed by each university's own procedures, although there are a minimum of requirements as far as academic qualifications are concerned.

Portugal

Schools cannot; teachers are recruited in a national selection process.
Staff management is free in theory because in the case of

	hiring staff Universities are funded according to a formula based on factors like academic staff–student ratios, and the number of attending students. The Minister of Education fixes the number of permanent positions based on the number of students and their distributions among the different study programmes. Universities are also free to hire non-academic staff for particular projects using their private income.

2.3. Are schools or universities entitled to choose freely among applicants with necessary qualifications?

The Netherlands	In theory, yes, but subject to restrictions, such as the obligation to re-appoint former teachers who have worked in their schools and are at that time receiving unemployment benefit. The so-called 'participatiefonds' restricts the dismissal of personnel from schools.
Belgium	The choice among applicants with the same qualifications is limited. A primary system exists. Provincial and municipal councils, as organizers of official schools, or the heads of a school of the Community have a duty to account for their choice. In higher education the institutions' boards are fairly free to choose between qualified applicants within the sketched framework. They are required to work out a procedure which they then have to respect. They have a legal duty to justify why someone is appointed.
France	–
Germany	No. Universities: mixed system (see above).
Austria	No.
England and Wales	In the maintained schools sector, teachers are required to hold qualified teacher status (Education Reform Act 1988), and must not be prohibited (by virtue, for example, of certain types of misconduct) from employment as a teacher as a result of a direction in the 1988 Act. The new General Teaching Councils for England and for Wales will be charged with the maintenance of a Register of teachers. An important innovation will be a requirement that

	headteachers hold a specific 'professional headship qualification'. In addition there is a mass of employment protection and anti-discrimination legislation. In the University sector, there is generally no legal requirement regarding qualifications, although in certain subject areas – notably medicine, dentistry, veterinary surgery – the relevant professional bodies lay down requirements as to the qualifications of those employed in the clinical sector. Anti-discrimination legislation will apply to the University sector as it does in the schools sector.
Ireland	Yes. No exams. The objects, functions and academic freedom accorded the universities is provided by the much-amended University Act 1997.
Denmark	Non-public schools: yes. Public schools: the municipality council decides. Youth education: see above. Higher education: see above.
Sweden	–
Spain	–
Portugal	Hiring of new staff must be preceded by public competition. The university is free to choose among the applicants but only under the limits prescribed by the law governing hiring of civil servants.

2.4. Is autonomy granted with respect to the fulfilment of the educational objective? Can schools or universities independently organize their curricula, decide autonomously on the numbers of students per class, etc?

The Netherlands	Central Government control may be exercised by imposing qualitative or quantitative standards for the educational process in schools and/or for the results they produce. The Primary Education Targets Decree describes for every subject the level of knowledge, understanding and skills that pupils should have attained when they leave primary education. Registration of the progress of these pupils is obligatory.

Attainment targets have also been established for the basic secondary education subjects. These provide a description of minimum qualities in the areas of knowledge, understanding and skills. For the second phase of secondary education there will be a change in the near future: there will be a choice of four profiles (see report) and a new form of secondary education in the concept of learning to learn: Project Studyhouse (to allow differentiation in classical lessons and time in which the pupils have to work for themselves).

Schools for general education and preparatory vocational education will have to offer 'learning routes' in vocational education. Since the 1996 Act on Vocational Training and Education the institutions themselves are responsible for examinations in the entire field of secondary vocational education (with the exception of examinations for the core subjects).

Higher Education and Research Act: includes the objectives and the general structure of education. Universities and Higher Education Institutes have central-entry systems. Restrictions are put on the maximum intake every year (labour-market problems).

The institutions determine their own curricula and their own examination procedures.

Belgium

The Flemish Community sets forth a set of basic competences and development goals which have to be reached by a certain group of pupils after a certain educational period. Inspection controls the results of the overall educational process, no longer the process itself. The schools have to work out a curriculum in relation to the basic competences and development goals. This curriculum must be approved by the government. Schools have to work out a school action plan that reflects, among other things, the pedagogical project. The government indirectly influences the number of pupils per class. The government determines the structure of education.

The universities and the non-university higher education centres are free to develop the curricula of their study programmes. However, there are limits set out in the Acts.

France

L'affectation des élèves dans les écoles est en principe de la compétence du maire de la commune. Il agit en pareil cas en

qualité d'agent de l'Etat et il délègue souvent l'exercice de cette compétence au directeur de l'école concernée. Dans les établissements secondaires, elle relève de la compétence des autorités déconcentrées de l'Etat, très généralement l'inspecteur d'académie au niveau du département. Cette affectation obéit à un principe de carte scolaire largement définie à partir du domicile des candidats. Le ministère a cependant atténué la rigueur du principe en instaurant, depuis une quinzaine d'années, des procédures de « sectorisation souple », qui permettent, sous la responsabilité de l'inspecteur d'académie, des dérogations au secteur.
Dans les universités: Il est interdit toute sélection à l'entrée en premier cycle, sauf dans quelques disciplines (essentiellement celles du secteur santé et certaines formations technologiques. Les universités fixent une capacité d'accueil dans chacune de leurs formations et elles sont obligées d'inscrire tous les candidats qui se présentent, tant que cette capacitré n'est pas atteinte. Lorsqu'elle l'est, il appartient au recteur d'académie, autorité déconcentrée de l'Etat, de répartir les candidats ensurnombre, en particulier en fonction de leur domicile, de leur situation de famille et des préférences qu'ils ont exprimé. En troisième cycle, la sélection est en revanche admise.
Il faut distinguer la décision sur les curricula et les questions d'organisation interne. L'Etat dispose en France du monopole de collation des grades. En revanche, les établissements scolaires et universitaires disposent d'une autonomie qui s'est élargie en matière éducative et pédagogique.
Les Universités peuvent délivrer deux types de diplômes: des diplômes nationaux, (en particulier ceux qui correspondent aux « grades » dont l'Etat a le monopole de la collation, licence, maîtrise, doctorat) dont le cadre est largement réglementé par l'Etatc'est au nom de celui-ci qu'elles les délivrent et il leur accorde pour ce faire une habilitation pluriannuelle renouvelée périodiquement après examen d'un dossier destiné à vérifier le respect des exigences posées par les textes. Cela n'interdit cependant pas une certaine souplesse dans l'interprétation des contenus des enseignements dispensés, où la latitude laissée aux enseignants est coutumièrement très grande. Les Universités peuvent par ailleurs délivrer des diplômes

d'université, dont elles déterminent alors librement le contenu et les conditions de validation. Mais les diplômes de cette seconde catégorie ne peuvent pas porter des noms qui permettraient une confusion avec les grades « protégés ».

Germany

Schools have to teach within the framework set by curricula laid down by the Ministry of Education of each 'Land'. The number of pupils per class is defined by the Ministry of Education.

The curricula are influenced by the state-examinations at the end of the studies in Higher Educational Institutions. New courses of studies require the permission of the Ministry of Science.

The number of students are laid down by the conditions set by the Law on Higher Education of the 'Land'. Because of the numerus clausus and numerus fixus, the Higher Educational Institutions are not free to determine the numbers of students.

Austria

Regarding autonomy in curricular matters, schools may vary from the standard curriculum within a given framework. Schools may indepently decide on the size of classes or on the size of groups in which individual subjects are going to be taught.

The autonomy of universities with respect to the educational objective is ruled by the Act on Studies at Universities with all principles for the structure of studies and for the contents of study schemes. The Act further defines the various categories of subjects and types of exams in an abstract manner. Concerning the contents of the studies the law only contains provisions for their purpose, for their duration, and for the number of hours available per semester. Thus, the law is oriented towards regulating necessary resources and procedural guarantees in order to safeguard the rule of law concerning the admission to universities and exams. Within this legal framework the study commissions are free to take decisions on curricula. This refers to the structure of studies into two or three phases, their division into several branches, and the laying down of a catalogue of obligatory and non-obligatory subjects. This also applies to rules on exams which define the types and methods of exams. The supervisory power of the Minister of Science and Traffic does not extend to a material examination of the study schemes (Art. 15 par 3). The realization of this broad legal autonomy concerning the fulfilment of the educational objective depends, however, on the available personal and financial resources. This also limits the principal freedom of study commissions to decide on the number of students per class.

The legal framework concerning the fulfilment of the educational objective of classes and institutes of the non-university sector in higher education in Austria is even more open than that for universities. The respective Act provides for a minimum duration of studies and a minimum number of hours for studies which must be offered during this period. It demands a final exam and lays down its type and general structure. All other decisions are assigned to the autonomy of the respective institution, which must provide a study scheme and rules for exams.

England and Wales

In schools within the maintained sector, curricular autonomy has been relatively limited since the introduction of the national curriculum, initially under the Education Reform Act 1988. The contents of programmes of study and assessment arrangements are set out in considerable detail in substantial documents for each subject within the national curriculum accompanying the relevant Orders.

The primary statutory provisions relating to the national curriculum are now to be found in the Education Act 1996, Part V. The school curriculum shall be 'balanced and broadly based'; it should promote 'the spiritual, moral, cultural, mental and physical development of pupils at the school and of society'; and it should prepare pupils for 'the opportunities, responsibilities and experiences of adult life'. It is provided, further, that the basic curriculum for every maintained school shall include religious education for all registered pupils, subject to parental right of withdrawal; and, in the case of secondary schools, sex education. In primary schools, the governing body has a discretion as to whether sex education should be provided.

In Universities, there is no legal regulation of curricular content or aims. However, in certain subject areas – for instance, law, medicine, dentistry, veterinary surgery,

	engineering – the relevant professional bodies lay down certain requirements regarding curricular content and subject-area coverage. In all areas of University teaching there is, however, increasingly detailed audit and inspection of the entire teaching and examination process by way of periodic 'teaching quality assessment' under the auspices of the Higher Education Funding Council. In the context of research conducted at Universities, many consider that the traditional concept of academic freedom has been significantly eroded in the past decade by virtue of a range of developments, including the abolition of the 'tenure' of established academic staff and selective funding based upon periodic assessments by the Higher Education Funding Council of research quality in Universities.
Ireland	In schools there is a national curriculum which must be followed. There are recommended figures of enrolment for maximum and minimum numbers in class.
Denmark	Non-public schools: pedagogical foundations do not have to be approved by the ministry. Public schools: a ministerial order defines 'central knowledge and proficiency areas' (CKP). The Act on public schools is a framework that does set some boundaries, e.g. minimum and maximum numbers of lessons, maximum number of pupils per class, but the municipalities and schools are left with a large degree of autonomy. Youth education: is governed by a framework laid out by Parliament which lays down the overall framework for the various types of general upper-secondary education including aims, subjects and examination forms. Higher education: general admission requirements and examinations are laid down by the Ministry of Education for the higher education programmes.
Sweden	All schools are free to build up their organization. For universities and university colleges tuition fees are forbidden. They can raise funds by gifts, research grants and contract teaching.
Spain	For non-university general education the existence of various educational authorities requires mutual cooperation in the question of objectives content, methodology and

assessment criteria, all coming under the heading of 'curriculum' in Article 4.1. of the General Educational System Act. Central government is responsible for establishing the basic aspects of the curriculum in order to guarantee a standard training.

The drawing up and approval of study and research syllabuses is an essential component of university autonomy (University Reform Act). The government, at the suggestion of the university's Council approves the general guidelines of syllabuses to be followed in order to obtain official qualifications, as well as their standardization. The universities following these guidelines draw up and approve the syllabuses.

Portugal

Schools have curricular autonomy implementing national curricular plans. They may promote professional guidance activities. Schools may also define their own methods of pupil evaluation.

Universities may fulfil their educational objectives autonomously. They are free to create, modify and close down study programmes, they decide autonomously the number of students per class, but they must take into account the staff/student ratios in order to keep the number of staff within the prescribed limits.

2.5. Autonomy of resources: are schools/universities free to determine the raising and expenditure of financial resources? Do they have facilities to raise money through sponsoring or through other means, etc.? Are they able to charge tuition fees?

The Netherlands

Primary Education Act: Admissions must not depend on the financial contribution of the parents. (The only exception relates to certain extra-curricula activities.) Pupils/students older than 16 must pay annual tuition fees. Sponsoring and contract-activities are allowed.

Belgium

All institutions receive money from the Community in relation to the number of pupils or students. Competition is inevitable in a system of funding based on the number of pupils. It is forbidden to undertake acts of unfair competition. Tuition fees are not charged, as compulsory education is free.

Non-university higher education centres receive a global envelope: this is a certain amount of money for personnel and administration together. Universities and non-university higher education centres can receive money from the government or private companies for research and societal service on a contractual basis. They can also participate in profit and non-profit associations. But these two alternative ways of funding are bound by stringent legal conditions. Tuitions fees are allowed, but the maximum is rather low.

France

A côté des dotations de fonctionnement attribuées par les collectivités publiques, les établissements scolaires et universitaires peuvent bénéficier d'autres types de ressources.

En raison du principe constitutionnel de gratuité de l'enseignement, ils ne peuvent décider librement de « taxer » les étudiants ou les élèves par des droits financiers. Le montant des droits d'inscription à percevoir par les universités est fixé par arrêté du ministre et la jurisprudence administrative a rappelé à plusieurs reprises que tout droit supplémentaire ne pouvait être que facultatif et devait en outre nécessairement correspondre à une prestation particulière sortant du cadre ordinaire de l'établissement.

Cependant, les établissements scolaires peuvent bénéficier de ressources propres: taxe d'apprentissage versées par les entreprises, à un taux fixé par la loi, pour le financement des activités de formation technique ou professionnelle; ressources provenant des activités de formation continue des adultes ou de la vente d'objets confectionnés. Par leur nature, nombre de ces ressources sont loin de concerner à un degré important tous les établissements.

Les universités peuvent disposer de ressources provenant de legs, dons, fondations, rémunérations de services rendus, fonds de concours, participation des employeurs par le biais de la taxe d'apprentissage (formations technologiques et professionnelles) et subventions diverses, en particulier des collectivités territoriales.

Germany

Schools receive their money from the State (salaries) and from the local community (costs for building and equipment). Schools in some Länder have the right to earn their own money via sponsoring or private school-clubs. The resources of the Higher Educational Institutions are provided more and more by a lump-sum system (salaries

are already fixed by law). Financial resources for research projects can be accepted from foundations, other state institutions and also private firms.
Tuition fees are not allowed at present, but new discussions are under way which may change this situation.

Austria

Only private schools are allowed to raise tuition fees. Public schools are free of charge (with the exception of contributions to teaching aids, but not in compulsory schools). Financial contributions may be raised for the non-instruction part of all-day forms of schools, the maximum amount being fixed by means of an ordinance. Sponsoring is permitted but must be used for educational purposes.
More than 98% of the financial resources of Austrian universities are covered by the state budget. The Minister of Science and Traffic, however, takes the final political decision as to precisely how to distribute the financial means according to the law, as adopted by the Parliament. The annual distribution of financial means by the minister differentiates between accomodation and posts for personnel and equipment and running costs (Article 17 paragraph 4 Act on the Organisation of Universities). The effective dimension of financial autonomy thus depends on how detailed these ministerial allocations are. Universities are free to raise money through sponsoring and any other means in accordance with general laws. The extent of this money will not, however, surmount the role of supplementing the state contribution to the university budget. Universities are not allowed to charge tuition fees.
The holders of classes and institutes of the non-university sector in higher education (Fachhochschul-Studiengänge, Fachhochschulen) are not constrained in their financial autonomy by legal norms, apart from general laws. In practice, no class of this sector could exist in Austria without the considerable financial involvement of the State. The State can thus influence the development of the non-university sector in higher education in Austria in material, qualitative and quantitative regard without any legal determination, just by using the instrument of their recognition. This instrument has also been used by non-admitting classes and institutes to charge tuition fees.

England and Wales

Schools in the maintained sector are financed through

	their local education authority on the basis of a 'budget share' allocated to each school by the maintaining authority. Maintained schools are prohibited from charging fees, with limited exceptions. In practice, however, many schools do seek and obtain donations from parents and engage in a range of fund-raising activities. Universities are funded through Higher Education Funding Council grants; tuition fees paid by students through the Research Councils; through contracts with the private sector; and through the fruits of extensive fund-raising activities.
Ireland	Some schools supplement the funding of the school with sponsored walks and cake sales. University students no longer pay fees per se.
Denmark	In general the Danish education system operates with a large degree of financial support. Often the funds will be given to a private self-governing institution, which is not part of the public hierarchy. Almost all types of public education are free. For institutions that offer alternatives to the public system, there will often be a user-charge to supplement the state subsidies. Basic educational institutions are not forbidden from performing income-generating activities but these may not lead to unfair competition and must have a close link with the ordinary activities. The public school is funded by the municipality. They can accept private sponsorhip. Youth education: the county council sets out a financial framework. The school board may decide on the distribution of the framework budget adopted by the county council. Universities may use any profits that may come from their research or by offering special courses. All institutions are financed by the State and no tuition fees can be charged.
Sweden	The municipalities are given financial resources for their task in general. Independent schools are entitled to financial support by the municipalities.
Spain	Autonomy of resources in non-university state schools is

recognized in the General Educational System Act and the Public Participation, Evaluation and Administration of Educational Centres Act. They may freely assign income obtained for services other than those raised by taxation. Each school's Council has the power to approve its budget and subsequent administration. Private schools are run according to the type of legal entity they are, be they companies, educational trusts, educational cooperatives or any other type of legal entity recognized by law as competent to impart education.
Universities enjoy economic and financial autonomy within the framework established by the University Reform Act. The highest proportion of their income is an annual subsidy from the Autonomous Community. They are subject to financial control by the Management Council and by the courts of justice or similar bodies in the ACs that have them.

Portugal

Schools have a private budget. Laws permit some school revenues such as bookselling, bank interest, etc.
Universities are free to determine the raising and expenditure of their private resources. They can also raise money through sponsorship, through contracts and can even hold shares in private companies. Bank loans are not freely permitted for public Universities: in this case they must obtain the approval of the Minister of Education.

2.6. Autonomy of organization for schools?

The Netherlands

Public schools are circumscribed by bodies such as the municipality.
Private schools have freedom of organization; the competent body is the school board. Freedom of organization applies to both public and private schools, but to a different degree, in that the State cannot interfere in private schools in denominational matters. The State must be cautious when interfering with the pedagogical autonomy of private schools as well as public-authority schools.

Belgium

Free education: educational legislation intervenes in the internal organization of the institutions. It imposes participation organs; of parents, teachers, the local com-

	munity, etc. The government has tried to rationalize the structure of education. Community education: The Community Education Act redrew the whole structure of community education. The major competences are attributed to the intermediary level or to school groups. Official subsidized education: the political organs of the local authorities determine the manner in which their schools will be managed. The Non-university Higher Education Act regulates the participation organs. Regulation of the participation organs of universities established by law is quite detailed. In practice the participation organs of free universities are very similar.
France	See above.
Germany	There is no right of schools to make decisions regarding how to organize the decision-making process in their school, or how to share powers between committees and between teachers and headteachers. All of these matters are regulated by the School Act of the Land.
Austria	–
England and Wales	The conduct, internal organization and running of a school are generally under the direction of the school's governing body.
Ireland	There is a high degree of autonomy in the organization of schools.
Denmark	Primary and secondary education: school boards set out principles for schools' work. Youth education: schools organize themselves within a framework laid down by the minister. Higher education: institutions can organize themselves freely, recognizing the obligations to establish various types of boards, with a broad representation of interest groups.
Sweden	All schools are supervised by the National Agency for Education. State institutions are under the supervision of the National Agency of Higher Education. Independent institutions can legally defend themselves against actions by the State.

Spain

Non-university education: State schools have autonomy to decide on their mode of organizational management (Public Participation, Evaluation and Administration of Educational Centres Act). They set up and approve an educational project which defines their objectives, priorities and procedure, following the School Council's guidelines.
Direct-grant schools may endow their educational project with their own style. Their organization, as far as management bodies are concerned, is governed by the Regulatory Right to Education Act.
University organization: the election process, powers and legal basis of these bodies are always decided by the university statutes, which are required to comply with the minimum requirements imposed by the University Reform Act.

Portugal

The new legislation for Autonomy and Administration allows a redistribution of competences for the several organs: the assembly, the executive board, the pedagogic council and the administrative board. Schools may also enter into Autonomy Contracts with the Central Administration for the extension of their competencies and responsibilities.
The autonomy of the faculties depends on the statute of each university, and is mainly a result of tradition. Usually that tradition is respected and its main aspects approved in the statutes of the University.

2.7. Are schools or universities entitled to defend their autonomous sphere by legal means against the state or government? Do schools have the legal capacity to appeal against acts of a supervisory authority?

The Netherlands

The school and university boards are legal persons which can defend their autonomous sphere by legal means against the inspectorate, the minister and other governmental agencies. Every action of the Minister or the Inspectorate which has legal effect may be challenged in an administrative court.

Belgium

Legal action against the government is only possible if education is organized by a body which is independent from central government.

France

Les principes applicables à cette question sont ceux qui

régissent, de façon générale, le problème de la tutelle. L'autorité de tutelle, qui peut être soit une autorité de l'Etat central, soit celle de la collectivité de rattachement, ne peut pas exercer un pouvoir de sanction qui ne lui serait pas reconnu par un texte. En cas d'abus de sa part, l'établissement public peut saisir le juge administratif d'un recours contre la décision abusive.

Germany

The areas which may be the subject of autonomous decisions are described by law. Schools do not have the right to appeal against acts of the Ministry of Science.
Higher Educational Institutions may have the right to appeal against acts of the Ministry of Science.

Austria

Schools have no legal capacity to appeal against measures taken by the supervisory authority. School autonomy does not provide an exemption from the principle to comply with instructions.
According to Article 8 paragraph 5 of the Act on the Organisation of Universities the university organs have legal capacity in supervisory procedure and the right to lodge a complaint against the final supervisory decision with the Austrian Supreme Administrative Court. Whether they are entitled to defend their sphere of autonomy by other legal means depends on the acceptance of a legal personality under public law for universities.
In the non-university sector in higher education in Austria the Council (Fachhochschulrat) has legal capacity in supervisory procedure and the right to lodge a complaint against the final decision with the Austrian Supreme Administrative Court. No ordinary legal remedy against an administrative decision of the Council exists. The applicants for the recognition of a class or the holders of such a class concerned by a withdrawal, are restricted to lodging a complaint with the Austrian Supreme Administrative Court or the Austrian Constitutional Court, respectively, depending on the subject of the complaint and the general procedural rules for access to these courts.

England and Wales

In principle it would be possible to defend any unlawful interference in the governance or conduct of a school by a local education authority or the Secretary of State by way of an Application for Judicial Review in the High

Court. In recent months, the conduct by the Office of Standards in Education (OFSTED) of school inspections has given rise to considerable dissatisfaction on the part of individual school governing bodies, and it may be possible to envisage legal challenge by way of judicial review in this context, although this is probably unlikely. A significant recent development in this context has been the appointment of an Adjudicator to adjudicate over such disputes between school governing bodies and OFSTED.

Ireland

The process of Judicial Review of administrative action is available to schools and teachers.

Denmark

Any educational institution defined as a self-governing institution will be regarded as being a different legal person from the State and may defend its legal sphere against the State. Educational institutions that are not defined as self-governing form part of the hierarchical structure of the State and thus will have to abide by the decision made by a superior body.

Sweden

The indepedent schools can appeal against negative decisions by the Agency for Education. For public schools the Agency can make critical observations but cannot make any binding decisions.
State institutions cannot legally defend themselves against the government. Independent institutions can legally defend themselves against the State.

Spain

State schools under a public authority are not, in principle, regarded as institutions with power to directly contest decisions taken by the educational authority. Direct-grant schools in the case of disagreements with the educational authority are subject to the complaints procedure (Regulatory Right to Education Act). The procedure consists of a Reconciliation Committee. If there is no agreement an application may be made to the courts. Private schools can apply direct to the courts provided they have complied with procedural rules.
The university community has the right of autonomy. Decisions enjoying legal status made by Central Government and the ACs cannot be directly contested by the universities, but they can be contested indirectly by challenging decisions.

Portugal	No. Any university is entitled to defend its autonomy by legal means against the State or the government. The court has the right to decide.

3. Individual autonomy

3.1. How much latitude of discretion is granted to teachers/professors in educational matters (content of education and methodological decisions)?

The Netherlands	The teacher is fairly autonomous in pedagogical matters but has to work within the criteria set by law and by the school board. Public school: the teacher has to uphold the positive neutrality of the religion or philosophy of the private denominational school.
Belgium	The teacher is a member of a pedagogical team, which reduces his/her freedom. This team works out a pedagogical project and pursues a local school policy. Within this team, the school board and teachers will make at least informal agreements on the means to realize their project and their policy. The area left are the margins where the teacher can act autonomously. For non-university higher education centres the discretion of the teacher is much greater than in primary and secondary education. In the universities, academic freedom is attainable, although it does not have an explicit legal basis, but there is a tendency towards less freedom.
France	Compte tenu de ce qui a été dit précédemment, le pouvoir des enseignants sur le contenu de l'enseignement de l'enseignement secondaire est très limité sur le plan juridique. Il porte pour l'essentiel sur les compléments éventuels aux programmes: comme la lourdeur de ceux-ci est souvent dénoncée, cela indique la difficulté qu'il peut y avoir à les augmenter. En revanche, le fonctionnement de l'enseignement français est caractérisé par une large application d'un principe de liberté pédagogique des enseignants qui donne à ceux-ci de grandes possibilités de choix des méthodes pédagogiques qu'ils appliquent; ceci se manifeste par exemple dans le pouvoir laissé à chaque établissement dans le choix des manuels scolaires.

Germany

Schoolteachers are bound by the curricula set by the Ministries of Education. By School Acts of the Länder freedom of teachers in methodological matters is often guaranteed, but may be limited by school decisions.
Higher education: academic freedom of the professor includes freedom of methods and also the right to develop their own opinions.

Austria

In matters of methodology and didactics, teachers are subject to instructions from their superior, the principal, although Article 17 Basic Law obliges the individual teacher to carry out his/her teaching. This provision cannot overrule the duty to comply with instructions.
By the constitutional guarantee of Article 17 paragraph 1 Basic Law on the General Rights of Nationals 1867 persons who prove to be able and qualified for scientific teaching have freedom concerning the contents and methods of their teaching. The borders of the freedom of science lie in the general laws. The freedom of scientific teaching is limited by prohibitions emanating from the Penal Code. The guarantee covers teaching at universities, but not at classes and institutes of the non-university sector in higher education (Fachhochschul-Studiengänge, Fachhochschulen). The legal competence of Article 43 paragraph 2 No. 2 of the Act on the Organisation of Universities 1993 for the Dean for Study-Affairs (Studiendekan) to issue directives does not refer to the contents and methods of teaching. His/her competence is restricted to the maintenance of the operation of the studies according to the study schemes.
Article 3 paragraph 2 No. 1 of the Act on Classes of the Non-university Sector in Higher Education recognizes the plurality of scientific opinions in teaching and of scientific methods, as well as the principle of freedom of teaching, as principles which must be observed in structuring classes which belong to this sector.
Nevertheless, directives by the responsible authorities must respect the individual pedagogical freedom of the members of the teaching staff concerning the contents and methods of their teaching.

England and Wales

In maintained schools, the discretion enjoyed by teachers is limited by the constraints of the National Curriculum. As initially promulgated following the Education Reform

	Act 1988, the National Curriculum programmes of study were widely criticized for their excessive detail and high level of prescription. However, the National Curriculum has now been significantly modified and made considerably less prescriptive in content, thereby giving teachers rather more (though still limited) professional discretion. In the University sector, teachers enjoy very substantial discretion in respect of course content, though every Department, Faculty and University will adopt rigorous mechanisms for the scrutiny of course content; and course delivery and the examination process are subject to detailed scrutiny through periodic teaching quality assessment exercises under the auspices of the Higher Education Funding Council. Schools have less autonomy. Universities have a higher level of autonomy.
Denmark	–
Sweden	This is a question for discussion within the profession.
Spain	The margin of discretion enjoyed by teachers is constitutionally guaranteed by the fundamental right of academic freedom. But academic freedom has to co-exist with the educational centre's own ideology or character.
Portugal	Teachers' discretion is only granted for pupil evaluation. Teachers are free to define the content of education and methodologies. A full professor has the right to coordinate the disciplines and so still has more freedom than a lower-ranked professor

3.2. Is the head of a school (university) or any of its bodies entitled to issue instructions in professional matters to the teaching staff?

The Netherlands	The head of the school may give instructions to the teachers. The position of a teacher in a higher education institute is guaranteed better thn those of a teacher in school. Academic freedom is protected by the Higher Education and Scientific Research Act. The teacher is free within the constraints set by the organization, the curriculum and the scientific standards to advance their own points of view and to choose teaching methods.

Belgium

New act initiatives can clarify the relationship between the headteacher and the teachers. The headteacher has to work out a function description. There will be a triennial evaluation of the teachers. So the way he/she fulfils tasks and uses his/her pedagogical autonomy can be controlled.
The relationship between teachers and professors and the head of the institution is similar to the relationship in primary and secondary education understanding that this relationship is more decentralized on the level of the faculties (in the universities) and the departments (in the hogescholen).

France

Il reste très prégnant le refus, tant par les enseignants individuels que par leurs organisations syndicales, du développement de tout pouvoir pédagogique au profit du chef d'établissement. Ce refus va de pair avec la reconnaissance exclusive des compétences pédagogiques au profit des corps d'inspection, considérés comme indépendants de toute hiérarchie administrative.
Le directeur d'école appartient au même corps que les autres enseignants et il a surtout des compétences de coordination et d'animation. L'école est cependant dotée de deux collégiaux, le conseil de l'école qui dispose de véritables pouvoirs de décision, notamment sur le réglement intérieur de l'école, et le conseil des maîtres, qui a surtout des pouvoirs d'animantion pédagogique.

Germany

No answer.

Austria

Yes. See above.
Apart from the borders, the superiors within the structure of a university are legally entitled to issue instructions to the teaching staff, depending on the legal status of the respective category to which the actual member of the teaching staff belongs, and depending on the superior's sphere of competence. These instructions are solely related to professional matters.
The same situation applies to the teaching staff at classes and institutes of the non-university sector in higher education (Fachhochschul-Studiengänge, Fachhochschulen) and is defined by the legal structure the respective holder has chosen for the organization. The barriers for the contents of instructions given by the holder, the head of

the teaching staff, or the head of the Board of Institute of the Non-university Sector in Higher Education (Fachhochschulkollegium) are considerably less restrictive than in the university sector, as has been noted in 3.1 above.

England and Wales — At school level, the headteacher has overall responsibility, subject to the governing body, for academic matters, and power to issue instructions to teaching staff.
The head of a university where academic control would normally be devolved to Faculty or Departmental level, is subject to more general supervision by the University Senate (or equivalent body).

Ireland — School principals have a role in the guidance and direction of teachers.

Denmark — Primary and secondary education: the school board has the right, in cooperation with the headteacher, to lay down principles. The Act on public schools confers a number of obligations on the headteacher.
Youth education: the headteacher is in charge of everyday management but has no right to intervene in the methodological choice of the individual teacher.
Higher education: the head of an institution has the power to instruct an academic employee to perform a specific task, but must do so with respect to the employee's free choice of scientific and/or pedagogical methods.

Sweden — The headteacher of the school is pedagogical leader of teaching and has the task of drawing up a local working plan based on the curricula, national objectives and the education plan.
The head of the department can determine a teacher's presence in the department and the extent of the teaching load within the limits of the collective agreement. The individual teacher has freedom to choose methods, but is bound by the syllabus.

Spain — State schools: teaching staff are responsible for the programming of teaching activities.
Direct-grant schools: the school council participates in the application of the pedagogical scheme of the school and approves the programming.

	Private schools: they may set up in-house regulations governing educational matters. University sector: University departments are responsible in their role as co-ordinatiors of teaching and other activities for the organization and development of research. The Faculties, Higher Technical Schools and Training Schools manage and administer all university teaching leading to the granting of academic qualifications. The syllabuses, the programmes determined by each department and the specifications decided by each teacher make up the content of the teaching of university students in a way that accepts various alternatives but which can in no way violate the individual teacher's freedom of academic expression.
Portugal	Only if decided by school organs. There are scientific and pedagogic bodies that may issue instructions in professional matters to teaching staff (but the resistance is high).

3.3. Do the teachers/professors participate in the universities' or schools' self-governing bodies?

The Netherlands	Education Participation Act: every educational institution is required to set up a participation council to give advice and make proposals. Higher Education and Scientific Research Act: Higher education institutions also have a requirement to set up a participation council.
Belgium	Teachers of subsidized schools are represented in the participation council of the school. These organs have no real decision-making power. Teachers in Community schools are represented in the school council. They may represent the school if they are elected. In the universities and their faculties it is a tradition that the staff is involved in the policy of the institutions. In the non-university higher education centres the teachers are represented in the academic council and the departmental council.
France	Dans les Universités, les enseignants sont représentés dans les trois conseils créés par la loi: leur proportion en leur sein est fixée par les dispositions de la loi de 1984

(environ 40% dans le Conseil d'administration, qui est l'organe essentiel en matière de détermination de la politique générale de l'université et en matière budgétaire; plus de la majorité au conseil scientifique, qui détermine la politique de recherche de l'université). Dans les E.P.L.E., les enseignants constituent environ le tiers du Conseil d'administration.

Germany	Yes. Teachers are always involved in decisions of the school commitees. Professors in higher education have their own committees.
Austria	There are no self-governing bodies at school level in a constitutional sense. On the level of ordinary legislation there are bodies of the school partners consisting of parents, pupils, and teachers. These bodies are called School Community Committees (cf. School Instruction Act) chaired by the principal. The structure of the universities according to the Act on the Organisation of Universities 1993 can be characterized as installing a two-fold system of monocratic and collegial organs. At all levels of the university structure a proportionate number of representatives of the various categories of members of the teaching staff is included by means of elections to the respective collegial organ. Members of the teaching staff (sometimes a limited number) may stand for election to all monocratic organs. At classes of the non-university sector in higher education (Fachhochschul-Studiengänge), due to the comparably wide field of organizational discretion of the respective holder, besides the grouping of of persons to a teaching staff, a self-governing body, which embraces all or some members of the teaching staff is not required by law. The establishment of such a body falls within the autonomy of the respective holder. In case of an institute of the non-university sector in higher education (Fachhochschule) the Act on Classes of the Non-university Sector in Higher Education provides for the establishment of a board (Fachhochschulkollegium). Members of the teaching staff may be elected as chairperson of this board.

England and Wales	The composition of maintained school governing bodies: there are either one or two teacher governors in addition to the headteacher and a representative of support staff. In universities, members of academic staff actively participate in virtually all the University's committees, including the Senate, the Council and the Court (terminology varies from one university to another).
Ireland	At the moment teachers do not yet have a self-governing body.
Denmark	Primary and lower secondary education. Yes. Two representatives of the teachers must participate. The school board must act within the framework set by the municipality, which has to respect the framework set up by the law. Youth education: academic staff also participate in the various bodies that are specified for individual youth education. Higher education: academic personnel also form part of the governing bodies (20% of the board).
Sweden	For public schools there is a local board of education comprising municipal politicians. The teachers are entitled to appoint three of thirteen members of the board. The rector is also a member of the board.
Spain	Management bodies of state schools are regulated by Regulatory Right to Education Act. The school council is composed of academic bodies of the school representatives of the city or Town Council and a certain number of parents, students and teachers. It decides on the syllabus, guidelines for extracurricular activities etc. Teachers are involved in the self-government of the universities (part of the right of university autonomy). They may elect the rector. The management Council is the body involved in the management of the university. It may not take decisions on academic matters.
Portugal	Teachers have a significant participation in all school organs. Academic and non-academic staff participate in the universities' and faculties' self-governing bodies.

4. Consequences of autonomy

4.1. If educational institutions can act autonomously, how are general aims or values like quality and unity of the education guaranteed?

The Netherlands — The unity of the system is guaranteed by laying down minimum standards, by procedures prescribed by law, by formulation of attainment targets and by the Education Inspectorate. Law also contains Articles concerning quality control by the school boards themselves, including a mandatory complaint commission attached to the school, for parents and pupils.

Belgium — There are some minimum standards of knowledge and skills that every pupil must reach. The inspectorate are less interested in a detailed control of the education process, more in a global quality approach of each institution. The inspectorate does not control pedagogical methods.
In the non-university higher education centres and universities they are required to constantly internally evaluate the quality of education. Externally, the institutions of each sector of the higher education level are required to jointly organize a periodic evaluation of the global quality of similar programmes. The global examination is executed by the so-called Commissions of Visitation in the universities and the Commissions of Evaluation in the non-university higher education centres. The government oversees that there is adequate evaluation and observes how the institutions deal with the results of this evaluation.

France — L'unité et la qualité de l'éducation sont garanties, dans les établissements scolaires, par l'existence de corps d'inspection existant au niveau national, régional ou local. Au niveau national, coexistent deux inspections générales, l'Inspection Générale de l'Education Nationale, chargée de l'évaluation de l'activité pédagogique et l'Inspection Générale de l'Administration de l'Education Nationale, chargée du contrôle administratif et financier. Dans les secteur universitaire, il existe un Comité National d'Evaluation, créé par la loi du 26 janvier 1984, organisé par deux décrets du 21 février 1985 et 7 décembre 1988. Composé de dix-sept membres indépendants,

choisis par la communauté scientifique, le Conseil d'Etat, la Cour des Comptes et le Conseil Economique et Social, il est chargé d'examiner et d'évaluer l'ensemble des activités des E.P.S.C.P. Ses rapports sont publics.
Il a par ailleurs existé au ministère une Direction de l'Evaluation et de la Prospective, créée en 1987, dont une partie des tâches ont été reprises en 1996 par la Direction de la Programmation et du Développement. Dans cette dernière direction, les tâches d'évaluation du système éducatif ont été fortement réduites.

Germany

Unity of education should be attained under the School Act.
In the schools new systems of control and quality-assessment try to combine a kind of internal evaluation by the school with external evaluations from the Ministry of Education. The level of quality-control in this new system should be a 'school-programme' in which schools must describe their aims and goals in advance. This should be the standard.
Centralized examinations are still under consideration.
Unity of education should be attained under the Acts on Higher Education. Systems of quality control are organized with respect for academic freedom.

Austria

Curricula are based on ordinances laid down by the School Organisation Act. They are binding, but schools can focus on specific priorities. They may replace some areas, but not the total number of weekly teaching hours, which remains a fixed number.
The Act on the Organisation of Universities 1993 provides for two major instruments in order to guarantee the achievement of general aims or values like the quality and unity of Austrian education at universities. One instrument should be seen as the creation of a mechanism for cooperation between Austrian universities, the other instrument lies within the supervisory function of the Minister of Science and Traffic.
The curatorium of universities (Universitätenkuratorium), which consists of four recognized experts from inside the universities and four from outside, both groups appointed by the Minister of Science and Traffic, is established to advise the Minister in his decisions with regard to Austrian universities. Thus, it primarily has a

coordinating function, which relates to quality as well as budgetary matters, restricted however, to an advisory power. Similarly, the activities of the rectors, vice-rectors, and chairpersons of the supreme collegial organs of universities are coordinated by the Conference of Rectors. This conference gives opinions on all university matters and projects of laws and ministerial decrees referring to these matters. It consists of the rectors and their deputies and is also restricted to an advisory function. The Act further provides for the creation of conferences representing the various categories of the members of the teaching staff at universities in order to coordinate the activities of their representatives. The powers of these conferences are also limited to advice and expert opinion.

The power of supervision of Austrian universities is in the hands of the Minister of Science and Traffic. The Act on the Organisation of Universities extends this power to the control of the observance of laws and decrees, as well as the fulfilment of the tasks of the university. The power includes the right of information on all university matters, but also the duty of universities to submit to ministerial inquiries. The supervisory power is connected with the sanctions overturning university decisions or refusal of ministerial approval, where such approval is provided by law. Apart from this, the Act on the Organisation of Universities 1993 provides for annual reports on the university organs concerning the fulfilment of the tasks of the universities on all university levels. The minister is specifically entitled to evaluate universities or studies and their development and may rule by decree on the evaluation of achievements at the universities.

Concerning classes of the non-university sector in higher education (Fachhochschul-Studiengänge) the coordination regarding the achievement of general aims or values takes place by means of the policy of recognition or withdrawal of recognition by the Council of Institutes of the Non-universitary Sector in Higher Education (Fachhochschulrat), the decisions of which are subject to approval by the Minister of Science and Traffic. Besides, the Council is submitted in a comparable manner with universities to the supervisory power of the Minister of Science and Traffic. Concerning institutes of this sector

	(Fachhochschulen) the coordinating policy is exercised direct by the Minister of Science and Traffic in agreement with the Minister of Education and Cultural Affairs, combining decision-making and supervision.
England and Wales	The scope for autonomy at school level is limited by the (arguably too) prescriptive nature of the contents of the national curriculum programmes of study. None the less there is still scope for autonomy and professional expertise in many aspects of the delivery of the curriculum, and accountability and quality assurance are regarded as of the utmost importance. The key mechanism for quality assurance in schools is the periodic inspection of the school by OFSTED under the School Inspections Act 1996.
Ireland	By school inspections at primary level; by state examinations at secondary level.
Denmark	Primary and lower secondary education: various types of evaluation. Local democracy also plays a key role. Public schools: central knowledge and proficiency areas are a tool to ensure unity. The Centre for Quality Assurance and Evaluation of Higher Education should contribute to quality assurance of higher education programmes.
Sweden	The quality and unity of education is guaranteed by the national curriculum, syllabuses and time schedules. The institutions are under supervision by the National Agency of Higher Education. The Agency makes quality audits, Quality assessment of different levels of education, supervises how the institutions adapt to legal demands, supports pedagogical development activities, gathers statistics and make investigations by request of the Government.
Portugal	School autonomy must respect basic statute law. Quality of graduate programmes is evaluated according to the law. Evaluation was introduced by the Portuguese rector's Conference in 1993 and approved by Parliament: Law 37/94. Research is evaluated by the Ministry of Science and Technology. After evaluation increase or decrease in funding is decided.

Spain	Non-university education is subject to control by those responsible for education in the respective Central and Autonomous Community, with the aid of the 'State Education Council'. There is a high degree of autonomy in the university sector, coordinated and planned by the Ministry of Education and Culture, with advisory input from the Universities Council. On a regional level political coordination is undertaken by the Minister of Education and Culture of that AC. The Autonomous Community exercises political control, which at a state level is exercised by the Spanish Parliament.

4.2. Is autonomy necessarily linked with a supervisory power?

The Netherlands	Yes. The Education Inspectorate with regard to primary and secondary schools, and by the institutions of vocational and higher education themselves in the form of examination institutes or so called 'visitation' committees.
Belgium	The recent reform has reduced the supervisory power. The inspectorate inspects the quality of primary and secondary education, ensures that the institutions respect the educational legislation and advises on the recognition and funding of schools. For the higher educational institutions, there is a Government Commissioner who ensures that the institutions do not infringe the law or endanger the financial balance of the institution.
France	Il existe une tutelle qui s'exerce sur les établissements publics. Dans le second degré, les règles sont différentes pour ce qui concerne l'action éducatrice et le reste de l'activité des établissements. Dans les universités, les statuts doivent être transmis au ministre après leur adoption. Les décisions et délibérations réglementaires ne peuvent entrer en vigueur qu'après leur transmission au recteur d'académie, dont les services assistent aux réunions ordinaires des Conseils d'administration. Aucune approbation préalable n'est donc nécessaire. La connaissance des décisions ainsi acquise permet au recteur d'intenter, le cas échéant, les

actions juridictionnelles qu'exigerait une éventuelle illégalité. Au cas où l'exécution de la mesure attaquée peut compromettre gravement le fonctionnement de l'établissement, le recteur peut en suspendre l'application pour une durée de trois mois. Enfin, le recteur a le pouvoir d'arrêter le budget au cas où il n'est pas voté en équilibre par le conseil d'administration.

Germany

Schools: the old system was a system of supervision by the Ministry of Education which also included supervision of the individual teacher. There now is a new system (see above).

Austria

Every school is subject to school inspection. Schools following their own curricula at a certain level are also inspected. The inspectorate may issue instructions to individual teachers or the principal.
According to the existing legal situation concerning universities and classes or institutes of the non-university sector in higher education (Fachhochschul-Studiengänge, Fachhochschulen) autonomy is necessarily linked with a supervisory power.

England and Wales

School autonomy in England and Wales may be traced to many possible origins, but delegated management and delegated budgetary responsibility initiated under the Education Reform Act 1988 is perhaps the most obvious starting point. School autonomy has since been developed and refined in many respects, but has been paralleled by significant supervisory and controlling trends on the part of LEAs and the central department. LEAs have powers to issue 'warning notices' to schools where they are concerned over the quality of educational provision; they may appoint further governors or may withdraw budgetary devolution; and the LEA is directly involved in the process of target setting for each school Similarly, the Secretary of State has important powers of intervention at individual school level under the same Act, and may ultimately direct the closure of a school which is severely failing. The Secretary of State also has a significant role to play in approving, modifying or rejecting LEA education development plans – a process which directly links the central department to the 'front line' at the level of the LEA and the individual school. All of

	this involves a significant element of monitoring and control from above: a central feature of this process of monitoring and control is OFSTED.
Ireland	Yes.
Denmark	If the input is very specified the control on the output can be more relaxed.
Sweden	Yes. The National Agency for Education has a supervisory duty to ensure that the provisions of the Education Act are complied with.
Spain	There is an educational inspection system of each administration complemented by the National Quality Assessment Institute in which the educational administrations are involved. The universities are subject to the supervision of the various university bodies and the Management Council.
Portugal	The Ministry of Education may use the Education Inspection Services. Supervisory powers of the Ministry of Education have been increased by the new legislation governing public universities.

4.3. What are the relations between autonomy, responsibility and accountability? Is autonomy necessarily connected with quality control within autonomous educational institutions?

The Netherlands	More autonomy implies that the school boards are more responsible for their results. Internal as well as external quality is necessary. In vocational education a quality assurance system has been introduced. Institutions must make progress reports every two years. For higher education quality control is a responsibility of the Minister of Education/Education Inspectorate as well as of the so-called 'visitation committees'. The committees carry out regular research on the quality of the study programmes; the task of the Education Inspectorate is limited to controlling the procedures followed by these committees (meta-evaluation).
Belgium	Autonomy necessarily seems linked with responsibility. This is most clear in the field of financial autonomy. The institution receives a budget and has to manage it. The

institution is responsible for the policy choices made and it will be disciplined if it infringes the law. It seems that autonomy is necessarily linked with at least a less active role for the government in controlling educational quality.

France

Il n'existe pas d'organes internes d'évaluation au sein des établissements.

Cependant, comme on l'a vu au 1.1, la réforme Jospin-Lang de 1982 autorise les universités à mettre en place en leur sein des procédures internes d'évaluation et ceci n'a pas été jugé incompatible avec le principe d'indépendance des professeurs de l'enseignement supérieur.

Germany

No answer.

Austria

See above.

Both the Act on the Organisation of Universities 1993 and the Act on Classes of the Non-university Sector in Higher Education provide for quality control within the respective institutions. Universities are obliged to include guidelines concerning the conducting of evaluation measures in teaching and research in their basic statutes. Similarly Article 12 paragraph 2 No. 8 of the Act on Classes of the Non-university Sector in Higher Education required a scientific evaluation of the respective class as a precondition for its recognition by Council and Minister.

Concerning responsibility and accountability, the institutions fall under the supervisory power of the Minister of Science and Traffic and under the control of the Audit Office of the Austrian Parliament (Rechnungshof).

Ireland

There has to be a reasonable balance between autonomy and accountability.

Denmark

No answer.

Sweden

The National Agency for Education has the task of developing, evaluating, following up and supervising schooling in Sweden. The Agency also make survey controls by Educational Inspectors.

Yes. Quality controls are conducted by the institutions themselves but also by the Agency.

Spain

In the non-university sectors the degree of autonomy is

lower and a greater power is exercised by the Regional Ministers with educational responsibility.
In universities the relationship between autonomy and responsibility and the rest of the educational institutions is highly diverse. Particularly noteworthy is the degree of awareness shown by society towards its university: regional government members tend to be part of the university community.

Portugal	All members of school organs have disciplinary civil and penal responsibilities. The supervisory model increases the responsibility of the Universities' Heads. External audits are now compulsory and the reports must be sent to the Ministry of Education.

4.4. If there are recent trends in your country with respect to autonomy of educational institutions: Is there a tendency towards enlargement of autonomy or towards more government control? Why is it so? (examples)

The Netherlands	School boards have been made more responsible for the quality of primary educational processes, and municipalities for local coordination between education and other social sectors. The State still has a general responsibility for the functioning of the system but the educational institutions, with the local government, are held responsible for their achievements. Schools have gained autonomy in the field of financial matters. All educational institutions except primary schools now are financed on a lump-sum basis. Schools will operate more efficiently if they are master of their own finances. This has led to a greater scale, that is, more institutions under one school board. Pedagogical autonomy for primary and secondary schools is decreasing. The State imposes all kinds of additional obligations with regard to the aims of education, the output to be achieved, the role of participants and the duty to cooperate with municipalities and other school boards. In a larger organization it is more difficult for a school to maintain its philosophy or religion.
Belgium	Trend to more autonomy at all educational levels but also movements in the other direction by introducing function descriptions and evaluation procedures.

France

Le principe d'autonomie et le principe de subsidiarité se frayent progressivement, mais difficilement, un chemin dans l'organization du système administratif français. On voit bien le développement important qu'ils ont connu depuis les mesures prises à partir du début des années 80. Mais on voit aussi la difficulté de leur conciliation avec les principes d'égalité qui caractérisent l'enseignement français.

Germany

The developments granting more autonomy for the single school are quite different from Land to Land. A general trend in direction of more autonomy may be observed. The question of more State control is not yet under discussion.

Austria

The autonomy of schools is not so much an autonomy but rather a way of decentralizing decision-making power. Schools may take more matters into their own hands but they remain under the full supervision of the school administration. Because of the power of superior administrative units to overrule decisions it is not possible to talk about autonomy in connection with schools. Nevertheless pupils and parents assume a more active role in the decision-making process. The latest reforms may well be seen as a step towards promoting the independence and self-responsibility of citizens.

There is a tendency in Austrian policy towards enlargement of autonomy of universities. Autonomy has been recognized as a means to strengthen the personal responsibility and accountability of universities, to activate the innovative potential and to reduce a contra-productive bureaucratization. The quality of the fulfilment of the tasks of universities can be improved by strengthening university autonomy. The autonomous administration of scarce financial means by universities themselves led to a transfer of decisions concerning conflicting demands and interests to inter-university forces.

Concerning the non-university sector in higher education, no legal basis existed until the adoption of the respective Act in 1993. This Act signals a remarkable change in the orientation of Austrian policy concerning the tertiary sector in education. A whole complex of education has been established considerably removed from State involvement and has been translated from experimental

	development into practice. There is a sign of deep confidence of the Austrian state in the creative force of autonomy.
England and Wales	Under the School Standards and Framework Act 1998 in particular, there is a significant expansion of external and centralized control from the level of the central department down through the LEA to the level of each individual school. This Act may, indeed, be viewed as a major centralizing measure, which is arguably a most significant current trend in the governance and the delivery of education in England and Wales.
Ireland	There is a body planned for first- and second-level education. There is a definite movement towards more government control at university level (Universities Act).
Denmark	There is a clear tendency to reduce autonomy. The establishment of an evaluation centre for higher education was the first indication. At this moment a National Centre of Evaluation for all areas of the education system is being prepared. However a large degree of autonomy continues to exist in the education system. There is also a newly launched quality project containing methods and tools for overall quality development. It is not obligatory to use the system.
Sweden	There is a tendency towards support for increasing autonomy. 1990–1994: development towards autonomy 1995–1998: reverse action Now: the situation has been stabilized.
Spain	Traditionally schools have enjoyed lesser autonomy and they are heavily under the power of politicians. Since 1980 a change has begun but it is still in an initial phase. The situation is marked by a heavy dependence on the educational authorities and the school's very scant financial and decision making autonomy. Older universities have a more consolidated system of autonomy.
Portugal	Tendency is towards an enlargement of school autonomy.

More freedom in finance and human resources management, transfer of patrimony to the institutions and allowing free contracts for staff using private funding was a welcome move towards more autonomy but also towards more responsibility.

WOLFGANG MANTL

Academic Freedom and Autonomy of Educational Institutions: Conflicts and Concordances[1]

1. Diagnosis of the status of universities and educational institutions

As the saying goes: 'The wise man says: I have looked for truth. The fool says: I have found it.' This saying expresses the problems of our educational institutions and the specific role played by the universities: the never-ending search for knowledge, on the one hand, and character-building, education and culture, on the other hand.

The school is the centre of educational systems and an important, if not the only place where character-building occurs. This latter role has traditionally been taken over by the family. Education, however, as a process of teaching and learning consists mainly of cognitive elements, whereas, character-building includes emotive, affective and normative elements. And it must be pointed out that with regard to character-building it is the teacher's personality which serves as a model and example for the pupils.

The number of 'educationalists' has steadily increased throughout history: today it embraces parents, teachers, pupils, peer groups, circles of friends, and religious groups. The fading influence of political parties and other organizations has been superseded by the media, above all by television and by the Internet. If there are crises in education – and there are – I am convinced that there is no point in fixating on a scapegoat, e.g. by blaming freedom for these problems. The real difficulty of our topic is that the schools and the universities

[1] Talk given at the Conference of the European Association for Education Law and Policy on 'Autonomy in Education' in Salzburg on 18 December 1998. – I owe a debt of gratitude in particular to Walter Berka/Salzburg and to the young scholars from Graz who have assisted me in the preparation of this essay: Thomas Koller, Hedwig Kopetz and Klaus Poier.

Walter Berka, Jan de Groof and Hilde Penneman (eds.). Autonomy in Education, 93–103.

are an integral part of an epoch, and not part of a pedagogical and scientific 'paradise' where crises do not exist.

If we now take a look at the sciences, they represent the practical aspects of life as well as the theoretical ones, going beyond the naïve daily life experience. 'Sciences are the organized transcending of the borders of the individual experience.'[2] And I would add, the borders of daily life experience.

The centre of sciences for research and teaching is the university. Austria is experiencing intensive and accelerated changes at the end of the millennium. These changes are not regarded by many people as liberation, but as threat. It is an understandable human reaction to attempt to escape from challenges through illusions; these can be seen as relief from pressure and responsibility. We could say the flags of symbolic signals are raised.

More exhausting, but also more sensible than symbols and illusions is a widespread programme of qualification. Therefore we need an inevitable positive attitude towards requirements of performance and the recognition of élites. Both performance and élites require a solid educational system from kindergarten through to university, especially in the creative years up to thirty. This requires the recognition of general knowledge as the knowledge which remains with us when everything changes around us. All those involved, parents and teachers, students, assistants and professors must be convinced of the necessity of a qualification initiative, which can only exist in an atmosphere of freedom. This calls for autonomy. What we need is a sober, but in itself very humane work ethic without utopian or populist phraseology.

The public expects, above all, heavily regulated, entirely syllabus-bound and strictly timetabled schooling, and not cultural and scientific institutions from the universities. And particularly the democratization of modern life, with its promises of equality, raises these expectations and elevates them to self-evident rights. It used to be a basic fact of the continental educational system that schools and universities generally offered higher social standing and social security.[3]

The specific identity of universities is created by the outcome of research and the fertile combination of research and teaching. In this connection – as Ralf Dahrendorf once said – quality should be the 'guiding star'.[4] One big

2 Peter Graf Kielmansegg, 'Politische Orientierungshilfen. Von Nutzen und Nachteil der Politikwissenschaft für das Leben', *Die politische Meinung*, 33 (1988), no. 239, July/August, 16.

3 An academic degree, indeed, increased the chances of having a career from 1960 to the end of the eighties, but today graduating from a university no longer guarantees any professional success.

4 Ralf Dahrendorf, 'Leitstern Qualität. Zur Diskussion über Eliten, Universitäten und technischen Fortschritt', *Die Zeit*, 39 (1984), no. 11, 19 March, 32.

problem, however, is the continuing quality assurance measured by international standards (evaluation). As we are not dealing with simply structured problems, for which there are clear solutions or clear algorithms, we need a setting of freedom, of autonomy and of performance.

Possessing only specialized knowledge will not secure a professional future for professors, assistants and students. Only the best theory of today will be a good practice for tomorrow. In fact, the practice of today is only the theory of yesterday, after all. The university must offer general knowledge with additional qualifications above all the command of languages both of the mother tongue and of foreign languages, especially English; but also computer skills and interpersonal and emotional intelligence, in order to produce 'provisions' without early expiry dates.

Walter Berka describes the latest developments with the following statement:

> 'With respect to higher education the Austrian educational policy has passed several cross-roads within the last few years. If one tries to identify the comprehensive issues decentralization, deregulation and a trend toward more competition are the dominating features.'[5]

The latest amendments of laws pertaining to schools on the one hand and the University Organization Act of 1993 (UOG 1993) as well as the University Studies Act of 1997 (UniStG 1997) on the other hand are an attempt to answer these challenges before the turn of the century. Regarding the universities, they can justify their special legal status only if they are not considered to be simply 'schools'. All the university claims for academic freedom and autonomy are based on their outcomes of research.

A new competitor for the universities is the 'Fachhochschule',[6] which I see as a positive challenge to force the universities to become aware of their identity. It is not the solution for universities to become better 'Fachhochschulen'. Schools always have elements of restrictions for both teachers and pupils. This is exactly why we are trying to liberalize even the pre-university educational system.

The Humboldtian university, with its connection between research and teaching in the biggest possible academic freedom, brought with it an exemplary success story. Particularly the universities in the German-speaking world became models for the entire world in the 19th century, as well as for the up-and-coming universities of the USA, as the historian Henry Adams, a relative of two US-Presidents, reported in his memoirs about Harvard University.

5 Walter Berka, 'Development of education law in Austria. Part II: Higher education', *European Journal for Education Law and Policy*, 1 (1997), 107.

6 A new institution of higher education at university level, but explicitly 'practice-oriented'.

The universities experienced the most difficult time of their existence during the Napoleonic era when the number of universities decreased by half, a setback from which they only recovered a century later.[7] This new rise then was closely connected with the Humboldtian idea.

In any case, the university has always been the successful historical response to the sceptical question whether or not sciences can be organized. – Yes, the sciences can be organized within the brilliant invention of the university, and it is in this construction different from a school.

Of course, the university never simply rested on its laurels; the university was constantly challenged by the social and political environment surrounding it. At present, increasing costs and a lack of sufficient resources especially for basic research as well as for the humanities strengthen the pressure for justification by the universities. Autonomy should not be a euphemism for the administration of packages of austerity measures.

2. Academic freedom and autonomy today: the liberal heritage

In the impressive tradition of modern times the last two centuries of enlightenment with their liberal achievements deserve a special place in history. The philosophy of freedom is part of market economy, of judicial independence and – this is our topic – of academic freedom. The liberal system of academic freedom reveals a basic trust in the social and cultural productivity of freedom. And this basic trust found its legal shape in the construction, that academic freedom is formulated in the fundamental rights catalogue, which enjoys validity without any requirement of a two-thirds-majority (Gesetzesvorbehalt).

Let us look a bit at the legal construction of academic freedom and autonomy:[8] Article 17 of the Basic Law of 21 December 1867 on the General Rights

[7] Manfred Eigen, 'Die deutsche Universität – Vielfalt der Formen, Einfalt der Reformen', in: Manfred Eigen et alii (eds), 'Die Idee der Universität. Versuch einer Standortbestimmung', Berlin 1988, 78.

[8] An instructive analysis and a comprehensive survey both of court decisions and secondary literature on academic freedom are presented in the jurisprudential doctoral thesis of my disciple Eva P. Stifter, 'Evaluierung universitärer Leistungen im internationalen Vergleich' Graz 1999, *passim*. – At this point the following earlier publications should also be quoted: Bruno Binder, 'Die verfassungsrechtliche Sicherung der Wissenschaftsfreiheit in Österreich', *Wissenschaftsrecht, Wissenschaftsverwaltung, Wissenschaftsförderung*, 6 (1973), 1–26; Werner Hauser, 'Universitäre Studienplanung. Eine integrierte verwaltungsrechtliche und verwaltungswissenschaftliche Studie', Wien 1995; Friedrich Koja, 'Wissenschaftsfreiheit und Universität', Salzburg 1976; Gerhart Wielinger, 'Die Freiheit der Wissenschaft': Art. 17 StGG, in: Rudolf Machacek, Willibald P. Pahr and Gerhard Stadler (eds), 40 Jahre EMRK. Grund- und Menschenrechte in Österreich, Vol. II, Wissen und Werte, Kehl-Straßburg-Arlington 1992, 175–194.

of Citizens provides: 'The sciences and their teaching are free'. The fundamental right of academic freedom was implanted into the bureaucratic state of the old monarchy and it should have created a sphere of freedom which, however, was not completely free from influence of the state.

Autonomy is only constitutionally guaranteed for a part of the educational system. The Basic Law of 1867 grants academic freedom in the said Article 17 (1), which represents the basis of the relative university autonomy in Austria. Apart from that, Section 2 (2) of the University Organization Act (UOG) of 1993 stipulates by a constitutional provision that universities are within the framework of acts, regulations and budget allocations entitled to fulfil their tasks autonomously. Section 7 (1) of the UOG 1993 empowers the universities constitutionally to issue individual basic statutes and regulations and Section 13 (2) of the UOG 1993 provides that the universities are no longer bound by directives of the ministry. Although universities remain dependent public institutions, they are no longer subject to administrative regulations.

Autonomous decisions can be taken, e.g. with regard to the following issues: recruitment of the staff and election of the university organs, financial matters and evaluation. But it must not be ignored that some bureaucracy is inevitable. Let us hope it will not become too extensive eventually: 'lean administration' must be the goal.

Schools, however, have to follow the administrative hierarchy. This means they are bound by directives from superior agencies and controlled by a supervisory authority. The constitutional basis thereof can be found in Article 17 (5) of the Basic Law, which is restricted by Article 17 (1): 'The state is empowered to supervise and to direct the entire educational system.'

The Constitution guarantees – as mentioned before – the freedom of scientific teaching and research (Article 17 (1) of the Basic Law). This academic freedom embraces the right to do scientific research, to take notes as well as to publish and teach its results. In the beginning, only persons with a venia docendi were considered to be holders of this right. This opinion was changed in 1977 through a decision of the Constitutional Court (8136/1977). Nowadays everybody who does research is protected by this fundamental right. Apart from that, this decision provided that Article 17 of the Basic Law did not have any relation at all to any specific form of university organization. Article 17 (1) of the Basic Law, which is directed against violations by the state, is considered to be an absolute fundamental right prohibiting any restriction by law. Yet, it is not granted without limitations, such as the general legal order or the right of supervision by the state laid down in Article 17 (5) of the Basic Law.

A teacher's educational freedom[9] is constitutionally granted, in so far as

[9] A paper of fundamental importance on this issue is: Walter Berka, 'Die pädagogische Freiheit des Lehrers als Rechtsproblem', *Juristische Blätter*, 100 (1978), 571-587.

everybody is authorized to found schools and teach there (Article 17 (2) of the Basic Law). In state schools, however, teaching is considered to be an administrative act and for this reason determined by the principle of legality (Legalitätsprinzip). Pedagogical freedom to a small extent is stipulated in Section 17 (1) of the School Instruction Act (SchUG), which is not part of the Constitution.

Autonomy[10] is granted to universities to a certain extent. In this context it mainly means that universities are not bound by regulations of the Federal Minister, but are entitled to issue binding directives of their own. The right to promulgate individual statutes and the independence from administrative directives can therefore be considered the main parts of autonomy.

If the legal diagnosis does not match every liberal expectation, it can be stated that the liberal state subject to the rule of law (Rechtsstaat) in its historical and in its present shape has been 'generous' to the universities. That is to say, compared with other areas, the universities do not have the same density of regulations.

Since the UOG 1993 was passed, the university has found itself in a phase of transformation regarding its organization, perhaps the biggest change since the epoch of liberalism. The transformation is also characterized by the adoption of managerial skills in order to increase the effectiveness and the efficiency of the universities. There is a clear difference between strategic organs (e.g. Senat, Fakultätsversammlung) and executive organs (e.g. Rektor, Dekan, Studiendekan). This transformation has been accelerated by the emergence of the competition from the Fachhochschulen and the non-university research centres.

It should be emphasized that the legal genesis of the UOG 1993, but also the present discussion, especially among non-jurists, is often accompanied by a naïve autonomy pathos. Autonomy – and this cannot be stressed enough – must be autonomy in a realistic sense and not anarchy or arbitrariness. The

10 A standard series of reference books about juridical problems of Austrian universities including the topic of autonomy is *Beiträge zum Universitätsrecht. Schriftenreihe des Forschungsinstitutes für Universitätsrecht und Universitätsmanagement der Johannes Kepler-Universität Linz.* This series has existed since 1983 and has been edited by Rudolf Strasser at Manz Publishers (Vienna). 21 volumes have been published up to 1999. – See also Bernd-Christian Funk, 'Legalitätsprinzip und Rechtsquellensystem im neuen Universitätsrecht. Inhalt und Reichweite der Rechtssetzungsautonomie der Universität unter besonderer Berücksichtigung der Beziehungen zwischen Kollegialorganen und monokratischen Organen', *Plenum, Zeitschrift der Österreichischen Rektorenkonferenz* (ÖRK), no. 1/1994, 3–26; Günther Winkler, 'Die Rechtspersönlichkeit der Universitäten. Rechtshistorische, rechtsdogmatische und rechtstheoretische Untersuchungen zur wissenschaftlichen Selbstverwaltung'. Wien–New York 1988. Cf. also the leading decisions of the Constitutional Court 8136/1977 and 13.429/1977.

tension between individual and collective freedom can also be found here. When misinterpreted, autonomy can lead to self-justification of local and regional mediocrity. This is not an improbable assumption if you remember how certain persons and groups try to extend the committee-systems of the UOG 1975. Freedom can be overshadowed by misuse. The temptation is great to produce insufficient achievements and to pursue one's own individual or particular interests. This is true for all those involved in a university, from student to professor.

The tension between collective autonomous entities and individual academic freedom is inevitable, because the complexity of modern sciences demands structured cooperation that is more than the sum of individual wishes or spontaneous or informal arrangements. Academic autonomy should lead the university organs to the power to act and not to chaos of eccentric capriciousness or a camouflage for deeply rooted incorrect networks (Filz).

Academic teaching is necessary – and this fact has been recognized as a duty of the university only in the last 30 years by my generation, but the most important characteristic of universities, in comparison to all other educational institutions, is research. All reforms only make sense if universities remain the centre of research. Therefore research-oriented teaching is extremely important, whereas on the other hand permanent research without teaching is unproductive.[11] Therefore I argue that research-oriented further education must be made available for our alumni. At the present time this is a gigantic deficit in Austria.

It worries me that research could emigrate from the university. There are already many demanding long-term research projects concentrated in the Austrian Academy of Sciences and not at the university.

The core of the Humboldtian idea is the inspiring combination of research and teaching. A separation could be fatal. What I fear is that research would then only take place at Oxford and Harvard and everywhere else only 'reproductive' teaching would be the norm.

Austria would then become, in many scientific disciplines, a colony of western research-findings and might even degenerate to a mere 'workbench'. Therefore I am strongly in favour of effective evaluation and for maintaining the 'Habilitation'. Without this procedure the identification of excellence would become even more difficult. The 'Ver-Beamtung'[12] would increase and the challenge to achieve excellence would decrease. The requirements for appointment would drown in a sea of bureaucracy.

[11] This view is often expressed by the prominent German philosopher Jürgen Mittelstrass, member of the Austrian Advisory Board for Universities. See e.g.: 'Die Wirklichkeit im Lichte von Ideen. Ein Plädoyer für Wissenschaft als Kultur', *Die Zeit*, 41 (1986), no. 21, 16 May, 56.

[12] i.e. most members of the academic staff attempt to become irrevocable civil servants.

In this connection, a short word about the Austrian Advisory Board for Universities, the Vice-Chairman of which I am. This board should serve as an independent body of experts. We certainly cannot create miracles, but can at least set up warning signs and give rational advice in order to strengthen existing potential through synergy. The goal of the Advisory Board is to be a 'generator of progress'. An important aspect of our work is also to design a realistic picture of the Austrian Universities.

Looking at the universities should not prevent us from noticing the changes taking place in the other educational institutions. For the first time in the history of the Austrian schools, which go back to the era of Maria Theresia, the strictly regulated paradigm of public schools has been left behind and new concepts such as decentralization, regionalization, deregulation and autonomy have begun to play an important role.[13]

Above all here we also find transformation processes in the 1990s. In the latest amendments to the School Organization Act (SchOG) of 1962 particular elements of autonomy were implanted into the law:

(a) autonomy in curriculum matters;
(b) autonomy concerning the number of pupils per class (group);
(c) autonomy concerning the time of instruction; and
(d) autonomy concerning financial matters.

As a consequence of this development a market-orientation and a positive

[13] A large number of studies exists in the field of school autonomy, not only on legal, but also on pedagogical issues. Cf. e.g. Christian Chvosta, 'Autonomie im Bildungswesen. Organisationstheoretische Aspekte der österreichischen Schulentwicklung'. Linz (diploma thesis) 1997; Renate Deininger, 'Schulautonomie und Teilrechtsfähigkeit: Reformansätze im österreichischen Schulwesen', Österreichisches Jahrbuch für Politik 1997. Wien-München 1998, 753–771; Rainer Fankhauser, 'Development of education law on schools in Austria' (1993–1996). Part I: Schools, *European Journal for Education Law and Policy*, 1 (1997), 101–106; Gerhard Friedrich, 'Autonomie der Schule. Ein Organisationsentwicklungskonzept'. Wien 1993; Reinhard Gande, Hans Putzer and Hubert Schwetz (eds), 'Schulautonomie. Ein Handbuch für die Praxis'. Graz 1994; Heike Hennebichler, 'Schulautonomie in Österreich'. Wien (diploma thesis) 1996; Geraldine Kraus, 'Autonomie. Herausforderung für Bildung und Weiterbildung'. Graz (diploma thesis) 1997; Theo Öhlinger, 'Verfassungsrechtliche Möglichkeiten und Grenzen der Schulautonomie', in: Herbert Haller et alii (eds), 'Staat und Recht. Festschrift für Günther Winkler', Wien–New York 1997, 731–749; Peter Posch and Herbert Altrichter, 'Schulautonomie in Österreich', 2nd edition. Klagenfurt-Wien 1992; Nikolaus Severinski, 'Schulautonomie und die Schulkrise der Gegenwart. Elemente einer liberalen Theorie der Schule'. Wien 1992 and Werner Specht, 'Autonomie und Innovationsklima an Schulen. Rezeption und Wirkungen der Schulautonomie an Hauptschulen und allgemeinbildenden höheren Schulen'. Graz 1997.

competitiveness among schools should have been initiated. Behind this is not only liberal optimism, but also the lack of resources of the state. There is hope that the influence of political parties will decrease. The roots of success in this direction will lie in the possibility of schools to obtain partial legal personality, to rent their rooms, to raise funds and to allow advertizing from outside companies.

So we can see that in schools and universities we must find, for every case, the optimal relationship between freedom and obligation.

3. Consequences and conclusions

Quality and unity of the educational system should not be diminished by autonomy but increased. In order to guarantee these values, evaluation programmes and a supervisory power should be established. Whereas the supervisory power is meant to guarantee unity and compatibility of the system, evaluation programmes are used to maintain quality.

Autonomy stricto sensu means complete self-determination, the right to issue one's own directives, acts and regulations without any supervisory power. This may be a concept for certain matters, but it is not entirely adequate for a national educational system. If a state is obliged to offer its people the possibility of education – and Austria is obliged to do so – it has the right and the duty to maintain and supervise the educational institutions. However, decisions should be taken as decentralized as possible in order to guarantee a consideration of local profiles. Relative autonomy should therefore be linked with a supervisory power.

Everybody wants to act autonomously, fewer people are ready to accept adequate responsibility but hardly anybody is willing to be accountable. Since the entire society, this means the state itself, is highly interested in educating its population in the best way possible, the state cannot abandon its accountability in educational matters. On the other hand, the state is obliged to decentralize and deregulate if these measures improve the fulfilment of the educational tasks. Therefore schools are entitled to demand more autonomy. In order to guarantee compatibility and continuity of education within more or less independently acting educational institutions, the establishment of quality controls (evaluation) seems to be an appropriate tool as well as supervision by the state.

Austria is, in general, characterized by taking the principle of legality (Legalitätsprinzip) almost too seriously, which ends in an enormous number of acts and regulations requiring a huge bureaucracy. As a consequence, deregulation and decentralization are demanded and necessary constraints to the budget of the Austrian State justify these proposals.[14]

[14] Cf. Wolfgang Mantl (ed.), '*Effizienz der Gesetzesproduktion. Abbau der Regelungsdichte im internationalen Vergleich*'. Wien 1995.

In Austria there is nowadays a clear tendency towards enlargement of autonomy with respect to educational institutions. One example represents the above-mentioned University Organization Act of 1993 (UOG 1993) which is today in the process of implementation. Other examples are the recent amendments to the School Organization Act (SchOG) of 1962 and School Instruction Act (SchUG) of 1974 creating new possibilities for a decentralized and more autonomous school administration.

In the discussions of education in Austria there are specific topics which would be impossible for me to cover here: free access (without 'numerus clausus'), no tuition fees, introduction of Bachelors' degrees (three years), installation of evaluation, research-oriented further education and the necessity of a true cost-consciousness.

However, there are some topics which must not be neglected as they are – so to speak – in the shadow of public awareness. This is why I would like to concentrate my final remarks on them:

(a) It would be reasonable to subject new measures, especially on the level of regulations, to a monitoring after two to five years.
(b) The evaluation should be balanced between qualitative and quantitative methods in a model of optimization. We have now a strong tendency towards quantitative methods in order to get comparable figures, identification numbers and indicators. This is undoubtedly necessary but hardly sufficient.
(c) The flexibility and mobility at Austrian universities still leave a lot to be desired. There is something like a 'cocooning' of students, assistants and professors in their region and its university. This phenomenon is similar to the Landesuniversitäten in the 18th century. Nowadays there are different reasons for the said 'rootedness': e.g. the workplace of the spouses.
(d) In the near future it will be necessary – following the Anglo-Saxon model – to 'bind' the alumni to their university, faculty or school respectively, much more than is done now. Universities must offer special programmes to their alumni. They represent a big pool of experience, of job chances for the students, and of potential donors. In the USA an alumnus refers to 'his' university in almost every conversation and even more in his curriculum vitae.
(e) We must find the optimal balance between oral and written types of teaching and examinations.
(f) The increasing character of the universities as 'schools' makes the prominent 'research-professor' redundant and overqualified, as his justification exists e.g. in very freely-shaped seminars. In any case, to profile of the highly gifted assistants would also become very difficult in such school-units. Admittedly the mediocrity would be justified by a university with the character of a school.

(g) The big changes at the turn of the millennium demand a new cultural position of the universities in their surroundings of academies of sciences, non-university research centres, 'Fachhochschulen' and institutions of adult education, but in this context we must not underestimate the impact of the media. With all the reforms it must be seen that the acceptance of the sciences – uncontested during the last two centuries – is no longer self-evident. Universities must present their corporate identity and their outcomes in effective target-group specific public relations work. Only in this way can fund-raising function – as done in the USA.

Considering all issues discussed we cannot help arriving at the conclusion that the vision and the wish of Karl Jaspers will remain valid, that through the universities the brightest consciousness of our times should flourish.[15]

[15] Karl Jaspers, '*Die Idee der Universität*'. Berlin–Göttingen–Heidelberg 1961, 1.

ELSA HACKL

Decentralization of Higher Education and Autonomy

CONCEPTS OF THE CHANGES IN HIGHER EDUCATION

The past quarter century has seen massive changes in higher education. In analysing the reasons and scope of the developments four terms have been developed, namely:

- '*Mass higher education*' which refers to the expanding demand for higher education and hence its regionalization and diversification which necessitates new ways to secure standards and quality.
- The '*enterpreneurial university*' which relates to the transformation of the internal culture of higher education institutions and the way they interact with society due to a diversification of clients and income.
- The '*audit society*' which refers to the changed role of the State, from that of a provider of higher education to that of its auditor.
- '*Internationalization*', which refers to the fact that universities, too, are less and less national institutions and their interaction abroad is no longer mediated by the nation state.

Like the concepts mentioned above the real changes have only gradually emerged and have not yet come to an end. It is not surprising, therefore, that we conceive of higher education as a system in flux. We may even get the impression that the speed of change is increasing, with new laws, White Papers and Commission Reports flourishing, so that even researchers in higher education find it difficult to follow the changes taking place all over the world. And we may tend to see the reforms of the 1960s and 1970s, in retrospect, more as attempts to accommodate the new demands on higher education within the traditional framework of the system or as mere amendments but not as the radical transformation which by now becomes apparent.

One of the most pressing challenges facing universities today is how to meet the expectations which different groups of society place upon them and

Walter Berka, Jan de Groof and Hilde Penneman (eds.), Autonomy in Education, 105–109.

hence to secure the universities' resources whilst maintaining the recognized tradition of autonomy and disinterested service. Under these circumstances I think it is about time to reconsider the concept of autonomy and clarify it. I am therefore most grateful that this conference has been organized.

Traditionally, universities (or institutions which formed part of the higher education sector) have been distinguished from other educational institutions by their 'autonomy' which meant both the individual right to freedom to teach and to do research and the institution's self-government. Both are interrelated and may enhance as well as undermine each other. The national higher education systems differ widely with regard to the emphasis put on one or the other of the two concepts and the degree to which they have been applied. This is due to the different historical developments, not only of higher education, especially of its role for professional life, but more generally of the organization of society. But in any case, the individual freedom of the scholars as well as self-government has been linked closely to the nation state. It is the State or government which has to refrain from intervention and it is the State that has to prevent others from doing so.

From self-government to institutional autonomy

We may notice that in the course of the changes taking place in higher education a new term has been coined, that of 'institutional autonomy'. I maintain that this term is not identical with what was formerly meant by 'self-government'. The latter relates to universities' internal management, their responsibility to look after the internal affairs of the academic community. The term 'institutional autonomy', in comparison, refers, in addition, to universities' responsibility to interact with their environments. It includes their capacity and responsibility to manage the demands of different external stakeholders and is a prior condition of response to competition. The additional dimension increases the scope of self-government.

It has been argued that the additional responsibility of universities to provide services for other stakeholders beside the State strengthens universities' autonomy by making them less dependent on state budgets. However, it raises a lot of questions. What are the effects on the freedom to teach and to do research? Does it increase the tension between self-government and individual autonomy which has always been inherent in the two concepts? And in what way will the responsibility of universities to provide their services to different clients affect academic labour and production? Will it be possible to organize and manage higher education institutions in a way which still allows for long-term enquiries or will the necessity to be responsive entail that 'practice relevance' becomes synonymous with 'immediate relevance'?

The authors of the books from which I borrow the concepts I used at the beginning to describe the changes analysed and did empirical work to answer these questions.

Transforming higher education in Austria

I will, instead, concentrate on a specific case of decentralization and self-government. By 'decentralization' I mean both:

- decentralization in the sense of regionalization to widen access to higher education, research and development; and
- decentralization as devolution of power from the State to the institutional level.

I draw my example from Austria. First, because it is the system I am most familiar with and secondly because it is an example for a fundamental change, as up to very recent years higher education institutions have been state institutions with no legal responsibility.

Traditionally, the Austrian system of education has been regarded as just another branch of bureaucracy, being characterized by close-meshed legal regulations, by public funding and, last but not least, by the teachers' status as civil servants. With higher education, due to historical reasons, to the small size of the country with only eight million inhabitants, and to the unbalanced regional distribution of higher education institutions, the responsibility lies with the federal government and not, as in most federal states with the regions. Universities which until five years ago were the only degree-awarding institutions are federal institutions and are mainly funded from the federal budget.

The traditional governance of universities and their status as dependent state institutions was first challenged by the increased importance of contract research – and later on of continuing educational activities – which eventually, in 1987, resulted in an amendment to the Act on University Organisation which empowered universities and their units to finalize research contracts and manage the income thereof on their own responsibility.

Only a few years later, a further increase in the demand for higher education, for greater equity with regard to social and regional access, together with budgetary constraints and a widespread doubt about the efficiency of the existing system, resulted in a reform process which emphasized 'deregulation, 'decentralization' and 'diversification'.

In the course of this reform process new institutions, based on private law, have been set up to offer 'practice-oriented' degree courses. Standards and quality of the latter are secured by accreditation and assessment procedures.The federal government subsidizes the courses applying a capitation formula, which has also been new in Austria as the money to universities had been distributed by line budgets. The Act governing the new sector provides for the freedom of staff to teach and do research and 'autonomy as inherent to universities' but does not state, in detail, its scope. It was clear, therefore that the implementation needed to be monitored carefully.

What are the experiences that have been gained so far?

At the start of the new sector, in 1994, most institutions running courses were 'associations'. Gradually they changed their legal status and formed 'limited companies' which, from the point of legal determination, transparent responsibilities and clarifying court decisions, is preferable. The members or shareholders of these associations or companies are predominantly regional governments, municipalities and chambers. The fact that 'privatization' is one in the legal sense though not in the economic sense, is understandable from a tradition without major private sponsorship in education and where demands of the economy of education have been mediated by the social partners.

With regard to the allocation of responsibilities in the new institutions, a 'dual system' is evolving. There is a division of labour between the company management, responsible for finanacial and administrative matters, and the teaching staff. The latter is responsible for academic affairs (curriculum design and development, coordination of teaching, matters concerning the learning of individual students). The appointment and dismissal of staff is a joint responsibility, staff development an issue as yet only little addressed.

The Act on the new sector would have allowed for both options, that of a 'unitary system' where the same management is responsible for financial and administrative matters as well as academic matters, which in the latter case is not subject to directives of the shareholders, and the above-mentioned 'dual system'. It has been via the interpretation of the Act, chiefly by the accreditation body, but also by those running the courses, that the 'dual system' has evolved. Those involved drew from their experience from the traditional university management, where, in Austria, the responsibilities have been split up in a similar way between the State and the academic bodies. The change, therefore, has been less radical than some might have envisaged. As it works, it may, however, be an example that it is more appropriate to develop an education system along its own tradition, than to break entirely with it.

This is the point where I would like to turn briefly to the reform of universities: in 1993 a new Act on University Organisation increased their self-government and strengthened the role of the rector. However, universities remained dependent state institutions, chiefly because no agreement was reached concerning the appointment, status and power of the rector. Recently, the issue of an increased institutional autonomy and a 'semi-privatization' of universities is discussed again and a ministerial proposal has been drafted. Again, one of the main controversial questions concerns the position of the rector who should be the responsible manager for both administration/budget and academic affairs. It may be useful to consider the traditional separation of power in Austrian universities. Broadly speaking, this consisted in a separation of the academic sphere supervised by the rector and the administrative/financial domain subject to directives of the Federal Ministry. One might object that it is precisely this division of responsibilities and tasks which needs reforming. I think this is not the case: the objective of the reform – as I understand it – is to strengthen the institutional level, to make universities autonomous and responsible – and to allow a 'steering-at-a-distance' policy of the government. A 'dual system' at the institutional level does not contradict this objective.

When speaking about the new sector in Austrian higher education, I drew from the experiences gained during the first four years of its existence. It is obvious that a 'pioneering period' is always exceptional. In a case where a project is well received – as I think the new institutions have been – there is much identification of all those who are involved. Without this dedication a project cannot start off. However, for institutions to flourish it is important that the different actors concentrate on their respective responsibilities and make clear that there are different interests and tensions, so that they can be dealt with. Both sides, the company management and shareholders, respectively, have trespassed on each others' competences occasionally and will do so again. In that case, where higher education institutions are 'learning organizations' they will, however, be able to cope with it.

Literature

Burton R. Clark (1998) Creating Entrepreneurial Universities: Organizational Pathways of Transformation, Pergamon.

Michael Power (1994) The Audit Explosion, London.

Peter Scott (1995) The meanings of Mass Higher Education, Buckingham.

Sheila Slaughter and Larry L. Leslie (1997) Academic Capitalism. Politics, Policies and the Entrepreneurial University, Baltimore and London.

Martin Trow (1978) Problems in the Transition from Elite to Mass Higher Education, Berkeley, Calif.

Research projects done for the Federal Ministry for Science and Transport:

Walter Berka (1998) Autonomie im Bildungswesen. Eine Untersuchung zu den juristischen Konsequenzen des Autonomiebegriffs im Bildungswesen.

Anton Pelinka und Hubert Sickinger (1998) Autonomie im Bereich des Höheren Bildungswesens. Autonomie aus politologischer Sicht.

Christian Zib (1998) Mögliche Rechtsformen für postsekundäre Bildungseinrichtungen.

BÄRBEL DORBECK-JUNG

Opportunities and Limits of Institutional Autonomy in Public Universities – a Comparison of Governance Structure Regulation*

1. Introduction

Most European universities have undergone remarkable changes over the past ten years. A 'managerial turn' seems to have taken place. As a consequence of mass education, financial budget cuts and general discussions on deregulation and decentralization in public administration, the emphasis at the moment is on quality control and the effectiveness of higher education rather than on democratic decision-making. The universities' institutional autonomy is affected by the changes in its environment. Old governance structures have been reformed and new regulation has been introduced in many European countries. So far, it is not clear whether the basic functions of institutional autonomy are supported or restricted by the new governance structures. If the reforms affect basic values of higher education, problems of legitimacy may arise.

The aim of our contribution is to explore problems of institutional autonomy that may result from changes in the regulation of governance structures.[1]

* I thank J.G. Rasmussen, M. Götsch, and M. Moeller for their comments on an earlier version.

[1] In universities the concept of autonomy is associated with freedom of science and self-governance (see Walter Berka in this volume). Freedom of science can be understood as 'the expression of the mutual and shared responsibility of the government, the community, the scientific institutions and scientists for the development, production and dissemination of scientific knowledge' (Zoontjes 1993: 440). The term 'autonomy' in the sense of self-governance is derived from the old Greek word 'autonomia', which refers to the drafting of a city's own laws. The term 'autonomia' consists of the words *autos* (self) and *nomos* (rule, governance or law).

Walter Berka, Jan de Groof and Hilde Penneman (eds.), Autonomy in Education, 111–147.

In universities, autonomy is attributed to individuals, professionals and institutions, and is seen as support for basic tasks. Our analysis will focus on the opportunities provided by the regulation of governance structures to implement self-regulation, control and democratic decision-making at public universities, as well as on the restrictions this involves. To get a clearer insight into the problems of institutional autonomy we will compare the Dutch, Danish and Austrian regulations. Our paper is arranged as follows:

In the *second section* we conceptualize the concepts of institutional autonomy and university governance structure (2.1). The concept of institutional autonomy is mainly based on Selznick's institutional theory (1992). In Selznick's approach, autonomy is associated with ideas on institutional integrity, standards of accountability and democracy, and the concept of responsive regulation. Our study sees governance as an interactive social process of exerting influence (Dorbeck-Jung & De Jong 1998). According to Selznick's institutional theory, university governance structure regulation can lead to problems of legitimacy[2] if it does not leave enough room for self-regulation, if it does not provide clear responsibilities and effective control, and if it does not comply with standards of democratic decision-making. In line with these ideas, we inquire whether governance structure regulation offers opportunities to implement self-regulation, control and democratic participation and how these opportunities are restricted. Having conceptualized institutional autonomy and governance structure regulation, the basic concepts will be operationalized (2.2). This operationalization yields a comparison scheme (2.3).

The *third section* gives a description of Dutch, Danish and Austrian university governance regulations on the basis of our comparison scheme. The *fourth section* deals with comparison and analysis. The comparison will indicate whether there are similar or different opportunities and limits of institutional autonomy. Our analysis results in conclusions regarding problems of institutional autonomy at universities (*fifth section*).

2. Conceptualization

2.1. *Institutional autonomy and governance in Selznick's institutional theory*

The conceptualization of institutional autonomy is based on Philip Selznick's social theory (Selznick 1992). At the very heart of Selznick's approach lies the concept of 'moral institutions'. Institutionalization is associated with the realization of values. According to Selznick, 'moral institutions' adhere to the values

[2] Legitimacy is regarded as the moral acceptance of regulation (De Jong & Dorbeck-Jung 1997: 195). In our contribution moral acceptance refers to basic values of universities and to the societal values in which their tasks are embedded.

of integrity, autonomy, accountability, and responsibility. Integrity is interpreted as remaining faithful to self-defining principles. To pursue integrity means to incorporate the objectives of an institution, its unifying principles and its moral claims into decision-making. In the case of universities, these basic objectives are: freedom of science, democracy, equality, and effectiveness (Dorbeck-Jung 1997b). These objectives are reflected by the policy goals that are the aim of governance structure regulations. The support of institutional autonomy is seen as a means to achieve these goals. In modern constitutional states, governance structures are bound to requirements of democracy to prevent any undue accumulation and abuse of power. Governance structure regulations are also related to requirements regarding effectiveness and efficiency. In contemporary developments of higher education these demands have been stressed in order to cope with the increase or decrease of student numbers, economy measures, and competitive pressures. In Selznick's approach, the integrity of universities is fostered by institutional autonomy as well as through internal and external control. Autonomy means that values can be protected and effectiveness and efficiency can be achieved by isolating institutions from outside pressures and leaving ample room for self-regulation. Autonomy is derived from the idea that these institutions serve public ends and do so best when protected from political interference. However, to ensure the recognition of moral issues and the exercise of self-restraint there must be mechanisms of internal and external control. Effective control requires controllability of action. Summarizing, we conclude that institutional autonomy can only be studied in relation to the social values, responsibilities and measures of effective control at stake.

In Selznick's theory, *responsive decision-making* is typical of the approach of 'moral institutions'. Such responsive regulation aims to solve public problems. Selznick assumes that problems can be solved more adequately through self-regulation and negotiation than through legislation and hierarchic steering. Responsiveness, however, denotes critical and controlled problem-solving. As Nonet and Selznick put it: '*A responsive institution retains a grasp on what is essential to its integrity while taking account of new forces in its environment*' (Nonet & Selznick 1978: 77). Responsiveness requires the integration of multiple interests. It is associated with ideas on *governance*, since '*to govern is to accept responsibility for the whole life of the institution. Governance takes account of all the interests that affect the viability, competence, and moral character of an enterprise*' (1992: 290). The concept of governance is in turn related to ideas on reasonable decision-making, such as participation, dialogue and balancing of interests. Democratic aspects play an important part here.[3]

According to Selznick, institutionalization is based on the normative order and history of an organization. Formal acts (i.e. the adoption of a rule or

[3] See also De Groof *et al.* 1998.

statute) are regarded only as a starting mechanism of institutionalization. Beyond the formal structure lies what Selznick calls 'thick' institutionalization (1992: 232). The idea of 'thick' institutionalization includes both the official design ('formal structure') and the informal structure ('organic structure'). The informal structure consists of attitudes, relationships, and practices that arise in the course of social interaction. Together, the formal and informal structure constitute the operative reality of institutions.

According to Selznick's theory, governance structure regulation can lead to problems, if little room is left for self-regulation, if no effective controls are provided, if democratic decision-making is not facilitated, if academic freedom is restricted, and if formal and informal structure diverge. Reflecting on the reasons for the various problems, we assume that some of them are created by conflicting values of higher education. Governmental responsibility for the quality of education and research that requires intensive public regulation and control, affects academic freedom and institutional autonomy. Institutional autonomy can also violate academic freedom if, for instance, teaching and research methods are restricted by regulations imposed by university bodies. The demand of democracy can clash with the requirements of effectiveness and efficiency, if, for example, democratic governance turns out to be more expensive than decision-making which involves less participation.

Summarizing, we can conclude that when analysing problems of institutional autonomy we should pay particular attention to the relations between the formal and informal structures of university governance regulation. This analysis is based on the opportunities the regulation of governance structures leaves for self-regulation of universities. Within this context we also explore the limits imposed on autonomy by government regulation. Moreover, we investigate whether such regulation restricts individual academic freedom. Secondly, we focus on the regulation of control. Here we explore whether control limits self-regulation and whether it is effectively designed. In this context, attention will be paid to the question whether responsibilities are clearly designed within the university governance structure. We also look at the democratic aspects of governance structure, including the tension between democratic decision-making and the effectiveness and efficiency of higher education.

2.2. *Research strategy*

To investigate the opportunities and limits of institutional autonomy we have to operationalize the basic concepts we introduced above, which are the concepts of governance structure, control, and democratic participation. Above we defined governance as an interactive social process of exerting influence whose main aim is the integration of various interests. A governance structure is seen as a set of (formal and informal) rules that is produced and reproduced by the organizational actors (Giddens 1984: 25). Rules are defined as standards for human conduct. Formal rules are based on formal authority, while informal rules are regarded as the actual standards of conduct (Dorbeck-Jung 1997a: 204). Formal rules allocate powers of governance to certain specific *actors*. From the legal perspective governance powers refer to *competences* of regulation, daily management,[4] policy-making, controlling, advising, and democratic participation.

Regarding the interactive perspective our definition implies, we focus on the *relations* between the various actors which are in charge of university governance. This means that we have to obtain an insight into the actors involved in university governance and the relations between them. Within universities, actors of governance can be either individuals or organizational sub-units or entities ('corporate actors'; Binsbergen *et al.* 1994: 223). In governance structures of universities, the following relationships can be distinguished: the relationship between government (ministry) and the central level of the university, the relationship between the central level and the decentralized levels of the university (faculty, department, or institute), and relationships between various decentralized levels (i.e. faculty and departments). Our broad definition of governance also includes the relationship between the decentralized level and the employees (teachers, researchers, and supportive staff).

Governance structures are related to the coordination of distinctive tasks.[5] Coordination can be achieved by means of government regulation, legally conditioned self-regulation and pure self-regulation (Dorbeck-Jung 1997a). Legally conditioned self-regulation is characterized by the following three aspects (Eijlander 1993):

1. certain basic and structural conditions are imposed by law;
2. private institutions are given autonomy in order to specify the legal framework by means of self-regulation; and
3. government control is restricted to the output of regulation.

When discussing the concept of *control* we mentioned internal and external control. Here control is considered as *external* if the members of the controlling bodies are from outside the university. *Internal* control refers to controlling activities within the university. Controlling actors can be located at the same

4 Governance and management are distinguished on the basis of their institutional context (Kwikkers 1997: 59). Management refers to methods originating from the private sector, and governance is used to indicate how a public system is organized and managed. For the purpose of this paper, we will mainly use the terminology of governance.

5 Governance structures are also defined as '*the ways in which an organization divides its labour into distinct tasks and then achieves coordination between them*' (Binsbergen *et al.* 1994: 220).

or at different levels of governance. Control can be exercised both by corporate actors (ministry, boards, councils, review bodies) and by individual actors (Minister, Director, Dean, students, employees, etc.). The term 'controls' refers to supervision rather than the formulation of regulations. The main focus of supervision is to audit regulations. It also involves the right or duty to approve or consent to regulations. From the point of view of democratic decision-making, however, the right of approval is seen as a participatory activity. Supervision also involves the right of complaint, if this can result in auditing activities.

Effective control requires the independence of controlling actors, the sanctioning of powers and the transparency of regulations, as well as the access of controlling bodies to relevant information.

Regarding the concept of *democratic participation* the aspects on which we will focus are election and co-governance.[6] As far as possible we include informal aspects that refer to the distribution of powers in reality and to the facts of democratic participation. The concept of *election* refers to the traditional rights to vote for and to be elected in governing bodies. *Co-governance* refers to the power of approval and consent to regulations and the right of being consulted in the regulation process. The extent and methods of democratic participation are reflected in models of leadership. These are the systems of representative, mixed and executive leadership (De Boer *et al.* 1998b: 154). This distinction is based on the distribution of powers within governance structures. In systems of representative leadership, most of the formal powers reside in the representative council(s). If these formal powers are spread out more or less evenly over the representative assembly and the executive actors, De Boer *et al.* speak of *mixed leadership. Executive leadership* means that most of the formal powers are allocated to the executive actors (i.e. Executive Board). According to the characteristics of democratic participation, executive leadership, for example, can be seen as less democratic than mixed and representative leadership.

To sum up, this operationalization has provided us with the following issues and aspects for our description and comparison of university governance regulation:

- formal and informal rules;
- corporate and individual actors;
- powers of actors;
- relationships and levels of governance;
- internal and external control;
- three modes of regulation;

6 Kwikkers distinguishes similar elements of democratic participation (election, communication, and selection; see Kwikkers 1997: 60).

- two aspects of democratic participation; and
- three forms of democratic leadership.

2.3. *Comparison scheme*

As we stated above, our operationalization has provided basic issues and aspects needed for the description and comparison of university governance structure regulations. To clarify the national situation in the various countries we intend to discuss, we start with some *general remarks*. These remarks will also be included in our comparison and analysis of problems of institutional autonomy. We begin by giving a survey of the reform of governance structure regulation, including information about reasons of the changes and policy goals. Secondly, we give an outline of the formal governance structure; here we list the actors involved, their major tasks, their mutual relationships, and the levels of governance. We describe the effects of the formal structure and the informal structure as far as possible. Since the informal structure is strongly related to the organizational culture of universities, an outline of the main characteristics of this culture is provided including changes as compared to the situation which existed before the governance structure reform. Hence our general remarks will refer to:

- recent reforms in governance structure regulations (reasons for changes, policy goals, forms of democratic leadership);
- the formal structure (levels of governance, actors, major tasks, relationships);
- the effects of the formal structure and the informal structure (including organizational culture).

Regarding the description and comparison of opportunities of institutional autonomy, our main subjects are the *competences of self-regulation* attributed by the formal structure to certain actors in certain relationships on a certain level of governance, as well as the informal rules in so far as they deviate from the formal rules. We will also focus on the competences held by actors outside the university (i.e. the regulation authority of the minister of Education). In our comparison we will investigate whether regulation competences are extensive, comprehensive and detailed. We are aware that institutional autonomy and self-governance do not just refer to powers of regulation, but also to autonomous decision-making on budget, planning, and university staff. To limit the complexity of this paper, we will focus on the competences of self-regulation that are seen as the core of institutional autonomy. The description and comparison of control refers to *competences of internal and external control actors* with respect to auditing, approval, and complaining. Considering the effectiveness of control, we explore whether the controlling authorities can be seen as independent actors, whether they are authorized to impose sanctions, whether self-regulation is made transparent and whether the supervisory bodies are authorized to have access to relevant information. We also investigate whether the controlling powers are formulated explicitly or implicitly. Looking at aspects of *democratic participation*, we investigate whether and by whom members of governing bodies are elected or appointed and how long their term is, and whether there are any procedures in place for the election and re-election of such bodies. Regarding co-governance, we look at the powers to regulate approval, consultation, hearings etc. As far as possible we regard the informal rules of democratic participation that indicate the real power structure.

Regarding the subjects of self-regulation, control and democratic participation we assume that it could be relevant whether the regulations are formulated either explicitly or implicitly. We suppose also that institutional autonomy is either enlarged or restricted by extensive, comprehensive and detailed regulation competences.

Here we will use the following comparison scheme:

1. General remarks
    - recent reforms in governance structure regulations (reasons of changes, policy goals, forms of democratic leadership);
    - the formal structure (levels of governance, actors, major tasks, relationships);
    - the effects of the formal structure and the informal structure (including organizational culture).
2. Autonomy and self-regulation
    - competences of self-regulation (extensive?, comprehensive?, detailed?);
    - regulation competences of other actors (extensive?, comprehensive?, detailed?);
3. Control
    - competences of internal control (audit?, approval/consent?, complaints?);
    - competences of external control (audit?, approval/consent?, complaints?);
    - effective control (independence of controlling authorities?, sanctions?, transparency of self-regulation?, access to relevant information?);
4. Democratic participation
    - establishment of governing actors (election/appointment?, term?, procedure of election/re-election?);
    - co-governance (approval of regulation?, right to be consulted or to be heard?).

Our description of the national situation is based mainly on legal documents, on legal doctrine, and on empirical studies concerning the effects of national university governance structure regulation. Here we will use a multidisciplinary approach that involves a broad view on legal sources. To meet the methodological requirements of comparability, we have selected countries that purport to hold similar views of the need for reform of university governance structures, with similar perspectives based on a similar perception of the governance problems that result from changes in the environment of the various universities. As such we will employ a problem-oriented approach to comparative law (Dorbeck-Jung 1995; 1997b). As far as reforms in the governance structure reforms of European countries are concerned, comparable developments took place in The Netherlands, Denmark, and Austria (De Boer *et al.* 1998a).

3. Description of governance structure regulations

3.1. *Dutch situation*

3.1.1. *General remarks*

In The Netherlands, the reform of the governance structures of the ten public universities took place quite recently. In March 1997 the new Act on the modernization of university governance structure (MUB[7]) became effective. Due to the decrease in the number of students and budget cuts, a more business-like governance structure was introduced, since the old structure no longer seemed capable of effectively supporting the processes of higher education and research and coping with the new developments of higher education.[8] This is why the title of the MUB refers to the modernization of university governance structures. Its Explanatory Statement mentions three main policy goals.[9] These are: the improvement of the quality of primary processes within universities, the strengthening of the governance power of the university as a social organization, and enhancing its self-sufficiency. When comparing the old and the new structure, we arrive at the following changes (De Boer *et al.*, 1998b: 63):

- Executive powers *vis-à-vis* the Council at both the central and faculty levels have been enhanced.
- The University and Faculty Councils have become representative advisory bodies for students and employees, instead of bodies with a strong governance role.
- Governance and management tasks have been integrated.
- The research groups ('vakgroepen'), which were quite powerful before, have disappeared (at least formally).

[7] 'Wet modernisering universitaire bestuursorganisatie' – MUB (Act on the Modernization of University Administration), 1997, 117.

[8] See also Explanatory Statement, p. 2.

[9] Explanatory statement, p. 1.

- A new governing body was introduced, the Supervisory Board (comparable to a 'board of trustees').

Considering the strengthening of the powers of the Executive Board and the Dean, we may conclude that the Dutch university governance structures have moved from a system of mixed leadership to a system of executive leadership. According to De Boer *et al.*, the Act partly codifies a current practice of executive leadership (De Boer *et al.* 1998b: 161). As De Boer et al. put it:

> *the results of our surveys suggest that the new Act will not revolutionise the everyday practice of university and faculty decision-making. The changes will be incremental rather than revolutionary.*

The *formal structure* of the Dutch governance regulation of public universities arises first and foremost from the MUB. The MUB is a part of the Act on Higher Education and Scientific Research (WHW[10]). It consists of 52 provisions on the main features of the governance structure of public universities, on the structure of education and research, reversal of decisions of faculties, on Research Institutes and schools, and on the systems of participation in decision-making. On the basis of the MUB, other formal rules were created regarding governance and management at both the central and decentralized level of universities (University and Faculty regulations). In addition to the MUB, Article 23 of the Dutch Constitution also refers to governance regulation, since it formulates a general governmental responsibility for education (Akkermans 1996: 1). This governmental responsibility implies financial aspects, regulation and control.

Four levels of governance can be distinguished in the Dutch situation. They are the government level, the central level and two decentralized levels. Governance relationships concern relations between the Minister of Education and Research and the central level of the universities, relations between the central level and the decentralized level of the Faculties, and relations between Faculties and staff and students. According to the MUB, the minister can bring his influence to bear in his relation with the Supervisory Board of the public university. At the central level, the MUB allocates tasks and competences mainly to the Executive Board, the Supervisory Board, and the University Council(s). The Executive Board has three members, including the Rector (Vice-Chancellor[11]) of the university.[12] The Chairman of the Executive Board is appointed by the Supervisory Board. The Supervisory Board consists of at least three and at most five members,[13] whereas the Councils have 24 members

[10] 'Wet hoger onderwijs en wetenschappelijk onderzoek' (Higher Education and Scientific Research Act), Bulletin of Acts, Orders and Decrees, 1992, 593.

[11] In this contribution we use the term 'rector'.

[12] Art. 9.3. Section 1 MUB.

[13] Art. 9.7. Section 1 MUB.

at the most. At the first decentralized level, actors of governance are the Dean of the Faculty, the Study Commission and the Faculty Council. The number of members of the Study Commission and their appointment is stipulated by faculty regulations. The Dean is authorized to give mandates with respect to the organization of teaching, research, and management.[14] According to Article 9.19 of the MUB, the full professors are responsible for the development of the research and teaching subjects with which they are commissioned. Except for the Dean, the Rector and the professors, the MUB refers only to corporate actors. Executive powers are allocated mainly to the Executive Board and to the Dean. As such this formal structure has a hierarchical approach to the powers and responsibilities of governance. The MUB mentions two models of counselling. In the first model, that of *undivided* counselling, student and staff members participate in one council; the second model, that of *divided* counselling, involves two councils (one made up of students and one consisting of employees). According to the Act, it is up to the Executive Board to decide on the system of student and employee participation.[15] The advisory tasks of the councils refer mainly to employment issues, while the powers of the Study Commission concentrate on matters of education programmes and courses. Advice can be given at the request of governing bodies as well as at its own initiative.

The formal structure of the Dutch public universities can be outlined as in Figure 1.

To obtain an insight into the *effects of the MUB*, its implementation was studied from May 1997 to May 1998 by an advisory group. The outcome of this study emphasizes the tension between the models of executive and mixed leadership (Klankbordgroep 1998: 14). The report argues that too much emphasis on effective governance and management can hamper the acceptance of new governance relations. Reflecting on the fact that most universities adopted a managerial approach, the study indicates that the quality of management must be a point of further concern. The report states that the new system of counselling has not yet led to any re-arrangement of co-governance and advisory functions. The systems of participation are not yet in balance. The relation between the Supervisory Board and the representative advisory bodies must be clarified. The report also indicates that little value is attached to the students' right of complaint. On the basis of these findings, the advisory group formulates questions for the evaluation of the MUB that will take place within the next years. Since the new system of governance structure has only been operating for a short time, it is not yet clear whether its informal structure corresponds to the formal one. To understand this informal structure, we should be aware

[14] Art. 9.12., 9.17. MUB.

[15] Art. 9.30 MUB.

Figure 1: Formal governance structure of Dutch public universities[16]

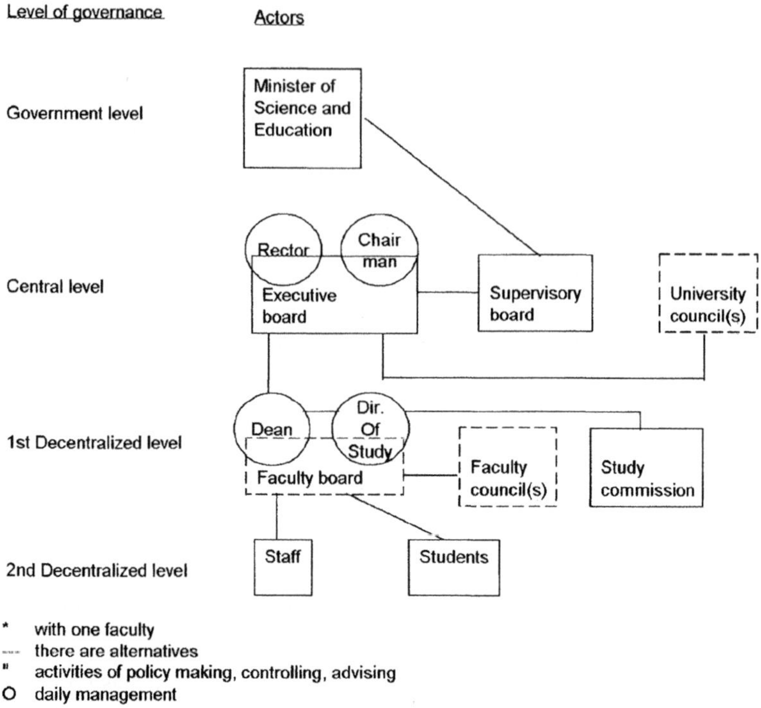

that the traditional organizational culture of Dutch universities is characterized by a high degree of informal communication and a low degree of formal hierarchy. Much importance is attached to individual autonomy and participatory decision-making.

3.1.2. *Autonomy and self-regulation*

According to Article 1.6 of the WHW, academic freedom is attributed to teachers, researchers and students. Institutional autonomy is not explicitly formulated by the Dutch constitution or by the WHW and MUB. It can be based on certain policy documents to which the Dutch Higher Education Act refers. It is also incorporated in the regulation approach of the MUB. In line

[16] To reduce the complexity of presentation the figure includes only main governance actors. It does not refer to particular governance activities or functions. According to our broad definition of governance ('exerting influence'), we include a decentralized level of actors (professors, students) that may exert influence on governance (though they do not have decisive competences).

with the concept of 'steering from a distance', the minister's powers of governance are rather limited. Assuming that the most adequate governance structure of a university cannot be designed adequately through government regulations, the MUB leaves much room for self-regulation. According to the explanatory statement, this approach fits with the general government policy of deregulation, decentralization and the globalization of rule-making.[17] Regarding the generality of the legal framework established by the MUB and the room this leaves for self-regulation, the regulatory approach can be characterized as *legally conditioned self-regulation.*

The Act provides a legal framework for university governance structures. This framework formulates a clear structure of responsibilities, leaving plenty of room for self-regulation at both the central and the decentralized level of the universities. At the central level, self-regulatory powers are mainly attributed to the Executive Board. Here, the powers of self-regulation involve education and research policies, specific issues of governance and management, the structure of participation of employees and students, the appointment of the Chancellor, and the tasks and composition of the Board of Promotions. Specific matters of governance also pertain to the decision of the Executive Board whether only the Dean is charged with the governance of a Faculty or whether others are also responsible (such as the Director of Studies). Concerning matters of organization and co-ordination, the Executive Board is also authorized to establish directives that are put to the Deans.[18] At the first decentralized level the Dean is empowered to impose his own regulations regarding the organization of teaching and research, including the governance and management of Research Institutes. Issues and procedures involved in the collective right of students to complain[19] are laid down in faculty regulations. The MUB does not formulate more specific regulation competences of the minister that could limit self-regulation.

3.1.3. *Control*

Regarding the *competences of internal control*, we must look at self-regulation at the central and decentralized level of the university. At the *central level*, self-regulation of the Executive Board is subject to internal control by the Supervisory Board. This Board is in charge of the governance and management activities of the whole University.[20] Its tasks, however, are not purely related

[17] Explanatory Statement, p. 7.

[18] Art. 9.5 MUB.

[19] Art. 9.28 MUB. This right of complaint of a group of students is a new phenomenon within the formal rules of university governance structures. Complaints can be made in cases the university has neglected its duties *vis-à-vis* students. As such it refers mainly to bad quality of curriculi, courses, and teaching.

[20] Art. 9.8 Section 1 MUB.

to control. The Supervisory Board is also in charge of advising the Executive Board. It is authorized to approve the university's strategic documents and system of counselling. Since the controlling activities of the Supervisory Board are related to government control, they can also be seen as a form of external control. At the central level, self-regulation is also controlled by the university Council(s), since their consent is required for certain policy documents and regulations of the Executive Board.[21]

At the *decentralized level*, self-regulation is controlled primarily by the Executive Board. According to the MUB, the Dean is accountable to the Executive Board.[22] If faculty regulations conflict either with law or the general interest, the Executive Board is authorized to reverse or overrule them.[23] If the Faculty neglects its governance and management tasks, the Executive Board is authorized to take appropriate action.[24] These measures are only valid if they have been approved by the Supervisory Board. Internal control is also exercised through the faculty Council(s), the Study Commission, and groups of students. Like the council(s) on the central level, the consent of the Faculty Council(s) is (are) required for certain regulations. The Study Commission's capacity of control lies in its competence to assess the implementation of the regulations of education programmes and exams.[25] According to Article 9.28 of the MUB, students have a collective right of complaint. Groups of students are authorized to appeal to the Dean regarding the duties the university has towards them (i.e. the viability of curricula, and high-quality education).

External control is exercised by the Minister of Education and the Dutch Audit Office. Within the controlling activities of the minister, the Supervisory Board plays an important part. According to the MUB, this body is accountable to the minister.[26] Regarding the self-regulation of quality evaluation of education, another government control is provided by authority of the Higher Education Inspectorate.[27] The Dutch Auditing Office checks whether the policy of public universities is correct and effective.[28] This means that the Office is also charged with the control of self-regulatory activities.

Regarding the *effectiveness of control*, the independence of controlling bodies is partly stipulated by the MUB. Some provisions of the MUB state that

[21] Art. 9.33 MUB.

[22] Art. 9.16 MUB.

[23] Art. 9.24 MUB.

[24] Art. 9.27 MUB.

[25] Art. 9.18. Section 1b MUB.

[26] Art. 9.9 Section 1 and 2 MUB.

[27] See Arts. 5.1, 5.2 WHW.

[28] Arts. 51, 57 Accountability Act ('Comptabiliteitswet') 1976 (Bulletin of Acts, Orders and Decrees 671).

governance actors should not be members of other governing bodies.[29] Since the Supervisory Board is seen as a controlling body of the ministry as well as a governance actor of the university, the independence of its members is questionable. In the MUB explicit sanctions are provided concerning the competence of the Executive Board to overrule faculty regulations as well as to take measures if the faculty neglects self-regulation. Sanctions are implicitly provided in the context of the competences to suspend or dismiss a governance actor.[30] The negligence of self-regulation can be one of the grounds for suspension and dismissal. If the Supervisory Board does not comply with its duty to control, the minister is authorized to discharge its members. Regarding self-regulation of quality evaluation, the minister can terminate a programme or stop funding if self-regulation has not led to an improvement of a low quality for the past few years or if self-regulation violates the provisions of the WHW.[31]

Considering transparency of self-regulation we conclude that most of the provisions of the MUB with respect to governance powers and responsibilities are clear and intelligible. They are more well-defined than in the old system. This is the case with respect to the Supervisory Board and the Dean. The competences of the Executive Board, however, are more vague. The demarcation between the competences of the Chairman of the Executive Board and the Rector as well as between those of the Executive Board and the Dean are not clear. Regarding the power relation between the Chairman of the Executive Board and the Rector, the MUB does not provide explicit regulations. With respect to the second power relation, the MUB stipulates that the Executive Board is in charge of policy, while the Dean's organization and management competences refer to the content of education and research. It is not clear, however, whether the Executive Board's competence to give directives to the Dean interferes with this rule. Similar questions arise in the relation between the Dean and the professionals. The demarcation between the professionals' responsibility with respect to the content of research, programmes and teaching[32] and the Dean's competence to give them directives is not well-defined. According to Article 7.59 WHW, the Student Statute must be published. Other products of self-regulation are published in line with the universities' rules and practices. To facilitate controlling, the Supervisory Board and the Dean are legally obliged to inform the minister respectively the Executive Board.[33]

3.1.4. *Democratic participation*

In the Dutch situation, most governing actors are not elected but appointed. The members of the Supervisory Board are appointed by the Minister of Education for a period of four years. According to the MUB, the minister

[29] For example Art. 9.3 Section 7 MUB regarding the Executive Board.

[30] For example Art. 9.3 Section 2 MUB.

[31] Art. 6.5, 15.1 WHW.

[32] See Art. 9.19 MUB.

[33] Arts. 9.9, 9.16 MUB.

appoints a member who is trusted by the University Council.[34] The Supervisory Board is authorized to appoint and suspend the members of the Executive Board. The Supervisory Board is authorized to lay down the period of appointment. The Dean is appointed by the Executive Board. The Executive Board formulates the period of appointment. Full professors are appointed by the Executive Board. After a probationary period of one year they are granted a permanent position. The appointment of the members of the Study Commission as well as the number of members is formulated within the faculty regulations. The MUB stipulates only that half of the members must be students.[35] The members of the Study Commission are appointed by the Dean.

The members of the University and Faculty Councils are elected by the group of staff or students to which they belong. In cases of conflicts about participation, a Disputes Commission can be set up by the Executive Board and the Councils.[36] This Commission consists of three members and three substitute members. One of the members and substitutes is elected by the Executive Board while the second member and substitute are elected by the University Council.[37] Both these members together elect the third member who acts as Chairman, as well as the third substitute member. The members of the Disputes Commission are elected for a period of four years. Re-election is possible. Regarding co-governance, we mentioned the authority of the various councils to agree on self-regulation. The University Council is also heard before the Supervisory Board appoints a member of the Executive Board.[38]

3.2. *The Danish situation*[39]

3.2.1. *General remarks*

In Denmark, the governance structures of the eleven public universities were reformed in 1993 to be able to cope with a number of changes. These changes involved an increase in the number of students, the growing importance of universities in state budgets, changes in curricula, increased importance attached to research, a far wider graduate labour market, and general reforms in the structure of the Danish state with respect to decentralization (Rasmussen 1998: 183). In addition there were many complaints about the distribution of power. In the old structure the power of governance was concentrated at the

[34] Art. 9.7 Section 2 MUB.

[35] Art. 9.18 Section 3 MUB.

[36] Art. 9.40 MUB.

[37] Art. 9.39 MUB.

[38] Art. 9.3 Section 3 MUB.

[39] The description of the Danish situation is mainly based on the publications of Rasmussen (1995, 1998) and the translation of the Danish UA 1993 (Order no. 334 of 27 May 1993).

faculty level. At the central level, the real power of the Senate was quite low. The old system of broad democratic participation in decision-making was seen to be very time-consuming and rather inefficient; that is why the old law appeared to be out of date. The demand for legal reform of university governance structure resulted in the University Act of 1993. The main policy goals of the Act are to make the university more efficient and to transfer tasks from the Ministry of Education to the universities. To reach these goals the 1993 University Act places more emphasis on university autonomy, on executive authority, and on hierarchical chains of command. The old law was more collegial in orientation. When comparing the old and the new University Acts, we see as the main changes:

- a shift of the internal power structure (more power to the central level and more authority to leaders on all levels);
- changes in resource allocation (budget model and increasing external funding of research);
- minor decentralization from the state to the universities; and
- the addition of external members to the Senate and Faculty Boards.

Regarding its forms of leadership, the Danish university governance system seems to have shifted from representative leadership to executive leadership. The *formal structure* of Danish university governance is primarily created by the University Act of 1993 (UA 1993). The UA consists of 14 provisions, relating to: general matters, the management of the institution, the Faculty Councils, the Deans of the faculties, the Departments Boards and their Heads, Study Boards and Study Directors, economic issues and other matters. On the basis of this Act, other formal rules such as the University Statutes are established. According to our view on governance levels of universities, the UA 1993 distinguishes 5 levels of governance: the government level, the central University level and three decentralized levels (faculties, departments, staff and students). Actors are the Minister of Education (government), the Rector and Senate (central level), the Dean and Faculty Council (first decentralized level), the Department Boards and their Heads, the Study Board and the Director of Studies (second decentralized level), staff and students (third decentralized level). Hence, the UA 1993 refers both to individual and to corporate actors. The Danish governance structure can be outlined as in Figure 2 (Rasmussen 1998: 185).

The new Danish approach attributes the executive power to the Rector, the Deans, the department heads and the Directors of Studies. According to Rasmussen, these actors are situated in a more or less traditional hierarchical governance structure, each leader acting as Chairman of a Board: the Senate, the Faculty Council, the Department Board and the Study Committee (Rasmussen 1995: 336). The new situation reduces the number of members of the Senate and the Faculty Board to 14 (and a chairman) as a maximum. They

Figure 2: Formal governance structure of Danish universities[40]

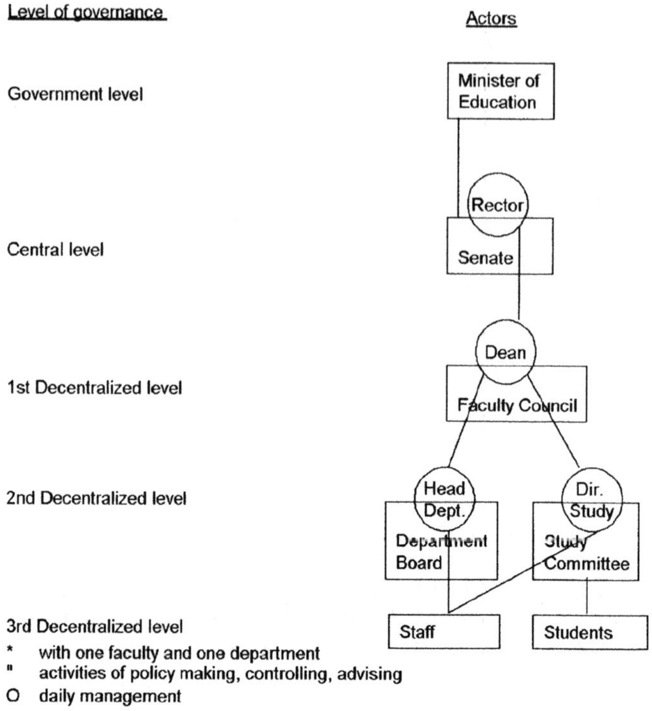

can also contain less members as long as the balance between students, academic and administrative staff is maintained. According to Rasmussen,

> '*The division of responsibility according to the law places the ultimate formal power at the top of the hierarchy-in the hands of the Rector. But at the time the power of decision making with respect to a number of specific areas is placed in the various decentralized bodies.*'
>
> (Rasmussen 1998: 186)

Comparing the *informal structure* with the legal framework of the University Act 1993, Rasmussen concludes that no major efforts have been made to evade

[40] To reduce complexity, the formal situation is only based on the Danish University Act. As other regulations might establish governance actors (i.e. advisory councils according to Danish Labour Law), the figure is not complete. This is one of the reasons why the three figures on the Dutch, Danish and Austrian formal governance structures are not comparable.

the formal rules. The new regulations are followed where they correspond with existing trends among the professionals. Rasmussen admits, however,

> '*that there are differences between the formal and the informal structure. The students do not fully use the new formal possibilities of influence; the technical and administrative staff still pursue old informal ways of influence; and the areas of power are only partially occupied by management at the department and study level*' (1998: 195).

In line with this trend, he speaks of an ongoing 'cold war' between the formal and informal systems (1995: 343). Tasks regarding the allocation of staff, coordination and routine administrative functions are informally defined responsibilities of the faculty staff. The informal structure appears to be an organizational structure with professional and semi-professional groups interacting in a culture that is characterized by hierarchy to only a minor degree. This culture is seen as being based on informal relationships and very few rules compared to the ideal of the present legislation (Rasmussen 1998: 197). According to Rasmussen, the organizational culture of Danish universities can be characterized by a high degree of informal communication, a low degree of formal hierarchy and a relatively high level of influence on the part of the various participants within the university academic staff, students and technical and administrative employees (Rasmussen 1995: 338). Regarding the central level, Rasmussen concludes that the role of the Senate seems much like that of the former and larger Senate looking like an assembly of elected representatives (1995:339). Centralization in the sense of a redistribution of power between the Senate and the Faculty Councils has only partially taken place. The influence of the Study Committees and Directors of Study, however, has increased.

3.2.2. *Autonomy and self-regulation*

According to Article 1 Section 2 of the UA 1993, an institution of higher education shall safeguard academic freedom and contribute to the dissemination of knowledge on its research methods and results. Individual autonomy is also stipulated with regard to a free choice of methods. The Head of Department may direct members of the staff to perform certain tasks, while always taking into account their free choice of research methods.[41] The Act is regarded as a general legal framework that leaves ample room for self-regulation. As such the regulatory approach can be characterized as a legally conditioned self-regulation. Institutional autonomy is also stipulated regarding study programmes, research, and publicity.[42] Each university decides on the study programmes it wishes to offer and its intake of students. It also decides on the

[41] Art. 7 Section 3 UA 1993.

[42] Art. 1 Section 3–5 UA 1993.

type of research it wishes to perform. The universities are empowered to set limits on publicity, lectures or oral examinations.

Self-regulatory powers are located at both the central and decentralized levels of governance in universities. At the central level, the Rector is authorized to make proposals for Statutes concerning the more detailed rules for management of the institution, activities of administrative bodies, and elections. The Senate establishes the guidelines for long-term teaching and research activities and development of the university.[43] The Rector lays down more detailed rules on disciplinary measures *vis-à-vis* the students.[44] At the decentralized level, the Faculty Councils establish guidelines to regulate day-to-day management by the Dean.[45] The Department Board also sets out guidelines for the activities and development of the department.[46] The Study Committee is authorized to draw up proposals for curricula.[47]

According to the UA 1993, the Minister of Education establishes general guidelines on the study programmes and on the admission to these programmes.[48] The Minister decides on the universities' proposals of study programmes. He/she may also lay down general regulations pertaining to quality control (including the role of external examiners), the awarding of doctoral degrees, the appointing of academic staff, complaints to the institution from students (including deadlines for complaints in connection with examination and tests), and grants and conditions regarding student organizations. Within these general guidelines, the Study Committee is authorized to make exceptions to the ministerial ordinances and to the curricula referred to in these ordinances.[49]

In connection with the allocation of teaching activities of the university, the minister formulates rules to calculate the number of students that count as active full-time students.[50] He is also authorized to lay down rules about the allocation of responsibilities for the maintenance and administration of buildings (especially regarding the property of the universities).[51] He may formulate special measures for universities or parts of universities that are charged with special assignments, or in cases where such measures are called for.

[43] Art. 3 Section 1 UA 1993.
[44] Art. 4 Section 2 UA 1993.
[45] Art. 6 Section 1 UA 1993.
[46] Art. 7 Section 2 UA 1993.
[47] Art. 8 Section 4 UA 1993.
[48] Art. 2 Section 2 UA 1993.
[49] Art. 8 Section 6 UA 1993.
[50] Art. 9 Section 4 UA 1993.
[51] Art. 9 Section 7 UA 1993.

3.2.3. *Control*

The *internal control* of self-regulation is exercised by the Senate, the Faculty Councils, and the Study Committee. At the central level, the Senate approves proposals for Statutes that include detailed rules for the management of the universities and core activities.[52] At the decentralized level, controlling powers are formulated in a general way. The Faculty Councils approve the development plan and budget of the faculty within the framework laid down by the Senate.[53] More specifically, they are authorized to approve curricula.[54] The Study Committee approves teaching plans, including the allocation of teaching resources.[55] Specific competences concerning the control of self-regulation are not stipulated. According to Danish Labour Law advisory councils are established with respect to labour affairs. These bodies can also be involved in the control of this specific subject of self-regulation.

External control is exercised by the Minister of Education and the Danish Auditing Office. The Minister is authorized to approve the Statutes of the university and agreements of a non-commercial nature with self-governing institutions and organizations that are affiliated with the institutions and whose main objectives are linked to the objectives of the institution (i.e. contracts with *cantines* or book shops).[56] He may also approve exceptions to the provisions of the Act if proposed by the institution.[57] Control of the Auditing Office refers to self-regulation activities of the universities concerning financial matters.

Control through complaints is provided for by the UA 1993. As mentioned before, complaints of students have to be in accordance with regulations laid down by the minister. Complaints of a legal nature on university decisions in accordance with the Act can be brought before the minister.[58] He can decide that a decision should be brought before a special Appeals Committee and whether this body shall have the final administrative decision-making power in the matter.

Considering *effective* control, the independence of the controlling authorities is not explicitly stipulated in the UA 1993. It can be derived implicitly from the composition of the governing authorities. Sanctions are implicitly provided concerning the authorities to suspend governance bodies which will be seen under 3.2.4. The provisions of the UA 1993 are seen as being clearer and less complex than the 41 provisions of the UA 1973 (Rasmussen 1998: 194). The responsibilities of the various governance actors are well-defined. However,

[52] Art. 3 Section 2 UA 1993.

[53] Art. 5 Section 1 UA 1993.

[54] Art. 5 Section 2 UA 1993.

[55] Art. 8 Section 4 UA 1993.

[56] Arts. 3 Section 2, 10 Section 2 UA 1993.

[57] Art. 12 Section 1 UA 1993.

[58] Art. 11 Section 1 UA 1993.

there are still areas of ambiguity, especially between the authority of the heads of departments and the directors of studies on allocation of teaching resources and on the improvement of teaching quality. The promulgation of Statutes and other products of self-regulation is encompassed by Article 4 section 1 of the Danish Act on Open Administration that enacts a right to open insight in documents received or produced by public authorities as part of their activity. To facilitate external control, the minister can demand information from institutions for budgetary purposes.[59] A right of access to information concerning self-regulation is neither explicitly nor implicitly stipulated by Danish law.

3.2.4. *Democratic participation*

To a large extent the Danish university governance structure is based on elected Boards and their Heads. At the central level, the Senate is the supreme authority of the university. Since it consists of 5 members representing the management, 2 members representing the academic staff, 2 members representing non-academic staff, 3 members representing students, 2 members from outside the university and the Rector (ex officio Chairman) it can be typified as a largely representative body.[60] The Rector is elected from professors and associate professors in full-time positions for a term of four years. Whether and how often the Rector can be re-elected is laid down in the Statutes.[61] The Faculty Council includes representatives of the academic staff, of the non-academic staff and of students in a proportion of 2 : 1 : 1.[62] It has two external members appointed by the relevant National Research Council and by the relevant National Advisory Board on Higher Education. The Dean is the ex officio chairman of the faculty council. He/she is elected from the permanent faculty staff for a term of 4 years.[63] If at least three-quarters of the members of the Faculty Council find that the Dean substantially ignores the decisions taken regarding the development plan and budget of the faculty, it may recommend to the Rector that the Dean's term of office be ended. In special cases such as ones mentioned above, the Rector is authorized to call a new election for the office of Dean, the Faculty Councils, the Department Boards and Study Committees before the election term has expired. In special cases, the Minister of Education decides that a new election for the office of the Rector is to be called. The same applies to the Dean with regard to new elections for the offices of Head of Department and Director of Study. The Department Board normally consists of the Head of Department (Chairman), two members elected

[59] Art. 9 Section 9 UA 1993.

[60] Art. 3 Section 4 UA 1993.

[61] Art. 4 Sections 4,6 UA 1993

[62] Art. 5 Section 5 UA 1993.

[63] Art. 6 Section 3 UA 1993.

from members of the permanent academic staff and one member of the technical-administrative staff.[64] The Head of Department is elected from among the department's permanent academic staff, normally for a term of 3 years with the option of re-election. Study Committees consist of an equal number of teachers and students with a maximum of 10 in all.[65] The teachers are elected for a term of 3 years with the option of re-election by and from among teachers attached to the relevant area. The students are elected for a period of one year. If at least two-thirds of the members of the Study Board apart from the Chairman find that the Director substantially ignores decisions regarding curricula that have been approved, it may recommend to the Dean that the Chairman's term of office be terminated.[66]

Regarding *co-governance*, the powers of the Senate, Faculty Councils and Department Boards to approve regulations were already mentioned above. The Senate also has the right to comment on all matters of significance for the organization, and it is obliged to discuss subjects brought before it by the Rector.[67] The Faculty Council has a right to comment on all matters of significance to the faculty as well as in matters that involve the relationship between two or more groups from different fields or between departments and Study Committee within the faculty. Before the Minister of Education lays down regulations, the universities affected by them shall be given the opportunity to comment, if the proposal does not originate from them.[68] The university is legally obliged to consult the Study Committee on drafts of ministerial ordinances for study programmes, drafts of general rules pertaining to examinations, marking and teaching, and other matters that concern teaching.[69] The Faculty Council has the right to comment on all matters that are important to the faculty.[70]

3.3. *The Austrian situation*

3.3.1. *General remarks*

In Austria, the governance structures of the 12 public universities were reformed in 1993, when a federal Act was adopted concerning the organization of the universities.[71] It became effective in 1994. The need for reforms was related to

[64] Art. 7 Section 5 UA 1993.

[65] Art. 8 Section 2 UA 1993.

[66] Art. 8 Section 8 UA 1993.

[67] Art. 3 Section 3 UA 1993.

[68] Art. 2 Section 3 UA 1993.

[69] Art. 8 Section 5 UA 1993.

[70] Art. 5 Section 1 UA 1993.

[71] Bundesgesetz über die Organisation der Universitäten (UOG 1993), Bundesgesetzblatt (BGBl) no. 805/1993.

the increase in student numbers, budget cuts, changes in public administration, and profound criticism of the old legal structure. Critical remarks on the UA 1975 concern its complexity, its lack of any clear and effective decision structure and too many detailed government regulations that inhibit the innovation of universities. In the old structure governance power was almost entirely situated in the collegial bodies; the position of the Rector and Dean was a weak one. It was only at the institutes that the power of decision was attributed to the Head and not to the institute's Council. Since the institutes were rather small, their organizational structure appeared to be fragmented. Because the budget rules and appointments of academic staff were formulated by the Ministry, criticism arose about the inflexibility of this approach. The impetus for the reform came from outside the universities. Like the UOG 1975, the new Act was one of the most controversial and fiercely debated Acts in Austria (Pechar & Pellert 1998). In the academic year 1994/95 it was implemented in five universities, extended to include five more in 1995/96 and put into effect in the remaining ones in 1996/97. The main policy goals of this Act were to make the Austrian universities more effective and efficient and create possibilities for innovation and quality improvement (Bundesministerium für Wissenschaft und Forschung 1993: 170–191). To reach these goals, the autonomy of universities was enhanced. Institutional autonomy was also seen as a means to realize deregulation and decentralization. Comparing the UOG 1993 with the UOG 1975, the main differences are ((Bundesministerium für Wissenschaft und Forschung 1993: 184):

- a shift of the ministerial powers to the institutions (i.e. self-regulation, budget, appointment of academic staff);
- strengthening of the position of the Rector and Dean; and
- the setting-up of an external National University Board.

Regarding the forms of leadership the new Austrian system of university governance can be characterized as a system of mixed leadership and as an approach of 'soft managerialism' (Pechar & Pellert 1998:144). In the Austrian situation, mixed leadership is based on a balance between the traditional collegial decision-making structure (an Academic Senate chaired by the Rector) and a stronger management structure. At the institutional level, this involves an executive body chaired by a President.

The formal structure of the Austrian governance regulation was primarily created by the UOG 1993. This Act consists of 90 provisions concerning the organization of universities. In 17 sections general provisions, provisions with respect to personnel, Curricular Committees, institutes, faculties, management, academic services, the National University Board, and penalties are formulated. On the basis of this Act, the Statutes of the universities are established. According to the Act, five levels of governance can be distinguished. These are the governmental, the central and three decentralized levels of the universities.

At the government level, governance actors are the Ministry of Science and the National University Board. At the central university level, the actors in governance are the Senate, the University Council, the Rector, the University Assembly, the four assemblies of staff members as well as the Directors of Administration, EDP and Library. At the first decentralized level faculties are discerned. In the faculties, the Faculty Board, the Dean, the Dean of Studies and Curricular Committee are governance actors. The third decentralized level is composed of institutes that are coordinated by the faculties. Here the Institute Assembly and Head represent the governance actors. At the fifth level (or third decentralized level) the actors consist of staff members and students. To summarize, the UOG 1993 refers to a great many corporate and individual actors. The Austrian governance structure can be outlined as follows (Figure 3).

According to the UOG 1993, the universities are directed by the Senate and the Rector.[73] Executive powers are allocated to the Rector, the Dean, the Head of the Institute, the Dean of Studies as well as to the Senate, the Faculty Board, the Institute Assembly, and the Curricular Committee. Formal power is thus shared by Executive Boards and their chairmen. Members of the Senate are representatives of full and assistant professors, students, the chairman of the committee of non-academic staff, Rector and Vice-Rector(s), Deans and the university director.[74] The number of members depends on the number of faculties, students, and Vice-Rectors. Members of the Faculty Board are representatives of full and assistant-professors, students, non-academic staff, and the Dean.[75] According to the Act, the number of members must not exceed 42. The Institute Assembly consists of the same categories of members.[76] Here, the Head of the institute is a member of the assembly. Members of the Curricular Committee are the same numbers of representatives of full and assistant professors, students, and one member from outside the university.[77] The National University Board is a body of the federal government. It consists of four members from inside and outside the university.[78] The University Assembly elects and discharges the Rector and Vice-Rector(s). The number of its members

72 To reduce the complexity only main actors of governance are included in the figure. The formal situation is only based on the UOG. As other regulations might establish governance actors and activities (i.e. a student right of complaint), the figure is not complete. This is one of the reasons why the three figures on the Dutch, Danish and Austrian formal governance structures are not comparable.

73 § 50 Section 1 UOG 1993.

74 § 51 Section 2 UOG 1993.

75 § 48 Section 3 UOG 1993.

76 § 45 Section 2 UOG 1993.

77 § 41 Section 5 UOG 1993.

78 § 83 Section 1,4 UOG 1993.

Figure 3: Formal governance structure of Austrian universities[72]

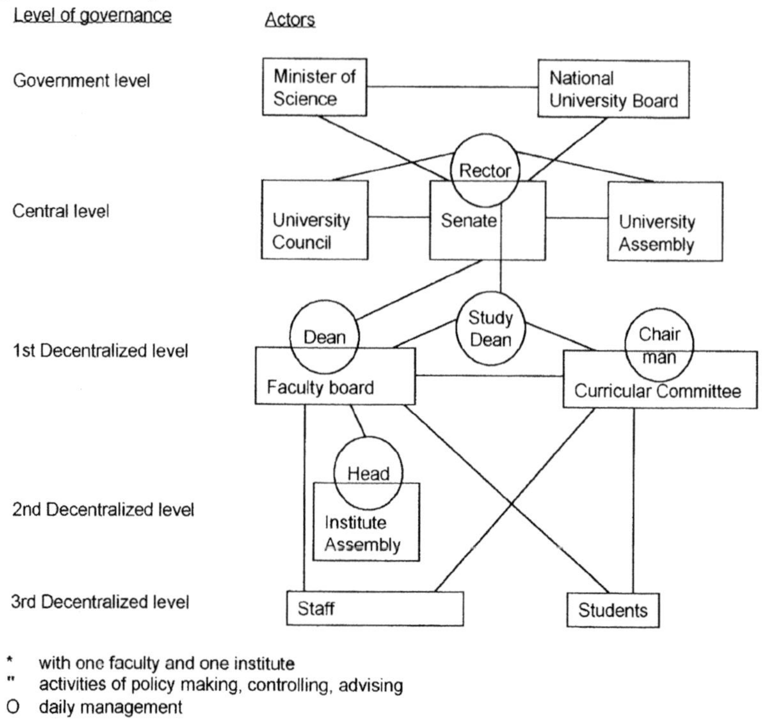

are laid down in the University Statute.[79] The University Council consists of the same number of representatives of regional bodies, of the economy, and senior students.[80] The four assemblies of staff members of Austrian universities (rectors, professors, academic staff and other employees) coordinate and support specific activities of the universities.[81] Regarding its forms of leadership, the Austrian system can be classified as a model of representative leadership rather than a model of mixed or executive leadership.

Since the UOG 1993 has not been evaluated until now, no insights exist as yet into the effects and development of the *informal structure*. Following Pechar & Pellert's analysis, we shall assume that the informal structure has not changed very much, since it seems that the reforms have not yet been incorporated into the normative structure and the 'symbolic side' of the universities (Pechar &

[79] § 55 Section 2 UOG 1993.

[80] § 56 Section 3 UOG 1993.

[81] §§ 84, 85 UOG 1993.

Pellert 1998: 146). The organizational culture of Austrian universities is characterized as paternalistic, highly formal, hierarchical and conservative. This could mean that the informal structure corresponds to the formal structure. It is not clear, however, whether the old formal structure has remained or whether it changed in the direction of the UOG 1993. Important factors here are that the market model and the approach of strengthening institutional autonomy have been rejected by the majority of Austrian academics. Academic freedom is still more or less seen as an individual right of full professors, and institutional autonomy is linked to an imposed institutional leadership and management. Gradually, however, some changes may be taking place in the informal structure,. As Pechar & Pellert put it: '*The initial stages of implementation of the UOG* 1993 *have encouraged first steps toward a new culture of institutional management*' (1998: 150).

3.3.2. *Autonomy and self-regulation*

In the Austrian situation, individual and institutional autonomy have been stipulated by law. According to Article 17 of the Austrian Constitution, 'Science and teaching are free'. Article 1 section 2 UOG 1993 states that academic freedom is one of the leading principles in the fulfillment of the university's tasks. The academic freedom of professors is explicitly formulated where freedom of teaching and the free use of university facilities for scientific research are concerned.[82] According to Article 7 of the UOG 1993, institutional autonomy is realized by the Institute's competence to formulate a University Statute. This Statute contains provisions on the organization of the university, its bodies and employees. The Act formulates 15 subjects of self-regulation (i.e. the numbers and tasks of Vice-Rectors, the establishment of institutes, procedure of elections). Self-regulatory powers, however, do not include the regulation of competences to take decisions. These competences are laid down exclusively by the UOG. Self-regulating power is attributed mainly to the *central level* of the university. The Senate is authorized to issue and modify the Statute, and also to formulate regulations of order for all collegial bodies of the university.[83] It sets out the general directives with respect to the activities of the Rector.[84] It regulates access to and use of the university services. At the central level, the Rector lays down binding directives with respect to the activities of the Deans and Study Deans.[85] The University Council sets out regulations of order.[86] At the decentralized level, the work organization of the institute is regulated by the Institute Assembly. This Assembly is also authorized to set general directives

82 § 21 Section 2 UOG 1993.
83 § 15 Section 7 UOG 1993.
84 § 51 Section 1 no 11 UOG 1993.
85 § 52 Section 1 no 2 UOG 1993.
86 § 56 Section 2 UOG 1993.

for the activities of the Head of the Institute.[87] The Faculty Board is authorized to formulate general directives regarding the activities of the Institute Assembly, the Dean, and Dean of Studies.[88] The Curricular Committee is authorized to regulate examination.[89]

Referring to the Austrian interpretation of legality, the UOG 1993 is seen as a legal framework that leaves much room for self-governance (Funk 1996: 5, Stolzlechner 1996: 25). From the point of view of the Austrian legal tradition, the principle of legality is differentiated here, i.e., laws and by-laws function as a limit to self-governance rather than as a condition. As such, the room left by the UOG for self-regulation is quantitatively and qualitatively higher than in other institutions of Austrian public administration.

3.3.3. *Control*

The Austrian approach to the control of universities can be seen as a complex interactive and complementary legal institute of internal and external relations of supervision (Funk 1996: 18). Generally, the procedure of supervision is formalized and powers are allocated to the administrative bodies. *Internal control* refers to decisions on planning, budgets and appointments of professors, Deans, Rectors, and the Heads of institutes. Internal self-regulation is subject to general supervision by the Rector,[90] who is in turn answerable to the Senate.[91] The *external control* of self-regulation is exercised by the Ministry of Science and the Austrian Court of Auditors.[92] In Austria, the need for the external supervision of self-regulation is derived from the constitutional principle of legality. According to Article 18 of the Austrian Constitution, public administration can be exercised only on the basis of law. The binding of self-regulation to law requires the supervision of the Federal Government as established by law. The general supervision authority of the Federal Minister of Science was formulated in Article 8 of the UOG 1993. This provision also authorizes the minister to reverse any self-regulatory activities that are not in accordance with the task of the body in question, or in cases where procedural rules were not observed. More specifically, the minister approves the Statutes of universities and directives proposed by the Assemblies of Rectors.[93] In cases where such approval is withheld, the Senate and Assemblies may apply to the Constitutional Court. Complaints of students are not regulated in the UOG 1993.

[87] § 45 Section 1 no 2,5 UOG 1993.

[88] § 48 Section 1 no 13,14 UOG 1993.

[89] § 41 Section 3 no 10 UOG 1993.

[90] § 8 Section 1 UOG 1993.

[91] § 52 Section 4 UOG 1993.

[92] See § 17 Section 10 UOG 1993.

[93] §§ 7 Section 3, 84 Section 5, 85 Section 7 UOG 1993.

Regarding the *effectiveness* of control, the independence of the members of administrative bodies is stipulated by the UOG 1993.[94] Sanctions are implicitly provided by the competence to recall actors of governance. Moreover, a general competence of the minister is stipulated with respect to the failure to perform certain governance tasks.[95] If the Senate does not establish a University Statute, the Minister of Science will urge the Senate to do so. If the Senate does not respond, the minister himself is authorized to formulate this Statute. The same competences apply to the tasks of other university governance bodies (including the task of self-regulation). Here, the administrative body at the higher hierarchic level of the university is authorized to urge performance of this regulatory task and perform this task itself, if necessary. Considering transparency, the powers of self-regulation appear to have been clearly formulated. According to Article 9 section 7 of the UOG 1993, the University Statute and other products of self-regulation must be published in the university's official Bulletin. The Minister of Science and the Rector are entitled to have access to relevant information. The Act also formulates the duty of all bodies to supply this information.[96] The Rector is obliged to inform the Senate.[97] The supply of information to the University Council by the Senate and Rector is regulated under the University Statute.[98]

3.3.4. *Democratic participation*

The Austrian university governance structure largely consists of elected bodies. The University Council and the National University Board, however, are not elected. The members of the University Council are appointed by the Senate,[99] while the members of the National University Board are appointed by the minister for a term of 6 years.[100] Regarding the constitution of administrative bodies the UOG 1993 includes a general provision,[101] which formulates the principles of the constitution of these bodies and some details of the election procedure. The election procedure is specified by the University Statute. According to particular provisions of the Act, the Chairperson of a collegial body is elected and recalled by this body. In all cases, a Chairperson is appointed for a term of two years. The Act regulates also the election and recall procedures of Rectors, Vice-Rectors, Deans, Deans of Studies and

[94] § 13 Section 2 UOG 1993.

[95] § 12 UOG 1993.

[96] § 8 Section 2 UOG 1993.

[97] § 52 Section 4 UOG 1993.

[98] § 56 Section 1 UOG 1993.

[99] § 56 Section 3 UOG 1993.

[100] § 83 Section 4,6 UOG 1993.

[101] § 14 UOG 1993.

Chairpersons of administrative bodies.[102] The Rector is elected and recalled by the University Assembly on the basis of a proposal by the Senate for a term of 4 years.[103] This period can be extended by two more years. The Dean and Dean of Studies are elected and recalled by the Faculty Board.[104] Re-election is permitted. The Dean is elected for a term of four years on the proposal of the Rector. If the proposal of the Rector is rejected by the Faculty Board, a new list of 3 candidates must be drawn up by the Senate. This proposal cannot be rejected by the Faculty Board.[105] The Dean of Studies is elected for a period of two years. Professors are not elected but appointed. However, the Chairman of the Appointment Committee is elected by its members.[106]

Considering the subject of *co-governance*, the participation of administrative bodies in the formulation of the University Statute is not provided in the UOG 1993. As mentioned before, this Act stipulates only that the Minister of Science must approve the University Statute.

4. Comparison and analysis

4.1. *General remarks*

When comparing the *reforms in governance structure regulation* that were implemented in The Netherlands, Denmark, and Austria, we can conclude that the reasons for changes, policy goals and regulation approaches are very similar. Due to similar changes in the environment of universities (growth and decrease in the number of students, economy measures, discussions about quality, general developments in public administration concerning deregulation and decentralization and changes in the labour market), institutional autonomy is strengthened in the new university governance acts of these countries to improve the effectiveness and quality of higher education and research. At first glance, in all the three countries the forms of democratic leadership seem to have shifted from representative to executive leadership. On closer observation, however, this only applies to the Dutch situation. Since the Danish Senate, Faculty Councils and Department Boards are representative bodies and formal powers are widely distributed, here we can speak of mixed leadership. In the light of the broad executive competences of the Austrian collegial bodies, the powers of the Rector and Dean appear to be quite limited. This is why we classified the Austrian approach as a model of representative leadership.

[102] § 15 UOG 1993.

[103] § 53 Section 4,6 UOG 1993.

[104] § 48 Section 2,3 UOG 1993.

[105] § 49 Section 3 UOG 1993.

[106] § 23 Section 1 UOG 1993.

Regarding the *formal structure*, it is striking how different the number of provisions and their contents are. The Dutch Act on the Modernization of University Governance Organization consists of 52 provisions, while the Danish University Act includes 14 provisions and the Austrian ninety. It is remarkable that all three countries speak of deregulation in the present situation. If we look at the regulation culture of each of these countries, this might be the case. If we interpret deregulation as the reduction of rules, this took place mainly in the Danish and Dutch situation. In Denmark the number of provisions was reduced from 41 to 14 in the UA 1993, while in The Netherlands this was reduced from 77 to 52 provisions in the MUB. Considering the *levels of governance* we see some variation among the three countries. In Denmark and Austria, one more decentralized level of university governance was established than in The Netherlands. In all the three countries the *governance actors* are corporate and individual actors. Comparing the new and the old legal governance structure of The Netherlands we conclude that the changes here are more than incremental as De Boer *et al.* state.[107]

Though the *effects* of the various laws have not been evaluated systematically, the empirical studies that were done so far indicate that these are similar. A general conclusion is that changes take place rather slowly and the old structure still dominates university governance at least partly. Rasmussen's study of the Danish case shows that slow changes of informal structure stem from an organizational culture of universities to which the new structure does not fit (Rasmussen 1998). Rasmussen's conclusion is also confirmed by the Austrian situation. Though the changes in governance structure in the Austrian University Organization Act of 1993 are less dramatic than in earlier drafts, the opposition of academics against the new organizational structure seems to be still quite high (Pellert & Pechar 1998). In sum, our comparison indicates that there may be large differences between the formal and informal structure in all three countries.

4.2. *Autonomy and self-regulation*

In the three countries individual autonomy is stipulated by law. The legal status of individual autonomy, however, is different. In Austria, individual autonomy is established by the Constitution and by the University Organizational Act, while in The Netherlands and Denmark it is only formulated by the University Acts. A right of institutional autonomy is not explicitly stipulated in any of the three countries. Its guarantee can be derived from the legal and policy documents that deal with the new governance structures. The policy goals of all three countries present the strengthening of institutional

[107] See 3.1.1.

autonomy as a means to deal with changes in the environment and the demands of universities.

In all three countries, the new regulation approach is characterized by a model of legally conditioned self-regulation that leaves ample room for self-regulation. Looking at the features of this approach, this conclusion is quite a striking one. Regarding the requirement of a general legal framework, the Austrian approach still seems to use mainly the system of government regulation; the UOG 1993 contains many detailed provisions on this. Moreover, self-regulation is subject to the approval of the minister. The amount of room that is left for self-regulation seems quite limited. By contrast, in the Dutch situation the legal framework appears to be quite a general one, leaving plenty of room for self-regulation. Self-regulation is subject only to monitoring, and does not require any approval on the part of the minister. The Danish situation lies somewhere in between, since here approval by the minister is stipulated and the minister's regulation powers are formulated more specifically than in the Dutch situation. Thus we conclude that we can speak of legally conditioned self-regulation only in the Dutch and Danish approaches. From the Austrian perspective, however, these approaches do not comply with the tradition of legality. According to the Austrian constitutional provision and doctrine of legality, self-regulation requires approval by the minister at the very least.

4.3. *Control*

In all three countries, the control of self-regulation is realized through complex interactive systems of checks and balances. Control is provided both through similar and through different bodies and powers of supervision. The controlling functions of the Dutch and Danish Councils at the central and decentralized levels of the universities are very similar. In The Netherlands, however, the powers of *internal control* of self-regulation are formulated more explicitly than in the Danish situation. In The Netherlands internal control seems to have been established more extensively and comprehensively than in Austria and Denmark. Regarding the few controlling powers of the Dutch Minister of Education, extensive internal control can be regarded as a compensation to maintain a balance of power. In The Netherlands the Supervisory Board was given the central authority regarding internal control. By contrast, the corresponding Austrian authority (National University Board) was established as a body of external control. In all the three countries, self-regulation of the faculties is controlled by governance authorities at the central level of the university (Executive Board, Senate, and Rector). We must realize, however, that the subjects of control are quite different. For example, in the Dutch situation this form of control refers to various faculty regulations, including the students' right of complaint.

The *external control* of self-regulation is provided most extensively and comprehensively in the Austrian situation. This can be explained by the Austrian interpretation of the principle of legality we mentioned before. Here, a clear responsibility was established of the minister to control self-governance. In Denmark, external control was provided less extensively and comprehensively than in the Austrian situation but still more strongly than in The Netherlands. It is interesting that the Danish UA 1993 also stipulates the minister's authority to approve agreements of the universities of a non-commercial nature with self-governing institutions. From the point of view of the Austrian and Danish approach, the Dutch regulations of external control seem to be rather limited.

Considering the *effectiveness of control*, the independence of the controlling authorities is explicitly formulated in Austria and The Netherlands. In the Austrian situation, the independence of administrative bodies is laid down by the UOG 1993. In The Netherlands, independence has been regulated more implicitly in provisions that stipulate that governance actors must not be a member of another governing body. In the Danish situation, the need for independence can be derived from the composition of the controlling bodies. It can be laid down in university statutes. In all three countries, sanctions are provided implicitly through the regulations regarding the suspension, recall, and dismissal of governance actors. In the Austrian case, sanctioning is regulated more explicitly through the minister's general competence to overrule the University Statutes. A similar competence was established in The Netherlands regarding the Executive Board's competence to overrule faculty regulations. In The Netherlands the minister is authorized to stop funding under special circumstances if universities refuse to regulate quality control. Considering the transparency of self-regulation, most of the provisions of the three countries seem to be clear. Intelligibility of self-regulation is rather high in Austria, since the subjects of the University Statutes are set out by the UOG 1993. In the Dutch and Danish situation, however, some self-regulatory powers are not clearly formulated and outlined. In The Netherlands, the self-regulatory powers of the Executive Board are rather vague; no clear distinction is made between these powers and the self-regulatory powers of the Dean. A similar problem exists in the relation between the Head of the Executive Committee and the Rector. In the Danish situation, a clear distinction between the powers of the Head of Department and the Director of Studies is also lacking. The need to publish self-regulation is clearly formulated by the Austrian UOG 1993. In the Dutch situation, the University Act (WHW) stipulates that University Statutes must be published. Other products of self-regulation are published according to university regulations and practices. In Denmark, the need to promulgate self-regulation follows from the Danish Act of Open Administration. The right of access of controlling authorities to information on self-regulation is provided for by the Dutch and Danish laws. In Denmark, the minister's right of access to information concerns self-regulation that refers to budgetary matters.

4.4. *Democratic participation*

Regulations regarding democratic participation differ greatly among each of the three countries. Regarding the way governance actors are established, *elections* play an important part in Denmark and Austria. In Denmark all governance authorities are elected. In Austria only the members of the University Council and the Board of Trustees are not elected. By contrast, in the Dutch situation most governance actors are appointed. Here only the members of the university and Faculty Council(s), and the members of the Disputes Commission are elected. In all three countries, governance actors are elected or appointed for a period of 2, 3 or 4 years. In Austria the procedure of elections, the possibility of re-election and new elections are laid down by law, while these matters are partly subject to self-regulation in The Netherlands and in Denmark. *Co-governance* is extensively regulated in the Danish situation, whereas in Austria there are hardly any provisions of co-governance. The Danish regulations refer to the authority of actors at all levels of the university governance structure to approve and comment on self-regulation. In Austria the approval of self-regulation is limited to the minister's competence to approve the University Statute. In The Netherlands, co-governance refers mainly to the rights of the various councils to be consulted.

5. Conclusion

In this paper we aimed to explore legitimacy problems of institutional autonomy that might arise from changing governance structure regulations. Elaborating on Selznick's institutional theory we assumed above that governance structure regulation can lead to problems, if (1) not much room is left to self-regulation, (2) effective controls are not provided, (3) democratic decision-making is not facilitated, (4) academic freedom is restricted, and (5) formal and informal structure diverge. The following problems are indicated by the description and comparison of the Dutch, Danish and Austrian governance structure regulation:

1. Regarding the amount of room that is left for self-regulation, problems may arise in the Austrian situation. We realized, however, that less government regulation activities would require another approach to the principle of legality. The comparison shows that the Austrian legal profession can draw inspiration from the Danish and Dutch models of legally conditioned self-regulation.
2. Effective controls of self-regulation are provided in all three countries. The different approaches to self-regulation indicate that leaving more room to self-regulation requires more control. The Dutch regulations show how compensation can be provided by a sophisticated system of internal control.

It is not clear, however, to what extent there is a need for compensation through extensive external control. Considering the measures taken to publish self-regulation of universities, the Dutch and Danish legal professions can draw on the Austrian provisions, which are clearer and more specific than the Dutch and Danish ones.

3. Regarding democratic decision-making, the Dutch approach seems to be problematic. Comparing the Dutch situation with the Danish and the Austrian regulations, the Dutch provisions with respect to democratic participation are very limited. Here, the Dutch legal community can learn from the Danish approach that introduces executive leadership without neglecting democratic participation.
4. In the Dutch situation, the possibility to restrict academic freedom seems to be provided by the comprehensive powers of the Executive Board and the Deans to give directives to faculties and respectively to the staff. Since the subjects and limitations of these directives have not been clearly formulated by law, they may also refer to the choice of research and teaching subjects.
5. Our comparison indicates that the formal and informal structures of governance regulation are different in all three countries. For this reason we conclude that more attention needs to be paid to the evaluation of formal regulations and possibilities to improve the situation. We showed that problems stem from the fact that the formal structure does not fit in with the organizational culture of universities. Moreover, there is a lack of trust and motivation amongst professionals. Rasmussen's empirical studies of the Danish situation indicate that changes take place very slowly in universities even if reforms are not revolutionary. This does not mean, however, that reforms should not take place. It only shows that university governance structure reforms must focus primarily on changes in the organizational culture and the building of motivation and trust at the shop floor instead of placing too much emphasis on the legal structure. Otherwise the strengthening of institutional autonomy will lead to undesirable side-effects, which should be avoided by any wise legislator.

Literature

Akkermans, P.W.C. 1996. 'Rector en dekanen: respresentanten of bestuurders?' in Akkermans, P.W.C. et al. *Een nieuwe universitaire bestuursvorm.* Deventer: Tjeenk Willink. 1–22.

Binsbergen et al. 1994. 'Comparing Governance Structures of Higher Education Insititutions' in Goedegebuure, L. & Van Vught, F. (eds.): *Comparative Policy Studies in Higher Education*, Utrecht: Lemma. 219–248.

Boer, De H. et al. 1998a. Introduction to *Higher Education Policy* 11 (1998).

Boer, De H. et al. 1998b. 'On boards and councils; shaky balances considered. The governance of Dutch universities.' *Higher Eduction Policy* 11 (1998). 153–164.

Bundesministerium für Wissenschaft und Forschung 1993. *Universitäts-Organisationsgesetz '93. Materialien zur Hochschulreform.* Wien.

De Groof, J. et al. 1998. *Democracy and Governance in Higher Education.* LRP Series Vol. 2. The Hague: Kluwer International.

De Jong, H.M. & Dorbeck-Jung, B.R. 1997. *Juridische Staatsleer.* Coutinho: Bussum.

Dorbeck-Jung, B.R. 1995. 'The conceptualization of comparative Educational Law' in De Groof, J. (ed.): *The Legal Status of Teachers in Europe.* Leuven-Amersfoort: Acco. 125–135.

Dorbeck-Jung, B.R. 1997a. 'Setting Priorities in Dutch Legislative Policy' in Boorsma, P.B. et al. (eds.) *Public Priority Setting: Rules and Costs.* Dordrecht: Kluwer. 201–216.

Dorbeck-Jung, B.R. 1997b. 'Comparing regulations of higher education quality evaluation'. *European Journal for Education Law and Policy 1*, 91–100.

Dorbeck-Jung, B.R. & De Jong, H.M. 1998. *The Legitimacy of Governance in the State.* Paper for the Conference of The Netherlands Institute for Governance. Noordwijkerhout: November.

Eijlander, P. 1993. 'Zelfregulering en wetgevingsbeleid' in Eijlander et al. (eds.) *Overheid en zelfregulering; Alibi voor vrijblijvendheid of prikkel tot aktie?* Zwolle: Tjeenk Willink, 129–140.

Funk, B.C. 1996. 'Die Aufsicht über Universitäten nach dem UOG 1993' in Strasser (ed.), *Die Universität nach dem UOG 1993*, 1–19.

Giddens, A. 1995. *The Constitution of Society.* Cambridge, Polity Press.

Klankbordgroep 1998. *De kanteling in het universitaire bestuur.* Rapport van de Klankbordgroep Invoering MUB. Den Haag.

Kwikkers, P. 'Governance through check and balances'. *European Journal for Education Law and Policy 1*, 57–79.

Nonet, P. & Selznick, P. 1978. *Law and Society in Transition. Towards Responsive Law.* New York: Harper & Row.

Pechar, H. & Pellert, A. 1998. 'Managing change: organizational reform in Austrian universities'. *Higher Eduction Policy 11* (1998), 141–151.

Rasmussen, J.G. 1995. 'Management in Danish Universities. New Legislation and Organisational Change'. *Higher Education Management* 7 (1995) No. 3, 335–344.

Rasmussen, J.G. 1998. 'New rules of university governance in Denmark'. *Higher Eduction Policy 11* (1998), 183–199.

Selznick, P. 1992. *The Moral Commonwealth. Social Theory and the Promise of Community*. Berkeley: University of California Press.

Stolzlechner, H. 1995. 'Das neue Satzungsrecht der Universitäten' in Strasser (ed.), *Untersuchungen zum UOG* 1993, 25.

Zoontjes, P. 1993. *Vrijheid van wetenschap*. Zwolle: Tjeenk Willink.

CESARE ONESTINI

The European Union Programmes and School Autonomy: a Reciprocal Process

The European Union today is focusing on the consolidation of its internal market, on the launch of the common currency and on the widening of its border to an increasing number of candidate countries.

At the same time today's European Union is more than a common market and it's more than an economic area: as a result of various overlapping factors – amongst which the literature singles out, for example, spillovers from the core economic concerns relating to the common market, consolidation through juridification and juridical activism on the part of the European Court, external pressures linked to international competition – the Treaty of Maastricht and the Treaty of Amsterdam have legitimized intervention in a wide number of policy areas, introduced the concept of a common European citizenship and created the preconditions for a progression of European integration along the lines of 'variable geometries' of countries deciding on a set of minimal common rules and standards but keeping some flexibility to decide how far or how fast to progress on the integration path.

As a result of these relatively recent developments, aspects of social policy as well as aspects of education and training have been proposed as subjects for European co-operation. On a more general level, and going beyond the development of specific programmes or actions, we can see that any major national reform is today analysed in a European 'context', in terms of examples of experiences to be emulated or in most cases as a justification or a push for the introduction of an innovatory proposal. The 'European context' goes beyond the political process and also permeates various analyses offered regularly by the media and by commentators.

It can further be said that analysing a reform proposal in a European context today is not simply an academic exercise in looking for reference points but includes a real analysis of how the intended reform or redefinition at the national level will improve the chances of the country to cooperate effectively

Walter Berka, Jan de Groof and Hilde Penneman (eds.), Autonomy in Education, 149–154.

and efficiently in that sector with other Member States. This slower but significant event is at work also in the traditionally national domain of education and training: even if treaty-based competencies for the Union in such fields are still rather limited – and consequently – European programmes in these fields are limited, the political dialogue and the implicit development of common understandings and common goals is progressing.

1. The development of EU programmes in the field of school education

- Juridical basis:
  - action plan of 1976;
  - interventions of the European Court establishing university studies as training related to the single market and the free movement of workers and legitimizing community interventions in this field; and
  - intensification of European schemes in the 1980s in the field of vocational training and qualifications, recognition of diplomas, university exchanges, training to enterprise links.
- From pilot actions to the SOCRATES programme:
  - launch in 1995 of the framework programmes SOCRATES and Leonardo da Vinci;
  - five-year programmes with the ambition of touching in a comprehensive approach the fields of education (as a whole) and that of vocational training;
  - EU, EEA, candidate countries;
  - creation of a network of national agencies for European programmes; centralized and decentralized procedures;
  - strengthening of European associations; and
  - synergy with new initiatives such as the taskforce for educational multimedia, the action plan 'Learning in an Information Society', the White Paper *Teaching and Learning*, the Green Paper *Obstacles to Mobility*, new council conclusions and pilot schemes (quality of higher education, truancy, multicultural issues, violence in schools, etc.).
- A first evaluation of the involvement and participation of schools in SOCRATES:
  - for schools SOCRATES was the first real opportunity of taking part in a European cooperation programme (COMENIUS and LINGUA actions);
  - very high levels of demand relative to means available: not entirely expected due to limited resources to each school, no pupil mobility, difficulty of creating multilateral partnerships, no specific incentives for teachers in terms of hours spent on the project or career development;
  - level of roughly 10,000 schools a year active under SOCRATES; and

- at the same time the European progammes had to establish common rules for schools and teachers subject to different educational systems, having different levels of access to resources, of decision-making possibilities of receiving a grant or not, of linguistic abilities, of experience of international contacts etc.

All of this has meant that the European Commission faced a difficult task of defining general guidelines that could accommodate the different traditions without negatively influencing the development of a joint programme. The question of school autonomy is therefore one of obvious interest to the Commission: the success and one of the implicit objectives of European programmes for schools is the promotion of autonomous action for schools. Access to European cooperation starts with an autonomous decision of a school, endorsed by the head of the school, and in partnership with other schools in partner countries.

2. School autonomy as an emerging priority in Member States

Different traditions, converging trends

- After a quick reading of current reforms in the field of autonomy for schools in Europe, the diversity of debates and traditions is striking: it is however obvious that over the last ten years the theme of autonomy has become a buzzword in the majority of the Member States.
- Latest example : in Italy the law 59/97 of 1997 has opened a new period of fundamental reform for Italian schools. Schools will be granted legal personality, headteachers will see an increase in their responsibilities and decision-making, and each school will be able to set priorities for, for example, the timetable or the use of resources.
- However, as noted in the OECD/CERI publication of 1996 on 'Evaluating and Reforming Education Systems':

> Devolution of administrative responsibilities to regional and local level or to single institutions is an obvious trend almost everywhere. But it is often compensated by control mechanisms at national level ...: this is why in fact autonomy of single schools has not increased while their responsibilities have gone up.

Examples of interpretations of 'school autonomy' in some Member States

- We have, for example, Scandinavian countries which from the end of the 1980s and starting with Denmark, have produced reforms that have focused firstly on decentralizing the education system giving more responsibilities to local authorities. Within a broad framework-regulation, municipalities have responsibility for various aspects of management and guidance of schools in their territory. Variations do result, such as the figure of a joint head of school for various schools in areas of low population density or different decisions in terms of allocation of resources. Central government does not carry out inspections but relies on reports of local authorities on how national objectives are arrived at by each school.

- The German example offers a model of a federal system with responsibility for schools in the hands of regional authorities (a constitutional guarantee in fact). The administration of the school in Germany is on three levels: the Ministries of Education of each Land have in fact decentralized offices in the department (Oberschulämter) and in local authorities (Schulämter). German Länder use their autonomy to introduce new pilot experiences which may vary from Land to Land: as a result, individual schools may have different margins of autonomy whether we look at Bavaria or Bremen due to the Land constitution and Land laws. Länder autonomy is limited though by constitutional provisions which guarantee equal treatment for all German pupils, which require recognition of diplomas and periods of study and which force the Länder into close cooperation. It can also be observed that on the whole and irrespective of the Land, school policies within each Land are relatively centralized and schools have often little margin.
- Reforms in the UK offer us yet another interpretation of autonomy which does not refer to decentralization but that focus on the option for each school to 'manage itself'. As a result some schools have decided to opt out of local education authority control and have taken the title of 'self-governing/grant-maintained' schools. The 1988 reform and successive legislation have in parallel strengthened the role of the National Curriculum for all schools, defined common minimal standards, restructured the national inspection system, and ranked schools in terms of achieved results. School autonomy is therefore autonomy to choose which administrative and management means to adopt to achieve better results within the framework of a unified curriculum and to improve its own standing within the league tables. Headteachers in self-governing schools become more and more managerial figures with financial responsibilities for investments, personnel policy and fund raising, following central government procedures for obtaining grants (usually in competition with other schools) but also looking from sponsors and donations.

From these brief examples we can see that some of the essential components for the definition of school autonomy can be summarized under the following headings:

- curriculum;
- financial resources;
- personnel policy (teaching and administrative staff); and
- pupil and parent involvement.

3. Are the European Union programmes promoting school autonomy?

European programmes for schools promote the following aspects of school work:

- Project-based approach in European programmes developing:
  - school own initiatives;
  - transnational contact and exchange;
  - financial implications for the school: managing the grant, accounting, producing reports; and
  - developing the project from one year to the next.
- Focus on the professional development of teachers: teacher training and European programmes:
  - in service training modules; and
  - individual initiative.
  - Headteachers as managers:
  - decisional responsibilities;
  - study visits; and
  - prioritizing.
- New technologies and the restructuring of learning and teaching:
- use of Internet in a great number of projects;
- specific EU initiatives in this field (multimedia educational software, *Netd@ys*, Learning in the Information Society); and
- use of new technologies for new learning methodologies (second-chance schools).

On the whole it can be seen that European programmes offer opportunities for schools to act autonomously, to make decisions and to receive – limited – financial resources.

4. Is school autonomy reinforcing European Union programmes?

- New interlocutors: schools can be seen as interlocutors for European programmes, able to mobilize some own resources to maximize the impact of their participation in European activities and to follow-up the European dimension beyond the limited financial contribution of European programmes.
- Participation of schools in the programmes is moreover eased by their level of autonomy, by their ability to review their use of resources and their flexibility in integrating participation in European programmes within their curricular activities.

5. The new SOCRATES programme and the school as an autonomous institution

The new SOCRATES programme (2000–2006) will focus on the development of a European plan (the COMENIUS Plan) for every school taking part in the programme. In the COMENIUS Plan the school will present its European objectives and will have an opportunity to set priorities for European cooperation which are in line with the specific needs of the school, which have been agreed and discussed with teachers, pupils and parents and which will allow the school to evaluate and review its objectives for European cooperation.

The aim of the Commission is to present Europe as the framework for school planning for the years to come: autonomous schools which take responsibility for their autonomy and look beyond the confines of national curricula to include considerations of the European dimension of education will be the building blocks for the new European school programmes.

ANTÓNIO PEDRO BARBAS HOMEM

Education Law and Legal Methodology

1. Historical origins of education law

I.

In the 16th century, philosophers and thinkers who called themselves humanists showed a major concern with education. Erasmus from Rotterdam was certainly one of the very first to idealize the function of education of human spirits and bodies.

In works such as the *Treaty of the Art of Education to all* (1657), by the Moravian Commenius (Jean-Amos Komensky (1592–1670)), education began to be understood as a subject of philosophy and theology.

The basic idea that human nature could be improved by education and learning is a conclusion that we can take from these authors. The optimistic belief in human nature created the idea that it was possible to progress in human knowledge, an idea in contrast with the medieval concept of science and education.

In the Middle Ages the nature of science justified the idea that a unified knowledge of all disciplines was possible. Theology was regarded as queen of sciences and scientific knowledge described as a tree: all branches belonged to the same tree; theology gave the roots to all sciences. That is the reason why a university should be understood as a universal representative of all the sciences, under the influence of theology. The distinction between a university and a *studium generale* in respect of the factors which distinguish the university could not be found. That is the reason why some institutions began as *studium generale*, before being recognized as universities. The basic sciences studied in those universities included theology, law and medicine.

From the Middle Ages to the 19th century philosophers such as Wilhelm von Humboldt (1767–1835), saw the university as an 'exemplary life form'.

The idea of university was a small model of the greek *Polis*: a correct form of society with its own intrinsic values and a moral standard for knowledge.

Walter Berka, Jan de Groof and Hilde Penneman (eds.), Autonomy in Education, 155–167.

During the Middle Ages and the Renaissance the Portuguese university was dependent both on the State and the Church and it was only in the 19th that relations between University and Church broke down, as a consequence of the principle of separation between State and Church.

Until the 19th century university was attended only by children of the privileged sectors of society: nobles or trades-men, with a specific prohibition of the children of those persons who did manual work (i.e. persons working with their hands).

II.

The medieval perception of science was also based on the idea of congruence between theory and practice: the concept of prudence (*prudentia*) was used to define the idea that theological knowledge should be enforced by all sciences, like law, physics or chemistry.

The humanists proclaimed a major distinction between theory and practice.

One of them, the French philosopher and politician Jean Bodin, realized the distinction between theory and practice as a consequence of a logical motive: we could distinguish theoretical knowledge, empirical knowledge and poetry: theoretical knowledge presiding with the sciences; empirical knowledge related to professional activities; poetry allowing for human happiness and fulfilment (Jean Bodin, *Exposé du Droit Universel. Juris Universi distributio*, a. c. L. Jerphagon, S. Goyard-Fabre and R. M. Rampelberg, PUF, Paris, 1985).

The logical treatises published during the 17th century had these same ideals of directing the spirit and reasoning according to a methodological approach (*art de penser, art d'étudier*).

This concept of university justifies the reason it neglected empirical research. It was only in the 18th century that the Enlightenment produced a reform of the university, allowing for the introduction of the new political and juridical ideas and doctrines allowing for a new empirical research. This also was the case in 'royal societies and academies'.

Anyway, university did not split into a research part and a teaching part: university teaching was still regarded as application of dogmatic exegetic and syllogism.

Socially, university was responsible for selecting the élite of power: this is also clear when we take into account the fact that in the 20th century most of our leading politicians came out of the university: eminent professors of law and nowadays also of economy are always seen as candidates for ministries and relevant posts in the administration.

III.

In the *siècle des lumières*, the Enlightenment was responsible for the introduction of a new paradigm. Human reason – and no longer God's will – was regarded as the origin of knowledge. The philosophers adopted as a *motto* an old Latin proverb by Horatio: *sapere aude*. 'Sapere aude: Have the courage to use your one mind and knowledge! This is the motive of Enlightenment' (Kant, *Was ist Aufklärung*, A 481).

We should understand these philosophical ideas in conjunction with the trust of politicians and jurists in absolutist kings: kings who were able to reform society and establish a new State, based on an individual right to happiness.

While medieval philosophy was based on the idea of stability of society and law, in the 18th century we can find a new perspective of human improvement through education: the idea of progress and the belief that an evolution of human civilization is possible is a topic of Enlightenment philosophers (Peter Stein, *Legal Evolution. The Story of an Idea*, Cambridge, 1980).

IV.

The philosophy of the Enlightenment produced a new vision of law and legal science (Barbas Homem, *The 'Science of Legislation'*, Lisboa, 1996). The Italian jurist Gaetano Filangieri (1752–1788) can be recognized as the first to use this optimistic view of education into a project of legal reforms. In a major work of European legal culture – *The Science of Legislation* – he tried to establish the methodological basis and criteria for the codification of all legal subjects (Filangieri, *La Scienza della Legislazione*, I–V, Milano, Giuseppi Galeazi, 1784–1791).

Education law is a part of this project, divided into several parts, mainly legislation; economic questions; criminal jurisprudence; and education and morals.

We can also find an identical concern with education law in a project of codification of public law in Russia. The *Instructions to write a new code of legislation* by Catherine the Great specifically mentioned education as a subject to be included in this work (Barbas Homem, *The Science of Legislation*).

In Portugal, we can find these ideas at the end of the 18th century in the project of a *Public Law Code* (which the Napoleonic invasion made impossible to approve). The Portuguese jurist and law professor António Ribeiro dos Santos proposed that education law should be included in the Portuguese Code of Public Law, here making a distinction between 'education of reason', a concept which included 'moral education' and 'domestic education' – and 'public education' – education of all public servants (António Ribeiro dos Santos, *Notas ao Plano do Novo Código de Direito Público de Portugal*, Coimbra, Imprensa da Universidade, 1844).

The influence of the doctrines of *science of the state* should be noted: higher education was basically directed towards public servants.

But all these ideas on the value of education demanded a new legal methodology. The idea of codification of laws was accepted throughout Europe as a legal consequence of this power of reason and of enlightened kings.

Voltaire, the French philosopher and friend of some of the European monarchs, wrote: 'Voulez-vous avoir des bonnes lois? Brulez les vôtres et faites-en de nouvelles' (v. Voltaire, *Dictionnaire Philosophique*, in *Oeuvres Complètes*, Paris, A. Sautelet, 1827).

All of these visions on legal evolution and progress explain a 'passion for law', which justifies private proposals for codification of law (Simone Goyard-Fabre, 'L'idée de loi dans les lumières françaises', in Jean-Marc Trigeaud (dir.), *Philosophie juridique européenne. Les institutions*, Roma, Japadre, 1988, 87 ff.). We should take into account that private proposals preceded the approval of Constitutions and Codes in the 19th and 20th centuries.

We can find here the doctrinal foundations of a new concept of State and a new concept of law: (a) 'État de droit', meaning the idea that the State was created by a legal instrument (the social contract, the Constitution); and (b) the science of law was seen as a *science of legislation.*

The 18th century science of legislation led to the codification of public and private law, beginning in that same century with the Constitutions and codes of public law.

IV.

These founding grandfathers of Education Law were responsible for a legacy in legal culture. The liberal Constitutions approved in Europe and America since the 18th century have some provisions regarding education.

Based on the value of human life and personality, freedom of education was seen as a major individual right – strongly connected, if not a consequence of, other basic rights to freedom such as freedom of conscience, of religion and freedom of speech.

Freedom of education was also connected to the right to education: the strong belief in the function of the State led, in Europe, to the beginning of a public service of education, at least in primary education.

V.

During the 20th century education began to be not only a topic of internal legislation, but also a concern of international treaties. The international dimension of education dates from the Universal Declaration of Human Rights. According to the Universal Declaration of Human Rights education must aim towards understanding, tolerance and friendship among all nations, races and religious groups, and it will then support the activities of the United Nations in maintaining peace.

European countries have ratified several conventions on human rights: Conventions on educational issues that have 'force of law' include universal and regional conventions: Universal Declaration on Human Rights (1948);

European Convention on Human Rights and Fundamental Freedoms (1950; 1st. Protocol, 1952); UNESCO Convention against Discrimination in Education (1960; entered into force on 22 May 1962); International Convenant on Economic, Social and Cultural Rights (1966; entered into force on 3 January 1976); and International Convention on the Rights of the Child (1989; entered into force on 2 September 1990). We can also refer to: International Convention on the Elimination of All Forms of Racial Discrimination (1965; entered into force on 4 January 1969); Convention for the Protection of the World Cultural and Natural Heritage (1972; entered into force on 17 December 1975); Convention on the Elimination of All Forms of Discrimination against Women (1979; entered into force on 3 September 1981); and Convention on Technical and Vocational Education (1989; entered into force on 29 August 1991).

It is acknowledged that most democratic constitutions assure a more accessible protection of human rights then the one that is guaranteed in international conventions, which ensure just 'minimum rights'. Nevertheless, we should remember that in some cases international treaties have the same status as internal law; in Spain and Portugal, international treaties are considered internal law, although there are some doubts if they have a supra-law value. In Portugal, the Constitution provisions relating to fundamental rights shall be interpreted and applied according to the Universal Declaration on Human Rights; the Spanish Constitution goes beyond this point, because it also states that fundamental rights should be interpreted in conjunction with other conventions and treaties ratified by Spain. Because of these criteria, the constitutional judge in Spain and in Portugal must bear in mind the European Convention and the interpretation of the Articles of the Convention by the decisions of the European Court of Human Rights.

VI.

In this process education began to be regarded not only as a matter of law, but also a matter of courts. It is not only a question of juridification of conflicts in education, but also a problem of judicialization of conflicts.

Access to courts is a basic right enshrined in all modern Constitutions. Access to court is a fundamental guarantee in any constitutional programme of human rights protection: access to the courts has been recognized not only for the defence of rights but also for the defence of social rights. We should distinguish some questions about access to court in educational matters: it is an institutional guarantee, in the sense that all persons whose rights have been violated can appeal to a court; but this guarantee poses the problem of the internal guarantee of access to court, against two major interferences: a law which declares that a person cannot appeal to a court against an administrative decision; a court decision which declares judicial review inadmissible; access to constitutional court is not a general guarantee. In Portugal, each judge has the right and the legal duty to refuse to comply with an unconstitutional law (judicial control of legislative action).

The influence of courts and jurisprudence in modern democratic countries has led some to question if we are facing a 'justice state' (Püttner) or experiencing a transition from a liberal state based upon parliamentary laws to a state based on constitutional justice (Böckenförde, *Staat, Verfassung, Demokratie*, Frankfurt-am-Main, Surkamp, 1991).

2. The philosophical background of education law

I.

In the modern *democracies of fundamental rights* (Fikentsher) we have to recognize the value of educational rights and duties. Moreover, we should also enforce social rights and constitutional principles, such as the principle of equality in education and the principle of justice.

Government goals expressed in the Constitution and in international treaties have been interpreted by constitutional court decisions as social rights, thus as rights of individuals, protected by the legal system. Constitutional principles such as the principle of equality have been accepted as a criterion for educational policies and, accordingly, the nature and structure of other basic rights has been revealed by constitutional court decisions by a different process of debate: from a single basic right to an implicit right; from a constitutional principle to a constitutionally protected social right.

II.

We may use the philosophical idea of Ronald Dworkin to describe the criteria of education law: 'taking educational rights seriously' is not only a task for Parliaments and Governments, but also for judges, teachers and the administration (R. Dworkin, *Taking Rights Seriously*, Cambridge, Harvard University Press, 1977).

Sometimes, as Dworkin notes, the task of implementing basic rights and constitutional and legal principles is not a task for an ordinary man: it is, in fact, a task for Hercules, a judge who can use all his strength to implement the principles of a democratic state (Dworkin, *Law's Empire* and Dworkin, *The philosophy of law*, Oxford University Press, 1982).

III.

The theory of justice is also an important component of the philosophical basis of education law. Not in the sense of a formal and procedural theory of justice, as it is the case of Rawls (John Rawls, *A Theory of Justice*, 10ª., Oxford

University Press, 1990), but in the sense that we should look for substantive principles of justice. In fact, it is no longer possible to rely on discretionary powers of administration and courts in the application of principles of justice (see de Groof, Neave and Svec, *Democracy and Government in Higher Education*, Kluwer Law International, 1998, 47 ff.). Eradication of abuse of power, subjectivity and irrationality is a dimension of the principle of justice.

In fact, there are specific items in education which make provision for the essential role of pluralism of institutions in the building of a society based on merit: the distribution of access to education and education assets is a task for a democratic society in order to fulfil cultural, economic and social democracy. We could use one of Walzer's concepts to say that the *sphere of justice* in education must be based on application of social rights and constitutional principles (M. Walzer, *Spheres of Justice. A Defense of Pluralism and Equality*, New York, Basic Books, 1983).

3. Legal methodology and education law

I.

Legal methodology is no longer considered as *science of legislation* (about *legislating*, see Peter Noll, *Gesetzgebungslehre*, Rheinbeck, 1973; H. Hill, *Einführung in die Gesetzgebungslehre*, Heidelberg, 1982; U. Karpen (ed.), *Legislation in European Countries*, Baden-Baden, 1991; Dominique Remy, *Légistique. L'art de faire les lois*, Paris, Romillat, 1994; Gomes Canotilho, 'Relatório sobre programa, conteúdos e métodos de um curso de teoria da legislação', *BFDC*, LXIII (1987), 405 ff.).

Until the Second World War, the science of legislation was based on structural political principles: separation of powers; superiority of the legislative power; rule of law (*principe de legalité*); equality. The opposition between interpretation and application of legal rules were based on the methods of legal science.

II.

In our time we find a strong distrust of legislators and in the law-making process.

In a certain way we are familiar with some inconvenient consequences of legislative action: too many laws and lack of coordination, sometimes the result of political consensus, but not possible to implement in daily practice. That justifies proposals for de-codification, de-legalization and de-regulation. Some authors even question if were are entering the age of *de-codification* (Irti).

We should mention that the perplexity of our times concerning the function of law in a democratic state is strengthened by the fact that Constitutional courts can declare that parliamentary or government acts are not valid.

In fact, we see the function of courts as a function of implementation of fundamental rights and constitutional principles.

We should also mention the two judicial methods of implementing the Constitution: (a) from a legal principle to a legally protected right; (b) from a fundamental right to an implicit right.

Some authors even regard constitutional clauses on human rights as general principles, allowing for a specific process of implementation by courts, especially by the Constitutional Court.

IV.

In a way, we could consider a return to some of the motives which inspired the 18th-century philosophers and are nowadays at the heart of modern sociology: instead of insisting on projects of codification of laws – of education laws – we could talk of two major tasks for legal methodology:

(a) make observations on the process of implementation of education legislation;
(b) establish the basis for doctrinal and conceptual codes of education law.

In the first case we must evaluate how laws are being implemented by courts, administrations and schools and we can pose several questions: why do laws or legal provisions need to be replaced? What went wrong? What is the economic and social cost of the new laws?

The other important aspect is the need for a consensus, mainly on the meaning of legal concepts, on the interpretation of social rights and on the interpretation of legal principles.

In fact, it is difficult to accept a normative and binding codification of education law, in a time when everything seems to change daily. Autonomy of universities and of schools warrants a conclusion. The idea of subsidiarity in education strengthens this point of view, but without any doubt, all these ideas would seem to be contradictory to the principle of equality as it was understood at the beginning of the century: all schools and universities should be considered equal and record the same equal treatment by law and by the administration.

4. Autonomy in education law as a challenge to legislators

I.

In recent Constitutions such as the Portuguese and the Spanish ones, autonomy of universities was declared a protected right of the university. Academic freedom is the legal justification for autonomy of universities, that is, freedom to teach, study, research.

It is remarkable that in a recent reform (Constitutional Law 1/97) to the Constitution, autonomy of universities was linked with the process of universities' evaluation.

The Portuguese Constitution reads: 'According to law, universities have statutory, scientific, pedagogical, administrative and financial autonomy, with regard to the evaluation of quality of teaching'.

However, we cannot find in the Constitution a definition of university and a statement of the requirements to create one.

The Portuguese law on autonomy of universities (Law 198/88 of 24 September 1988) reads:

> The universities are centres for the creation, transmission and diffusion of culture, science and technology which, through the linked action of study, teaching and research, are integrated into the life of society (Art. 1/1).

But we find no definition of the courses and knowledge required to create a university. The characterization of university usually identifies the following imperatives: (a) unite research and teaching; (b) unite science and general upbringing; (c) unite science and general upbringing (Habermas, 'The Idea of the University – Learning Process', *New German Critique*, 41; Parsons and Platt, *The American University*, Cambridge, Mass.; Marcelo Rebelo de Sousa).

II.

It is a challenge for the modern university to satisfy all these demands from the State and society, from the students and from teachers: the participation of students in the decision-making process is also a Constitutional provision.

So, the democratization from within the institution makes the autonomous university a sort of federation of interests. In fact, the conflict between all of these groups – faculties, professors, students, all with specific interests to be protected – allow us to speak of a 'state of war' each time the university has to decide relevant matters, such as its annual budget or students' or professors' disciplinary measures.

Autonomy and democratization cannot be separated. However, modern universities have to satisfy a vast number of demands, from outside and inside the university. Not only the demands of teachers and students, but also from the community and private industry.

Autonomy of universities seems to be a better way to engage professors, students and community in a common project. The principle of subsidiarity also concerns the relations between the State and educational institutions, not only in the classic way of delegation of powers and tasks, but also as a guarantee of autonomy against State interference. One of the most important consequences is the recognition of a right of appeal to court in respect of government acts which affect autonomy. So the principle of subsidiarity is more than a political guideline: it is a binding principle and a right of the autonomous body.

III.

We could discuss the nature of this constitutional principle: is it a fundamental right of the university or an institutional guarantee?

The basic idea is that it protects a fundamental right of the university. Thus autonomy cannot be seen as a social right or a state duty to be implemented as long as the State wants. It is a fundamental right, established in the interest of the universities, not only a social right depending on government programmes. On the contrary, government must respect universities autonomy and, although a legal framework is possible, law must respect the right of each university to organize itself internally in a way which seems best fitted to its purposes.

The legal consequences of autonomy of universities has not been determined. We could think of autonomy as a *long road*, meaning that the concept of autonomy needs to be seen according to the conditions of society and time. We should be able to interpret the concept of autonomy by its interactions with the actual conditions of society and education.

Anyway, some of the legal conditions of autonomy of education are detailed: (a) each university is a legal entity with legal personality; (b) each university has financial and administrative autonomy; (c) each university has cultural, pedagogical and scientific autonomy.

(a) *The university as a legal entity*
As a legal entity, the university also has judicial personality: it can be plaintiff or defendant in a civil or administrative court without any interference by the government or the minister.

One other right of universities contained in the Portuguese Constitution is the right of the universities to be heard by the Government and Parliament prior to the adoption of any legal provisions relating to the university. There is a legally binding provision stating that universities shall advise on the creation of new public universities.

(b) *Financial and administrative autonomy*
The limits of this administrative autonomy are not clear, but we should recognize at least two basic conclusions about the content of this right to administrative autonomy: (a) the right to freely adopt a basic statute (university statute); (b) the right to choose a particular form of organization.

The interpretation given to administrative autonomy of universities maintains that for each university we recognize the right to choose the way they want to be organized, with faculties or with departments; to decide which staff should exist, and which competence they should have.

The nature of this right was, in some universities, extended or transferred to faculties or organic units: some universities' statutes do recognize the right of the faculty to autonomy and, in this case, the faculty has its own statute and a right to adopt its own organization and process of working.

That admits the conclusion that some of our universities are in fact a *federation of faculties* (Marcelo Rebelo de Sousa), each one with legal powers and rights similar if not identical to the university. In these cases, the rector of the university is specially responsible in the field of finance, presiding over the senate of the university – the organ responsible for the allocation of financial resources.

In the area of financial autonomy, the universities own and use their assets without limitations other than those established by law, freely manage the funds that are annually allocated to them in the state budget, and may receive their own income and manage this through private budgets, according to the criteria established by themselves.

We can extract from the Constitution some legal criteria about the relation between state and higher education institutions: (a) the principle of equality, and the principle of equality in education implies equality of public universities in access to public funding; (b) the principle of trust in a democratic state prohibits any form of discrimination between universities that is not based on objective criteria.

Basic criteria for the allocation of financial resources adopted in Portugal are based on the ratio of students to teachers. There are different ratios relating to different courses – such as medicine or law – research units, libraries, old buildings or national monuments belonging to a university. Thus, these are objective criteria and discussion is focused on other criteria concerning distribution of permanent staff: how many professors, how many assistants, and so on.

(c) *The cultural, pedagogical and scientific autonomy of each university*
Scientific autonomy gives the universities the capacity to freely define, programme and carry out research and other scientific and cultural activities.

Pedagogical autonomy includes the right to create, suspend and cancel courses. Even more, the law guarantees that universities are autonomous in matters of designing study programmes and subject contents, defining educational methods and selecting methods of evaluation knowledge. According to this, it is uncertain if the State could impose a minimum curriculum as a requirement of state recognition of diplomas, even in the case where the State respects freedom of universities to regulate teaching methods (for Spanish constitutional court decisions, Antonio Jimenez Blanco et alii, *Comentario a la Constitution. La Jurisprudencia del Tribunal Constitucional*, Madrid, 1993). Although the fact that diplomas have national validity can justify state regulations, in order to guarantee quality of higher education institutions. Universities autonomy does not exclude the limits that are imposed by the existence of other rights and freedoms, and the need to harmonize all of these rights and freedoms with the nature of a public service of education. We should accept state regulations on university curricula and other pedagogical and scientific requirements as conditions for government recognition of diplomas, as diplomas are valid and recognized throughout the country and in Europe. Democratization of culture and education is a legal obligation of the State (Arts. 73.°, 74.°, 75.°; of the Portuguese constitution).

IV.

Autonomy has also some limits.

We should also consider the status of students. The government goal of defending the right of access to university is not an individual right and, therefore, we cannot recognize a right for each student to attend the university of their choice, if systems of *numerus clausus* fixed by the government on admission to public universities can be considered as based on objective criteria, respecting students: qualifications and skills.

A system of tuition fees in public universities is legal: it is a government goal imposed in the Constitution as well as in international conventions, to establish free education progressively. However, as the Constitutional Court decided, this social right does not mean an individual right to demand free higher education.

V.

The constitutional recognition of freedom of education made possible the existence of private higher education.

The right to establish a private university is a dimension of freedom of education, but can be limited by law. Among these legal limits, official recognition is only awarded to institutions case by case. But limits for this legislation on private universities also eisst in the equality principle: education law cannot discriminate between public and private universities and impose different standards for private universities.

However, the concept of autonomy should mean different things when we talk about private universities. Private universities' autonomy needs to be harmonized with other rights and freedoms, such as the right of ownership, also contained in the Constitution and in international conventions. Thus, regrding the Constitutional programme of autonomy of private universities, the question 'who should run private universities'? has two different answers: (a) the owners (stockholders, foundations, etc.); (b) the teachers and students. The Portuguese law on private universities tried to harmonize these rights in a coherent model: owners are responsible in all economic matters, including a right to veto decisions that can affect the institution; in all pedagogical, cultural and scientific matters we can refer to autonomy of the university.

VI.

It is a mere statement of facts that modern constitutions and laws regarding universities are not based on any philosophical concept of university and higher education knowledge.

All medieval, modern and romantic concepts of university as an 'exemplary life form' was replaced by some pragmatic ideas on the function of education and of educational institutions.

But I believe that we should look for more than these politically oriented ideas on the function of universities and education. As the philosophers of the Enlightenment wrote, we should *dare to know*.

Approach of Issues

JAN DE GROOF

Gaining Independence: 'Autonomy' versus 'Centralization' in the Higher Education of the Flemish Community?

There are different ways of serving,
but only one Spirit
(1 Cor. 12:4)

1. Introduction

1. Juray Svec, authoritative rector of the Comenius University in Bratislava, and representative of Central and East European rector conferences in multilateral organizations, explains what '*autonomy*' meant there: 'having no tanks on campus for six months.' In the new democracies, the concept is discussed with greater modesty.[1]

American university administrators for their part reiterate that *good management* is particularly obvious during a period of economic scarcity.

As far as Europe is concerned, the question of the 1990s seems in particular to consist of specifying which agency is tenable as having the *responsibility* for academic research and education. It is thus a call for the distribution of authority and of tasks, for autonomy. More a matter of administration and general culture and of a sense of responsibility and transparency, than of legislation and jurisprudence, however relevant and pregnant these things may

[1] Or, to mention another example: why was it insisted that there be a guarantee of *academic freedom* for universities written into certain constitutions? Example: See our contribution 'Some comments and questions on rights dealing with education in the R.S.A.; On section 29 of the constitution and the draft South African schools bill,' in the collection *Education under the new Constitution in South Africa*, Leuven, ACCO, 1996, pp. 55–104.

Walter Berka, Jan de Groof and Hilde Penneman (eds.), Autonomy in Education, 171–200.

be.[2] An assessment that presents itself both to the government and to the universities.[3]

These considerations are therefore not limited to setting standards, they also affect management.

The aim of this contribution is mainly to raise questions, most probably somewhat audaciously, and certainly provocatively, relating to future policy; to take up the role of a critical 'interference transmitter', which – after all – is what every academic and university ought to be.

A somewhat forgotten assignment, if one considers the ubiquitous silence of rectors in fundamental debates – except to defend corporate interests, as appears to be the time-honoured custom.

Harvard's former President, Derek Bok, wrote:

> Armed with the security of tenure and the time to study the world with care, professors would appear to have an unique opportunity to act as society's scouts to signal impending problems long before they are visible to others. Yet rarely have members of academy succeeded in discovering emerging issues and bringing them vividly to the attention of the public![4]

The universities should be urged to place public social responsibility explicitly on the agenda. 'Autonomy' is pre-eminently 'personal and positional' – a lost imagined truth? In this discussion, personal engagement does not remain off limits. In this debate one must cast neutrality aside in order to call attention to the value-related aspects of the topic of 'gaining independence'.

Thus, one must immediately ask about the authenticity of the university and how university administrators[5] apply the (academic) *critical approach* to their own environment. There is also the fundamental question of how '*innovation*', the key to modern academic policy, is being sought.

One must ask about the balance between an 'unpretentious but active government' and the higher institutions of education in the Flemish Community.

2 It will be useful to consult the comparative constribution of Kwikkers, P., 'Governance through checks and balances. An approach to drafting regulations for higher education and research,' in the splinter new periodical *European Journal for Education Law and Policy. Journal of the European Association for Education Law and Policy*, 1997, vol. 1, nrs 1–2, The Hague, Kluwer Law International, p. 57 ff.

3 One must however guard against a perpetuation of the growing confusion between 'regulation' and 'administration or management', and also, even if it is a little more tedious, between 'management' and 'supervision'.

4 *Universities and the Future of America*, Durham, 1990, p. 105.

5 Some of which, and this usually applies to the rector, may not particularly be called 'professional university managers'.

Ultimately, this topic affects the essence of the (old and modern) European dimension of higher education.[6]

2. The history of universities and their administrative autonomy

2. The question about the implications of the autonomy of universities can hardly be said to be a recent one. It is a question of 'all times': with variable results as well.

May I refer you to the pertinent historical study, including the fascinating study of the Flemish historian, De Ridder-Symoens, *History of the Universities in Europe* in its various volumes.[7]

In contrast with primary and secondary education, the governing powers showed interest in universities quite soon after they came into existence, and became involved in the current issues of the time, also in the management of the university.

During the Christianization of Europe in the late Roman period and the Middle Ages, higher education was provided in schools connected with cathedrals and monasteries.

The three pillars of society during the Middle Ages were the Church, the State and the University: *sacerdotium, regnum, studium* (the ecclesiastical, the secular and the intellectual powers). The power relationships changed often, and in the 12th century some schools, to strengthen the power of the Church, regrouped themselves into real *corporate bodies*, a unification (*universitas*) of persons who perform common tasks and who wish to defend their interests.

These corporate bodies grouped school masters and students, and were provided with a special statute in the cities. The had to receive their recognition as a university, however, from the 'competent authority'. Since these pre-university schools were in the hands of the Church, this competent authority was the Pope.

A 'university', according to the definition of canon law, was

> an institution for higher education, recognized or established for that purpose by the Pope, the members of which enjoy all privileges that were granted to them by the Pope, the degrees of which are recognized in all Christendom on the declaration of the Pope.

Throughout Europe the first, often prestigious, universities came into being.

6 Read: Guy Neave, 'In quest of a continuity: The European dimension in the history of higher education', *European Journal for Education Law and Policy*, 1997, vol. 1, p. 49 ff.

7 Rüegg, W., 'Themes' in De Ridder-Symoens, H., *History of the Universities in Europe, Vol. 1: Universities in the Middle Ages*, Cambridge, 1992, *vol. 2: Universities in Early Modern Europe (1500-1800)*, Cambridge, 1994.

The original calling of the university community consisted of the advancement of intellectual pursuits on their own merits on condition that there was actual freedom. To that end, of course, the university required access to sufficient financial means and material resources, and for this, was dependent on external agencies.

It was only after some time that the universities gradually extracted themselves from the guardianship of the Church in their internal organization and intellectual authority. In concrete terms this means there was a progressive *secularization* of the faculty, the students, the content and approach of the study material, as well as the authority over, and the control of, the university. The highest secular authorities concerned themselves with the university at the expense of the influence of the Popes. Around 1500 one could hardly still refer to it as an 'ecclesiastical institution' although the influence of the Church continued to be felt.

3. The main motive for the interest of the secular powers, Kaisers, kings and princes, was the intellectual and individual contribution the university could make to *strengthen governmental institutions* against the centrifugal power of the rural aristocracy and the urban citizenry.

The universities were always found to be intermingled with the politics of the state of the territory where they were located. As a centre for the training of the intellectual and administrative, the religious and political élite in the State and mini-states, they were expected to provide fame and glory for the sovereign. He felt responsible for good management and the *interference of the sovereign* was felt through the establishment of state universities (for example, Naples in the 13th century), and an increasingly greater control of the professors and students, as well as the content of education and financial management.

The dependence of the professors expressed itself, for example, in the allotment of a fixed salary rather than payment by the student, and in the erosion of privileges and freedoms.

The internal coherence of the academic community weakened and the civil government capitalized on malpractices (absenteeism, corruption, blameworthy behaviour) by 'laying down the law'.

With the rise of the *modern state* in the 16th century, the universities had to integrate themselves into the prevailing political and religious 'ideology' of the State. The civil government decided on the 'orthodoxy' of the university.

The enlightened despots of the 18th century also wanted to reorganize and governmentalize the university. The century of *Enlightenment* provided a new concept of a university: more scientific, adapted to the pedagogic renewal, socially useful and often laicized as well. Education and science were expected to cross-fertilize each other: the training of the young was to be built on a solid scientific foundation. New universities were established. In particular, the universities of Germany had that profile, including the university of Berlin, established in 1810 by Wilhelm Von Humboldt.

Under the *ancien régime* the universities did not have that scientific profile; they limited themselves to the distribution of scientific discoveries and did not appear able to modernize themselves and to adapt to scientific and professional needs. They were labelled as retrograde, and they opposed 'progress' in the fields of science, religion and philosophy. The reactions were diverse.

In France the *revolution* first abolished the universities. Napoleon later called the entire French school system a 'university', the *lycea* secondary schools and the faculties for the training of teachers, jurists and physicians, were all dependent on a central government in Paris. During the course of the 19th century the university turned to the 'Humboldtian' model (the interweaving of science and education).

Just about everywhere in Europe, governments also established separate schools outside the university, partially to capitalize on the industrial revolution: schools for engineers, military men, veterinary surgeons, schools for economics and administration, fine arts, etc.

The reform of university education advanced only very slowly, and also in this period it was not under impulse of the universities themselves, which usually reacted guardedly to new challenges.

In some European countries university reform took on concrete forms, partially in the 19th century, and often higher technical schools were integrated into the university – except in France where, in spite of attempts in 1896 and also after the legislation of 1968, the specialized schools retained their independence.

In other matters, French reform followed the line of the European universities: pluri-disciplinary, autonomous, participative management on the part of the personnel and a separate legal (external) personality.

In most of the states of Europe, to enhance the scientific potential, important separate scientific institutions were often established as well. Their relationship with the universities remains even now an issue for future university policy.

From this historical study on the concept of the modern university in Europe, it is obvious that the reform of university education advanced only with great difficulty and usually not under the impulse of the universities themselves.

Usually the political government, as defender of the interests of society, had to take the decisive initiative to bring the passivity of the universities to an end.

3. A few basic principles and a confession. Some international comparisons

4. May I first – and I do so without hesitation – confess my faith in 'the Flemish model'. A striving for balance, a *modus vivendi* between higher technical schools and universities on the one hand and the government on the other.

'The university as the excellent handmaid of society' on the one hand; the government and its minister, the *servus servitorum*, as guarantor for that mission, and for the independence of universities which their calling demands, on the other hand.

What is the substance of this balance, roughly speaking?

The legislator establishes the general legal framework, the principles of programming (and no doùbt in the future also of rationalization since the universities themselves refuse to draw the proper conclusions with regard to thinly or unpopulated departments or fields of study), access to education and ratification of the studies, financing of the institution (operation, investments, research, social sector) and its personnel, financing in consideration of the student, the basic pattern of the (academic, financial, social) statute of the various branches.

The government must also see to it that the goals of academic education are accomplished. One may have a look at the shortest but inexhaustible art. 5 of the decree, if one wishes to engage in creative 'interpretation of law' for the benefit of universities.

The university may not turn aside, for example, to become merely a research institute or a narrowly specialised higher technical school. One of the specific characteristics of the Flemish (European oriented) concept is precisely the refusal to make a selection between the '*researcher discipline based loyalty*'[8] and the '*teaching, institutional loyalty*',[9] in accordance with the American school of thought.[10]

Or – in the same vein – a mortgage could also be placed on the academic mission by the deletion of historical, philosophical or cultural curriculum content.[11]

In this context, may I refer once more to a statement by one of the most brilliant minds of our time, the language philosopher, Georges Steiner, who in his famous '*Bluebeard's castle*'[12] wrote:

> We know now that formal knowledge and the numeric distribution of educational systems is not necessarily accompanied by an increase in rationality and morality. Libraries, museums, theatres, universities and higher technical schools, in which the transfer of the arts and the exact sciences takes place, can prosper right beside concentration camps.

[8] Characteristic of the American top (research) universities.

[9] Of overriding importance for *community colleges.*

[10] The standard article in this area remains: Gouldner, A., 'Cosmopolitians and locals', in *Administrative Review Quarterly*, 1957, vol. 1, nr 2.

[11] In this connection, remember the controversy some time ago in the medical faculty of UCA and in the law faculty of UG.

[12] G. Steiner, *In Bluebeard's castle: some notes towards the redefinition of culture*, New Haven: Yale University Press, 1971.

5. What can we conclude from this?

The government must help the university (and higher technical school) not to deny its mission.

At the same time, the university must be able to develop its own strategic management, with a view to planning, searching for strong and weak points, leadership, vision, communication, evaluation, and personnel management. Each institution ought to profile itself, as it were, in *forum internum* and in *forum externum*.

This balance does not allow for any centralism. No detailed central steering of conduct by the government with respect to education and research. A new application of the '*trust principle*' of civil law. But neither may there be obstinacy on the part of institutions. Or to employ another judicial principle: the application of the 'loyalty principle' to community regulations.

And above all: The university and higher technical school must – precisely because they are '*enclaves of self-management*' – give account for the investment entrusted to them by society. The recent Flemish legislation, with its stipulations of application, is permeated by this.[13]

At a recent OESO meeting, a minister said: 'Any university autonomy ends where the state subsidy is larger than zero.' I will refrain from applying this witticism to the Flemish higher technical schools and universities, albeit not without mentioning that the Flemish universities obtain only a very limited portion of their global income from private sources (very few *grants* from *alumni*, there are contracts with companies, but then again gifts and legacies are only minimal ...).

In some institutions the private contribution is stagnating or even decreasing.

To the extent that the private universities – at their own request – want to keep pace with the public universities, the subsidy system will also be used as a '*handy management tool*'.[14] It goes without saying that the explicit *equality principle* in educational affairs, in accordance with art. 24 of the Constitution, further enhances a *more uniform approach* on the part of the Community, regardless of the legal nature of the institution.[15]

[13] Veny, L., *De regelgeving op het academisch onderwijs; De rechtspositie van de Vlaamse universiteiten en van hun personeel* (Doctoral dissertation); De Groof, J., '*De gewijzigde regelgeving voor de universiteiten in de Vlaamse Gemeenschap - Het globale kader*', T.O.R.B., 1992–1993, nr 1, p. 6 c.v.

[14] *Cf* Craenen, G., *De bestuurlijke zelfstandigheid van de universiteiten in België, Preadvies voor de Vereniging voor de vergelijkende studie van het recht van België en Nederland*, Zwolle, 1986, p. 33.

[15] In this regard, see the position taken in our book *De grondwetsherziening van 1988 en het onderwijs*, Brussels, 1989, p. 233; specifically in connection with the discusson of the constituent regarding the autonomy of the universities, *ibidem*, p. 173–175.

6. Because of the monopoly which the universities hold with regard to the ratification of academic diplomas and because of the fact that the basic financing of the universities is based on government money, the Belgian constitutional judge designated them as a '*public service*' (organic or functional). This also appears to be the case in the other European member states, according to the authoritative commentator on legislation on higher education in the United Kingdom,[16] D.J. Farrington.

The observation which is often made in other member states of the European Union, namely: 'The changes in the funding of higher education produced an unprecedented degree of central control over the university sector at the expense of institutional autonomy,'[17] can hardly be applied without modification to the Flemish model, however.

To a certain extent, the distinction between higher and non-higher education continues to be relevant in this regard.[18]

'Government policy' concerning academic education and research can certainly, at least in the European context, hardly be labelled as 'superfluous,' as the Anglo-American literature[19] sometimes does.[20]

16 *The Law of Higher Education*, Butterworths, London, 1994, p. 86, stating that as a consequence of various procedures and as stipulated by the European authorities, a 'body governed by public law' is to be define as:
'(i) established for the specific purpose of meeting needs in the general interest, not having an industrial or commercial character; and
(ii) having legal personality; and
(iii) financed, for the most part, by the State, or regional or local authorities, or other bodies governed by public law; or subject to management supervision by those bodies; or having an administration, managerial or supervisory board more than half of whose members are appointed by the State, regional or local authorities or other bodies governed by public law.
It seems reasonably clear that institutions of higher education fall within the definition of bodies governed by public law.'

17 Harris, N., *Law and Education: Regulation, Consumerism and the Education System*, London, 1993, p. 94.

18 Verhoeven asked the question, to what extent the measures with a view to autonomy of the educational instituations at the 'school pact' level were also actually considered to be such: Verhoeven, J. and Gheysen, *Scholen en nieuwe voorschriften. Een evaluatie door directie, leerkrachten en ouders*, Centrum voor Theoretische en Onderwijssociologie, KUL, 1994.

19 Since the tendency is stronger there for private law to have the upper hand as soon as private money and (for example, immobile) property come into discussion. It is well-known that even the public universities obtain only a portion of their regular operational costs from public financing sources. Guy Neave once defined the points of difference as follows: 'the British view being that the scholars own the property and the American that the founders own the property and the scholars!'.

20 In the process going to great lengths in an attempt to make an accurate distinction between the terms *public oversight*, *public control*, and *public supervision*, depending

Comparing the American concept with the *continental European* tradition, the following three significant differences can, in any case, be put forward: American institutions are characterized by a very limited governmental 'interference' with the curriculum and the content of the courses of study, they are only (sometimes very) partially dependent on governmental financing (in any form whatever) and their quality control is separate from the government.[21]

7. The question must be continually raised as to whether the lines of authority have not been exceeded. The administrative and the constitutional judges try with difficulty to detect criteria which hopefully will help the legislator himself find a way to respect the careful balance. The new legislation also appears to continually question whether there is danger of some imbalance (in one way or another).

A study would indicate — although it would be a good idea to test it systematically – that the *Flemish concept* is entitled to its own position in the European context, but that it certainly is most closely related (to return to the imposed terms of the title for this contribution) to the decentralised administration, characteristic of the *German* model ('the State as guardian of the free exercise of science') than to the central administration that conforms to the French model ('higher education is a department of central governmental organization').

Beyond that, in our concept, features can also be found of the *American and market-orientated model*, but the *European* pattern predominates: general accessibility, uniformity of the education offered and of the administrative organization, relevance of public law, ratification of the studies, etc.[22]

---

on the terminology one uses. Concerning this terminology that covers their classification of the relationship between the university and the government, see Neave, G. and Van Vucht, F.'s books *Prometheus Bound*, 1991, Oxford, Pergamon and *Government and Higher Education Relationships across three continents*, 1994, Oxford, Pergamon. Both publications for their part opt for the distinction *state control/state supervisory model.*

[21] See, among others, the comparative-law work of Zoontjens, P., *Vrijheid van wetenschap: juridische beschouwingen over wetenschapsbeleid en hoger onderwijs*, Zwolle, 1993, p. 485.

[22] One must concur with the proposition according to which European comparative-law research, and in some respects also educational research on higher education often does not penetrate to actual comparisons but tends to get stuck in descriptions: Goedegebuure, L., Van Vucht, Fr., 'Comparative higher education studies: The perspective from the policy science', in *Higher Education*, 1996, vol. 32, nr 4, p. 371 ff. See in this regard the various publications of J. Jallade; also: Zoontjens, Paul, 'Klunen naar het eind van de eeuw. De hervormingen in het Nederlandse wetenschappelijk onderwijs', T.O.R.B., 1996–1997, nr 3, pp. 171–177; It can also be fruitful to have a look at the publications of the European Education Law and Policy Association: *Subsidiarity and Education. Aspects of Comparative Educational Law. First Report of the European Educational Law Association. / Mobility and education.*

4. The claims of the autonomy principle

(a) *The functionality of 'autonomy'*

8. 'Autonomy': authors and education practitioners attach divergent and one-sided definitions to it.

In Flemish policy documents as well, several meanings are employed, including *the* independence from the community, or the principle of 'Selbstverwaltung', or 'academic freedom'. They are distinct concepts, although aspects of the same reality.

Often the concept *'substantive autonomy'* is placed beside *'procedural autonomy'*:

> Substantive autonomy relates to the power of the institution to determine its own goals and programs, while procedural autonomy has to do with determining the means by which these goals and programs will be pursued.[23]

The concept *academic* freedom touches the individual task of education and the research of the academic, whereas *institutional* autonomy relates to the status of self-governing groups ('units') of academics within the institution.[24]

It goes without saying that these concepts are related to each other, and certain criteria are cited to measure the so-called degree of autonomy: the exclusion of non-academic external influence on the administration of the university, freedom of allocation of resources, freedom of choice in hiring staff and regulating their terms of employment, the selection of students, autonomy in planning and ratifying the curriculum, in establishing quality goals, in academic methods, etc.[25]

Thus, autonomy is not a goal in itself – although in some debates certain administrators zealously intermingle goal and means – but it is a technique, a potential, for realizing the distinctive mission. 'The mission' which one would expect every university or higher technical school to be able to state precisely. The ambiguity of the content of many such (specification) documents, fails to confirm this, however.

The legal status of teachers in Europe. Second report of the European Educational Law Association. / The legal status of minorities in education. Third report of the European Educational Law Association.

23 Berdahl, R., 'Academic freedom, autonomy and accountability in British universities', Stud. High. Ed., 1990, nr 2, p. 170 ff.

24 Tight, M., 'Institutional autonomy', in Clark, B. and Neave, G., *The encyclopedia for higher education*, Oxford, 1992, p. 1384 ff.

25 For example, Ashby, E., *A study in the ecology of higher education*, London, 1966, p. 296 ff.

It bears repeating, that in the framework of this book we are limiting ourselves to higher education, and for a long time institutions of higher education have been granted significantly more independence than was usual at the other levels. The origin lies in a tradition that developed in the 18th century, the principle of academic freedom: the researcher and his environment must be free in the determination of the content and the method of research.

Even so, a good deal of movement can also be detected in primary and secondary education – including things pertaining to educational theory.[26]

In the previous issue of the *Cahiers voor onderwijsrecht en onderwijsbeleid* more attention is given to this.[27]

(b) *Autonomy requires the recognition of the principle of co-responsibility*

9. In Flemish higher education, by way of exception, mention has been made of actual 'exclusive' or 'competitive' jurisdiction – if I may use the terminology of constitutional law.

An OESO study on decentralization of education policy estimated the central jurisdiction at 19% for matters pertaining to non-higher education.[28] For the rest it is significantly lower. I noted, for that matter, during the abovementioned study day of the Vl.I.R. that Karel Tavernier had no suggestions ready for further 'decentralization' of areas of authority.

But neither does the government limit itself, however, to purely co-ordinating tasks or only to the defining of minimum conditions concerning the educational programme, administrative organization, personnel management and planning. The government also determines to what extent results have been achieved and whether they are in compliance with the minimum conditions (*output*, even if it is in a differentiated manner, for example, in things concerning scientific research) and whether they, to a certain extent in any case, were accomplished in an appropriate manner (*process control*).

As far as the latter is concerned (namely, *process control*), I have already defined certain aspects of this more precisely myself, for example, relative to the observance of legal requirements, the institution's own statutory standards in that regard, and also the observance of the general principles of good management.[29] Moreover, I feel that I am in good company with one of the

[26] De Groof, J., 'Omtrent de pedagogische vrijheid', *Nova et Vetera*, 1995–96, nr 1–2, pp. 138–174.

[27] See Coppieters, P. *et al.*, *Responsabilisering van de school*, Deurne, 1998, pp. 53–59.

[28] OESO/CERI, *Les processus de décision dans 14 systèmes éducatifs de l'OCDE, Paris, 1995.*

[29] 'Academische personeelsbeleid: vrijheid in gebondenheid', in De Groof, J., *Personeelsbeleid aan de Vlaamse Universiteiten*, Deurne, 1995, p. 172.

proponents of the liberal school in university management, Prof. Walter Nonneman, who recently wrote (1996) in an UFSIA memorandum:

> The evaluation of the quality of education is an aspect of integral quality care. Rather than concentrating on after-the-fact quality control, IKZ focuses on the development and improvement of the processes that produce services.

Thus, government may not take to itself the role of the administration of the institution, unless a reorganization or restructuring becomes imperative.

It must invite the institution to define its goals explicitly, to accountability, to budgetary orthodoxy, to integration of quality control in personnel management and in the allotment of scientific funds. But it may not itself decide on the concrete allotment of the funds granted, since the university or higher technical school itself must be considered to have the required expertise in the areas of financial management and of educational and science-related policy.

Wielemans, whose contributions (among others) in the *Tijdschrift voor Onderwijsrecht en Onderwijsbeleid* are obligatory reading for those involved in (higher) education, writes in his contribution for *Prometheus Bound* about higher education in the Flemish Community:[30]

> The remote control of higher education by government has been, and remains, the norm. Consequently, the autonomy of higher education in general and the universities in particular is rarely curtailed by direct government intervention.

This relationship between the university/higher technical school and the government has ushered in the next phase of the refinement of the basic standards of freedom of, and right to, education and freedom of science. It requires the mutual fine-tuning of government regulation and of self-regulation (self-regulation which, on the part of the institution, evidently leads to over-regulation, but that is another topic).

I call this the system of *co-responsibility*, which bears within itself the orchestration between autonomous institutions and the government.

All too often, however, university administrators prove to be incapable of leaving their own stronghold and accepting their co-responsibility for the future of all higher education within the Flemish Community. Too often a survival strategy is followed, which, however, is seldom fruitful for prospective policy in relation to general (educational) interests.

10. It cannot be denied that the Coens decree, dd 12 June 1991, as modified

[30] Which he wrote in cooperation with Johan Vanderhoeven: 'Market Impact and Policy Drift: Belgian Higher Education', in Neave, G. and Van Vucht, F.A., *Prometheus Bound. The Changing Relationship Between Government and Higher Education in Western Europe*, Oxford, 1991, p. 11.

later, had the intention of bolstering the autonomy of universities. Since this concept was almost carbon-copied for the higher technical schools, this also applies *mutatis mutandis* largely for them.

The law on academic degrees and the enumeration of subjects for each study cycle has been abolished; the organizational authority for universities of the Community was transferred and their freedom of management structures written into the decree (as for all universities); physical standards no longer exist, the government only requires a long-range plan and a physical inventory; there is retention of operational surpluses and the possibility of certain internal transfers of financing channels, etc.

After 1991 other deregulations or decentralization modifications were carried out: the terms of seniority for ZAP, the abolition of the 70% rule for AAP people, a commencement with the full-time temporary ZAP position, etc.

The most recent 'train' of decree regulations extends this trend further.

The Flemish model, an excellent product for export, that does need some fine-tuning, even modifications in some regards, is serving as an inspiration for educational systems in other countries, including the supervisory organisms, to the sorrow of those who are envious of it. This will be evident from the book that will be published shortly in cooperation with the 'popes' of higher education in Europe, Ulrich Teichler, Guy Neave, Roel In 'T Veldt and Jury Svec.[31]

(c) *The enrichment consequences of autonomy*

11. The following generation will look back and decide, however, whether in this decade universities also reacted so conservatively to new challenges as they did previously.

The risk is not minor. This has already been shown by the opposition of universities (and their vassals in the Flemish Parliament) to the introduction of the '*Quality Care*' section in the general decree, dd 12 June 1991, (original version) and possible sanctions in this area (namely, holding back subsidies when there is a clear unwillingness to act on objective findings, or when a systematic lack of quality is detected).

Only the recent *audit*, presently in progress, concerning the implementation of quality analyses ('meta-evaluation' by the government) gained the unreserved approval of the universities relative to quality control. Previously the initiatives were experienced as a 'burden', a 'hindrance for autonomous institutions', not as the natural counterpart of independence. It is no exaggeration to state that

[31] De Groof, J., Svec, J. and Neave, G., *Democracy and Governance in Higher Education*, Kluwer Law International, The Hague, 1997; The first volume in this series is: In 'T Veld, R., Fussel, H.P. and Neave, G., *Relations between State and Higher Education*, Kluwer Law International, The Hague, 1996.

without 'gentle pressure' from the government, such mechanisms would have come into being only with great hesitancy. Elsewhere, however, the discussion about the failure of the universities in the accomplishment of academic standards could lead to a legal summons (and in some cases to compensation for damages[32]) or even to criminal prosecution, as is the case in new democracies.[33]

Another sensitive example was the long-sustained opposition to the (now zealously praised) *overhead*, and also the aversion to giving up the 'complete university' concept.

May I introduce a little parenthesis?

For twenty years, without interruption, I have attended the academic opening and the ceremony on the occasion of 'Lichtmis' at the Catholic University of Leuven, and for several years now also that of the University of Gent, in addition of course to the universities I am able to follow by virtue of my profession. In Gent also for a particular reason: namely, because there the minister invariably articulates his policy viewpoint in a brilliant manner.[34]

His criticism of the lenience of the universities, whether citing OESO reports or not, in his address for the academic years 1996–1997 and 1997–1998 was stinging. The lack of innovation in the realm of education, the too one-sided interest in current-generation students, the lack of a radical reduction in contact education, etc.

One still regularly hears the proposition that there is no demand for 'open higher education', but how closed our institutions remain for some challenges.

These analyses have been known for some time, certainly in the first international indicators report 'Education at a Glance' (1991). These indicators also demonstrate that the trailing behind of the Flemish Community in the educational participation of adult students in the structural organization of permanent education is not just *alleged*, but is *proven* beyond any doubt. Our country is dawdling along at the very rear, just in front of Greece.

And I will not go into the other *challenges* in the new international, socio-economic and cultural context.

I conclude in this regard that autonomy is beneficial for meeting the quality requirements of education and research, for advancing the social function of scientific service, and for competing with other spheres of science. These are not static items of data, however.

[32] A discussion which for the time being is not being carried out frequently. *Cf* Whincup, M.H., 'The exercise of university disciplinary powers', in *Education and Law*, vol. 5, nr 1, 1993, p. 26 ff.

[33] *Cf* De Groof, J., *Comments on the Law on Education of the Russian Federation*, Leuven, 1994.

[34] Van Den Bossche, L., 'Universitair beleid in een kantelfase', T.O.R.B., 1997–1998, nr 1, pp. 48–52; 'Het universitaire landschap in Vlaanderen in de jaren negentig en daarna', T.O.R.B., 1995–1996, nr 4, p. 239.

One does not approach such things from a so-called 'survival strategy' – a term that university administrators regularly use[35] in the light of former or impending revisions of the financing rules.

For some, the autonomy of universities is synonymous with the *raison d'être* of the university.[36] Maybe it is a 'gift'. In any case, it *is* the giving of a *difficult assignment.*

(d) *Autonomous personnel management*

12. In my contribution for the collection already mentioned, *Het personeelsbeleid aan de Vlaams universiteiten,* interspersed with stories with which – may I express it somewhat coarsely – rectors like to console themselves, I was in a position to approach university legislation from the viewpoint of its deregulation, its lack of legal security, the conflict with the 'general university' interest through the promotion of particularisms.

The analysis developed there indicated that the legislator provides the universities with real opportunities for autonomous and flexible personnel management, to be combined with the quality approach.

I refer, among other things, to:

- the promotion of opportunities for young academics ingrained in the decree;
- the free determination and the individualization of the academic's task; and
- the end of the blind domination of seniority and of obligatory uniformity in wages, on condition, of course, that the differentiation be objectivized.

Some modifications certainly are needed to further modernize 'academic' personnel policy, and these are certainly not limited to the introduction of the *right of dismissal,* in conformity with the report of the external commission concerning quality care in scientific research of September 1996.

The question can also be raised as to what arguments – beyond the theme of tradition and the affiliation with other venerable professions – can be made to prevent tampering with *permanent appointments,* or the drawing up of different *personnel profiles.*

Thus, it can already be regretted that the legal renewal that is defined as 'epoch-making' (by means of Education Decree VIII) to allow full-time members of the ZAP to be appointed (just) temporarily, was made possible only

35 In the light of former or impending revision(s) of the financing rules. Especially at a time when fixed costs are too high, this leads a number of institutions to occupy themselves with their own viability. The contradition for the universities is that this narrow 'margin of freedom' occurs excactly at a time when the university should find itself in a period of (intrinsic) expansion. University administrators, like shopkeepers, pleading for their 'own store'?

36 According to Wielemans, W. and Vanderhoeven, J., *op. cit.*, p. 19.

'with a view to a permanent appointment', and this after the completion of a trial year. This looks more like the 'torpedoing' of the introduction of the (fully fledged) system of full-time employees with limited duration – an evident aspect of personnel management.

No doubt also from conservativeness, one prefers not to tinker – in the area of education at least – with the division of academic education into a *first and second cycle,* which is unparalleled in western higher-education systems.

Although one must keep in mind that for any modification in the duration of the studies for obtaining a diploma, an appeal must be made to 'cooperative federalism' in the light of the federal authority in this area.

5. Some rather annoying questions concerning autonomous administration, both for the universities and for the government

(a) *Several examples from the institutions*

13. A broad margin of autonomy has thus been granted to the universities.

May I somewhat critically raise the question as to whether fruitful use has also been made of it in all circumstances?

(1) Can it be denied how necessary it proved to be to stop the explosion of *advanced academic courses* by means of a different financing policy?

As the irony of fate would have it, the adaptations of the decrees relating to this point, as questioned by the court of arbitration, were what gave occasion for the revision of the basic financing itself.

Also within the third cycle of the academic landscape, nothing was seen except lack of consensus among Rectors and a lack of elementary distribution of tasks and planning. Such incapacity already existed with regard to the organization of the academic courses since the governmental agreements dating from the early seventies. They obliged the universities to define programming rules to prevent further uncontrolled growth in university education.

Self-regulation capacity at the macro level seems to be a perilous assignment.[37]

Competition, described positively as a stimulant for growth and quality, as an antidote for self-satisfied esconcement in monopolies, presents itself in education and science in different terms than in relation to economic activities, and that also applies to scientific pursuits to a certain extent.

And is there not a danger of the same lack of constructive competition, but a raising of the bids – for example with a view to obtaining fresh money – with respect to continued education? A question of self-regulation at the *macro* level.

[37] See also *infra.*

Already institutions are draining off former advanced courses to the lucrative sector of 'continued education'.

(2) A second example: who still denies the salutary effect of the legislative and governmental measures dating from 1994 and 1995 in respect to two other components of the mission, namely *service* and *scientific research*?

As a result, the universities (finally) gained the capacity for insight and internal control, and a resultant improved management.

The community would no doubt also appreciate it if the universities of their own free will would draw up an ethics clause in connection with contracts with industry, as is customary in the top American universities.

(3) Previously I already launched several suggestions concerning *personnel management*, including the voluntary limitation of the number of permanent appointments. I can refer to the series of concrete suggestions in this area in the above-mentioned book on 'Autonoom personeelsbeleid aan de Vlaamse universiteiten'.

(b) *The urgent need for 'legislation evaluation'*

14. On the other hand, neither can it be denied that a 'legislation evaluation' is needed to determine whether certain legal ordinances do not hinder responsible autonomous administration.

It can therefore only be welcomed that the decision is being considered to have each section subjected to a thorough investigation which would lead to a decree that is specific for each personnel category. This would certainly avoid a decree with a mishmash of provisions that must offer an ad hoc solution for all situations and circumstances.

In this regard the government must include more flexibility and autonomous management in the area of personnel management.

(1) This certainly applies for the *ATP statute*. The universities demonstrated that a more flexible system (via function classification and a career model) resulted in better management and furthermore, turns out less expensive.[38]

(2) Second example: the possibility – even if it is limited to a certain percentage – to appoint *contractual personnel for an indefinite term*, also in the statutory universities, in order to be able to meet fluctuating needs.

Great appreciation should be shown for the initiatives in this area that the Department is taking concerning the screening of statutes. The universities seem to react less readily. And the cooperation of the Auditor's Office also needs to be assumed in this area, which — this frightens some off – has proven

[38] Van Loon, F. and Derycke, H., 'Naar een personeelsbeleid aan de Vlaamse universiteiten', T.O.R.B., 1992–1993, nr 4, pp. 230–239.

its ability to make a constructive contribution to new interpretations and even to the drawing up of existing regulations, although the *consensus* is not given beforehand (for example with regard to the position of the Auditor's Office that the personnel of a free university has a statutory rather than a contractual affiliation).

(3) Another example of the evaluation of valid standards this time touches the 'self-regulation' on the part of universities.

Virtually all institutions have a so-called 'special academic framework', namely, academics who in principle are selected objectively, who voluntarily (i.e. without pay) carry out activities of instruction and research within the academic entities. In this regard there is a degree of incoherence present, and at the same time, the universities must be careful that the 'parallel formations' (to use terminology from the Financing legislation of 1971) do not cross each other, and that the university administrators can still find their way through the maze of statutes they have created themselves.

And by means of the obligation to have *internal coherence* – a modern principle of good management, as I tried to show elsewhere – I come to my next comments.

(c) *Several conclusions regarding the universities*

15. What are now at this point the honest consequences of a well-understood autonomy for universities, first from the viewpoint of the universities, then from that of the government?

In each case I will limit myself to conclusions that can lead to positive measures in the short term.

In some cases they express the 'uneasy relationship' between the government and the university, which Job Cohen speaks about, and which according to him originate largely from a certain 'dissatisfaction' that higher education summons up in recent years and which paradoxically enough is the result of successful policy.[39]

1. Self-standardization

16. For the universities, independence includes:

- first of all, really to be able *to draw up their own regulations* in implementing the strict legal provisions (and in most universities this is done quite completely; the university hospitals form a separate problem);
- and also to abide by them (and the adage *patere legem quam ipse fecisti* no doubt causes problems);

[39] T.O.R.B., 1995–1996, nr 3, p. 153 ff.

- and possibly to also be able to adapt their own management techniques, for example, relative to the distribution of authority between the board of governors and the board of directors in the community universities.

On the application of self-regulation within the academic sector there are not very many evaluations in existence, other than on an ad hoc basis. On the need for self-regulation there is a broad consensus; there is no paradox to be found between this form of standardization on the one hand and the 'withdrawing government' on the other hand.[40] Also from the most recent comparative educational and judicial research it is shown that self-regulation must form the core of quality control.[41]

Thus the parallel legislation and the principles of good management (including the observance of the equality principle, the accountability obligation, competition, personnel management, information obligation, etc.) force the university into that role.

It certainly must be taken into consideration that self-regulation is not unlimited. It is first of all limited by the general principles of good management, and second by a greater accountability obligation on the part of the institutions *and* a supervision thereof on the part of the government. Dutch legal doctrine has appropriated this viewpoint for a long time.

If government and legislator is serious about the autonomy of universities, the decree framework also needs to be investigated from this side as well. In that regard one should remember the wise words of In 'T Veld and co.:

> Legislation should utilise the self-regulating potential of professional organisations more than in the past. Self-steering of universities necessitates leadership by inspiration besides the use of methods for pricing and costing, planning and evaluation. The governance of universities in the next century will be characterised by hybridity and diversity, and new cultural patterns will emerge to ensure that universities remain the most attractive organisations in the world.[42]

2. Self-evaluation

17. Independence means guaranteeing the continual existence of a critical capacity within the institution. Applying quality care as a legal obligation and as a principle of good management to all aspects of the life of the university or higher technical school.

[40] *Cf* for example Goedegebuure, L., Kaiser, Fr. *et al., Higher Education Policy. An International Comparative Perspective,* Oxford, 1993, p. 340.

[41] *Cf* Dorbeck-Jung, B., 'Comparing regulations of higher education quality evaluation', in *European Journal for Education Law and Policy*, 1997, vol. 1, p. 91 ff.

[42] *Relations between State and Higher Education, op cit.*, p. 90.

One of the first guidelines from the 'Gids voor Visitatiecommissies' (guide for visitation commissions of the VNSU) is stated as follows:

> By a withdrawing government and by the promise of a greater autonomy, higher education is challenged to assume responsibility for quality care. Autonomy and quality care as two sides of the same coin.[43]

In this context, the suggestion could be launched to make the reports of the visitation commissions completely accessible, including the 'self-evaluation report', which would benefit the students as much as anyone – not as a means of recruitment, but as a proof of transparency. Immediately annexed to this could be a list of measures the administration of the institution proposes to develop in order to rectify any deficiencies. Such an 'implementation plan' would appear to be an essential ingredient of quality care.[44]

A brief parenthesis.

In this context, the question concerning the government/university relationship in The Netherlands was: can the government thoroughly investigate the *quality management plans* for each course of study separately or can the inspection only do this – as maintained by the rectors – with respect to the basic pattern? P. De Meijer, Rector Magnificus of the University of Amsterdam stated: 'It cannot be the responsibility of the Minister or of the Legislature to descend to the module of each separate course of study. That would be an expression of detailism and statism.'[45] He added to this, however, and this sounded less persuasive: 'Furthermore, we already have our own system of quality control: the visitation commissions. Now a new system is being placed on top of that.'

Furthermore, access to required information in this area must also be granted to candidate students.

> Consumers must have sufficient information about the likely outcomes of their choices before decisions are made; if this condition is not met then not only will they be prevented from at least attaining a second best outcome, but there will be no inducement for providers, faced with the loss of market share as customers seek satisfaction elsewhere, to improve the quality of their service/product.[46]

[43] Quotation originating from Vroeijenstijn. If it is formulated by a 'foreign expert' – although The Netherlands should be viewed more as part of the interior – it evidently sounds more weighty to some Rectors, although excatly the same wording was previously used in the Explanatory Memorandum for Flemish decrees.

[44] Compare with regard to The Netherlands: Westerheijden, D.F., 'Quality assessment in Dutch higher education. Balancing improvement and accountibility', *European Journal for Education Law and Policy*, 1997, vol. 1, p. 81 ff.

[45] *NRC-Handelsblad*, 24 January 1996.

[46] Parlour, J.W., 'Student charters in higher education', in *Education and the Law*, vol. 8, nr 3, 1996, p. 232.

If self-evaluation is defined as the most important stage in quality control, does not such an openness also apply to the *'self-evaluation reports'*, in spite of the hesitation of universities in this regard?

3. Co-operative model at the macro level

18. Independence requires more and more penetrating mutual co-operation among institutions.

- Certainly concerning the 'personnel union' of academics and to combat the practice of inbreeding which is profusely rampant in Flemish universities. Realize that the best universities *elsewhere* consider it a matter of honour to recruit their faculty chairmen and rectors – by means of profile descriptions – from other universities.
- Concerning the disposal of misconceived competition, for example, related to the illegitimate use of the 'Master's Degree', a finally understood hint now also for the higher technical schools.
- Concerning a radical decision in favour of mutual quality initiatives after the second cycle, rather than the formerly observed reluctant and modest beginnings of inter-university courses of study. Why should not the specialized advanced courses of study and the doctoral courses of study in principle only be recognized if they are based on an inter-university network – a suggestion that was already formulated by the editors of the general university decree of 12 June 1991 and apprehensively rejected by a large majority of the Flemish rectors?
- And it goes without saying, concerning the concept – expertly avoided so far – of *complementarity, task distribution, centre-of-gravity formation and specialization* among institutions, 'pre-conditions' for entering the European competition with success.

Of course, hesitation prevents me from referring to the wall of rejection to the concept, which every objective observer experiences as obvious and rejuvenating, of Flemish-Dutch cooperation in Limburg, or to refer to the troublesome concept of a confederate university in Antwerp.

I must be very careful not to even mention such things ...

We will have to wait for the further report of the (Catholic) 'Commissioner of the Flemish Government', honorary rector Roger Dillemans, but it can certainly be hoped that in this area, daring, and thus horizon-broadening proposals will be introduced. Certainly one should be able to assume that it will not remain a little clique of interested parties: one will want to keep in mind that the Flemish Council itself must pronounce upon this matter. One must also remember that the legal doctrine test, in the final instance on the part of the *quasi*-Constitutional Court, requires the drawing up of *objective norms and criteria* which should support the sketch of the future landscape.

4. Consistent application of the subsidiary principle, also internally

19. From the beginning of this contribution, it has been pointed out that *real* autonomy is situated in the independence and the critical attitude of the university and the individual academics. Administrative autonomy is *helpful to this end.*

The somewhat alluring aspect of a university is to a certain extent the mild and guided 'chaos' that may prevail there – a consequence of having an institution where *freedom* is defined as the highest good – the *unpredictable.* Education jurist, Prof. Job Cohen expresses this, applied to organizational theory, in his *foundation day speech,* on the occasion of the acceptance of the position of Rector Magnificus at the Rijksuniversiteit Limburg, in the following paradox: 'Certain inefficiencies in the administration of a university could turn out to be considerably more efficient than a strict hierarchical organized apparatus.'[47]

Also the amazing interaction between 'public' and 'private' comes in this category.

Further in this context: there is not very much international literature available on the internal administration and management of a university as an 'interface' between public and private welfare. Furthermore, some claim that the improvement of administrative techniques is more a topic for informal discussion between a rector and some of his disciples, with possibly a minister in attendance, at a *Faculty Club.* Informal discussions may indeed have a certain impact on policy,[48] yet other than the protracted discussions about the subdivision of the academic entities in subject groups and/or departments and the drawn-out disputes about the length of the mandate of a rector, the Flemish institutions have not given evidence of great inventiveness in the use of the *quasi*-complete autonomy that the general decree of 12 June 1991 gave them for the organization of their own administration.

One topic for the future, which the university will not be able to avoid, is the (re)distribution of areas of authority.

Each appeal of universities for further autonomy relative to the government is more credible to the extent that the university takes 'decentralization' *into its own bosom,* not just as an option, but as an actual pattern of behaviour.

The demand for the extension of the administrative powers of faculty councils is now under discussion in several universities. Far-reaching initiatives in this context have been taken by the administrative and academic authorities

47 'Professoren en Politiek', *Universiteit en Beleid*, vol. 9, nr 3, p. 6 ff.

48 Most probably this (portion of the interesting) discussion ends with the announcement that, regardless of how interesting such considerations of administrative science are, it is better to get on with the agenda of the day ...

of the University of Gent (RUG)[49] and one of the sister institutions within the Antwerp University, namely the UFSIA.[50]

This also includes, where relevant, the greater involvement of faculties in the improvement of quality and even in *values communication.* A good example of this (essential) mission of the university is the project: 'Knowing values. The place of values in the instruction of the Vrije Universiteit Amsterdam.'[51]

20. Responsibility must be placed on its main foundation, namely the *expertise* that is present.

This requires *unity* and *coherence* in administrative policy, which is also a principle (and the reference is relevant from several perspectives) from European community law, that appears to be applicable to autonomous institutions.[52]

Van Vucht means the same with his term 'collegiality':

[49] *Cf* a synthesizing article by Hoogewijs, R., Buelens, M. and Willems, J., 'Decentralisatie van beslissingsmacht. Reorganisatie van de centrale administratie aan de Universiteit Gent', *Tijdschrift voor Hoger Onderwijs en Management*, 1997, nr 3, p. 38. The authors obviously do not adopt a very critical attitude with regard to the implementation of the 'reformation plan'. To what extent have the principles outlined by the external 'organization agency' been carried out in reality?

[50] *Cf* The discussion memorandum *Academische reorganisatie UFSIA*, AV–UFSIA, 16 December 1997.

[51] By means of a detailed scenario, the faculties were invited to fill in their own content for the assignment to develop a profile: 'The VU views itself as an institution with complete conviction as a part of the ecumenical Christian tradition and has the mission, among others, of keeping this tradition alive. It is clear that the present population of staff and students stand only partially in that tradition. The values project should lead to an open exchange of values and opinions through which the ecumenical Christian tradition is also defined more clearly. In the project, which has a better communication of values in view, the VU goal therefore functions not as a moral obligation, but as a guideline and a challenge in the educational process relative to values communication. The accomplishment of a transparency of the ideological influence on scientific theories, practices and concepts is thus considered to be the most important result that can be pursued by means of the project.

The subsequent phase of the values project can make an important contribution to the creation of a clear profile of the VU as an academic institution for education and research. The tradition of Philosophical Education and the traditional involvement with problems of faith and society can receive a new stimulus by the project. At the same time it must be understood that an improvement in the quality of education in values communication does not tolerate an exclusively (Protestant) Christian composition or design. Values communication requires openness and respect for values pluralism, so students and instructors can broaden their scientific attitude to include ideological and philosophical decisions upon which they can reflect in a critical manner.'

[52] De Groof, J. and Friess, B., 'Opportunities and limitations for a European education policy', *European Journal of Education Law and Policy*, vol. 1, nrs 1–2.

> Universities must want to be more than a more or less random collection of disciplines and specialists. Universities must also want to be more than a group of isolated ivory towers. A university must strive for a certain social homogeneity and must want to really be an academic community of students, instructors and researchers. A university must first of all be a collegial context in which one is proud to work together toward the renewal of bases of knowledge. Crucial for this are mutual trust, communication and co-operation. Only on the basis of these can a university take the next steps in its development. Because to take the next steps, choices must be made, certainly in a university on a scale such as ours.[53]

I might also refer to an – also in this regard – unimpeachable source: Karel Tavernier wrote: 'The greater the decentralisation, the greater the necessity becomes to write explicit decentralization rules that define the limits for the decentralised decisions.'

The decentralized model, as established in the statutes or the charter and the organigram, may never obscure the final responsibility of the institution.[54]

This is also the debate that is being conducted in most of the *East European countries*: a separate faculty by itself can indeed not be called a 'University'.[55]

[53] *De nieuwe academische collegialiteit.* A speech given upon acceptance of the office of Rector-Magnificus of the Twente university, 13 January 1997.

Previously he rightly pointed out the danger of fragmentation: 'Independent academic units limit themselves to scientific communication with like-minded specialists outside their own institution and have no need for a discussion within the university. In addition to this, in our present universities to an increasing degree a non-intervention mentality seems to be coming into existence. Referring to the unavoidable tendency towards increased specialization and emic collegiality, scientists recoil from measuring each others' science. Each individual and each group has, according to the implicit reasoning, the right to a specialization of its own and collegiality forbids, as long as others do not interfere with my work, that I should interfer with their work' (Keller, 1983, p. 37). But with this approach, academic collegiality will be completely eroded away and any call for organizational autonomy and academic freedom lacks credibility. A collegiality that causes all discourse to cease may not wear the designation 'academic'.

[54] This rule, however, may not place a mortgage on the final responsibility of the institution's organizational management. Regarding the controversy about the force of the advice of the faculty/departmental council *versus* the decision-making autonomy of the Board of Directors (as organizational authority): see the judgement of the Council of State, and our comments in T.O.R.B., 1997–1998, nr 2.

[55] *Cf* the reports of several review commissions of the Council of Europe.

(d) *The unfulfilled promise on the part of the university: that of multidisciplinarity. Also room for a new 'scepticism'*

21. May a consideration also be allowed as an extension of the above? Attention has already been drawn repeatedly to the inability of the University to organize scientific research in a multidisciplinary manner, as well as integrating the instruction with more multi-disciplinary perspectives, possibly by organizing special educational sections.

European history is largely the story of the difficult dialogue between the various approaches to reality: mythology and religion, the criticism of philosophy, the emergence of the exact sciences.

The story of this discussion formed Western culture; an outstanding result of the confrontation of various approaches is the University.

The modern time, the *Enlightenment*, claimed that the age of religion would be replaced by the age of science.

In a poem, Goethe, declared *Prometheus* to be the herald of human autonomy, who had finished off deity, and I quote:

Hier sitz ich, forme Menschen
Nach meinem Bilde,
Ein Geschlecht, das mir gleich sei,
Zu leiden, zu weinen,
Zu genießen und zu freuen sich,
Und dein nich zu achten,
Wie ich!
Johann Wolfgang von Goethe, 1773

'Here I sit, forming men
In my image,
A race to resemble me:
To suffer, to weep,
To enjoy, to be glad –
And never to heed you,
Like me!'
Translated by Michael Hamburger,
in Goethe, Selected Poems,
edited by Christopher Middleton, 1983

Our time, and post-modernism, has radical criticism of such one-sidedness.

There is no longer room for one story. The sciences are developing alongside each other.

Gradually the understanding is growing that the historical responsibility of mankind – the disunity of mankind also has its limitations – requires a *dialogue* among divergent sciences. Crossing boundaries. Interdisciplinary. A coherent perception of the individual and society, an integrated world view. And this is demanding. Much more so than what is usually required in our academic centres. It requires on the one hand *openness*: the creation of space to allow interpolation *and* an interest in areas of study in other sciences.

Not accidental, but structured. Not without obligation, but engaged. A characteristic claimed to have been given by Christianity, namely, the ability to 'deny oneself', to put oneself into perspective.

Meanwhile, science itself has given rise to that purpose of dialogue. No scientist can escape confrontation with the findings of other areas of learning, unless he wants to end up in an *ethical vacuum.*

To a certain extent there is even a need for some scepticism about science and technology. In his little book,[56] Max Wildiers points out that in the team who developed the *atomic bomb* in secret at Los Alamos no one had been given the assignment to reflect on the consequences of the whole endeavour.

In his essay[57] Wildiers writes somewhat provocatively – as all scientists ought to do at times – that 'the technological project is willed to be one-sided, and to completely ignore mankind, all that is humane, and all the riches of the emotional realm'.

On the other hand, it needs to be asked whether the humanities can carry out their task with relevance and credibility without actively helping to determine the agenda of scientific criticism.

Or to formulate it by means of a witticism based on the statement of Cardinal Danneels: if the practice of science wants to take up an ethical position in the next century, it must be interdisciplinarily conceived and consulted.

No institution can ignore the discussion about the implementation of the new *synthesis* between the exact sciences and the humanities in the University and in science. How the education of students and teachers, how the exercise of science itself, will be affected by it, and finally, how society can be made more humane.

Neither can the task of giving concrete form to the multidisciplinary perspective in research and also in education be ignored by the government and its satellite institutions. How, for example, can multidisciplinary research be given a chance in the light of the present 'compartmentalization' of the FWO commissions?

(e) *And finally, several conclusions relative to the government*

22. What does institutional autonomy mean for the government? In a few brief strokes:

(1) First, a troublesome task for the government which, as governing body,

[56] *Afscheid van Los Alamos, Notities uit het nucleaire tijdvak*, Kapellen, 1989.

[57] *Het verborgen leven van de cultuur*, Leuven, 1988, p. 43.

must require quality care and also must promote, as a branch of the legislative authority, the *quality of the legislation.*

This will no doubt require the acceptance of a first suggestion: a little calm on the legislative front ... The general university decree of 12 June 1991 has already been modified fifteen times (plus two adaptations as a result of annulments by the court of arbitration); some articles six times (namely the most sensitive: financing, the 80–85% rule, and ... the cumulation regulation).[58]

According to established Belgian custom, some decrees are issued just a few weeks before the new academic year (such as the general practitioner decree).

I admit that the all-time record has not yet been reached of the School Pact legislation (with 60 legislative modifications in 30 years, and some articles, 20 times) but there *is* a need for legal security.[59]

Making modifications too soon to modifications that have already been modified too soon is at right angles to long-term planning – a *novum* in the above-mentioned decree.

But a consequence of this is that the universities must also resist the urge for a while to run to the government with lists of requests for modifications to the decree, and must limit themselves to testing any objections of the auditor's office for their judicial relevance.

(2) When there is new legislation, the government itself must employ the *subsidiarity* test.

Only allow what is essential to remain the object of central regulation, without however placing a mortgage on the mobility of academics and students, on the common Flemish and later European educational space.

The Flemish government should also submit a request for the modification of Art. 24 § 5 of the Constitution, which has been interpreted by the Council of State as follows: everything that has to do with education, can only be regulated by decree. From now on the decree needs to be able to limit itself to the basic pattern, and the large majority of the regulation can be looked after by decisions of the Flemish government.

At the same time, an old promise must be kept: what can be done just as well by the universities themselves, can be given a norm and does not have to be done by the government. Uniformity is only required if it has to do with basic rules. This raises the problem again of the preparatory editing of the

[58] See also Verstegen, R., 'De onderwijswetgeving in Vlaanderen. Een overzicht', in Verstegen, R. *et al.*, *Actuele vraagstukken van onderwijsrecht, Cahiers voor Onderwijsrecht en Onderwijsbeleid,* 1997, nr 2, p. 27.

[59] See De Groof, J., 'Onderwijs en regelgeving, Enkele notities'; Lecture before the 'Education' Commission of the Flemish Council on 22 January 1997, T.O.R.B., 1996–97, nr 4, pp. 201–208.

university decree and the interpretations it will be given later, in the final 'instance' also by the Court of Arbitration.

(3) Another pressing point: the government should apply the *coherence principle* itself. In this regard the current distribution of authority sometimes plays tricks on the universities.

I am referring, among other things, to the discrepancies within the autonomous sphere of authority of the Community between university policy and scientific policy; for example, with regard to financing, spearhead policy, and it is probably premature to cite the example of the 'Flemish Institute of Biotechnology'. In that regard the proposition can already be formulated that planning for academic education cannot ignore the management contracts between the Flemish government and the scientific institutes.

There are certainly discrepancies between the federal and the Flemish level – manifested by the intolerable dividing up of powers relative to scientific policy (have a look at the incoherence in respect to the regulation of the so-called 'Dehousse doctoral scholarships' and in respect to (university) development cooperation.

The assumption should be made that the next coalition agreement will end the debate in this area, to the advantage of (the primacy of) an intrinsic coherence with the authorized academic policy.

6. Two provocative propositions

23. This brief, somewhat polemic contribution will be concluded with two suggestions.

First: American literature shows that the plea of a university or college sounds unbelievable if it demands independence *both* from the government *and* from the user, the student.

The *accountability obligation* to the community and to the student body needs to be further refined. To a certain extent, the comment by Williams is justified: 'Decisions about higher education by any individual are equally irreversible and made only once.' He adds to this: 'The essential information feedback on an efficient market is absent.'[60]

'Final attainment levels' or 'development goals' as introduced by the legislator for non-higher education, will not be capable of being obtained for academic education just like that. It is written in the stars, however, that professional profiles and field of study goals for education at the academic level are being drawn up and the universities will also have to define their general and their specific goals.

[60] Williams, G., 'Higher Education', in Flude, M. and Hammer, M. (eds), *The Education Reform Act 1988: Its origins and implications*, Lewes, Falmer Press, 1990, p. 259.

And is it not to be recommended that universities make themselves more accessible for the professional groups who – in one way or another – will pass judgement on the quality of the education of the graduates? It is certainly remarkable in this area how one of the sections of the basic report with a view to the reformation of higher education in The Netherlands, *Hoger Onderwijs: Autonomie en Kwaliteit*[61] remains unread, and this in contradistinction to most of the other conclusions.

On the other hand, the national and international clubs of industrialists must be invited to convert their rather noncommittal attitude, as is recognizable in several reports and lectures, with regard to the future of higher education into a greater engagement.

Why should not, for example, the splendid column of executives, who have a seat in the management bodies to represent the outside world, be asked collectively to clothe their *commitment* with a greater thirst for action? A 'Parliament of Higher Education', with at the top of the agenda: participation on the part of the socio-economic environment in the financing of the operation, investments and research; also a discussion about the academic profiles and about a strategy for continued education; possibly also a discussion of some type of distribution of tasks among the laboratories ...

24. Second suggestion: Universities and higher technical schools are — according to the specialized literature – *complex professional bureaucratic organizations*. They must exercise their administrative freedom expertly while taking their own culture into consideration.

And one of their tasks is the development of techniques for the purpose of strengthening their own powers of management, especially at the moment when the fixed costs are too high and the institution is too involved with its own viability. The paradox of universities and higher technical schools is that this occurs at a time when higher education must face new challenges.

This also includes mapping out statistical management information, policy indicators and basic data for objective self-evaluation, necessary for a consistent administration.

Might consideration be given to starting a programme at the macro level that makes systematic *comparison* possible, not with a view to irrelevant 'ranking' – not in accordance with the present practices of the uninspiring American game (what is the rank by the way of the *McDonald University* among the 3,500 universities and colleges?)[62] – but with a view to the detection of strengths and weaknesses?

[61] Tweede Kamer der Staten-Generaal (Lower house of The Netherlands), 1985–1986, nr 19 253, 1–2, p. 36.

[62] See the somewhat critical observations and comparisons relative to personnel policy as a result of the *American Myth*, in our above-mentioned article in *Personeelsbeleid aan de Vlaamse Universiteiten*, pp. 49–52; supplemented by 'kanttekeningen' in T.O.R.B., 1997–1998, nr 4.

This could be done via the *incentive funding method*, as advocated, among others, by Minister Van Den Bossche, a well-known practice in other countries. In Scandinavia, for example, 10% of the whole scientific policy budget is allotted to the institutions that score best that year.

Also in this area the Department of Education and Scientific Research could take the initiative.

7. The final conclusion

25. Flemish higher education is subject to the policy that is found in all of Europe since the beginning of the 1980s. *Budget cuts* and planning, *accountability* and quality control, a regional entrenchment and an openness to the socio-economic environment, and above all autonomy for the institution and the formulation of questions regarding the task of the government.

Only conclusions were drawn somewhat more slowly in our area, especially by the institutions themselves.

The Flemish Community (now) no longer has 'the luxury of time'.

A strategy for higher education will have to rest on a partnership between autonomous institutions and a dynamic government. They are 'condemned to each other'.[63]

The conclusion: both are bound to each other in their servitude to society, but the community will demand an accounting as to how autonomy is utilized and whether the government's approach was too lax.

[63] Cohen, J., 'De ongemakkelijke relatie tussen Universiteit en Overheid', *Tijdschrift voor Onderwijsrecht en Onderwijsbeleid*, 1995–1996, nr 3, p. 156.

ANTONIO EMBID IRUJO

University Autonomy in Spain

(I) General introduction. The extensive doctrine of the constitutional tribunal on this question

University autonomy is recognized in Art. 27.10 of the Spanish Constitution (SC) as an essential attribute of universities. Thus, it is a constitutional concept which has proved fundamental for shaping the legal system for universities. Particularly interesting is the considerable intervention by the Constitutional Tribunal (CT) to define this concept and it is worth listing, as a start, the judgments handed down on this subject, and the matters treated, as a demonstration of this considerable intervention and also of the versatility of the concept.

Thus the fundamental judgment was No. 26/1987 of 27 February 1987, dealing with an unconstitutionality appeal lodged by the Basque Government against the Universities Reform Act, which defined the concept in legal terms, and far-reaching changes resulted. With this judgment as a basis, the CT has handed down others based on the fundamental aspects contained therein, and these have served at the same time to refine the concept: for example CTJ (Constitutional Tribunal Judgement) No. 55/1989 of 23 February 1989 (appeal for legal protection lodged by the University of Santiago de Compostela), No. 106/1990 of 6 June 1990 (on various questions of unconstitutionality regarding Act No. 5/1989 of 4 May 1989 concerning the reorganization of the university system in the Canary Islands), No. 130/1991 of 6 June 1991 (on a request for an injunction lodged by private individuals against a sentence handed down by the Valencia Court of Appeal concerning a decision by the University of Valencia to modify its coat of arms), No. 187/1991 of 3 October 1991 (on a request for an injunction against a High Court judgment concerning an appeal against the decision taken by the Autonomous University of Madrid to include the subject of Catholic Doctrine and Morality and its Pedagogy as an optional subject in its syllabus), No. 131/1996 of 11 July 1996 (on the powers

Walter Berka, Jan de Groof and Hilde Penneman (eds.), Autonomy in Education, 201–209.

of the State and the Autonomous Communities in the matter of the creation and recognition of universities) and No. 75/1997 of 21 April 1997 (on the use by the University of Valencia of the term 'Catalan' to refer to the co-official language of this Autonomous Community). Not to mention that alongside the legal process, there has been an ongoing labour in writings on the subject, some examples of which are shown at the end of this paper.

(II) University autonomy as a fundamental right. The holder of the right

There were two options, from a legal point of view, when deciding on the legal nature of university autonomy: as a fundamental right or an institutional guarantee. It is true that the institutional guarantee option would have meant constitutional protection for the university institution, but on a small scale, in that the shaping of the autonomy would have been in the hands of the legislators who, although acting within restrictions deriving from the Constitution, would have enjoyed a great deal of liberty in the designing of the specific content of the guarantee.

Conversely, to talk of a 'fundamental right' implies acknowledging that a subjective right is held by the Universities which in turn means that there is potential for legal recourse against any violation of the essential content of this right, as it stands in the Constitution, that may be committed by public authorities. Thus the latitude enjoyed by the ordinary legislator for the shaping of university autonomy is not so great, due to the existence of an essential content which, without exception, must be respected.

Of course, there are those who are sceptical about whether there really are any differences between a constitutional guarantee and a fundamental right. They maintain that a constitutional guarantee possesses a basic ingredient, immune to the legislator, which could coincide, *mutatis mutandis*, with the essential content of fundamental rights. However, it should be remembered that fundamental rights are protected by, among other things, the power to lodge an application for protection before the CT, something which, for those institutions protected only by a constitutional guarantee (such as local administrations in Spanish law), would meet with no success.

The CT resolves this dichotomy by opting for the configuration of university autonomy as a fundamental right of the Universities. For this, it uses various arguments, such as the actual location of the precept: Art. 27.10 appears in the first heading of the SC referring to fundamental rights; it also talks of the grammatical sense of the words used in Art. 27.10, which is not the same as that used by the SC for local autonomy. It refers to the drawing up of the SC, from which the drafter's intention in favour of its configuration as a fundamental right may be inferred. Finally, the object of university autonomy, which is the preservation of academic freedom or freedom of learning (which comprises the freedoms of teaching, research and study) is understood, both from an individual point of view (academic freedom referred to in Art. 20 SC) and a collective point of view, the university institution itself. From this collective aspect, it seems appropriate to speak of a fundamental right of the University, in the same way that there is a fundamental right (academic freedom) at an individual level.

This fundamental right belongs to the University as such. It does not belong to each one of its members nor to the universities as a whole. The holder of the right is the university community but, in the words of Leguina Villa,

> this does not mean that the CT has intended to transfer the ownership of this right from the University as an institution to a new legal entity which would be what might be called the university community. What it does mean is that, if we consider autonomy as a right, there is an identification or hypostasis of the university institution with its own indispensable or irreplaceable element, which is, in effect, its own academic community.

Article 27.10 of the SC, after recognizing university autonomy, states that it will be 'in the terms established by law'. This is a remit for the law-makers to define the content of university autonomy which, strictly speaking, places university autonomy within the framework of fundamental rights legally sanctioned. This gives the law-maker scope to create different modes of University, which however should respect the requirements of the essential content of this fundamental right, which consist of the guaranteeing of academic freedom and which, as far as the CT is concerned, are contained in the specification of University discretionary powers in Art. 3 of the University Reform Act (which I shall be dealing with in point 4). If the law-maker – or any other public authority – did not respect this essential content, this would give rise to the deploying of the constitutional remedies available, among which would be the appeal for protection, a resource which is possessed by the Universities. However, once the law-maker has had his say, for anything that he has not decided on, the University, in the words of the CT, 'has, in principle, full decision-making powers'.

Once the CT has definitely established the nature of university autonomy and its general configuration, it goes on to apply its consequences to various regulations which the University Reform Act – the object of the unconstitutionality appeal referred to previously – has decreed in the matter of University Statutes, Departments, the Management Board, the teaching staff, students and so on.

(III) University autonomy in the University Reform Act

Article 3 of the University Reform Act, after establishing the legal status of universities and their functions on a basis of autonomy, specifies the content of this autonomy. For the basic legislation of the Universities, autonomy comprises the drawing up of their Statutes and other internal regulations (power to make statutes and power to make regulations); the selection, appointment and dismissal of their managerial and administrative bodies; the drawing up, approval and management of their budgets (power to make budgets) and the administration of their assets; the establishment and modifications of their staffs; the selection, training and promotion of their research personnel and their administrative and services staff as well as the terms and conditions of their employment; the drawing up and approval of teaching and research syllabuses; the creation of specific structures to act as back-up for research and teaching; the admission of students, the rules governing their staying at the university and the verification of their knowledge; the granting of qualifications and diplomas; the setting up of relationships with other academic, cultural or scientific institutions, whether in Spain or abroad, and so on.

Any one of these powers described above are legislated for in the University Reform Act which at the same time may make reference to other rules of the legal system (for example, in relation to the administration of assets, Art. 53.2 of the University Reform Act states that this will be within the framework of general legal operations). What Art. 3 of the University Reform Act is saying, then, is that the University, as a consequence of its autonomy, must necessarily have control of the material aspects listed in Art. 3, but the amount of control is governed by the University Reform Act itself or its development or referral regulations (for example, there are regulations on the selection of teaching staff in the University Reform Act which clearly imply the non-exclusivity of the University in the selection process, but do imply its necessary involvement in it).

What is important to emphasize is that the outcome of TCJ No. 26/1987 of 27 February 1987, on the principle of university autonomy, is that Art. 3 of the University Reform Act does comply with the Constitution, by describing it as a quintessential element of the principle of university autonomy. In fact, in later constitutional legal proceedings – TCJ No. 196/1990, which I shall be quoting later – Art. 3 of the University Reform Act is considered to be 'a parameter of constitutionality' in that university autonomy is a legally configured right and requires the necessary and indispensable involvement of the law-maker. This identification as a parameter of constitutionality resulted, in the TCJ quoted, in the confrontation of Art. 3 of the University Reform Act with the Act brought before the Constitutional Tribunal (an Act of the Canary Islands Parliament on university reorganization in the Canary Islands which involved the creation of a new University), as a process to assert the respect for university autonomy shown by the Act in question.

(IV) University autonomy and the creation of new universities

The principle of autonomy might be seen as excessively ill-defined and subject to the vagaries firstly of the law-maker and subsequently of the Constitutional Tribunal which deals with the hypothetical violation of the principle's essential content. Therefore, it has been necessary to explain exactly what this principle is.

This task was undertaken by the Constitutional Tribunal in TCJ No. 26/1987 of 27 February 1987 and subsequently followed up by others. In TCJ No. 196/1990 of 6 June 1990, the Tribunal was able to confront the principle of university autonomy with the creation, as the result of the splitting up of an existing university, of the University of Las Palmas de Gran Canaria, evolving from the University of La Laguna, by Act of the Canary Islands Parliament. This question, although formally referring to the Canary Islands case, due to the potential duplication, at any time, of its content (as was the case later with the creation in 1996, by Act of the Valencian Parliament, of the University of Elche, evolving from the University of Alicante), is sufficiently interesting for me to quote now the arguments referring to university autonomy in the judgment. It was in this judgment, also, that the Constitutional Tribunal used Art. 3 of the University Reform Act as a 'parameter of constitutionality' to confront the precepts of the Canary Islands Act.

The Constitutional Tribunal's procedure was to examine, firstly, general complaints of violation of university autonomy which would affect the very nucleus of the constitutionally protected fundamental right, and then to go on to the confrontation of the legal configuration of the right, Art. 3 of the University Reform Act. With regard to the general aspect and the Tribunal's allegations of unconstitutionality, the Constitutional Tribunal declared that the principle of university autonomy had not been violated by the setting up of the university in question, because that autonomy

> does not include the right of universities to possess one or more specific centres, thereby making difficult or placing conditions on any decisions which may be the responsibility of the State or the Autonomous Communities in the question of the defining and organisation of the university system as a whole.

This is because, as the Constitutional Tribunal clearly states,

> the Universities' autonomy does not give them a sort of 'intellectual property' resulting from the number of centres, teachers and students which at any given time may make up these universities, since their autonomy is merely at the service of academic freedom in teaching and research, which is necessarily carried out within the framework of the effective availability of staff and materials for each University.

Similarly, the Constitutional Tribunal examined the possible violation of the principle of university autonomy as a result of the loss of teaching staff which could arise or from the point of view of the loss of property as a result of the assignation of assets to the new University. In both cases it was decided that the legislator had a free hand in the creation of a University which logically included the assignation of assets which was not discretionary but linked to the educational services to be provided by the new University. In addition, with regard to teachers, without wishing to make general declarations which would hold for all teachers, there was only one change to the statutes which would now occur with the new University.

The Constitutional Tribunal then went on to rule on the possible violation of some of the subsections of Art. 3 of the University Reform Act (the setting up or modification of staff, the selection, training and promotion of teaching and research personnel, the drawing up and approval of teaching and research syllabuses and the creation of specific structures to act as back-up to research and teaching), and it decided that there was no such violation. The creation of a new University does not prevent either of the two from setting up their staff, selecting their personnel or approving their syllabuses, and, with regard to the creation of specific structures, the organizational power reflected in this principle – and here the Constitutional Tribunal recalls its CTJ No. 55/1989 – refers to structures considered by the University Reform Act not to be basic, never centres which would be basic structures whose re-inscription could perfectly well be undertaken by the Act. In conclusion, both from the point of view of its constitutional content and of its legal configuration, the right of university autonomy had not been violated.

(V) Limits and powers of university autonomy: the national university system and the field of unrestricted decision-taking by university bodies. Autonomy and legal control

There are several powers and limits of university autonomy which may be inferred from the explanation given up to now. In Constitutional Law there have been new data which, due to their significance, I would like to examine very briefly here. It is possible that one aspect of university autonomy, the approval of syllabuses, could be limited by the existence of a national university system, and therefore the State could establish in its regulations a lowest common denominator for all Universities (CTJ No. 187/1991 of 3 October 1991).

Another instance was the ruling established by CTJ No. 130/1991 of 6 June 1991, which set out to establish the relationship between university autonomy and a basic principle of the Rule of Law, the judicial control of the activities of the Public Authorities, wherein the application of university autonomy was restricting the scope of this judicial control. In this case, a Court had annulled a decision taken by the University of Valencia to modify its coat of arms. On appeal by the University, the Constitutional Tribunal was to reaffirm the University of Valencia's decision, and declared at the same time that it was not possible for judicial control to interfere in – or usurp – the principle of unrestricted decision-taking by the University arizing from its autonomy. The Constitutional Tribunal set forth the case with these words:

> What is at stake in these proceedings is not so much the scope or material content of university autonomy, as the range of the judicial control of a specific decision taken by the said institution while exercising its autonomy

and concluded the judgment with a paragraph which I quote here in its entirety, both for its general relevance to the topic of this paper – university autonomy – as well as for its subsequent application in establishing the control – or restrictions and even exemption from control – of other state bodies equally protected by constitutional autonomy clauses:

> In a democratic State governed by rule of law, which proclaims liberty and political pluralism to be supreme values in its system, the natural form of expression of the notion and content that society – in this case, the university community – sees in the public interest at any given time, when it is a question of the adoption of decisions involving options of a mainly political nature – such as those adopted by the University Senate in the name of the university community and while exercising its autonomy – this public interest is made up of the majority decision taken by representative bodies in public debate and by means of established legal procedures, whose observance is at all times subject to the control of the Judiciary and the Courts. The Judiciary and the Courts are also responsible for the legal review of the powers granted or acknowledged by the University Reform Act to the Universities, so that neither the law nor university autonomy are violated. Thus, this judicial control, on the one hand, must comply with the legal configuration of university autonomy without imposing limits against the will of the drafter of the University Reform Act, and on the other hand, must respect the essence of freedom of decision, a result of autonomy, which in each case may be considered the most convenient or adequate for the interests of the University; but what is not within the competence of the judicial body is to place the control of legality within the confines of the appropriateness of the decision freely taken while exercising that autonomy, and overstep those confines, as has happened in this case.

(VI) Final reflections

Finally, I should like to conclude with a series of questions which I feel to be of particular interest at the present time:

(a) *The relationship between university autonomy and university funding.*

In other words, it is impossible to exercise all the powers inherent in university autonomy without adequate funding. In particular, this problem poses some very significant questions at a time when the Autonomous Communities have now all been vested with responsibility for University matters, with the corresponding cash funding from central government, and the Autonomous Community Parliaments will from now on decide on the future funding of their universities: the same amount as now, or more or, even, less. The budgetary powers of the Parliaments and the autonomy of the autonomous body will no doubt find themselves in conflict with the constitutionally guaranteed university autonomy, especially when, as I say, the initial state funding was guaranteed.

(b) *The relationship of the Management Councils and the Universities, whether in Autonomous Communities recently vested with responsibility for their universities or those who have had this responsibility for some time.* This relationship has always been problematic from the time of its configuration by the University Reform Act and one need look no further than CTJ No. 26/1987 to be reminded of this, when the Constitutional Tribunal annulled some of the Articles of the University Reform Act for having provided the Management Council with powers which were considered to be within the realm of the autonomy of the university community. There is no doubt that in the future, the whole question of who is the holder of the right to university autonomy will have to be cleared up, avoiding the easy way out consisting of considering the Management Council to be part of the University itself, and therefore co-holder of the right of autonomy. This would back up CTJ No. 26/1987 which gave shape to the concept I have quoted of 'the university community' as something distinct – although a component – within the concept of the University.

(c) *The dialectic between the autonomy of a University and the fundamental rights of some of its members*, particularly the academic freedom of its teachers. Specifically, this will have repercussions in the organizational area (departmental structure, powers to establish teaching guidelines), and in relation to the students (power to decide freely on the format of exams etc.).

(d) *The structure of University centres and Autonomous Community powers to create Universities and to decide on the location of centres.* The Constitutional Tribunal has already dealt with these questions, deciding in favour of the Autonomous Community (in the case of the splitting up of the University of La Laguna) against the University. However, I believe that there are still some questions left unanswered, and in particular, that there are measures, which in theory could be adopted by the Public Authorities, which could have an effect on the 'image' of a particular University, on its historical background in some cases, and could violate an ongoing policy of investment and research, and these measures might be considered, I would go so far as to say, to be violators of the guarantee of each University, to such an extent that it might be considered a completely different University to the one it has evolved from if the decisions of the Autonomous Community Legislature or Government were to be adopted, and this could be contrary to the guaranteed fundamental right.

LITERATURE

Embid Irujo, A., 'La autonomía universitaria y la autonomía de las Comunidades Autónomas', RAP 146, 1998.

Leguina Villa, J., 'La autonomía universitaria en la jurisprudencia del Tribunal Constitucional, en *La autonomia universitaria*, Boletin de Informacion Universitaria n° 1, ed. Consejo de Universidades, Madrid, diciembre de 1989.

Lopez-Jurado Escribano, B., *La autonomía de las Universidades como derecho fundamental: La construcción del Tribunal Constitucional*, de. Civitas, Madrid, 1991.

Souviron Morenilla, J.M.ª, *La Universidad española. Claves de su definición y régimen jurídico institucional*, Valladolid, 1988.

Tardio Pato, J.M.ª, *El derecho de las Universidades Públicas españolas*, 2 vols, Barcelona, 1994.

NEVILLE HARRIS

The Autonomy of the Teacher: Education Law and Educational Standards in England and Wales

INTRODUCTION

> 'To a unique extent English teachers have the responsibility and the spur of freedom'.[1]

This statement, made just over 30 years ago, acknowledges the autonomy of teachers in England and Wales at that time. It reflects the fact that traditionally teachers have enjoyed considerable freedom in their professional role. Moreover, it acknowledges that while teachers have always had duties arizing specifically out of their contract of employment, the most important duty resting with the teacher is the *moral* responsibility to develop and inform the minds of the children and young people who will be the next generation of adult citizens, in an appropriate manner. These aspirational aims of teaching are reflected in general legal responsibilities of the State. For example, we have the long-standing duty of local educational authorities in England and Wales to

> contribute towards the spiritual, moral, mental and physical development of the community by securing that efficient primary education, secondary education and further education are available to meet the needs of the population of their area.[2]

Similarly, we have the duty of local education authorities, school governing bodies and head teachers to ensure that the curriculum 'promotes the spiritual, moral, cultural, mental and physical development of pupils at the school and

[1] Plowden, *Children and their Primary Schools, A Report of the Central Advisory Council for Education (England)* (London: HMSO, 1967), Vol. 1, p. 311.

[2] Education Act 1996, s. 13(1), formerly Education Act 1944, s. 7.

Walter Berka, Jan de Groof and Hilde Penneman (eds.), Autonomy in Education, 211–223.

of society'.[3] These responsibilities mirror those in Article 29 of the UN Convention on the Rights of the Child: that the education of the child should be directed at, amongst other things, 'the development of the child's personality, talents and mental and physical abilities to their fullest potential'; the Article also refers specifically to other values such as racial tolerance and social responsibility and to 'the preparation of the child for responsible life in a free society'. Although not mentioned specifically in connection with the statutory duties in England and Wales referred to above, teachers have acted as de facto agents of the state or public authorities in this context.

Traditionally, teachers' pedagogical freedom went unchallenged: there was not perceived to be a conflict between the autonomy of the teacher and the power and responsibility of the State or the rights of the parent or the child. In consequence, the role of the teacher was largely unregulated. However, in recent years the legal and professional accountability of teachers in England and Wales has increased significantly and has been associated with a dramatic decline in their autonomy. In this paper, I will examine the various legal and policy issues surrounding the declining autonomy of the teacher and will assess the various initiatives designed to restore the status of teachers and enhance teacher recruitment, which has been in decline.[4]

Teacher autonomy under English law

In England, the legal status of the teaching profession has always been an ambiguous one. While teachers are employees whose conditions of employment are mostly laid down via legislation,[5] they have always retained a degree of independence over certain matters. For example, since the Education Act 1944,[6] the law has protected their religious freedom (a protection almost unique in England, although becoming universal following the enactment of the Human Rights Act 1998,[7] but a protection traditionally afforded with 'caution' by the

[3] Education Act 1996, s. 352(1)(a), (3) and (4).

[4] The legal status of head teachers is somewhat different to that of other teachers because their roles are more clearly defined under education law in general and their management functions, and the related powers and duties, are linked to those of governing bodies of schools. In this paper, therefore, I am addressing the position of ordinary classroom teachers, who of course constitute the overwhelming majority of the teaching profession.

[5] The Teacher's Pay and Conditions Act 1991 and, currently, the Education (School Teachers' Pay and Conditions) Order 1998 and the *School Teachers' Pay and Conditions Document*.

[6] Section 30.

[7] This will in effect require laws and actions to conform to, or be construed in accordance with, the European Convention on Human Rights.

English courts in the educational context).[8] Most teachers have a right not to participate in religious worship at school and not to give religious education there. Moreover, they are protected against discrimination on the grounds of their religious opinions in relation to such matters as promotion to senior posts.[9]

The question of teachers' autonomy arises in a variety of contexts which will now be discussed.

Discipline

Teachers have also enjoyed some autonomy over disciplinary matters. Their power to assert disciplinary authority over pupils is said to derive not so much from the implied delegation of parental disciplinary authority (the *in loco parentis* principle) but rather from their independent professional status as teachers. A report commissioned by the Government in 1989 recommended that this authority should be underpinned by a statutory right.[10] Although this has not happened, the power to use reasonable force in restraining disruptive pupils has recently been incorporated into statute.[11] This power does not apply to corporal punishment, which will shortly cease to be legally sanctioned in any school in England and Wales.[12] Overall, disciplinary authority within schools is hierarchical. The governing body has a duty to ensure that the school has a policy for promoting good behaviour and discipline among pupils, whilst the head teacher is required to determine the measures, including rules, to secure these objectives and to determine the standard of behaviour which shall be deemed acceptable.[13] Furthermore, only the head teacher may exercise the ultimate sanction of exclusion of a pupil from school – whether for a fixed

[8] As long ago as 1978 an English court referred to Art. 9 of the Convention in 1978, in a case concerned with the right of a Moslem teacher to attend religious services away from school on Fridays, during school hours. By a 2-1 majority the Court of Appeal held that his rights, while protected under the statute, could not prevail over those of the children and local education authority: *Ahmad v. Inner London Education Authority* [1978] 1 All ER 574: 'So, whilst upholding religious freedom to the full, I would suggest that it should be applied with caution, especially having regard to the setting in which it is sought' (Lord Denning, Master of the Rolls, at 578a–b).

[9] School Standards and Framework Act 1988, ss. 59 and 60.

[10] Elton, *Discipline in Schools* (London: HMSO, 1989).

[11] Education Act 1996, section 550A, added by section 4 of the Education Act 1997.

[12] School Standards and Framework Act 1998, section 131, laying down a new section 548 in the Education Act 1996.

[13] School Standards and Framework Act 1998, section 61.

term or permanently.[14] The ordinary teacher must therefore exercise his or her disciplinary authority within this regulated framework.

The curriculum

It is in the area of the school curriculum that teachers' traditional autonomy has been most weakened. Paul Meredith and I explained some time ago[15] how the post-1979 Conservative Government took control of the school curriculum and curbed teachers' autonomy in order, as they saw it, to prevent the progressive and egalitarian ideals which were being put into practice at that time from continuing to drag down educational standards. Even before the introduction of the National Curriculum, which has been phased in since 1989, legislation was passed to require the teaching of sex education to be aimed at encouraging pupils 'to have due regard to moral considerations and the value of family life'.[16] Also, in direct response to the alleged political bias that had entered teaching, legislation required political issues to be covered in the classroom in a 'balanced' way.[17]

The National Curriculum is, of course, even more prescriptive. The Secretary of State is empowered to prescribe the subjects to be studied (currently there are up to 10 in England, 11 in Wales). Although statute prohibits him from specifying the amount of time schools should spend on individual subjects, he can and does prescribe the 'attainment targets' which pupils must work towards, the programmes of study to be followed and the assessment arrangements for determining the ability of pupils by the end of each of the four 'key stages' between the ages of 5–16.[18] Reforms in 1994–1995 reduced the content of the National Curriculum a little, giving schools more flexibility by slimming down the compulsory curriculum, mostly outside the core subjects, and simplifying the assessment scales. Since 1997 the Labour Government has tightened up some areas of the curriculum by recommending that each school devotes a structured hour per day to literacy for all primary school pupils from September 1998 and has issued draft homework guidelines. A numeracy strategy, similar to the literacy strategy, is likely to be implemented fairly soon. The Government's aim is to ensure that by 2002 80% of 11 year olds reach the expected standard in English (only 56% did so in 1996) and that 75% of them reach the standard expected for their age in mathematics (compared with 55%

14 *Ibid.*, section 64.

15 N. Harris and P. Meredith, 'Success against the odds?: the legislative response to under-achievement in urban schools in England and Wales', paper at ELA Conference on urban education, Rotterdam, December 1997.

16 Education (No. 2) Act 1986, section 46; now section 403 of the Education Act 1996.

17 Education (No. 2) Act 1986, s. 45; now section 407 of the Education Act 1996.

18 Education Act 1996, Part V, formerly in Part I of the Education Reform Act 1988.

in 1996).[19] To make room for more time to be spent on the core subjects, primary school teachers have been informed that they will be able to reduce the time spent on art, geography, history, music and physical education. Baseline assessment schemes are also being introduced by law;[20] they will provide for assessment of children's abilities when they start primary school so that their progress can be monitored over the years. The Government hopes that they will facilitate measurement of the effectiveness of schooling.

Prior to its introduction, the Department for Education and Science promised that the National Curriculum would represent a 'framework' rather than a 'straitjacket' for teachers.[21] Yet at the start of the National Curriculum in 1989 many teachers 'felt that their freedom had been lost and their professionalism compromised'[22] and rightly claim now that the National Curriculum has had a constraining influence. Moreover, an equally strong challenge to teachers' professional autonomy has resulted from the power and willingness of the Secretary of State for Education to ignore the recommendations of teachers (including the statutory advisory bodies on which teachers were represented) when determining the curriculum, as happened on several occasions under the previous Government.[23]

Teachers are also subject to the curriculum policy for the school, whose determination is a matter within the authority of the local education authority and school governing body. Teachers are represented on the governing body, but will always be in the minority. In a majority of schools the head teacher has statutory responsibility for the determination and organization of the secular curriculum but must have regard to the governing body's and LEA's policy.[24]

Administration and bureaucracy

Another problem has been the administrative burden placed on teachers through various requirements on record-keeping and reporting under the National Curriculum. Indeed, the pressures faced by teachers in England and

[19] Department for Education and Employment, *Excellence in Schools*, Cm 3861 (London: The Stationery Office, 1997), Chapter 2.

[20] Education Act 1997, ss. 15–18; and the Education (Baseline Assessment) (England) Regulations 1988 (S.I. 1988 No. 1551).

[21] DES/Welsh Office, *The National Curriculum 5–16 – A Consultation Document* (DES/Welsh Office, 1987), p. 5.

[22] D. Hofkins, 'After the Act – a decade of change' (1998) *TES Primary*, 17 November, pp. 5–6.

[23] N. Harris, *Law and Education: Regulation, Consumerism and the Education System* (London: Sweet and Maxwell, 1993), pp. 62–63 and 204–205.

[24] Education Act 1996, ss. 370–374.

Wales have brought them into conflict with the State.[25] This is exemplified by the *Wandsworth* case in 1993.[26] Here, the second-largest teaching union balloted its members to determine whether they should boycott work in connection with the National Curriculum tests. The union complained that the National Curriculum had led to a 'massively increase workload' and that teachers were working an average of 52 hours per week, well beyond the contractual hours (35 per week). The local education authority argued that the teachers' complaint concerned the National Curriculum assessment process rather than workload per se: in other words, the authority complained that the teachers were using this dispute for political ends, to challenge the National Curriculum, and were not engaged in a legitimate trade dispute such as would make their boycott lawful. The Court of Appeal disagreed, regarding the teachers' primary concern as relating to workload.

This has not been the end of the matter, however. The teaching unions have continued to raise concerns about the bureaucracy associated with the National Curriculum and other areas of responsibility, such as providing for children with special educational needs. In 1997 the newly-elected Labour Government said that 'to give teachers time to focus on the important task of raising standards, we need to root out any unnecessary bureaucracy'; it proposed to set up a working group of teachers, education authorities and others to look into the issue.[27] One important aspect of this initiative was the fact that teachers were among the representative groups being asked to find solutions and make recommendations. The working group's final report, published in January 1998,[28] called for a systematic review of the administrative demands that the Government places on teachers (often on a statutory basis). The report also proposed a pilot scheme of reduced bureaucracy. The Department for Education and Employment published its guidance in June 1998.[29] Unfortunately, while it offers some practical suggestions, the guidance is weak and at times patronizing: for example, it advises that 'keeping documents short is a valuable discipline for both the author and the readers'. Furthermore, in

[25] D. Lawton, *Education and Politics in the 1990s: Conflict or Consensus?* (London: Falmer, 1992).

[26] *The Mayor and Burgesses of the London Borough of Wandsworth v. National Association of Schoolmasters and Union of Women Teachers* [1994] ELR 170.

[27] Department for Education and Employment, *Excellence in Schools* Cm 3681 (London: Stationery Office, 1998), Chapter 5, para. 30.

[28] Working Group on Reducing the Administrative Burden on Teachers, *Final Report* (London: DfEE, 1998). Management consultants conducted a study for the Group: Coopers and Lybrand, *Reducing the Bureaucratic Burden on Teachers*, Research Report 41 (London: DfEE, 1998).

[29] Department for Education and Employment, Circular 2/98, *Reducing the Bureaucratic Burden on Teachers* (1998).

many places it merely reports that the Government is still considering how to reduce the bureaucratic burden. Nevertheless, the guidance offers some commitments which have pleased teachers, although teachers are also looking for positive action by government.

One of the areas of particular concern to teachers, which is also referred to in the guidance, has been the inspection of schools. A considerable amount of paperwork is involved in preparation for an inspection under the direction of the Office for Standards in Education (OFSTED). These inspections are very important, because as Paul Meredith and I explained in 1997, schools which fail their inspection can be closed.[30] In June 1998 the Government announced that the proportion of comprehensive (non-selective) schools failing their inspections had increased and that up to 25 schools might be closed.[31] Powers to deal with such schools, and others with serious weaknesses and other problems, have been increased under the School Standards and Framework Act 1998.

The regime of inspection of schools in operation since 1993, which of course includes inspections of teaching, has been partly responsible for increasing the accountability of teachers for educational standards.[32] However, the inspections are very stressful for staff; and preparation for an inspection can greatly distract teachers from their teaching role in the weeks leading up to the inspection.[33] The inspections have also helped to engender a collective insecurity among many teachers, which has been intensified by government threats to dismiss teachers whose 'performance ... falls below acceptable levels'.[34] With this amount of pressure, it is difficult to see how school staff can be willing to effect the reduction in the time and effort that they put into preparation for an inspection that the government's guidance on reducing bureaucracy recommends.[35]

Legal action

In recent years, teachers' widespread sense of insecurity has also been heightened by the threat of litigation in the area of educational malpractice, particularly in relation to a failure to prevent children from the effects of bullying or

30 N. Harris and P. Meredith, 'Success against the odds?: the legislative response to under-achievement in urban schools in England and Wales', paper to ELA Conference on urban education, Rotterdam, December 1997.

31 J. O'Leary, 'Blunkett may close up to 25 failing schools', *The Times*, 3 June 1998.

32 N. Harris and P. Meredith, *op. cit.*

33 See generally T. Brighouse and B. Moon (eds), *School Inspection* (London: Pitman, 1995).

34 Department for Education and Employment, *Excellence in Schools* Cm 3681 (London: Stationery Office, 1997), Chapter 5, para. 3.

35 Above n. 29, paras 16–18.

to identify their special educational needs (such as dyslexia). The High Court in the case of *Phelps v. London Borough of Hillingdon*[36] found negligence where an educational psychologist employed by the local education authority had failed to diagnose a child's special educational needs, with the result that the child experienced psychological problems and a reduced level of both educational attainment and career opportunity. The High Court awarded £45,000 damages (compensation). The defendant appealed and the Court of Appeal overturned the decision. In doing so it was keen to stress the policy reasons for denying any extension of liability for negligence in relation to educational malpractice, citing a number of decisions of the US courts, and in particular the decision of the New York Supreme Court in *Donoghue v. Copiague Union.*[37] In that case the court had said that education enactments –

> were not intended to protect against the 'injury' of ignorance, for every individual is born lacking knowledge, education and experience. For this reason the failure of educational achievement cannot be characterized as an 'injury' within the meaning of tort law.

However, the *Phelps* decision has not fully resolved the potential liability of teachers in relation to educational malpractice. This is because an earlier decision by the House of Lords[38] upholds the possibility of bringing negligence claims against teachers in circumstances where they fail to investigate the reasons for a child's under-performance. The matter will not be fully resolved until the House of Lords decides on an expected appeal in the *Phelps* case.

Lawyers believe that teachers may also owe a duty of care to protect pupils from the psychological effects of bullying by other pupils:[39] although several such claims have failed, in one case in 1996 insurers settled a claim to avoid a legal precedent being set. Teachers have also been very concerned about the perceived risk of allegations of child abuse resulting from any normative physical contact with children in primary schools.

Consumerism in the education system

The relationship between teachers on the one hand and parents and pupils on the other has also been affected by the public policy trend towards opening up public services to the forces of competition. Competition has been fostered by legislation since 1980 giving parents opportunities to select schools and requiring schools and local education authorities to publish various categories of

36 4 November 1998, to be reported in [1998] ELR 6.

37 (1978) 407 NYS 2d.874.

38 *X v. Bedfordshire County Council* [and related cases] [1995] ELR 404.

39 J. Robinson, 'Damages for academic under-performance: pupils as plaintiffs', *Education and the Law* 9/2 (1996) 93–101.

performance information about schools, including the examination and assessment results of pupils. School inspection reports are also published. Demand for places at a school continues to have an impact on the funding it receives. While the development of consumerism has been pushed to the background by the present preoccupation with educational standards, it remains a potent force. Schools continue to be accountable in the education market for the standards that are achieved in them.

One feature of this consumer-based system is that relationships between teachers and parents or pupils are beginning to become more individualized, similar to private contractual arrangements. The English courts have confirmed that in the field of public education, where no charge for provision may be made, there is no binding contract between the education authority or school and the parent.[40] Nevertheless, the widespread introduction of non-legally binding 'home-school agreements', with an accompanying declaration signed by the individual parent and possibly the child, is set to occur.[41] Parents will not in fact be compelled to sign the agreement. The child or young person, if considered capable of understanding the agreement as it relates to him or her, may also be invited to sign. The agreement will set out the aims and values of the school and the responsibilities of both the school and the parents regarding the education of the child. It will also specify the school's expectations of its pupils concerning their behaviour. The agreement will not be legally binding in a contractual sense (the statute states this). However, it will have the effect of formalizing relationships between the school and the parents or pupils.

Partnership and competing rights

Home-school agreements are also said to be important in reinforcing the notion of partnership between parents and teachers, which the Government has acknowledged is crucial to any attempt to raise levels of attainment and improve pupil behaviour. Nevertheless, to many education professionals the law appears to have driven a wedge between the teacher and the pupil: first, by interfering with a natural relationship based on the principle, recognized in law, of *in loco parentis* – that the teacher acts as a quasi-parent to the child, with appropriate authority, responsibility and autonomy; and secondly, by undermining a fraternal approach which helps to encourage a feeling of mutual respect and trust between the teacher and the older pupil.[42] A strong illustration

40 *R v. Fernhill Manor School, ex parte* A [1994] ELR 67.

41 School Standards and Framework Act 1998, ss. 110–111.

42 As Pearce and Hillman say, 'Teacher-pupil relationships are a key determinant of the extent of [pupil] dissatisfaction. Young people specifically identify teachers treating them with a lack of respect as having a negative impact on their attitudes to school and their motivation to learn': N. Pearce and J. Hillman, *Wasted Youth* (London: Institute for Public Policy Research), p. 46.

of this is the way that the teacher is warned by the Department for Education and Employment against giving contraceptive advice to pupils below the age of consent in law without the parents' knowledge, on the (erroneous) grounds that only doctors are permitted to do this.[43] Moreover, in some cases parental rights are competing with the autonomy of the teacher. For example, the unconditional right of parents to withdraw their child from sex education at school, a right introduced in 1994 at the same time that the provision of sex education became compulsory, challenges the basic role of the teacher referred to earlier.[44] In this way, parents' rights also make it difficult sometimes for the teacher to act as a guardian of the rights of the child.

Modernization of the teaching profession

It is now important to examine the Government's reforms to the teaching profession and to assess their potential impact on the autonomy and status of teachers.

Modernization has become the buzz-word of the Labour Government elected to power in the UK in 1997. Legislation has already been enacted by the UK Parliament to modernize aspects of the social security system[45] and the Government recently published its Access to Justice Bill, which aims to reform the methods of publicly funding access by the citizen to the legal system and to modernize lawyers' professional practices. Now, the tide of modernization has reached the teaching profession. An official consultation document, *Teachers: Meeting the Challenge of Change*,[46] which has been heralded by the education press as 'the most significant event since the 1988 Education Reform Act',[47] aims to improve training and support, but above all to change the career structure of the teaching profession in England and Wales. It proposes increased rewards to teachers – in terms of career advancement and higher pay – in return for high levels of performance. (Ironically, a system of paying teachers by results, namely the results of pupils entered for examinations, was abolished almost exactly 100 years ago.) Some 5,000 'advanced skills' teachers (or 'super' teachers, as the press has described them) could be placed on a new

[43] Department for Education and Employment Circular 5/94, *Education Act 1993: Sex Education in Schools* (London: Department for Education and Employment, 1994). See N. Harris (ed.), *Children, Sex Education and the Law: Examining the Issues* (London: NCB, 1996).

[44] See R. Thomson, 'Sex education and the law: working towards good practice', in N. Harris (ed), *Children, Sex Education and the Law, op. cit*, pp. 99–112.

[45] Social Security Act 1998.

[46] Department for Education and Employment, *Teachers: Meeting the Challenge of Change* (London: DfEE, 1998).

[47] *The Times Educational Supplement*, 4 December, 1998, editorial, p. 14.

'leadership' grade. Eligibility for the rewards being offered would be based on the outcome of the new appraisal arrangements that would be introduced, involving an annual assessment of teachers' performance against agreed objectives. Some particularly talented trainees could be placed on a fast track for career progression. Anticipating criticism that such differentials could be divisive, as well as demoralizing for the unrewarded majority, the proposals also envisage that *teams* of staff and schools as a whole might be eligible for *collective* awards. The justification for the increased public expenditure involved in funding the new career structure (estimated to be in the region of £1.2 billion) is that, as the introduction to the paper itself explains, the Government will expect teachers to play a 'key role ... in raising standards' and so it must offer the profession 'bigger incentives for success'.

These proposals follow on from the Teaching and Higher Education Act 1998 which will shortly establish a General Teaching Council (GTC) in England and Wales (one for each jurisdiction). The functions of the GTC[48] are to advise the Secretary of State and others on such matters as teaching standards and teacher recruitment, to maintain a register of qualified teachers, and to issue and keep under review a Code of Practice laying down standards of professional conduct and practice expected of teachers. Although teachers will form a majority of the members of the GTC, employers, parents and others will also be represented and, as a consequence, the GTC's role could be as much concerned with the public accountability of the teaching profession as with professional self-regulation and support. As the Government has explained, these other groups' interest 'in contributing to the national debate on standards' will be recognised in the membership of the GTC.[49]

The message the Government wishes to convey in its modernization changes as a whole is clear. Having promoted a School Standards and Framework Act 1998 to set in place a new schools structure, under which schools and local education authorities will have increased responsibilities for improving standards of education, and having ploughed considerable additional resources into the schools system (for example, through a 'New Deal for Schools' programme providing £1 billion over four years and through support for Education Action Zones[50] and a national literacy initiative), the Government is now seeking a way to ensure that individual teachers will play their part. This is crucial to the Government, as it has staked a great deal politically on achieving success in its education policies. In particular, it has set national targets for improvements in numeracy and literacy for 2002, as noted above; and as a recent newspaper report explained, 'ministers have staked their careers on

[48] Teaching and Higher Education Act 1998, Part I.

[49] Department for Education and Employment, *Excellence in Schools* Cm 3681 (London: Stationery Office, 1998), Chapter 5, para. 35.

[50] These zones were discussed in N. Harris and P. Meredith, n. 30 above.

reaching target levels in the basics'.[51] The new teaching reforms raise the stakes for teachers as well. Teachers will know that if the national targets, or those set by their school,[52] are not met, the government is likely to pin responsibility for under-achievement among pupils on them.[53]

Conclusion

The Government has sought to rebuild the professional status of teachers in England and Wales not by restoring their traditional autonomy but by making them central to the drive to raise standards of education in England and Wales and by acknowledging their role as agents of social change: 'Good teachers can create the dynamic force which can turn round not only schools but whole communities', wrote the Prime Minister recently.[54] The modernization reforms are intended to establish rewards for the most effective teachers, to create the incentives to improved performance. Yet experience in other countries where such schemes have been operated, such as Sweden and parts of the United States, has not been altogether positive: the schemes have proved divisive and their operation has been highly stressful and burdensome for principals in conducting the evaluations and making recommendations.[55] Fear of similar

[51] D. Charter, 'Teachers told to cut subjects and raise literacy', *The Times*, 13 January 1998.

[52] These targets may be set under section 19 of the Education Act 1997: 'The Secretary of State may by regulations make such provision as [he or she] considers appropriate for requiring the governing bodies of maintained schools to secure that annual targets are set in respect of the performance of pupils – (a) in public examinations or in assessments for the purposes of the National Curriculum, in the case of pupils of compulsory school age; or (b) in public examinations or in connection with the attainment of other external qualifications in the case of [older] pupils'. The regulations, which came into force on 1 September 1998, require the targets for pupils aged 15 to relate to pupil performance in terms of the quantity of particular grades rather than performance by subject. However, subject specific targets for English and Mathematics must be set for pupils in the second key stage (age 8–11): the Education (School Performance Targets) (England) Regulations 1998. See also Department for Education and Employment, Circular 11/98, *Target-setting in Schools* (London: DfEE, 1998).

Targets may also be specified for reducing the levels of unauthorised absences of pupils (truancy): School Standards and Framework Act 1998, section 63.

[53] Recently a government adviser suggested that the targets for individual schools would be regarded as 'aspirational' rather than mandatory: 'Barber softens line on teachers': *The Times Educational Supplement*, 13 November 1998. This does not, however, reduce the moral pressure on teachers.

[54] Tony Blair, 'Forging an inclusive society', *The Times Educational Supplement*, 11 September 1998.

[55] K. Riley, 'And the winner is ...', *Guardian Education*, 8 December 1998, p. 4.

consequences in England and Wales have been expressed by teachers' leaders in response to the proposals.[56]

The Government knows that it is essential to its ambitious plans for the education system of England and Wales to re-build teachers' professional esteem and status. It also knows that the country's 400,000 teachers[57] have faced a never-ending flow of new initiatives to raise educational standards over the past decade. Generally teachers have not been well-supported in managing change – certainly not on the scale on which it has been occurring. A new duty on local education authorities to prepare plans on supporting the education of children with behavioural problems[58] and a new statutory limit on infant class sizes[59] are two of only a small number of recent changes that will assist teachers in their role. Teachers are now facing up to further reforms under the School Standards and Framework Act 1998, such as the introduction of Education Action Zones.[60] In my opinion, only when the reform of education is once again teacher-led, as it was 30 years ago, and teachers' autonomy in their professional role is restored, at least to a degree, will the current recruitment crisis and demoralization within the profession in England and Wales be ameliorated. It is naïve to expect higher pay and improved career status for some teachers to raise standards overall. Nevertheless, the Government is attempting to elevate the status of teachers in general, and this is a positive development. It is right that the Government should also be concerned about teachers' accountability. However, the Government also needs to look at the autonomy of the teacher to see whether it is part of the key to securing the improvements in the standards of education that are sought.

[56] 'Frosty on the fast track and anxious about appraisal', *The Times Educational Supplement*, 4 December 1998, p. 4.

[57] Department for Education and Employment, Press Notice 206/98, *Teachers in Service (January 1998)*, 27 April 1998.

[58] Education Act 1997, section 9.

[59] School Standards and Framework Act 1998, ss. 1 and 2.

[60] See N. Harris and P. Meredith, n. 30 above.

ANDRÉ LEGRAND

France: Une Autonomie Limitée des Etablissements Secondaires

L'Ecole est traditionnellement considérée en France comme une des institutions fondamentales de la République et cela entraîne un certain nombre de conséquences sur la conception même que s'en fait la société: d'une part, sur le rôle imparti à l'Etat central dans son organisation, au nom d'un principe constitutionnel qui n'a pas perdu son actualité, comme en témoigne son utilisation récente dans la querelle sur l'abrogation de la loi Falloux. Confronté à la question de savoir si le législateur pouvait octroyer une liberté totale aux collectivités locales de financer les dépenses d'investissement des établissements privés, le juge constitutionnel s'y est opposé en raison du risque qu'encourrait en pareil cas le principe d'égalité[1]. Là est d'ailleurs la seconde conséquence essentielle: le rôle essentiel attribué à l'Ecole dans la réalisation de l'égalité sociale. Dans l'Ecole de la III° République, aucun particularisme ne peut trouver place dans l'activité d'enseignement.

Certes, comme toute affirmation de principe, celles-ci méritent d'être nuancées; en particulier, elles exigent une distinction soigneuse entre les divers ordres d'enseignement: d'une part, comme le montre Claude Lelievre[2], des pans entiers du système éducatif sont toujours restés sous l'emprise du local: en particulier, toute l'organisation de l'enseignement primaire mise en place par la III° République, y compris le primaire supérieur, reposait sur de larges pouvoirs laissés aux collectivités décentralisées et aux établissements. D'autre part, notait en 1981 Maurice Jordy[3], 'dans l'école primaire de Jules Ferry, "l'école du peuple", a fonctionné et fonctionne encore selon un corpus de règlements uniformisés, le fait qu'elle se soit voulue, dès le départ, au service de la société

[1] Cons. Const. 13 janv. 1994, Vr B. Genevois, *Le principe d'égalité et la libre administration des collectivités territoriales*. R.F.D.A. 1994, 209.

[2] *Une cohabitation séculaire*, Les Cahiers pédagogiques, juin 1994, p. 16

[3] *Sur les chemins de l'autonomie*, Ministère de l'Education nationale, doc. mult., Mai 1981, p. 11.

Walter Berka, Jan de Groof and Hilde Penneman (eds.), Autonomy in Education, 225–232.

et largement ouverte aux besoins nationaux et même locaux, grâce à une sorte de symbiose de l'instituteur et des élèves avec leur milieu, a longtemps assuré à ses établissements une autonomie réelle, faite, avant tout, de la connaissance de l'environnement, d'ouverture, de la volonté de formation des futurs citoyens au civisme, c'est-à-dire à un apprentissage des responsabilités adapté au rôle moyen qu'ils étaient appelés à jouer. Au contraire, l'armature rigide, centralisatrice, en un mot napoléonienne, qui a longtemps été celle des lycées et collèges, si elle a imposé un modèle unique d'acquisition du savoir abstrait et de promotion des élites, n'en a pas moins laissé subsister une nette ségrégation entre ses institutions, strictement régies, surveillées et fermées sur elles-mêmes, et la vie de la société qui se déroulait au dehors'.

En généralisant l'accès au collège, la V° République donnait une extension inconnue jusqu'alors à ce second modèle. Emprise forte de l'Etat sur l'institution scolaire d'une part: comme le montre Antoinette Ashworth[4], l'Ecole de la V° République s'est caractérisée, pour des raisons diverses, mais toutes liées à la conception gaulliste de l'organisation politique, par une emprise croissante de l'Etat et une éviction corrélative de la société civile. Vision jacobine de l'organisation, qui se traduit dans la tendance incoercible à son uniformité: alignement progressif des 'petites classes' des lycées sur l'enseignement primaire, suivi de leur suppression en 1962; alignement des programmes des écoles primaires supérieures sur deux de l'enseignement secondaire, avant la transformation de ces écoles en collèges modernes. Plus tard; là où coexistaient plusieurs formes de collèges, correspondant *grosso modo* à la différence des milieux urbain et rural, la réforme Haby substituera, à la fin des années 70, une forme unique d'organisation, en généralisant le Collège d'Enseignement Secondaire.

Phénomène aux origines multiples, mais d'abord culturelles. Tout ceci explique que la notion d'autonomie des établissements secondaires n'ait qu'une histoire récente (I). Mais cela éclaire aussi la difficulté qu'elle éprouve à trouver réellement sa place dans le système français, malgré les déclarations de principe des divers gouvernements successifs depuis deux décennies.

I: Un développement progressif, mais récent

'Evoquer l'autonomie des établissements scolaires et universitaires constitue une gageure tant la notion d'autonomie est vague, voire controversée' cette formule de Bernard Toulemonde[5] résume d'abord l'insuffisance de l'approche juridique de la notion d'autonomie. 'C'est sur le terrain de la pratique, ajoute-t-il – dans lequel les éléments juridiques jouent un rôle parmi d'autres éléments

[4] *L'Ecole, l'Etat et la société civile en France depuis le XVI° Siècle*, thèse Droit, Paris II, 1989, doc. dact., 2 tomes.

[5] *L'autonomie des établissements scolaires et universitaires*, L'Administration de l'Education nationale, Economica, Paris, 1992, p. 85.

– que se joue l'autonomie'. En ce sens, la question de l'autonomie ne fait que révéler un des traits essentiels du fonctionnement de l'éducation en France, caractérisé, nous dit Jacques Lesourne[6] par la coexistence d'une 'abondance de règles formelles et d'une variété de pratiques informelles'. Mais, en nous incitant à une certaine méfiance vis-à-vis de la stricte approche juridique des phénomènes éducatifs, cela n'en complique pas moins l'analyse du phénomène.

A: C'est à la fin des années 1970 que la notion d'autonomie des établissements secondaires commence à susciter un intérêt dans les instances de l'Education nationale; plusieurs stages d'étude sont organisés au cours de l'année 1977–78 autour de l'Inspection Générale 'Vie scolaire', bientôt suivis de la mise en place d'un groupe d'études chargé d'une mission de mise en œuvre d'une politique de décentralisation par la définition des niveaux optimaux de décision[7].

Ce groupe allait rendre sa contribution en juillet 1980[8], mais le changement de majorité politique devait intervenir peu après. Le nouveau ministre de l'Education, Alain Savary, allait cependant accentuer le mouvement et ses premières décisions marquaient une volonté de rupture avec nombre de principes qui caractérisaient le fonctionnement de l'Ecole traditionnelle: la création des Zones d'Education prioritaires, dès les toutes premières semaines introduisait un principe de discrimination positive, rompant à la fois avec la vision habituelle de l'égalité et introduisait la notion de diversité au sein de l'institution scolaire.

Le ministre commandait d'ailleurs à un inspecteur général du groupe 'Vie scolaire' une analyse de la question[9]. A la suite de ce rapport, la circulaire de rentrée 1983[10] introduisait une nouveauté importante, en demandant la mise en oeuvre de projets d'établissement, 'traduisant la politique de l'établissement'. Deux dispositions méritaient une attention particulière: 'des dérogations à certaines normes ou prescriptions des circulaires nationales pourront être accordées par les autorités académiques à des établissements qui auront établi des projets ... Une réglementation nouvelle apportera, dans le cadre des horaires nationaux, des assouplissements sur certains points(horaires des disciplines, par exemple).' Ainsi s'amorçait un mouvement qui allait laisser aux établissements une part croissante de liberté dans la fixation des horaires et culminer,

6 *Education et société demain*, Min. de l'Educ. nat., Paris 1988.

7 Instructions du 21 sept. 1978, *B.O.E.N. n° 36* du 12 oct. 1978.

8 *Rapport de synthèse sur le développement de l'autonomie des établissements scolaires*, M.E.N. juillet 1980.

9 Luc Soubre, *Décentralisation et déconcentration des institutions scolaires*, rapport au ministre de l'éducation nationale, 1982.

10 Note de service n° 82–522 du 31 décembre 1982, *Vers une plus grande responsabilité des établissements scolaires*, B.O.E.N. spéc. N° 1 du 13 janv. 1983.

par exemple dans l'arrêté du 29 mai 1996[11], qui rendra la grille horaire de 6° entièrement indicative.

De nombreuses décisions développaient largement par la suite le principe de la responsabilisation des établissements: celles relatives à la rénovation des collèges reposant sur un projet local, celles qui instauraient une expérience d'assouplissement de la carte scolaire, celles qui aboutissaient à la mise en place d'une dotation globale horaire, qui délivrait les autorités académiques du carcan des normes uniformes dans le calcul des dotations en emplois attribuées aux établissements, etc. ... Tout ceci développait les thèmes de l'adaptation et de la souplesse, deux des maîtres mots de la circulaire de 1982.

B: Les raisons de cette conversion française à la notion d'autonomie sont multiples. La première est indubitablement liée à l'impopularité, au sein de la population, d'une institution généralement considérée comme l'un des parangons du blocage social. L'ère de 'l'Ecole contestée', dont parle Antoinette Ashworth, pour caractériser les rapports entre l'institution scolaire et la société civile sous la V° République, s'explique en particulier par la rigidité des procédures d'orientation des élèves.

Là encore, la période giscardienne constitua un tournant: déjà les programmes établis pour l'école primaire entre 1977 et 1980 suggéraient le recours aux modulations et aux variations dans leur application en fonction de la réalité des élèves. Le collège 'unique', mis en place par la réforme Haby en 1975, ne peut pas être un collège uniforme, répétaient ses promoteurs.

Mais là aussi, c'est Alain Savary qui donna l'impulsion décisive. Pour des raisons en partie circonstancielles: le projet de constitution d'un grand service public unifié, dans lequel la gauche envisageait de rassembler l'enseignement public et l'enseignement privé et qui devait aboutir aux grandes manifestations du printemps 1984 entraînant la chute du gouvernement Mauroy, obligeait le ministre, en même temps qu'il conduisait cette négociation, à imaginer l'antidote, en réintroduisant la spécificité de chaque établissement sous la forme du projet déterminant 'l'identité (de celui-ci), qu'elle fût spirituelle, pédagogique, culturelle[12]'. Mais la transformation obéissait aussi à des causes plus profondes, tenant aussi à l'évolution des idées. Dès la fin des années 70, Antoine Prost condamnait les méthodes traditionnellement utilisées pour les réformes, en souhaitant 'opposer à une régulation purement nationale...un mode nouveau de prise en charge locale des difficultés[13]'. Cela nourrira l'espoir de la possibilité de définir, au niveau de l'établissement, 'un bien public local ... Il existe, un service public local, conscient de son environnement mais aussi éclairé par des

[11] *B.O.E.N.*, n° 25, 20 juin 1996, p. 1737.

[12] Alain Savary, *En toute liberté*, Hachette, Paris, 1985, p. 137.

[13] *Eloge des pédagogues*, Paris, 1979, p. 124.

références éducatives et humaines plus générales (où l'on peut) développer le souci du local sans tomber dans le localisme[14]'.

C: Se développent dès lors, de 1982 à 1989, toute une série de décisions et de textes, qui visent à accorder aux établissements français une autonomie relative: les deux plus importants seront le décret n° 85–924 du 30 août 1985 et la loi d'orientation du n° 89–486 du 10 juillet 1989.

La loi insiste sur deux idées essentielles pour la notion d'autonomie; elle fait d'abord du projet d'établissement le fondement de la gestion du système et en impose l'élaboration à tout établissement primaire et secondaire. (art. 18): 'celui-ci définit les modalités particulières de mise en œuvre des objectifs et programmes nationaux. Il fait l'objet d'une évaluation'. 'Dynamique nouvelle pour les établissements', dira le rapport annexé à la loi, en constatant qu'un 'des problèmes majeurs posés à chaque école et à chaque établissement scolaire consiste à respecter les objectifs nationaux tout en prenant en considération. les élèves qu'ils accueillent dans leur diversité d'origine sociale, de culture, de niveau et de qualités personnelles'. En droite ligne avec ceci, la loi de 1989 consacre en outre la notion de communauté éducative.

Quant au décret de 1985, il consacre les deux éléments qui forment la base juridique de l'autonomie des établissements. En en faisant des établissements publics locaux d'enseignement (E.P.L.E.), il leur donne la personnalité juridique. A ce titre, le contrôle exercé sur leur fonctionnement relève d'une tutelle aux règles complexes, mise en œuvre à la fois par des autorités de l'Etat et des collectivités locales. Dans son titre II, il leur reconnaît par ailleurs une autonomie financière qui se traduit par l'existence d'un budget propre voté par le conseil d'administration. Par ailleurs, dans sa rédaction actuelle, qui résulte des modifications apportées successivement par les décrets n° 90–978 du 31 oct. 1990 et n° 93–530 du 26 mars 1993, l'art. 2 du décret de 1985 définit huit rubriques qui forment le contenu de l'autonomie pédagogique et éducative dont jouissent les établissements secondaires.

La discussion essentielle a porté et porte sur la présidence du conseil d'administration. Après débats, elle fut laissée au chef d'établissement, fonctionnaire d'Etat, nommé par le pouvoir central et soumis à son pouvoir hiérarchique, au lieu d'être confiée à une personnalité élue par le conseil. Malgré quelques velléités, vite étouffées, cette situation n'a pas été remise en cause par la suite. Cet exemple est caractéristique des ambiguïtés qui marquent la notion d'autonomie et qui expliquent la difficulté qu'elle éprouve à passer dans les faits.

II: Une difficulté à passer dans les faits

La notion d'autonomie est polysémique. En 1981, Raymond Mallerin pouvait déjà écrire ces phrases. 'La marge d'autonomie est à trouver au cœur d'une

[14] J.L. Derouet et Y. Duterco, *L'établissement scolaire, autonomie locale et service public*, ESF, Paris, 1996, spéc., p. 188.

série de contradictions dialectiques: liberté/règle, initiative/contrôle, participation/autorité, centralisation/régionalisation, communauté individualisée/service public national. Dans une certaine mesure les textes traduisent la difficulté et l'embarras de ces difficultés. L'on insiste tantôt sur la responsabilité et l'autorité du chef d'établissement, tantôt sur le rôle et l'importance du conseil d'établissement et des institutions de participation; l'on met en avant, tantôt l'importance du service public, tantôt les notions d'ordre et de discipline nécessaires à la bonne marche du service public, tantôt les vertus du dialogue. La fonction du chef d'établissement assume fondamentalement cette ambiguïté[15]'.

Quinze ans après, Bernard Toulemonde note à son tour que 'la marge d'autonomie dont jouit l'établissement varie de façon considérable ...: en fonction de l'attitude des autorités hiérarchiques et de tutelle, plus ou moins respectueuses de (cette) autonomie ...; en fonction du comportement de l'établissement lui-même ... On ne renverse pas aisément deux siècles de centralisation et le confort que l'on peut éprouver à renvoyer les décisions épineuses à la hiérarchie[16]'.

Ces contradictions irriguent en permanence le fonctionnement du système éducatif. Il est vrai que, souvent, l'établissement est tenté de s'affranchir des principes ou des règles du service public. L'exemple de l'assouplissement de la sectorisation pour les affectations est sur ce point caractéristique des dérives susceptibles de se produire: malgré les précautions prises par les textes, la relative liberté que se sont attribuée certains établissements a souvent abouti à l'émergence de pratiques de sélection implicite, qui portent souvent atteinte au principe d'égalité conduisant à une hiérarchisation des établissements.

Ces dérives s'expliquent fréquemment par l'indulgence dont elles bénéficient de la part de la société environnante. Les discussions autour de l'autonomie des établissements révèlent aussi certains des blocages de la société globale et expliquent les réticences qui s'expriment souvent en son sein sur le cours nouveau de la politique. Blocages souvent internes; l'une des principales discussions publiques porte sur les questions de la gestion du personnel, pour laquelle est souvent défendue, sur le modèle de l'enseignement privé, l'idée d'un renforcement du pouvoir du chef d'établissement sur la gestion de son personnel: suggestion présentée, du côté des syndicats, comme une remise en cause du statut de la Fonction publique.

Mais cette accusation, qui dénonce la propension à la déréglementation n'est pas l'apanage des agents. On la retrouve aussi chez les usagers quand ils dénoncent la disparition de la rigidité des normes nationales concernant les formes de regroupement d'élèves, ou la définition des horaires d'enseignement. On la retrouva aussi chez d'autres partenaires du système, lorsque le ministère, qui finance sur crédits d'Etat l'acquisition des manuels scolaires destinés aux

[15] *Sur les chemins ..., op cit.*, p. 22.

[16] *Le chef d'établissement d'enseignement du second degré*, A.J.D.A. 1996, 820–821.

élèves des collèges; modifia, pour la rentrée 1989, les conditions de remplacement des manuels usagés; alors que, jusqu'alors, une circulaire nationale définissait de façon uniforme sur le territoire national les niveaux de classe et les disciplines concernés, la décision fut prise de laisser à chaque établissement, au nom de l'autonomie, la liberté de choisir au niveau local les manuels à remplacer. Cette décision provoqua plusieurs démarches de protestation de la part des organisations d'éditeurs, dont elle désorganisait le planning de production.

L'un des aspects majeurs autour duquel ces débats tournent concerne évidemment l'importance attachée au principe d'égalité. De droite comme de gauche, les ministres successifs ont toujours été très sensibles à cet aspect. Ainsi François Bayrou, qui, peu de temps après son arrivée au ministère, dénonçait 'le danger d'un morcellement du système éducatif ... (le risque) qu'un jour quelqu'un, à gauche ou à droite, (décide) de morceler l'institution pour la rendre plus adaptable, plus souple, plus transformable. Soit en décentralisant brutalement ... Dans les débats qui ont eu lieu avant l'alternance, je me suis toujours opposé à cette conception. Je crois que, s'il faut créer des espaces de liberté, la forme nationale de l'éducation fait partie du modèle français et que l'homogénéité de notre société repose largement sur ce ciment[17]'. L'action gouvernementale elle-même est ainsi fréquemment empreinte de contradictions liées au souci, lié aux exigences constitutionnelles, de voir l'Etat garder la responsabilité du service public d'éducation. Cela explique sans doute la timidité des méthodes utilisées sur le plan juridique pour déterminer le contenu de l'autonomie, comme le montrent les dispositions du décret de 1985 précitées. 'Dès l'instant, écrivait Jacques Lesourne[18], où l'on parle de décentralisation, cela veut dire que l'on accepte un certain degré de diversité, de différence, et que l'on troque l'uniformité contre un certain montant de "variété", mais, en contrepartie, il faut préserver les éléments fondamentaux qui assurent la cohérence du système'. On peut lire cette déclaration comme un plaidoyer en faveur du principe de subsidiarité, mais telle n'est pas la méthode utilisée par les textes, qui définissent davantage les compétences locales en termes de compétences d'attributions que de droit commun.

***

La France ne s'est engagée qu'avec précaution dans la voie de l'autonomie des établissements secondaires. Pourtant, malgré les résistances politiques et sociales qui s'expriment fréquemment sur ce point, divers éléments indiquent que l'évolution est en marche: en particulier, la tendance récente, mais plus fréquente à la mise en cause des responsabilités individuelles en cas de problème, à

[17] Interview au *Monde* du 5 février 1994.

[18] *Education et société demain*, M.E.N/, Paris, 1988, p. 12.

commencer par celle du chef d'établissement[19], montre de plus en plus la difficulté à régler toutes les questions du fonctionnement du système éducatif par des normes nationales et uniformes. Et combien des questions de plus en plus importantes se poseront et se régleront au niveau de l'établissement.

[19] B. Toulemonde, *Le chef d'établissement*, *op. cit.*, p. 823.

ANTÓNIO ABREU

Lisbon and the New Model of Autonomy and School Management: the Municipal Perspective

Let me tell you the main points of a new model of autonomy and school management before presenting my opinion which, as you will note, is a critical one regarding this model.

This new legislation concerns the pre-school, basic school and secondary levels of State education. The basic school ends at the 9th year which corresponds to the duration of compulsory education.

Autonomy concerns the power given to schools to take decisions in areas of strategy, pedagogy, administration, finances and organization according to the school's educational project.

The government says that it is important to develop a new organization in education, in two fundamental areas:

- the autonomy of schools; and
- the system of decentralization (without referring to which decentralization ...).

Autonomy will incorporate several dimensions of the school:

1. Internal organization and its links with central and local levels of the administration;
2. Local powers being increased with corresponding resources;
3. The constitution of social and educational partnerships that guarantee initiative and participation of society.

The school will build autonomy in the community in which it belongs.

Autonomy should not be seen as a target in itself, but as a way to increase the quality of the state service in education.

The legislation introduces:

- the participation of parents, students and other bodies;
- the possibility of an *individual* director, instead of a collective board which has been our experience for the past 25 years.

Walter Berka, Jan de Groof and Hilde Penneman (eds.), Autonomy in Education, 233–237.

Autonomy contracts:

- the government described this process as *made with a culture of responsibility*;
- the legislation deals specially with pre-school and the first cycle of compulsory education in which schools have had no administrative support or budgets until now;
- the legislation includes the opportunity of *grouping schools*, according to their local experience and educational needs; and
- the *organization of educational administration* is based on the school and on educational territories, on the balance between identity and complementarity of educational projects and on the value of the *participation of* teachers and other school workers, students, parents and representatives of local power.

The *instruments of the autonomy process* are:

- the educational project;
- internal rules; and
- the activities plan.

The legislation emphasizes orientation principles of administration and management established in the Educational System Basic Law, such as democracy, participation, pedagogical and scientific criteria being stronger than administrative ones, elections to school bodies, state responsibility and other participants in the educational process, etc.

The *school bodies* are:

1. the Assembly;
2. the Executive Board or Executive Director;
3. the Pedagogical Council; and
4. the Administrative Council

each with different areas of responsibility.

Autonomy consists of two stages, each giving levels of powers and responsibilities according to the rules laid down.

These levels are negotiated beforehand between schools, the ministry and the municipal administration. From these negotiations comes the autonomy contract, containing a definition of targets and resources required to achieve them.

The regional service of the ministry decide on each contract proposal made by a school or groups of schools.

The Municipality of Lisbon currently cooperates, when requested by schools, in the introduction of the new system of autonomy, administration and management of teaching establishments, from pre-school to secondary education – *Decreto-Lei* (Decree-Law) no. 115–A/98 4th May 1998.

However, it has disagreed and continues to disagree with this new model (not because it objects to autonomy, which it has always supported). When the bill was being publicly and actively discussed in large assemblies, we said that it proposed a change in the nature of the school. It would become more like a company, with the teacher being like a manager, and a commercial relationship being developed with the community, which could create conditions for the privatization of parts of the state school system.

At the time, we suggested changes to this *Decreto-Lei* that were not accepted then, but which we have again put forward in the course of the ratification process that is proceeding in the *Assembleia da República* (the Portuguese Parliament).

The other municipalities in the Metropolitan Area of Lisbon, governed by different political majorities, including that of the Government party, also put forward serious doubts about this *Decreto-Lei.*

Be that as it may, the Municipality of Lisbon will remain involved in a process which is going to demand from everyone – City Hall, District Councils, teachers and parents – close attention in order to prevent diversions contrary to the interests of a high standard of state school teaching.

It is difficult to disagree with the basic concepts expressed in the opening section of this *Decreto-Lei.* Apart from the fact that it is formulated without a time frame and disconnected from concrete dynamics, we are entirely in agreement with the process of territorialization of social functions (education, health, social security).

However, this legislative initiative must be clarified and the questions below duly noted, for example:

- Why put an end to an experiment of democratic school management in operation since 1976, when democracy was growing in Portugal?
- From what perspective does the current Government deal with the reform of systems applying basic social rights: education, health, social security?
- How has this investment in the first years of schooling and the transference of powers in this area from central administration into local administration been processed?

Leaving aside, for reasons of economy, detailed discussion of the facts that are the origin of the respective proposals, we shall move on to direct reference to them.

There are no fundamental reasons that put into question the model of democratic management that has, over 20 years, always displayed flexibility in adapting to new realities, despite some limitations.

To formalize the representation of parents in the school bodies, the role of teachers was reduced to an almost subordinate position in schools.

The existing *Decreto-Lei*, even after public debate, still has some negative aspects, for example:

- in addition to the collective direction, introduction of the position of the single executive director;
- the demand, for these positions, for teachers with management experience which will reduce their recruitment base and the renewal of posts;
- the capacity to approve budgets has been given to the Executive rather than the Assembly (the Assembly has also not been given the power to ratify educational projects and internal regulations); and
- the Pedagogical Council has not been given:
  - the power to approve (and not merely propose) the school educational project;
  - the power to approve the internal regulations (under the proposal of the executive direction), but to reject them;
  - the power to give an opinion on the functioning of the school.

The perspective from which the Government intends to deal with the future realization of basic social rights now takes responsibility away from the State concerning the respective systems and even privatization. The *Decreto-Lei* allows for the contractualization of autonomy, requesting the school to obtain other sources of funding.

This may create unacceptable situations. For example (and this is already a reality), a school hires its sports pavilions to a certain company, and which are thus no longer freely available to the local community. There are other examples which create a commercial relationship with the community based on the use of infrastructures built through public investment and that will lead to the deterioration of the ties that have been so important between the school and the environment.

Finally, and still concerned with the contractualization of autonomy, the contract is made between three parties: the school, the Government and the municipality.

The municipalities in the Metropolitan Area of Lisbon have already decided not to subscribe to these contracts of autonomy until Parliament passes a new law on the powers of local councils.

Indeed, the powers given 14 years ago did not provide the respective financial means and the local councils

- either accept these responsibilities without means and, in some cases, are technically bankrupt or are unable to continue providing certain services (such as subsidizing meals in the first school years);
- or they do not accept them and the system today does not provide basic things such as subsidizing meals, leisure-time activities, a larger public pre-school network, the functioning of primary schools as well as kindergartens within the normal parental working timetable.

The negotiation of new powers for the municipalities in terms of education was preceded by an attempt to fill these gaps in the system. This is being done through agreements, problematic in terms of application, where solutions can be created for municipalities impossible under the current scheme of legal powers. These include limits imposed on current spending and staffing; the qualification of human resources and know-how of other levels of teaching that historically have always been in the hands of central administration.

It is significant that no restructuring of the education ministry has been announced at the same time as the so-called local educational councils will be created on municipal initiative, which should be instruments of decentralization of the education system.

We also must note that contractualization is a negotiation between the ministry and each school and it may increase differences that already exist, not providing, at the same time, special resources of teaching that so many schools need.

Nevertheless, this path towards a growing autonomy is historically desirable and inevitable and a significant step in the improvement of the quality of the educational system. It is important to take this step, however, without removing the State's responsibility, creating mechanisms allowing the coherence and suitability of the process of autonomy and the existence of human resources able to develop and expand that process. This guarantees the role of teachers and pedagogical councils as well as assuring the decentralization of the education system's administration through the profound restructuring of the Ministry of Education. Local Education Councils are sanctioned which constitute local structures for the administration of the education system.

HANS VISSER

Autonomy in Education

Summary of paper

1. *Some constitutional background*

Autonomy, and its mirror concept 'accountability', must be seen against the background of the Bill of Rights. The existence and content of the Bill of Rights suggest a fresh approach to autonomy in education. This new constitutional dispensation has had a profound impact on education and education law. For the first time a fundamental right to basic education has been introduced, placing certain positive, legally enforceable duties on the State in the provision of education.

The Bill of Rights also recognizes a right to further education which the State, through reasonable measures, must make progressively available and accessible. The special language provisions in the Bill of Rights give a right to receive education in the official language or languages of choice at public educational institutions provided that certain conditions are met – underpinning a degree of 'language autonomy' at public institutions.

In addition there is a right to establish and maintain independent educational institutions which meet certain requirements (and which the State is not obliged to fund). Naturally all the basic human rights mentioned in the Bill of Rights are also applicable in the field of public education and are directly relevant in the debate on freedom and autonomy.

As far as independent educational institutions (or private education) are concerned, the doctrine of horizontal application will ensure a certain measure of applicability of human rights.

Education is an area where the national government and the provincial governments have concurrent jurisdiction on legislative and policy issues.

The Constitution also prescribes cooperative government between various authorities – which means that autonomy at very level is affected.

Walter Berka, Jan de Groof and Hilde Penneman (eds.), Autonomy in Education, 239–242.

2. *Concept of autonomy*

Autonomy generally means self-government and freedom. The concept *accountability* must be considered in conjunction with autonomy. This refers to responsibility, or the duty to give an explanation. There are obviously different degrees of institutional autonomy and accountability. In a sense autonomy and accountability appear to be opposite concepts: greater autonomy implies lesser accountability. However, there are many other views on this issue. The basic premise is that obviously no role-player in education should have absolute or unrestricted autonomy and that a sufficient degree of accountability must also be present. The education system as a whole must reflect fundamental rights limiting the autonomy of the State and of other power-blocks. A healthy balance is to be achieved to ensure the fullest possible practical realization of the right to receive a proper education.

3. *Some possible areas of examination*

Autonomy in education can be examined on many levels and in many areas. Attention may be given to the autonomy enjoyed by (and the accountability of) functionaries, institutions and bodies such as:

- the national Minister of Education (especially on formulating national policy);
- the provincial 'ministers' of education and the heads of the provincial education departments;
- independent schools (private schools);
- the governing bodies of public schools;
- parents of pupils at independent and public schools;
- the professional managers of public schools (for example, the provincial head of education, the school principal);
- university councils;
- private institutions of higher education.
- rights of parents regarding home schooling.

4. *Governing bodies of public schools: general*

For the purposes of this paper it is obviously impossible to consider autonomy (and accountability) in regard to all the issues listed above. Particular attention is given to the autonomy of governing bodies of public schools. Subject to any other legal provisions, the governance of a public school is vested in its governing body. The governing body is the 'directing mind' of a public school in all matters which do not fall under the professional management of the school (which is the responsibility of the head of the education department and the principal of the school) or matters which have been entrusted to another decision-making body. Legal criteria which may be used in evaluating the autonomy of the governing body, include the following:

- How are members of the governing body appointed (or dismissed) and in terms of what principles and procedures do appointments take place?
- How is the governing body constituted (from what categories of persons)?
- Where does the balance of power in the governing body lie?
- To what degree are the members of the governing body subject to the instructions, mandates, guidelines or approval from any outside authority, constituency or person?
- What are the nature and extent of the discretionary powers of the governing body in directing and managing the school's internal affairs (personnel, administration, finances and programmes), as well as its external relations?
- To what external influences, procedures and controls will the governing body (and through them, the school) be subject?
- Does the governing body, or some of its members, have to submit a report to any person or body, what should be reported and what action may the latter take in regard to such a report?

5. *Governing bodies of public schools: autonomy in certain areas*

The legal autonomy of governing bodies of public schools in the following critical areas are briefly examined:

- appointment of educators;
- aspects of admission policy;
- power to formulate and enforce a code of conduct for learners which limit or restrict certain fundamental rights;
- finances of the school;
- developing a mission statement for a school;
- aspects of language policy; and
- aspects of religious policy.

6. *Some conclusions*

An examination of the autonomy of governing bodies of public schools in the areas listed above, demonstrates that although the legal basis for a reasonable measure of autonomy is present, the *de facto* position is that the State generally still interferes on an extensive scale in public school governance and thus limits the autonomy enjoyed by governing bodies in critical areas. The following reasons exist for this situation:

- the political will of the present government in desiring to eradicate all traces of racism, sexism and inequality in education;

- the complexities of the education transformation;
- the legacy of apartheid which produced an education system characterized by inequality and fragmentation;
- the inexperience and inability of many school governing bodies to undertake meaningful school governance.

As far as governing bodies of public schools are concerned, the issue of autonomy – and the maximum measure of autonomy to be enjoyed by these bodies – will probably only be settled once the transformation of the education system as a whole has been completed. In order to achieve such transformation education management development will have to occur. In this regard it has been recommended that schools, as the centres of teaching and learning, be placed at the *core* of education management and education management development, rather than at the bottom of a hierarchical and bureaucratic management pyramid.

ELMENE BRAY

Autonomy in School Education in South Africa: A Legal Perspective

1. Introduction

'Autonomy' is an important concept in law. However, it is probably more commonly used in a general context which reflects little about its specific legal content and application. In analysing its dictionary meaning, one finds a common denominator in the term 'self-governing' or 'self-governance'.[1] To determine the legal meaning of self-governance (autonomy), one has to examine the legal context in which an entity functions to determine its autonomy or the degree of autonomy it enjoys. In short, 'autonomy' or 'self-governance' refers to the way in which a variety of institutions and systems influence each other, but cannot perform the other's functions for its own account.[2]

This paper examines to what degree provinces enjoy autonomy in the new South African constitutional system, particularly with regard to education: a functional area shared ('concurrent') between the national and provincial government. After that, the focus is on school education only, in particular the autonomy or self-governance of the ordinary public school.

[1] 'Autonomy' – the right or state of self-government, especially when limited; a State or individual possessing autonomy; freedom to determine one's own actions. 'Autonomous' – possessing a large degree of self-government, living under one's own laws; independent of others. From Greek *autonomia* – freedom to live by one's own laws. *Collins Concise Dictionary (Plus)* (1989) ISB 0 00 433252-0.
Self-governed, autonomous, self-supported ... *Roget's Thesaurus The Everyman Edition* (1986) ISBN 0 7064 1651 1.
'Autonomous' – selfbesturend, selfregerend, selfstandig ... *Tweetalige woordeboek* (Bosman, Van der Merwe & Hiemstra) 1986 ISBN 0 624 02126 2.

[2] Bray, W. 'The legal status of the South African university' (1993). Unpublished doctoral thesis, University of South Africa.

Walter Berka, Jan de Groof and Hilde Penneman (eds.), Autonomy in Education, 243–269.

Constitutional background and development[3]

The Interim Constitution of 1993 paved the way for the 'final' Constitution (Constitution of the Republic of South Africa of 1996 – hereafter 'Constitution') which came into operation on 4 February 1997. The new constitutional system abolished the previous Westminster system of parliamentary sovereignty, and established a constitutional democracy in which the Constitution became the supreme law of the Republic.[4] All government bodies, including Parliament, are subject to the Constitution, and any law or conduct, including parliamentary legislation, inconsistent with it is invalid and can be struck down by the courts.[5] Other basic features of the Constitution include:

- A Bill of Rights (Chapter 2) in which fundamental human rights are protected.[6] The courts (with the Constitutional Court as highest court in constitutional matters) watch over fundamental rights and also maintain and promote the objectives and spirit of the Bill of Rights.[7]
- A democratic system of government in which democratic principles such as universal adult suffrage, proportional representation, regular elections, decentralization of authority (e.g. to public schools) and public (community) participation play a central role.
- Cooperative government (Chapter 3) which recognizes and distinguishes the three spheres of government (national, provincial and local), yet bonds them together in interdependent and interrelated relationships of governance.[8]

3 For more information on the constitutional transition in general see, e.g.: Du Plessis, Lourens and Corder, Hugh *Understanding South Africa's Transitional Bill of Rights* (1994); Corder, Hugh 'Towards a South African Constitution' 1994 *Modern LR* 491–533; Van Wyk, D., Dugard, J. *et al.* (eds) *Rights and Constitutionalism: The new South African legal order* (1994); Carpenter, Gretchen 'The Republic of South Africa Constitution Act 200 of 1993 – an overview' 1994 *SAPR/PL* 222–232; Venter, F. 'Milestones in the evolution of the new South African Constitution and some of its salient features' 1994 *SAPR/PL* 211–221; Cachalia, A., Cheadle, H. *et al. Fundamental rights in the New Constitution* (1994); De Villiers, Bertus (ed.) *Birth of a Constitution* (1994).

4 See e.g. ss. 1 and 2 (in Chap. 1, 'Founding provisions') of the Constitution; also Wiechers, Marinus *Staatsreg* (1981) 22; Corder, Hugh *op. cit.* 491–533.

5 S. 2. See Rautenbach, I.M. and Malherbe, E.F.J. *Constitutional Law* (1997) 15–17.

6 The right to education (albeit qualified, e.g. basic education, further education and the right to receive education in the official language(s) of choice where reasonably practicable): s. 29.

7 S. 39(1) provides that when the courts interpret the Bill of Rights, the values that underlie an open and democratic society based on human dignity, equality and freedom must be promoted. The courts must consider international law in the intepretation of the Bill of Rights and may consider foreign law.

8 Cooperative government (a new Chapter) envisages the adoption of legislation for the establishment of structures and institutions in which governments in various

Within this cooperative context peace, national unity and the indivisibility of the Republic must be secured by means of effective, transparent, accountable and coherent government. (See below.)

- A public administration (Chapter 10) in which, for example provincial education departments and public schools, are bound to govern according to democratic values and principles enshrined in the Constitution.[9]
- An aspiration to build one nation in which the diversity of interests in South African society is accommodated to ensure justice for all.[10]

Constitutional supremacy has fundamentally changed our approach to the interpretation and application of laws and the courts will now in terms of section 39(2) of the Constitution, ask certain questions when they interpret and apply ordinary laws. For example, what does the Constitution say and how do we give effect to the values and norms of the Constitution?[11] The Constitution is a value-laden document and enshrines a number of values and ideals which have been elevated to constitutional norms and all conduct must conform to these norms.[12] This means that the dated literalist approach to interpretation has had to make way for a normative approach in which the courts actively promote constitutional values and norms and pursue the ideals expounded in the Constitution.[13] All education laws are subject to this normative approach to interpretation.

---

spheres will cooperate and through which the principles of cooperative government will be given effect. In short, no watertight separation of powers or hierarchical levels of power exists between the spheres of government and their functions: Rautenbach and Malherbe, E.F.J. *Constitutional Law* (1996) 254–255.

9 In terms of Chap. 10 (a new Chapter), the administration in every sphere of government (including the public service), and of organs of state and public enterprises must be open and transparent, broadly representative, development-oriented and accountable: Burns, Yvonne *Administrative law under the 1996 Constitution* (1998) 68–69.

10 Rautenbach, I.M. and Malherbe, E.F.J. *What does the Constitution say?* (1998) 4–5.

11 e.g. s. 39(2) provides that when interpreting any legislation, and developing the common law or customary law, courts must promote the spirit, purport and objects of the Bill of Rights. This happens when laws affected by the Bill of Rights are interpreted. See Rautenbach, Rassie 'Constitutional perspective on higher education'. a paper presented at a symposium entitled 'Akademiese vryheid onder die nuwe bedeling vir hoNr onderwys in Suid-Afrika' at the University of Stellenbosch on 6 August 1998.

12 Botha, Henk 'The values and principles underlying the 1993 Constitution' 1994 *SAPR/PL* 233–244. (This applies even more in the case of the 1996 Constitution.)

13 A normative (purposive) approach is being followed to find the purpose of the Constitution. The 'purposive' approach was laid down in *S v. Makwanyana* 1995 6 BCLR 665(CC) para. 9 and followed in numerous subsequent cases. See also Davis, D., Chaskalson, M. and De Waal, J. 'Democracy and constitutionalism: the role of

Finally, all spheres of government, the public administration in general and organs of state, are bound by the values and norms enshrined in the Constitution. This means that the national and provincial education departments as well as public schools are bound by the Constitution and, particularly, Chapters 3 and 10: each must promote and develop its own distinctive character, but work together to improve their strength and effectiveness; each must practise open, participative and accountable government. Against this background, the autonomy (or degree of) of each entity to 'live by its own laws' has to be evaluated.

2. Provincial autonomy in education

Provinces in the constitutional context

The new constitutional system introduced a new uniform regional system (consisting of nine provinces) which integrated the previous regional institutions.[14] Provinces are therefore aptly referred to as the 'building blocks' of the new national state.

The degree of autonomy of regional institutions (*in casu* provinces) inter alia determines whether a particular state is a union or a federation.[15] But it must be borne in mind that modern states are complex and dynamic and a simple formula cannot encapsulate the strength and diversity of their powers. The South African constitutional landscape has changed and the state is no longer a classic unitary state, neither is it a formal federation.[16] Many federal

---

constitutional interpretation' in Van Wyk, D., Dugard, J. *et al.* (eds) *op. cit.* 1 *et seq.*; Botha, C.J. 'Waarde-aktiverende grondwetuitleg: Vergestalting van die materiële regstaat (1996) (unpublished LLD thesis, University of South Africa).

14 Rautenbach, I.M. and Malherbe, E.F.J. *op. cit.* (1996) 239–240. The provinces, self-governing territories and so-called 'independent' homelands of the previous regime were abolished and integrated into a new uniform regional system.

15 Rautenbach and Malherbe *op. cit.* (1996) 238, 258–259.

16 Klaaren, Jonathan 'Federalism' in Chaskalson, M. *et al. Constitutional law of South Africa* (1996) refers on 5.1 to 'a federal system with unitary features'; De Villiers, Bertus 'The Federal/Unitary debate: is there light at the end of the tunnel?' 1996 *The Human Rights and Constitutional Law Journal of South Africa* 11 at 11–14 where he observed that South Africa is not a federation but that some distinct federal elements are present. See e.g. the National Education Policy Bill case (*Ex parte Speaker of the National Assembly: In re Despute concerning the Constitutionality of Certain Provisions of the National Education Policy Bill 83 of 1995* 1996 4 BCLR 518(CC)) at para. 23 where the Court stated 'the provinces in South Africa are not sovereign states. They were created by the Constitution and have only those powers that are specifically conferred on them under the Constitution'.

characteristics have become part of our new democratic order and the institution of nine constitutionally anchored and protected provinces reflects one of the important federal characteristics of our constitutional democracy.[17]

A unique feature of provincial autonomy is that a provincial legislature has the capacity to adopt its own constitution (s. 142). Provincial constitutions may provide for provincial legislative and executive structures and procedures that differ from those provided for in the Constitution. Nevertheless such a constitution must comply with certain constitutional requirements and will have force and effect only if the Constitutional Court certifies that it has been adopted in accordance with the Constitution.[18] Notwithstanding this, Chapter 6 of the Constitution (Provinces) provides a complete blueprint for provincial government and it is therefore not necessary for any province to enact a constitution.[19] To date, only the province of the Western Cape has successfully adopted a constitution.

Cooperative government

Although provincial government signifies a strong federal dimension, the relationship of cooperative government binds all spheres of government together. Cooperative government (Chapter 3 of the Constitution) describes the relationship of cooperation of the different spheres of government and stipulates that each sphere is distinct, but also functions in an interdependent and interrelated relationship with each other. It is apparent that the principle of cooperative government which underscores participative decision-making among spheres of government that are unique in character and of equal importance in the relationship, does not fit comfortably in either the 'unitary' or 'federal' model

[17] See Elazar, Dan 'Form of state: Federal, unitary, or ...' in De Villiers (ed.) (1994) *op. cit.* 29–36 where he refers on 34 to the interim Constitution (and even more applicable to the final Constitution) ... '[i]t is explicitly not a federation and clear national supremacy is specified. Yet at the same time it is almost as clearly a federal arrangement in that the provinces are anchored and constitutionally protected in the document as are their powers ...'.

[18] See ss. 142–145. In *In re: Certification of the Constitution of the Province of KwaZulu-Natal, 1996* 1996 11 BCLR 1419(CC) the Constitutional Court declined on various reasons to certify, in terms of the interim Constitution, the constitution adopted by the provincial legislature of KwaZulu-Natal. In *In re: Certification of the Amended Text of the Western Cape, 1997* 1997 12 BCLR 1653(CC) the amended text (the first text was rejected) of the constitution of the Western Cape province was finally approved by the Constitutional Court.

[19] Malherbe, E.F.J. 'Provinsiale grondwette: 'n Barometer van provinsiale outonomie?' 1998 *TSAR* 344. The author emphasizes at 354–355 that the adoption of a constitution is a logical consequence of provincial autonomy. Provincial constitutions have to be adopted within the principles and framework of the Constitution and provincial legislatures must be encouraged to adopt their own constitutions; the Constitutional Court should not unduly hinder a provincial legislature in exercising this power.

of government. This principle illustrates clearly the hybrid nature of the South African state.

Cooperative government is the bedrock of governmental relations and underscores the values and ideals of the Constitution: it provides the ways and means to achieve democratic, participative, transparent and accountable government.[20] Throughout the Constitution various built-in 'checks and balances' are provided to promote, evaluate and control this fine relational balance.[21]

Provinces and education

Education (with the exclusion of tertiary education) is a functional area divided between the national and provincial government.[22] In short, a province is for all practical purposes in charge of all matters relating to school education in its province and provincial school laws will generally prevail over national school laws adopted by the national legislature. However, in a case where a conflict arises as to which law should prevail, a national law prescribing school norms, policy and standards which apply uniformly in the country (e.g. the National Education Policy Act of 1996 and the South African Schools Act of 1996 – SASA), should prevail over a provincial school law. Clearly in such a case a provincial school law cannot regulate national school norms and standards. National legislation on school education will also prevail when it is, for example, aimed at preventing unreasonable action by a province that could harm the economy or security of another province or the country as a whole.[23] Because of possible inconsistencies and conflict within this area of shared

[20] e.g. s. 41(1) inter alia provides that 'all spheres of government and organs of state within each sphere must ... provide effective, transparent, accountable and coherent government to the Republic as a whole; ... be loyal to the Constitution, the Republic and its people; ... respect the constitutional status, institutions, powers and functions of government in the other spheres; ... cooperate with one another in mutual trust and good faith by ... assisting and supporting one another ...'.

[21] e.g., the National Council of Provinces (ss. 60–72) forms part of Parliament and acts as a 'watchdog' to ensure that provincial interests are taken into account by the national government (e.g. school education bills that fall within the concurrent legislative powers of the national and provincial legislature, will be referred to the Council – ss. 76–78); the national government has an obligation to assist provinces by way of legislation and other measures to develop the administrative capacity required for the effective exercise of powers – s. 125(3); in the same vein, national and provincial government must by means of legislative and other measures, support and strengthen the capacity of municipalities to manage their own affairs – s. 154(1).

[22] S. 104(1) read with Schedule 4.

[23] S. 146(3).

legislative competence, detailed and complicated procedures are prescribed for discussing and solving them in a spirit of cooperation.[24]

In summing up: provincial legislatures function for all intents and purposes like the national legislature and have original legislative powers; for example, the Gauteng provincial legislature has promulgated its own school education law (Gauteng School Education Act of 1995) which is not subordinate to (or derived from) the national school education law promulgated by the national legislature (SASA).

The executive powers of the provinces vest in the premier who exercises these powers together with the executive council (*in casu* the member of the executive council (MEC) in charge of education who may delegate powers to the head of the provincial education department). Executive authority of a province corresponds in principle with that of the national executive authority, for example initiating, preparing and implementing provincial legislation, developing and implementing provincial policy and coordinating functions of provincial departments and their administrations.[25] A province has executive authority over national legislation in the concurrent functional area, only if (and to the extent that) it has the administrative capacity to assume effective responsibility for the administration and implementation of the national law. For example, Gauteng province must have the executive capacity to administer the SASA; if it lacks this capacity, an obligation is placed on the national government to assist it by way of legislation and other measures to develop the required administrative capacity for the effective exercise of powers.[26] When a dispute arises on the question whether a province has the executive capacity

[24] See also above. E.g. in the case of a bill dealing with norms and standards for schools in the country, the National Council of Provinces would have to determine whether the bill contains inconsistencies which would infringe upon school-education powers of the provinces. If it does, the bill would eventually have to be referred to a mediation committee – s. 78. In the case of conflict, the other legislation is not invalidated but becomes inoperative for as long as the conflict remains – s. 149. A dispute concerning the constitutional status or the demarcation of powers (e.g. concurrent legislative competence) and functions between national and provincial government, is decided by the Constitutional Court – s. 167(3); in the case of a dispute that cannot be resolved by the Court, national legislation will prevail over provincial legislation – s. 148. Two Constitutional Court cases have already been heard on inter alia the sharing of concurrent education powers between the national and provincial legislature in terms of the interim Constitution: *In re The School Education Bill of 1995 (Gauteng)* 1996 4 BCLR 537(CC); *In re National Education Policy Bill 83 of 1995* 1996 4 BCLR 518(CC).

[25] cf. ss. 125–141 on provincial executive authority with ss. 83–102 on national executive authority.

[26] See s. 125(3).

to administer a national school law, it must be referred to the National Council of Provinces for resolution.[27]

The preceding paragraphs illustrate some of the most important ways in which the national and provincial government cooperate in school-education matters. The concurrent functional area of education is certainly one of the best areas to illustrate the balance that exists (or should exist) between the 'self-rule' and 'shared-rule' basis of cooperative government. It should also reflect to what extent skewed governmental relationships impact on the capacity of a province to function autonomously in the area of provincial school education.

Are provinces autonomous in education?

The new South African constitutional democracy with its hybrid system of government has been designed to suit the South African context. It is embedded in norms and values, and ideals of reconstruction, reconciliation and participative government. It requires a deep respect for human dignity, freedom and equality. Traditional notions of strict separation of powers, hierarchical levels of government, and concentration of powers at national (central) level, in which meaningful participation by civil society was severely limited, made way for cooperative and participative governance in all spheres of government in a manner which recognizes each entity's unique character and promotes capacity-building, transparency and accountability to the benefit and advantage of all the people of South Africa.

Within this context the Constitutional Court held in *In re: Certification of the Constitution of the Republic of South Africa of 1996*[28] that the principle of cooperative government (*in casu* section 41(1)(e) and (g) which relates to respect for the constitutional status, institutions, powers and functions of government in all spheres; and the exercise of powers and performance of functions in a manner that does not encroach on each other's geographical, functional or

[27] S. 125(4). Provinces do not automatically enjoy full executive authority over every concurrent and exclusive functional area mentioned in Sch. 4 and Sch. 5. E.g., national government will continue to administer an existing national school education law until the President transfers it to the province. However, if the President refuses such a transfer, the province could adopt its own provincial school law to be executed by the provincial executive council.

[28] 1996 10 BCLR 10 1253(CC) paras 287–292, 469. This was the first certification case in which the Constitutional Court had to test the constitutionality of the 1996 Constitution against the Constitutional Principles of the interim Constitution. The Court held in para. 245 that the fact that s. 41(1)(e) and (g) applies to all spheres of government, does not result in Constitutional Principle XXII not being complied with. Principle XXII provides that national government may not encroach upon provincial government.

institutional integrity) does not encroach upon Constitutional Principle XXII and, therefore, does not invade provincial autonomy. In future this Constitutional Principle which prohibits national government from encroaching upon provincial government, will have to be taken into account when conflict arises between national and provincial government regarding concurrent legislative competences (s. 146 and Sch. 4).

Indications of provincial autonomy in school education

Some aspects relating to the status of the provinces and their role in intergovernmental relations have been highlighted and examples indicated how the identity of provinces is being secured in the field of school education – a concurrent functional area. Nevertheless, a province, through its own fault (e.g. corruption) or as a result of a lack of capacity, may lose its autonomy or some of it (see below). The following points illustrate a few areas of provincial autonomy (or the degree thereof) in school education.

- Intergovernmental cooperation and coordination must be seen as an ongoing process for the development of efficient goverment in all spheres. One way of achieving it is by sharing expertise, and through coherent planning and joint management of scarce resources.[29] For example, the equitable division of national revenue among the provinces is regulated by national legislation. Such legislation must consider, inter alia, that the provinces must be able to provide school education in their respective provinces (see below). Intergovernmental cooperation also addresses extreme disparities between respective provinces and help to rectify imbalances to raise the standard of education in those provinces, as well as provincial education standards in general.[30]
- A provincial legislature is elected directly according to an electoral system that generally provides for proportional representation. This ensures that most political parties are represented in the legislature (and executive) and directly involved in shaping school education according to the needs of the inhabitants of the province. In this way cultural, religious and ethnic differences in school education can be accommodated and better managed.[31]
- The legislative authority of a provincial legislature is entrenched in the Constitution (section 104) and provinces have the competence to adopt their own provincial constitutions. Provincial school laws are original laws because a provincial legislature has original legislative powers to regulate school education comprehensively. School laws are also not subordinate to national school laws. The fact that the adoption of school education laws is

[29] Burns, Yvonne *op. cit.* 70–71.

[30] See De Villiers, Bertus 'Intergovernmental relations: a Constitutional framework' in De Villiers (ed.) (1994) *op. cit.* 256 at 272–278.

[31] Rautenbach, I.M. and Malherbe, E.F.J. *op. cit.* (1996) 237.

shared between the national and provincial legislature simply emphasizes the fact that a different type of power (that of the national legislature) is required to govern school education in its national context.[32] Section 146 provides which law prevails in the case of a conflict but does not limit legislative authority. The Constitutional Court decided in *In re: National Education Policy Bill 83 of 1995* 1996 4 BCLR 518(CC) paragraph 14 (in respect of concurrent powers under the interim Constititon) that both spheres of government may freely make laws on concurrent functional areas.

- The national government must assist the provinces through legislation or other measures to develop the administrative capacity required for the effective exercise of their powers and performance of their functions in the provision of school education.[33]
- Within the framework of cooperative government the provinces enjoy constitutional status and protection.[34] There are express constitutional safeguards to protect the geographical, functional and institutional integrity of the province in its intergovernmental relations.[35] For example, the hierarchical structure in which a central level of government had the largest concentration of powers and was inherently more important, stronger and more efficient than the other 'smaller' levels, has been changed.[36] The new horizontal structuring of spheres of government, signifies that each sphere is equally important in its own jurisdictional area. This notion (also underscored in Chapter 10 of the Constitution) should safeguard provincial autonomy and develop its capacity to govern school education more effectively.

Encroachment upon provincial autonomy in school education

Encroachment upon provincial autonomy in education is caused by different reasons and manifests itself in various forms and degrees. The following points illustrate only a few situations and may differ from province to province.

32 Van Wyk, Dawid 'Subsidiariteit as waarde wat die oop en demokratiese Suid-Afrikaanse gemeenskap ten grondslag lê' in Carpenter, Gretchen (ed.) *Suprema lex Essays on the Constitution* presented to Marinus Wiechers (1998) 251 at 267–268.

33 Burns, Yvonne *op. cit.* 71.

34 e.g. under certain circumstances, provincial laws on concurrent matters are subject to national laws, but parliament does not have unlimited authority over those matters: Rautenbach, I.M. and Malherbe, E.F.J. *op. cit.* (1996) 258–259.

35 e.g. the institution of the National Council of Provinces in which the provinces have a direct control over the way in which their representatives vote in the Council – s. 65; special procedures for cooperation where inconsistencies or conflict may occur, as discussed above; s. 125(3) which underlines national government's duty to assist in the development of provinces.

36 e.g. although parliament has residual power to pass legislation on areas not covered in Schs. 4 and 5, it does not mean that parliament can exercise those powers. Parliament may indeed transfer those legislative powers to the provincial legislature or pass the legislation and transfer the application to the provincial executive: Van Wyk, Dawid *op. cit. Suprema Lex* 267–268.

- Provinces are partners in the cooperative relationship and therefore subject to the principles of cooperative government. A province, for example, may not encroach arbitrarily on the constitutional position and status of the national government. However, national government has far-reaching powers to intervene in provincial affairs and may even cut off provincial funds.[37] National legislation regulates provincial finance and provincial authority over such legislation has been diminished because the National Council of Provinces (in contrast to the former Senate) does not have to adopt such a bill in a separate sitting and thus, in effect, exercises a veto over it.[38] Provinces must receive an equitable share of the national budget and certain prescribed factors are considered in the distribution of the budget. Provinces themselves are responsible for the division of the provincial budget, and the revenue allocated to the education budget will depend on factors such as needs, the availability of financial and other resources and the priority of education in the province.

  In the light of the general financial crisis in school education and the crippling effect it has had on human resources and the economy in general, one has to question whether proper attention has been given to provincial education needs. For example, what is 'equitable' distribution and, furthermore, what is meant by 'national interest and needs,' 'fiscal capacity and efficiency' and obligations and ability of provinces to provide services and perform their functions? To what extent has the lack of financial resources generally, but particularly in education, influenced (and contributed to) the incapacity and inabilility of provinces to exercise their powers and perform their functions effectively? On the other hand, how effective is the supervision of national government over provincial government, and has enough been

37 In terms of ss. 214(1) and 227(1) national legislation must provide for the equitable distribution of the national income among, inter alia, all three spheres of government. Such legislation may be adopted only after consultation with the provinces and organized local government and after consideration of the recommendations of the Financial and Fiscal Commission. Factors that must be taken into account include: the national interest and needs; the assurance that the provinces are able to provide basic services and perform their functions; the fiscal capacity and efficiency of provinces and their developmental and other needs; economic disparities; and obligations of the provinces. All income received by the province must be paid into a provincial revenue fund and money may be withdrawn from it only in terms of legislative prescriptions. The form and detail of provincial budgets are prescribed by national legislation and a national treasury controls provincial finances – s. 226(1) and (2), 215 and 216.

38 cf. ss. 155–157 of the interim Constitution. The arguments of the Consitutional Court in *In re: Certification of the Constitution of the Republic of South Africa of 1996* 1996 11 BCLR 1419(CC) paras 422–422 on why the new provision in the Constitution does not constitute a diminution of provincial powers, is unconvincing: Rautenbach, I.M. and Malherbe, E.F.J. *op. cit.* (1996) 247–248, 259.

done to assist the provinces to develop their capacities (particularly education capacity)?

- As mentioned before, national government supervises the administration of the provinces. Provinces have executive authority over national legislation falling within the school education ('concurrent') domain (e.g. the SASA) only to the extent that they have the administrative capacity to assume effective responsibility. However, in the spirit of cooperative government, the national government is obligated to assist the province by way of legislation and other measures to develop the administrative capacity that is required for the effective exercise of its powers.[39] A dispute on the question whether the province has the administrative capacity to administer the particular national law, must be referred to the National Council of Provinces for resolution within 30 days. When a province does not fulfil its executive obligation (e.g. the application in the province of the national SASA, or regulations, norms and standards in terms of it), the national government may intervene by taking any appropriate steps to ensure that the obligation is fulfilled.[40]

  Once again, whether a province has the ability or capacity to administer the SASA, for example, depends to a large extent on the services (supervision, assistance, capacity-development, etc.) provided by the national government in the cooperative partnership. For example, if education facilities are not improved, professional expertise and management skills not developed, provinces will experience an ongoing battle to implement school laws, norms and standards effectively. Needless to say, a shortage of financial resources (as mentioned above) has a serious impact on capacity-building and efficiency.

Finally, it is apparent that provinces themselves must, in terms of the principle of cooperative government (Chapter 3) and the values and principles prescribed for the public administration (Chapter 10), strive towards their own development and capacity-building since they are not totally dependent on the national government for assistance. They have to claim, watch over and protect their autonomy in provincial education through the various procedures and mechanisms provided for in the Constitution for this purpose. Ultimately, a finely-tuned or balanced relationship in the 'self-rule' and 'shared-ruled' domain

[39] S. 125(3). This provision did not appear in the interim Constitution and must be read in the context of cooperative government: Rautenbach, I.M. and Malherbe, E.F.J. *op. cit.* 251–252.

[40] S. 100(1). These steps taken by the national executive include: issuing a directive to the province which sets out the failure and states the steps required to meet the obligation; assuming responsibility for the obligation to the extent that it is necessary to maintain essential national standards to meet minimum standards for the rendering of a service or to prevent unreasonable action by the province that would prejudice another province or the country as a whole.

provides the barometer for provincial autonomy (*in casu* in school education) and provinces have to guard that education powers and functions are exercised as closely as possible to their inhabitants.

3. Autonomy of public schools in education

Public schools in the constitutional context

South Africa's new constitutional democracy paved the way for a new democratic education system. This meant that the imperatives of democracy and human-rights protection had to be followed and finally culminated in the establishment of a single, non-discriminatory system of education which provides equal opportunity for all. Education reform forms part of the overall transitional process and many old educational structures have been transformed or are in the process of being changed. Apart from the purely constitutional challenges in education, the goverment and other education stakeholders were also confronted with another more practical and logistical problem, namely, the rationalization of the previously fragmented, diverse and unequal education system(s), into a single democratic system.[41]

This discussion deals with public schools: the emphasis is on the development of the new school-education system and the place of the public school in this system. After that, the autonomy (or degree of) of the ordinary public school is examined.

Public schools in the school-education system

Throughout the negotiations that eventually led to the establishment of the new school-education system, the various stakeholders and interest groups were given the assurance of the government's commitment to 'creating sufficient legal, political, linguistic and cultural space for all our varied peoples to live in peace together' and the 'active encouragement of mutual respect for our people's diverse religious, cultural and language traditions, their right to enjoy and practise these in peace and without hindrance, and the recognition that these are the source of strength for their own communities and the unity of the nation'.[42]

The Cabinet approved *White Paper* 2 as well as three other documents related to school education during 1995/96. The most important of these documents was the Draft South African Schools Bill of 1995. The mandate of

41 Department of Education. *White Paper on education and training* (1995).

42 Department of Education. *White Paper on the organisation, governance and funding of schools* (1995) (White Paper 1) 19, 22; Department of Education. *White Paper on the organisation, governance and funding of schools* (1996) (White Paper 2) 5–7.

the legal team which drafted this legislation was not only to draft legislation within the parameters of the constitutional framework, but to capture the core elements of the Constitution (e.g. fundamental rights) in the school system. The Bill was approved in September 1996 and came into operation in January 1997. The South African Schools Act 101 of 1996 (SASA) is the most important piece of national legislation pertaining to schools. Education (*in casu* school education) falls within the concurrent legislative authority of national and provincial government (discussed above), and with this statute the national legislature proposed to establish uniform norms and standards and school policy for all schools in a national context.[43] Provincial legislatures have all promulgated their own school laws to regulate school education in their respective provinces.[44] (Individual provincial school education laws will not be discussed.)

The SASA provides for school education in South Africa and deals in particular with the organization, governance and funding of schools. The preamble reads:

> WHEREAS the achievement of democracy in South Africa has consigned to history the past system of education which was based on racial inequality and segregation; and
>
> WHEREAS this country requires a new national system for schools which will redress past injustices in educational provision, provide an education of progressively high quality for all learners and in so doing lay a strong foundation for the development of all our people's talent and capabilities, advance the democratic transformation of society, combat racism and sexism and all other forms of unfair discrimination and intolerance, contribute to the eradication of poverty and the economic well-being of society, protect and advance our diverse cultures and languages, uphold the rights of all learners, parents and educators, and promote their acceptance of responsibility for the organisation, governance and funding of schools in partnership with the State; and
>
> WHEREAS it is necessary to set uniform norms and standards for the

[43] Other national laws which affect school education include: the National Education Policy Act 27 of 1996 which deals with the determination of national education policy and the monitoring and evaluation of education; the South African Qualifications Authority Act 58 of 1995 which provides for the establishment of a national qualifications authority to oversee the development and implementation of a national qualifications framework.

[44] e.g. the Northern Province School Education Act 9 of 1995; Western Cape School Education Law 10 of 1994; Gauteng School Education Act 6 of 1995. Provincial school-education legislation is not discussed in this paper.

education of learners at schools and the organisation, governance and funding of schools throughout the Republic of South Africa.[45]

The preamble reiterates, inter alia, the importance of equality of treatment and opportunities in a democratic education system, as well as the importance of education in eradicating poverty and creating economic well-being. Another important principle is that of responsibility by all education stakeholders in the organization, governance and funding of public schools. Through this 'partnership' relationship all education stakeholders (particularly the parent- and learner-community) have become more involved in the running of schools but have also incurred more responsibilities in that they, inter alia, have to contribute more towards funding to improve the quality of education in their school.

The public school as a juristic person

In terms of section 1 of the SASA, only two main categories of schools exist, namely public schools (ordinary public schools and public schools for learners with special education needs) and independent schools. Every public school is a 'juristic person' with the legal capacity to perform its functions in terms of the SASA (s. 15).

In terms of the law, legal relationships exist between persons. A 'person' in the eyes of the law can be a natural (human) person or an 'entity' such as a company, university or school. These entities are called juristic persons because, as in the case of natural persons, the law regards them as legal subjects and therefore having the capacity to be bearers of rights and obligations.[46] In terms of section 8 of the Constitution, a juristic person (also 'organs of state' in terms of s. 239) are bound by the the Bill of Rights and entitled to rights guaranteed in the Bill of Rights to the extent required by the nature of the rights and the nature of the juristic person.[47] Naturally, the juristic person also carries all the responsibilities and liabilities attached to its status (e.g. it has to fulfil its obligations, can sue and be sued in its own name – e.g. in the case of breach of contract).[48] It is obvious that a juristic person is not a natural person, and cannot perform all the functions of a human person. Unlike the natural person,

[45] The SASA comprises various chapters which deal with matters such as: Definitions and Application of the Act; Learners; Public Schools; Funding of Public Schools; Independent Schools; Transitional Provisions; General Provisions.

[46] e.g., a natural person may enter into a contract and purchase a car (a legal object). Similarly, the school may enter into a contract with another legal subject (a company) to purchase assets such as equipment and stock (legal objects).

[47] e.g. the public school is entitled to freedom of association and freedom of expression, although not unlimited or unqualified freedom (s. 36 may limit these rights as prescribed). On the other hand the school has no right to life.

[48] Hosten, W.J. *et al. Introduction to South Africanh law and legal theory* (1995) 542–544.

the juristic person has perpetual succession and will continue to exist as an entity despite any change that may take place in its constituent parts.[49] In terms of section 33 of the SASA, the MEC may by notice in the *Provincial Gazette* close a public school and thereby terminate its existence.

As a legal entity, the school participates in the law and may enter into different legal relationships with other legal subjects (natural persons or juristic entities). If it enters into a private contract to purchase sports equipment for the school, both parties will agree to the contractual terms on an equal and voluntary basis, each party fulfilling its own (private) interests. This contractual relationship is called a private law relationship. Since the school is a public school and functions in the public-education system, it operates primarily in the public-law sphere. Public law (or state law) regulates relationships between legal subjects and one subject is always an organ of the state and in an authoritative position. The relationship is therefore authoritative and coercive and performed with the public (education) interest in mind.[50] In this context, a public school may for all practical purposes be regarded as an 'organ of state' because it exercises public-education powers or performs public functions in terms of legislation: it is therefore part of the larger public administration of education.[51] Chapter 10 of the Constitution (Public Administration) provides that 'organs of state' (*in casu* public schools) must be governed by the democratic values enshrined in the Constitution and, inter alia, be development-oriented, and promote a high standard of professional ethics (see above).[52]

[49] *Ibid* 869–870. This means that the members of the governing body of the school may change and parents and learners come and go, but the school as a juristic entity remains intact until its existence is legally terminated.

[50] e.g. the minister must, after consultation with the MEC and by notice in the *Government Gazette*, determine the date by which election of members of governing bodies at all public schools in a province must be finalized (s. 54). Public schools are compelled to adhere to this notice because public education interests demand that schools function properly with duly elected governing bodies. It is also in the interest of public education that all learners receive compulsory basic education (a fundamental right protected by the State) and the parent (or responsible person) who fails to comply with this provision is guilty of an offence – s. 2(1) and 3(6). Wiechers, Marinus *Administrative law* (1985) (translated by Gretchen Carpenter) 7–9, 46–50; Kleyn, D. and Viljoen, F. *Beginner's Guide for law students* (1995) 101–102.

[51] 'Organ of state' is defined in s. 239 as, inter alia, (a) any department of state or administration in the national, provincial and local sphere of government, or (b) any other functionary or institution – (i) exercising a power or performing a function in terms of the Constitution or a provincial constitution, or (ii) *exercising a public power or performing a public function in terms of any legislation* ... (My emphasis.) See Rautenbach, I.M. and Malherbe, E.F.J. *op. cit.* (1997) 161.

[52] Other principles underlying Chap. 10 include: to promote efficient, economic and effective use of resources; people's needs must be responded to; the public must be encouraged to participate in policy-making; transparency must be fostered; good

The governing body

As a result of its abstract and fictitious nature, the school needs one of its constituent parts to formally act on its behalf and perform legal transactions in its name.[53] The SASA provides that the governing body of a public school acts on behalf of the school. For example, when the governing body suspends the learner in terms of section 9 from attending school, the action against the learner is taken in the name of the school and the school as a legal entity (not the governing body or its disciplinary committee) is legally responsible for this conduct (s. 9). The SASA provides in section 16(1) that the governance of a public school is vested in its governing body. Furthermore, the governing body stands in a position of 'trust' towards the school and this simply means that a relationship of trust (a fiduciary relationship) exists between the school and its governing body.

The governing body comprises representatives of all stakeholders (e.g. parents, educators, staff and learners) and although no prescription exists regarding the number of members, parents must comprise the majority vote (s. 23). Special provision is made for learner representation on governing bodies of secondary schools (ss. 11 and 32) and for the composition of the governing body of a public school providing education to learners with special education needs (s. 24).

All public schools must have governing bodies, and the MEC determines the process for the nomination and election of members of the governing body (s. 28).[54]

Capacity-building programme

Since local (school) communities share in the management of schools, they are also responsible for efficient and effective school governance through their representative governing body. The governing body is, in terms of sections 16, 20 and 36, responsible for the proper governance of the school and the provision of quality education at the school. It is therefore imperative that special training be provided for governing bodies (particularly parents) who have thus far had very little knowledge of or experience in the governance of a school.

---

human-resource management and career development practices to maximize human potential must be cultivated and the public administration must be broadly representative of the South African people (s. 195(1)).

53 Hosten *et al. op. cit.* 553–554.

54 The govering body elects its own office bearers (e.g. chair, treasurer and secretary) and the chairperson must be a parent not employed at the school (s. 29). Governing bodies also establish committees to assist them in their work and may even co-opt persons who are not on the governing body. The term of membership of a parent is a maximum of three years while learners and office bearers serve for a maximum of one year. Nevertheless, any member of the governing body or an office bearer may be re-elected or co-opted and no specific term is prescribed (s. 31).

To this effect section 19 of the SASA provides that out of funds appropriated for this purpose by the provincial legislature, the provincial Head of Department (HoD) must establish a programme to provide introductory training for newly elected governing bodies to enable them to perform their functions. Furthermore, continued training must be given to governing bodies to promote effective performance of their functions and to enable them to assume additional functions. The HoD must also ensure that principals and other officials of the education departments render all necessary assistance to governing bodies in the performance of their functions.

From the discussion above, it is clear that the purpose of the SASA, the nature of the public school and its governing body, and the provincial department's commitment to capacity building, all point to the principles underlined in Chapter 10 (Public Administration) of the Constitution. For example, the promotion of professional ethics, public participation in policy-making (e.g. the partnership relationship), transparency and accountability, broad representation and the need to redress the imbalances of the past, to name a few.

The values and principles underscored by the Constitution and education legislation also enhance the development of the principle of subsidiarity which advocates nearness or closeness of power to the people (e.g. the school as part of its community and therefore the most suitable entity to govern the educational needs and interests of its community), or, to the most practicable sphere of government (*in casu* the province in charge of provincial education).[55]

Functions of the governing body

All governing bodies must perform the functions listed in section 20. They include: to promote the best interests of the school and strive to ensure its development through the provision of quality education for all its learners; to adopt a constitution for the school and a code of conduct for learners; to develop a mission statement for the school; to support the principal and staff members in the performance of their professional functions; to determine school times consistent with applicable conditions of employment of the staff; to administer and control the school's property and buildings and grounds occupied by the school; to encourage parents, learners, educators and other staff to render voluntary services to the school; to recommend to the HoD the appointment of educators and non-educators subject to relevant employment legislation; to allow (at the request of the HoD) the reasonable use under fair conditions of the facilities of the school for educational programmes not conducted by the school; to discharge other functions consistent with the SASA as determined by the Minister or MEC. Governing bodies may also join voluntary associations representing governing bodies of public schools (s. 20(3)).

[55] Van Wyk, Dawid 'Subsidiariteit as waarde wat die oop en demokratiese Suid-Afrikaanse gemeenskap ten grondslag lê' in *Suprema lex op. cit.* 251.

In terms of section 21, a governing body may also apply to the HoD to be allocated any of the following functions: the maintenance and improvement of the school's property, buildings and grounds; the determination of the extra-mural curriculum of the school and the choice of subject options in terms of provincial curriculum policy; purchasing of textbooks, educational materials or equipment for the school; other functions consistent with the Act and any applicable provincial law. The HoD may approve such an application unconditionally or subject to certain conditions, or refuse such an application if the governing body does not have the capacity to perform such function. The decision by the HoD must be in writing and reasons must be furnished. A person aggrieved by the decision of the HoD may appeal to the MEC. The MEC may, by notice in the *Provincial Gazette*, determine that some governing bodies may exercise one or more functions without applying for the allocated functions, for example, in a case where the governing body has the capacity to perform such a function effectively and there is a reasonable and equitable basis for doing so (s. 21(6)). Furthermore, if the MEC decides that it is in the best interests of school education at particular schools, the governance of two or more public schools will vest in a single governing body, subject to certain procedures being followed (s. 17).

Any function of a governing body may be withdrawn by the HoD on reasonable grounds, provided the correct procedures have been followed (s. 2(1)–(2)). Although the HoD may in urgent cases withdraw a function immediately and follow the prescribed procedures afterwards, such action may also be reversed or suspended. An aggrieved person may appeal against the decision of the HoD to the MEC (s. 22(5)). In the case of a failure by a governing body to perform its functions (reasons for failure are not mentioned), the HoD must appoint persons to perform such functions (s. 25)).[56]

In furthering the interests of the school, a governing body must in terms of section 36, take all reasonable measures within its means to supplement the resources supplied by the State to improve the quality of education provided by the school to all its learners. This function underscores the principle of 'partnership' between the state and the school community. The governing body may determine and charge school fees provided it is adopted by the majority of parents at the general meeting of parents (s. 39). The resolution adopted by the majority of parents must provide for the amount of fees to be charged and equitable criteria and procedures for the total, partial or conditional exemption of parents who are unable to pay. The minister must issue regulations regarding equitable criteria and procedures for exemption of payment of school fees. Once the payment of school fees has been determined in terms of section 39, parents who must pay are liable to pay such fees and the governing body has

[56] There is no indication who these 'persons' would be but the HoD must ensure that a governing body is elected within one year after the appointment of these persons.

the power to enforce payment of fees on behalf of the school by process of law (s. 41). An aggrieved parent may appeal to the HoD against the decision of the governing body regarding exemption from paying school fees. In terms of section 38, a governing body must prepare a budget according to guidelines determined by the MEC, but before the budget is approved by the governing body, it must be considered and approved by a majority of parents at a parents' meeting.

The State's obligations towards public schools
In terms of section 34, the state bears overall responsibility for inter alia the funding of all public schools. This responsibility originated in the position of the modern state as an 'administrative state:' it provides for the development of public functions (i.e. health, education) through the establishment of infrastructures and the provision of resources.[57]

The state owns the immovable property of all public schools, except in the case of public schools on private property (ss. 55–57). The immovable property of former state-aided schools (e.g. Model-C schools) reverted back to the State in terms of procedures set in section 55(1). The SASA provides for an agreement with the owner of the private property on which a public school is situated and the minister must issue regulations regarding the minimum requirements of such an agreement. The agreement must provide inter alia for the provision of education and the performance of the normal functions of the school, the governance of the school including the relationship between the governing body of the school and the owner, and the protection of the owner's rights in respect of the property occupied, affected or used by the school (s. 14). In terms of section 57, a religious organization which is the owner of the private property of a public school, may require that the above agreement must recognize the religious character of the school. The State may even expropriate land for educational purposes, for example, the MEC is empowered to expropriate land or real rights in or over land for any purpose related to school education in the province but the correct procedures for expropriation and the determination of compensation must be followed (s. 58).

The State (minister) determines the norms and standards for funding and procedures to be followed (s. 35), and must furnish financial information to enable schools to plan their budgets for the next year (s. 34(2)). During the transitional period, assets and liabilities of a school (which became a public school) and which had vested in the school, will continue to vest in the school. Funds and other moveable assets of a school which belonged to the State, will remain at the disposal of the school and will devolve on the school on a date and subject to conditions determined by the minister (s. 52).

57 Henning, P.J. v. R. 'Die administratiewe staat' 1968 *THRHR* 1ff; Wiechers, Marinus *op. cit.* (1985) 9, 14.

Section 34 provides that the State must fund public schools on an equitable basis to ensure the proper exercise of the right to education of all learners and the redress of past inequalities in education provision. This provision reflects the State's responsibilities in terms of its position as protector of fundamental rights in a constitutional democracy: it recognizes and protects individual fundamental rights in terms of the Bill of Rights.[58] Section 60 provides for overall state liability and stipulates that the State is liable for any damage or loss caused as a result of any act or omission in connection with any educational activity conducted by a public school and for which such a school would have been liable but for the provisions of section 60. The provisions of the State Liability Act of 1957 apply to any such claim.

Finally, the State may terminate the legal personality of a public school. In terms of section 33, the MEC may by notice in the *Provincial Gazette* close a public school. The correct procedures must be followed and all assets and liabilities (subject to conditions of trusts, donations, etc.) devolve on the state unless agreed otherwise between the MEC and the governing body of the school (e.g. the case of a public school on private land).

Are public schools autonomous?

To determine whether a public school is autonomous (e.g. has its own unique powers of self-governance), one has to, as in the case of provinces, see autonomy (or the lack of it) within the relational context. First, the school's relationship with the province as the public-education authority (State) and, secondly, the public school's internal relationship (with the governing body representing the stakeholders). The relationship between the State and the school has been described, inter alia, as one of a partnership (participation and responsibilities are shared); within the school itself, a relationship of trust exists between the school and its governing body and school governance must be tested against the democratic values and principles enshrined in the Constitution.[59]

Indications of public school autonomy

The following illustrations of a school's autonomy are not exhaustive and varying degrees of autonomy may be found.

- In terms of the SASA, the public school is a juristic person with the legal capacity to perform its functions through its governing body. The primary objective of the relationship of trust is to serve the best interests of the

[58] Rautenbach, I.M. and Malherbe, E.F.J. *Your rights in the Constitution* (1994) 1ff.

[59] See the discussion of Chap. 10 (Public Administration) above. Also Visser, Hans 'Some principles regarding the rights, duties and functions of parents in terms of the provisions of the South African Schools Act 84 of 1996 applicable to public schools' in De Groof, Jan *et al.* (eds) *Human rights in South African education* (1997) 133–144.

school. As a juristic person the school exercises its autonomy (self-governance) within its own jurisdiction (the school and school-education activities). The governing body performs functions listed in the SASA (plus other functions not specifically mentioned) in compliance of the school's legal personality (e.g. policy making, financial administration, contracting, buying and selling, suing and being sued in the name of the school).

- The school establishes its own unique character in the community, and fulfils the needs and aspirations of the community through, inter alia, its admission policy, and cultural, linguistic and religious affiliations. The school achieves this autonomy through legitimate means (e.g. its governing body is representative of all its stakeholders with a majority vote to parents; a relationship of trust is maintained and democratic values and norms are practised according to the Constitution and relevant national and provincial school laws).
- The partnership relationship between the State and the public school manifests itself, inter alia, in the concentration of stakeholder representation in the governing body of the school and the practising of participative, transparent and accountable management and governance. The sharing of responsibilities and liabilities generates mutual trust, support and solidarity within the school, its community and society in general.
- The public school is empowered to manage and govern its educational and administrative functions on a day-to-day basis without undue interference from the State (*in casu* provincial or national education authorities). It has wide-ranging rule-making powers (e.g. to draft its own constitution and mission statement, admission policy, language policy and code of conduct); extensive powers to implement rules and regulations (e.g. to apply and implement its admission policy, code of conduct and disciplinary rules); and effective mechanisms to control these actions (e.g. internal and external 'due process' procedures to secure lawful, fair and reasonable conduct, and access to judicial (final) control by the courts).
- Special procedures of 'due process' (administrative-justice rules) have to be followed by the State (minister, MEC and HoD) in cases where they share (or interfere) in the powers and functions of the school. For example, the HoD may withdraw some functions of the governing body but only on reasonable grounds, and provision is made for appeal to the MEC; the MEC may close a public school but only after the 'due process' procedure has been followed.[60] Within the internal sphere of school administration, the

[60] In *OVS Vereniging vir Staatsondersteunde Skole v. Premier, Provinsie Vrystaat* 1996 2 BCLR 248(O) the court set aside the decision to suspend the payment of subsidies to state-aided schools (model-C schools) because the applicant had had a legitimate expectation based on an express promise given by the public authority, and the existence of a regular practice that the subsidy would be paid again to the schools. The *White Paper* (2) (1996) expressly stated that any necessary change in this regard would be preceded by prior consultation with the interested parties, but no such consultation had taken place.

same democratic process of 'due process' has to be followed: for example, an aggrieved parent may appeal to the HoD against the decision of the governing body regarding exemption from payment of school fees; the HoD must furnish the parent with reasons for the refusal to admit the learner to the school, and the parent or learner may appeal to the MEC against such a refusal; a learner may be expelled from school by the HoD provided he/she had received a fair hearing and was found guilty; the learner or parent may appeal to the MEC against the expulsion.

- Although the public school does not own the immovable property of the school (state-owned), it uses it to the benefit of the school and with the best interests of education in mind. There are special procedures of participation and consultation prescribed with regard to schools on private property and how to protect the rights and interests of both the landowner and the school.
- Public schools receive state subsidies on an 'equitable' basis but with due regard to the fulfilment of the learner's right to education and of redressing the inequalities of the past. However, the governing body has the responsibility to improve the quality of education in the school with additional funds generated in the community, as approved by the parents. The governing body has wide scope in generating such funds and the application of these funds.
- The school manages its own funds and prepares proper financial records. The records must be audited and statements submitted to the HoD as prescribed by the SASA.

Finally, in the light of the preceding paragraphs, one realizes that within the framework set by the Constitution and relevant education legislation (particularly the national SASA), public schools have much scope to acquire (and improve) autonomy within their own sphere. Similarly, the school has the obligation to protect and practise its autonomy in the interests of education in its community.

Encroachment upon the autonomy of the public school

It was mentioned earlier that autonomy (or the lack of it) must be gauged contextually (e.g. within the relationships that exist). The question is therefore: does the State encroach upon the autonomy of the school and, if so, to what extent? Only a few examples will be used.

- The State issues regulations, guidelines, norms and standards on various issues that fall within the powers of the school, or are 'shared' between State and school. Although these prescriptions are not always binding (e.g. guidelines on minimum standards) they are overarching and intended to establish uniformity and equal standards in the province or nationally. Many of these prescriptions may encroach upon the powers of schools and detract from their unique character, values and tradition. For example, the governing body is in charge of the admission policy and code of conduct and may develop a language policy for the school.[61] The governing body must adhere to prescribed procedures of consultation and participation in developing these policies. Nevertheless, the minister determines age requirements for admission to the school or different grades at the school and also determines norms and standards for a language policy. Does this mean that the governing body has to change the school policies that were approved by the stakeholders?

The Constitution of the school is developed in a similar way by the governing body but must comply with minimum standards set by the minister.[62] Another example is where the Minister issues regulations regarding equitable criteria and procedures for total, partial or conditional exemption of parents who are unable to pay school fees, and also sets guidelines to help governing bodies in matters relating to charging and collection of and exemption from paying school fees. The parents of the school have to decide with a majority vote on all these school funding issues at a general meeting and may even employ educators out of funds they have raised privately. However, they are not free to choose the educators they want to provide quality education in their school and are now restricted to lists supplied by the State in terms of the rationalization and redeployment of educators.[63] One does understand the role of the State in its partnership and developmen-

[61] cf. Potgieter, Johan 'The South African Schools Act, 1996: Comments on the functions of school governing bodies, with special reference to admission and language policies' in De Groof, Jan *et al.* (eds) *Human rights in South African education* (1997) 107–132.

[62] e.g. to what extent does the standards and qualifications of the National Qualifications Framework (NQF) with its strong centralized effect, impact on the freedom of expression (particularly academic freedom – s. 16(1)(d) of the Bill of Rights of the juristic person? Furthermore, the governing body issues rules regarding religious observances, subject to the Constitution and applicable provincial laws. Observances must be conducted on an equitable basis and attendance is free and voluntary – s. 8. Does it involve multifaith in every school and what does the admission policy determine (what can it determine and what are the practical implications)? Schools based on common religion and the right of learners not to attend religious education classes and practices encroach upon the right of persons to attend schools where religious education activities are compulsory. *In re: The School Education Bill of 1995 (Gauteng) 1996* 4 BCLR 537 (CC). This case dealt with the right to establish where practicable, educational institutions based on common religion, provided there is no discrimination on the ground of race in terms of s. 32(c) of interim Constitution. The Court held that the government is not obliged to create schools based on a common religion. It only guarantees to those who wish to establish such a school, the freedom to do so, provided there is no racial discrimination.

[63] cf. the *Grove Primary School v. Minister of Education and Others* 1998 4 SA 982(C).

tal role, but to what extent should it curb the initiatives and autonomy of the school in these issues?[64]

- The State has to fund public schools. The term 'equitable' distribution to schools must be interpreted in terms of the constitutional values and ideals and the relevant education legislation (e.g. to realize the right to education and redress inequalities). In terms of the partnership relationship, all governing bodies are responsible for raising additional funds to improve the quality of education for all the learners in the school. It is a fact that poor schools cannot raise additional money to improve the quality of their education and this restricts their autonomy and has far-reaching implications for juristic personality.

  The State also does not have sufficient funds for education (e.g. only 10% of the total education budget is allocated to learner spending and non-personnel costs). As a result of this, it cannot spend more money on capacity building or the provision of quality education. The new education system requires new norms and standards and proper skills and expertise from managers and governing bodies, but poor schools (the majority of public schools) will not be able to 'afford' these. Without financial resources the right to education is worthless.
- The capacity of a governing body to perform its functions (or apply for additional functions), is dependent upon its expertise and skills and the availability of funds in the community. On the other hand, the State has an obligation to provide training and continued training to governing bodies; if expertise and skills are not developed, public schools will always be dependent on the State (a type of 'forced' dependence or disempowerment).

Finally, public schools are juristic persons and as 'organs of state', must promote cooperative, transparent and accountable governance within their own spheres. They must know their 'rights' and how to use their powers and functions within the parameters of the Constitution and relevant education legislation. They must guard against encroachment upon their autonomy and against mismanagement and corruption in their own sphere.

4. Conclusion

The principles of self-rule and shared-ruled permeate the entire education sphere. When dealing with the relationship between spheres of government

64 See also *Beeld* of 9 Dec. 1998 'Boer stoot skool plat' where a public school on private land was bulldozed by the landowner. The relevant agreements and procedures in terms of s. 14 of the SASA have not been fulfilled and regulations on the matter (as prescribed in the SASA) have not yet been issued by the minister. An example of how the autonomy of the school is affected when the state fails to fulfil its obligations.

(national and provincial) it is referred to as 'cooperative government'. In the relationship between the provincial education authority and the public school, it manifests itself in the 'partnership' relationship. Both relationships are based on recognition of and respect for each other's distinct character, and working together in an interdependent and interrelated manner to achieve the best results for education through the sharing of scarce resources. Democratic principles such as cooperation, trust, public (stakeholder) participation, transparency and accountability are the building blocks for achieving the cooperative relationships.

It is apparent that self-governance (autonomy or 'self-rule') is protected in the different relationships and that much scope has been left for the development of community participation in decision-making in the 'smaller' spheres of public functioning (i.e. a province or a public school). This ensures that decisions are made as closely as possible to the people which enhances the political credibility and accountability of the decision-makers.[65] The promotion of self-governance (autonomy) in the spheres of government (or public functionaries) closest to the people, underscores the principle of subsidiarity: it endeavours to strike a balance in power sharing and promote good government.[66]

The Constitution provides the foundation for balance and self-determination in these relationships, but years of neglect and the apartheid heritage cannot be changed overnight. Although the need for effective government is high on the South African political agenda, subsidiarity and effectiveness should complement each other and will depend on the extent of powers vested in the spheres of government and public functionaries to fulfil their constitutional obligations. Provisions in the Constitution and relevant education legislation leave opportunity for the presumption of power in favour of the 'smaller' spheres. It is proposed that politicians and courts favour the term of subsidiarity and indicate that the 'smaller' sphere has power, unless it does not want it or cannot exercise it. In deciding on who can or will do it, the 'smaller' sphere must participate in the process. The shortage in skills and infrastructure in South Africa means that there will always be competition among spheres to

[65] De Groof, Jan 'The scope of and distinction between Arts. 126 and 127 of the Treaty on European Union and the Implementation of the subsidiarity principle' in De Groof (ed.) *Subsidiarity in education: aspects of comparative educational law* (1994) 77–114; Lenaerts, Koenraad 'Subsidiarity and Community competence in the field of Education' in De Groof (ed.) *op. cit.* (1994) 117–144.

[66] The principle of devolving political decisions to the lowest practical level (but not in the traditional fashion of 'top down' as if all powers are inherent or original at the centre or top) is referred to as the susidiarity principle. Subsidiarity relates to autonomy and self-determination of the individual (e.g. fundamental rights in the Constitution and the emphasis on human dignity, freedom and equality) and also to the relationship among different spheres (levels) of government: Van Wyk, Dawid, *op. cit. Suprema Lex* (1998) 254–259.

get the best – in this context the danger exists that the national government (or 'larger' sphere) almost always wins. Constructive deeds and words are needed from 'larger' spheres to empower 'smaller' ones to place the government in the hands of the people.[67]

[67] Van Wyk, Dawid *op. cit. Suprema Lex* (1998) 267–268.

Country Reports

European Association for Education Law and Policy – ELA

'Autonomy in Education' – ELA Conference, Salzburg, December 1998

National Reports – Questionnaire

I. *Theoretical background*

Educationalists have often put the concept of autonomy at the centre of their reasoning. Ever since Immanuel Kant declared the autonomy of the human will as the supreme principle of morality, a person's self-determination seems to be the ultimate goal of education. Considering this goal, it has often been postulated that the education process itself must be self-regulative. As Eduard Spranger put it in 1928: 'Learning and education will only be successful if teachers and students come together in freedom and the schools themselves are free.'

In this respect, autonomy seems to be an essential prerequisite for education, associated with the principle of pedagogical and/or academic freedom and deduced from specific conditions of the teaching process. On the other hand, the educational system does not exist within a vacuum; instead, it is exposed to various social influences. The State as well as different social forces, such as the economic or the political system or the churches, influence schools or institutions of higher education, thus making them more or less subject to heteronomous laws. In this regard, autonomy of education can probably only be a relative autonomy, whereas its limits are open and fluid.

Autonomy is also a legal concept. It indicates the independence of educational institutions or an area of pedagogical freedom for persons who act within the educational system. But as autonomy has its origin in philosophical and pedagogical reasoning, it is not always a well-fitted legal concept. Therefore, if used in a legal context, the notion of autonomy requires a precise setting. It must be made clear to whom autonomy will be granted and within which limits and for what purpose. If these different qualities of autonomy are not taken into account, misunderstandings will be likely to arise. It is the aim of the Salzburg conference to reflect the relationship between the pedagogical concept of autonomy and its legal consequences.

Walter Berka, Jan de Groof and Hilde Penneman (eds.), Autonomy in Education, 273–275.

II. *Questionnaire*

1. Constitutional legal basis

1.1. Is autonomy of the educational system or of some of its parts constitutionally guaranteed?

1.2. Does the constitution guarantee teachers' educational freedom or the liberty of scientific teaching (academic freedom)?

1.3. If autonomy is constitutionally granted: which notion of autonomy underlies the constitution?

1.4 Are there strict legal bases and describe it?

2. Autonomy of educational institutions

2.1. Is autonomy granted with respect to the organisation of educational institutions? Are schools or universities vested with a legal personality of their own? Have schools or universities individual constitutions of their own (basic statutes, basic charters)? Are these autonomously set up by the educational institutions or conferred onto them by the state or government?

2.2. How independently can they determine the recruitment of their personnel, etc.?

2.3. Are schools or universities entitled to choose freely among applicants with necessary qualifications?

2.3. Is autonomy granted with respect to the fulfilment of the educational objective? Can schools or universities independently organise their curricula, decide autonomously on the numbers of students per class, etc.?

2.4. Autonomy of resources: Are schools/universities free to determine the raising and expenditure of financial resources? Do they have facilities to raise money through sponsoring or through other means, etc.? Are they able to charge tuition fees?

2.5. Autonomy of organization for schools?

2.6. Are schools or universities entitled to defend their autonomous sphere by legal means against the state or government? Do schools have the legal capacity to appeal against acts of a supervisory authority?

3. Individual autonomy

3.1. How much latitude of discretion is granted to teachers/professors in educational matters (content of education and methodological decisions)?

3.2. Is the head of a school (university) or any of its bodies entitled to issue instructions in professional matters to the teaching staff?

3.3. Do the teachers/professors participate in the universities or schools self-governing bodies?

4. Consequences of autonomy

4.1. If educational institutions can act autonomously, how are general aims or values like quality and unity of the education guaranteed?

4.2. Is autonomy necessarily linked with a supervisory power?

4.3. What are the relations between autonomy, responsibility and accountability? Is autonomy necessarily connected with quality control within autonomous educational institutions?

4.4. If there are recent trends in your country with respect to autonomy of educational institutions: Is there a tendency towards enlargement of autonomy or towards more government control? Why is it so? (examples)

MICHAEL GEISTLINGER

Autonomy in the University and Non-University Sectors in Higher Education

AUSTRIAN REPORT

1. Constitutional legal basis

1.1 *Constitutional guarantee of the autonomy of universities and classes and institutes of the non-university sector in higher education in Austria*

Since 1993 the autonomy of universities in Austria has been constitutionally guaranteed by Article 2 paragraph 2 of the Austrian Act on the Organisation of Universities.[1] A comparable autonomy for the non-university sector in higher education, which was legally created in Austria for the first time also in 1993, is deduced from Article 17 paragraph 2 of the Basic Law of 21 December 1867 on the General Rights of Nationals in the Kingdoms and Länder represented in the Reichsrat.[2] Article 17 paragraph 2 reads: 'Every national who has furnished in legally acceptable manner proof of his qualification has the right to found establishments for instruction and education'. This provision is considered not only to form the constitutional basis for private schools in Austria, but also to establish institutes and classes of the non-university sector in higher education (Fachhochschulen, Fachhochschul-Studiengänge).[3] This constitutional guarantee is reflected at the level of general Austrian federal law by

[1] Universitätsorganisationsgesetz 1993, Austrian Federal Law Gazette (BGBl) 1993/805, as amended by I 1997/99.

[2] Staatsgrundgesetz über die allgemeinen Rechte der Staatsbürger für die im Reichsrate vertretenen Königreiche und Länder, Austrian Imperial Law Gazette (RGBl) 1867/42.

[3] See W. Berka, 'Autonomy in education'. Unpublished study for the Austrian Ministry of Science and Traffic. Salzburg 1998, p. 140.

Walter Berka, Jan de Groof and Hilde Penneman (eds.), Autonomy in Education, 277–294.

Article 12 paragraph 5 of the Austrian Act on Classes of the Non-university Sector in Higher Education.[4]

Under the predecessor of the Austrian Act on the Organisation of Universities 1993, the Austrian Act on the Organisation of Universities 1975,[5] a constitutional guarantee of the autonomy of universities did not yet exist. According to Article 1 paragraph 2 lit f of the old law, the universities were attributed autonomy only on the basis of a federal law below the constitution and subject to general laws.

Until the entrance into force of the Austrian Act on the Organisation of Universities 1993 (1 October 1994), the institutional autonomy of universities in Austria on the constitutional level was considered to be an emanation of the freedom of science, which is constitutionally guaranteed in Austria by Article 17 paragraph 1 of the Basic Law of 21 December 1867 on the General Rights of Nationals.[6] Article 17 paragraph 1 reads: 'The science and its teaching are free.' Before and after the adoption of the Austrian Act on the Organisation of Universities 1975, which introduced the organizational system of a so-called group-university, it was strongly disputed in Austrian constitutional doctrine, as well as between the Austrian Constitutional Court and the Austrian Supreme Administrative Court, whether this provision demanded a specific organization of the Austrian universities.[7] Whereas the Austrian Constitutional Court finally decided that Article 17 paragraph 1 of the Basic Law 1867 had no institutional reference,[8] the majority of Austrian constitutional doctrine continued to interpret this provision in a way that constitutionally guarantees a minimum standard of autonomous rights for Austrian universities.[9] This opinion is based on

4 Bundesgesetz über Fachhochschul-Studiengänge (Fachhochschul-Studiengesetz), Austrian Federal Law Gazette 1993/340, as amended by I 1998/72.

5 Universitätsorganisationsgesetz 1975, Austrian Federal Law Gazette 1975/258, as amended by 1978/443, 1981/341, 1987/654, 1988/745, 1990/364, 1991/623, 1993/103, 1993/249, 1993/804, 1995/297, 1995/509, 1996/655, I 1997/109.

6 See fn 2.

7 For details and further references see e.g. G. Wielinger, *Die Freiheit der Wissenschaft in Österreich* (The freedom of science in Austria), EuGRZ 1982, pp. 289–297 (293–296) *idem*; 'Die Freiheit der Wissenschaft' (The freedom of science), in: R. Machacek, W. P. Pahr, G. Stadler (eds.), *40 Jahre EMRK. Grund- und Menschenrechte in Austria* (40 years ECHR. Fundamental and Human Rights in Austria). Kehl *et al.*, 1992, vol 2, pp. 175–194 (184–192).

8 Collection of decisions of the Austrian Constitutional Court (VfSlg) 8136/1977.

9 See e.g. F. Koja, *Wissenschaftsfreiheit und Universität* (Freedom of science and university). Salzburg 1976, pp. 76–80; P. Pernthaler, 'Die Universitätsautonomie im Spannungsfeld von Wissenschaftsfreiheit, Bildungsanstalt und Forschungsunternehmen' (The autonomy of universities within the strained relations of freedom of science, educational establishment, and research enterprise), in: R. Strasser (ed.), *Organisations-, europa- und immaterialgüterrechtliche Probleme der Universitäten* (Problems of the universities relating to organisational law, European law, and Law on non-material goods). Vienna 1992, pp. 1–45 (4 f).

the historic organizational background at the time when the Basic Law was adopted and on the teleological reasoning that the effective guarantee of the individual freedom of science presupposes the adjudication of rights of autonomous decision to university organs.[10] Last but not least, both arguments, however, do not allow a more concrete final conclusion than stating that the freedom of science can be, but need not necessarily be bound to an institutional autonomy of the university. The contents of such a constitutionally required institutional autonomy depends on the purposes of this institution.[11]

1.2. *Constitutional guarantee of the liberty of scientific teaching (academic freedom) and of teaching within the non-university sector of higher education*

Article 17 paragraph 1 of the Basic Law 1867 constitutionally guarantees the liberty of scientific teaching. This guarantee means that scientific teaching must not be determinated by forces outside of science.[12] The guarantee protects against the suppression of different opinions within scientific teaching. The guarantee relates to persons who proved to be able and qualified for scientific research and teaching based on this research.[13] The guarantee, however, is not restricted to persons holding a *venia docendi.*[14]

The liberty of scientific teaching, guaranteed by Article 17 paragraph 1 of the Basic Law 1867, does not relate to teachers/professors at institutes and classes of the non-university sector of higher education (Fachhochschulen, Fachhochschul-Studiengänge). This follows from the specific purposes of Fachhochschulen and the different qualification profile for persons teaching at these institutes. Fachhochschulen and Fachhochschul-Studiengänge typically educate on the basis of scientific views and findings, whereas universities typically educate by science. The principle of unity of scientific research and scientific teaching forms the basis only for universities, not for Fachhochschulen and Fachhochschul-Studiengänge.[15]

1.3. *The notion of autonomy as granted on the constitutional level*

Autonomy of universities as granted by the constitutional provision of Article 2 paragraph 2 of the Austrian Act on the Organisation of Universities 1993[16] means the right to decide independently those public affairs which are linked

[10] See Berka (fn 3), pp. 31 f.

[11] See Berka (fn 3), pp. 33 f.

[12] See e.g. Koja (fn 9), pp. 15 f.

[13] See e.g. Koja (fn 9), pp. 28–47.

[14] See Koja (fn 9), pp. 31 f with further references and Berka (fn 3) p. 25.

[15] See Berka (fn 3), pp. 154 f.

[16] See fn 1.

to the picture of universities and scientific research and teaching as enshrined in the Austrian Constitution. The concrete shape of the provisions of the Act on the Organisation of Universities can serve to indicate the constitutional understanding.[17] The constitutionally guaranteed autonomy, in the sense of a right to self-administration of universities, is thus defined by their functions (concept of a functional autonomy of universities in Austria).[18] By the constitutional provision of Article 7 paragraph 1 of the Austrian Act on the Organisation of Universities 1993, universities are endowed with the right to adopt their own statute ruling on the constitution of organization in the framework of state laws and decrees. The application of the fundamental constitutional principle of legality[19] of all acts of the executive power in Austria, thus, is reduced concerning the self-administration of universities in Austria.[20] The self-administration and right of Austrian universities to have their own statutes not subject to directions, but within the framework of state laws and decrees, is only limited by supervisory competences of the Austrian Federal Minister of Science and Traffic on behalf of the State. Legal acts of an autonomous university organ are legal, even without a formal basis in general law, so long as they do not infringe precept established by a general law or decree. It is, however, constitutionally forbidden to reduce the autonomy of universities by laws below the Austrian Constitution.[21] University autonomy in Austria, thus, comes closer to the autonomy of churches and religious communities, as well as to the independence of broadcasting, than to the constitutional guarantee of self-administration of local communities.[22]

The autonomy of institutes and classes of the non-university sector of higher education in Austria (Fachhochschulen, Fachhochschul-Studiengänge) is part of the social autonomy and means the practice of social freedom. The State is confined to supervision comparable to supervision of private citizens, for example, in the field of economic supervision.[23] This supervision of the State emanates from its ultimate responsibility for all educational processes on its

[17] See Berka (fn 3), pp. 37 f.

[18] See Pernthaler (fn 9), pp. 9–12.

[19] Art. 18 Federal Constitutional Law (Bundes-Verfassungsgesetz), Austrian Federal Law Gazette 1930/1, last amended I 1998/30 with corrections by I 1998/35.

[20] This was the explicit will of the Austrian Government and Parliament when preparing the draft and adopting the law; see motivations of Art. 2 para. 2 of the draft law, in: Bundesministerium für Wissenschaft und Forschung (ed.), *Universitätsorganisationsgesetz '93*. Regierungsvorlage (Act on the Organisation of Universities '93. Draft by the Government). Vienna 1993, pp 193 f. See also M. Kostal (ed), Universitätsorganisationsgesetz (Act on the Organisation of Universities). Vienna 1993, pp. 37 f and Berka (fn 3), pp. 40–42.

[21] See Berka (fn 3), p. 36.

[22] See Berka (fn 3), p. 41.

[23] See Berka (fn 3), pp. 142 f.

territory according to Article 17 paragraph 5 of the Basic Law on the General Rights of Nationals 1867. This provision reads: 'The right to supreme direction and supervision over the whole instructional and educational system lies with the state.'

1.4. *Description of the legal basis of the autonomy of universities and of the non-university sector in higher education in Austria*

The legal basis of the autonomy of universities in Austria is designed by the Austrian Act on the Organisation of Universities 1993,[24] which has been supplemented concerning studies at Austrian universities by the Austrian Act on Studies at Universities.[25] The Act on the Organisation of Universities defines the duties of Austrian universities and the principles they have to follow when fulfilling their duties (Art. 1). The Act lays down the legal personality of universities as autonomous institutions of the Federal State of Austria and defines their representatives (Arts 2–4). The Act enumerates all Austrian universities and rules on the procedure for establishing their structure (Arts 5, 6). The Act defines the necessary elements of the university statutes, the adoption of which falls within the university autonomy, but has to be approved by the Minister of Science and Traffic (Art. 7). The Act lays down the supervisory power of the minister, the procedure which must be followed by the university administration (Arts 8–15), rules on the election of university organs (Art. 16), the university budget (Art. 17), and on the report and evaluation system (Art. 18). Chapter II of the Act on the Organisation of Universities 1993 (Arts 19–40) is dedicated to the staff of Austrian universities, Chapters III–VI, and XI cover the organs of the various structural levels of the universities. Chapters VII–X contain special provisions for several types of faculties (medical, veterinary science, theological faculties) and Chapter XII offers the legal scope to create inter-university establishments. Universities are entitled to honour persons by conferring specific offices, medals, and awards (Art. 82). An advisory university board of curators, four of the curators appointed from the university sector, four from outside, is established for Austria according to Article 84 of the Austrian Act on the Organisation of Universities. Last but not least, the Act provides for organs of coordination between the Austrian universities and their staff (Chapter XV).

The Austrian Act on Studies at Universities forms the legal framework for studies, classes, courses at Austrian universities (Chapters I and II). It defines the rights and duties of students, their admission to universities (Chapter III), rules on exams, and on academic degrees (Chapters IV and V).

[24] See fn 1.

[25] Bundesgesetz über die Studien an Universitäten (Universitäts-Studiengesetz), Austrian Federal Law Gazette I 1997/48, as amended by I 1998/38 and I 1998/131.

The legal basis for institutes and classes of the non-university sector of higher education in Austria (Fachhochschulen, Fachhochschul-Studiengänge) are contained in the Austrian Act on Classes of the Non-university Sector of Higher Education.[26] This Act defines the holders of such classes (Art. 2), the purposes and principles of the classes (Art. 3). It rules on the admission, rights and duties of students (Art. 4), on academic degrees (Art. 5), and establishes a specific authority, the Council for Institutes of the Non-University Sector in Higher Education (Fachhochschulrat) (Arts 6–10). The council falls under the supervisory power of the Austrian Minister for Science and Traffic (Art. 11) and decides on the recognition of a class. The recognition of an institution, which organizes classes of the non-university sector in higher education (Fachhochschul-Studiengänge) as an institute (Fachhochschule), takes place by ministerial decree (Art. 15). So far, no such institute has been established. In case of its establishment an institute (Fachhochschule) must install a specific board for the organization and execution of teaching and examinations at the respective institute (Fachhochschulkollegium) (Art. 16). The Act provides rules for the procedure of the recognition of classes and institutes, as well as for the deprivation of their status (Arts 14, 15, and 17).

2. Autonomy of educational institutions in higher education

2.1. *Organisational aspects*

The number and names of Austrian universities are fixed by the Austrian Act on the Organisation of Universities 1993 (Art. 5).[27] The highest level of the organization of these universities (faculties – Fakultäten) is prescribed by decree of the Austrian Minister of Science and Traffic in accordance with the Main Committee of one chamber of the Austrian Parliament (Hauptausschuss des Nationalrates). The university so far only has a right to a proposal for its structuring into faculties or for being heard (Art. 6 para. 2). Universities need not necessarily be structured into faculties. All other structural levels – departments are obligatory (Institute) – fall within the autonomous decision of the respective university (Art. 6 para. 3, Art. 7). Within certain legal limits, universities are free to establish sections at departments (Abteilungen).[28] Apart from this, universities are free to rule on their internal structure.[29]

The composition and election of the organs which represent a university

[26] See fn 4.

[27] See fn 1.

[28] Art. 46 para. 2 of the Austrian Act on the Organisation of Universities 1993 demands a minimum number of university professors at a department to entitle it to establish sections.

[29] So also Berka (fn 3), p. 43.

(rector, dean, senate, etc.), whether they are monocratic or collegial organs, are prescribed by law.[30] Autonomy concerning the central decision structure at Austrian universities, is thus considerably limited. The universities have a certain autonomous influence on the size of collegial organs, and on their election and activity by means of adopting election rules and standing orders, as well as on the numbers of vice-rectors (Vizerektoren) and vice-deans for study-affairs (Vizestudiendekane).[31] On the other hand, the influence of the Minister of Science and Traffic on the election of the central organs of universities has been eliminated, as can be seen, for example, from Article 53, ruling on the election of the rector. Thus, the organizational autonomy of universities centres on the autonomous election of the central monocratic university organs. Their structure, however, is prescribed by law. Concerning the structure, university autonomy focuses on the level of establishing departments.

Universities are considered to be institutions of the Federal State of Austria (Art. 2 para. 2). They are federal offices (Bundesdienststellen), which means collegial bodies, which comprise several persons for joint administration.[32] In Austrian legal doctrine it has been controversially discussed whether, and to what extent, this includes a legal personality of their own. Universities in Austria can no longer be considered to be corporations of self-administration under public law. On the other hand, they are vested with a limited personality under private law. By a decision of the Austrian Constitutional Court, however, the vagueness of the respective legal provisions has been replaced by court law recognizing the university as a legal person under public law.[33] The Austrian Supreme Adminstrative Court, nevertheless, continues to assume only a partial legal personality, which is based on the concept of self-administration of state organs.[34]

Universities are entitled to adopt basic statutes. The minimum contents of these statutes is prescribed by Article 7 paragraph 2 of the Austrian Act on the Organisation of Universities 1993. These statutes are adopted and amended autonomously, but are subject to the approval of the Austrian Minister of Science and Traffic (Art. 7 para. 3).

The holders of classes and institutes of the non-university sector in higher education (Fachhochschul-Studiengänge, Fachhochschulen) may be legal persons under public law, as well as under private law.[35] Consequently, the Act

[30] See e.g. Arts 13–16, 41–43, 45, 46, 48, 49, Chapters VI and VII, Act on the Organisation of Universities 1993.

[31] See e.g. Art. 7 para. 2 No. 2 and 5, Art. 43 para. 6, Art. 54, Art. 55, Act on the Organisation of Universities 1993.

[32] See Kostal (fn 20), pp. 36 f with further references.

[33] See Collection of Decisions (VfSlg) 13.429/1993.

[34] See decision of 22 October 1997, 90/12/0008.

[35] See Arts 2 and 15 of the Austrian Act on Classes of the Non-University Sector of Higher Education (fn 4).

on Classes of the Non-university Sector in Higher Education (Fachhochschul-Studiengesetz) only contains a few provisions with reference to the internal structure of the respective institutions. Article 12 paragraph 2 requires the existence of a teaching staff (Lehrkörper), which according to Article 12 paragraph 3 must consist of at least four persons with specific qualifications defined by this provision. One person must be nominated as head of the teaching staff (Leiter des Lehrkörpers) (Art. 12 para. 4 No. 2) and one person responsible for the development of the respective class (Art. 12 para. 3). All further legal structural prerequisites follow from the general law applicable depending on the legal form of existence chosen by the holder of a class or institute. This can be an association, a legal corporation, etc. An institute of the non-university sector in higher education (Fachhochschule) must establish a board (Fachhochschulkollegium), the composition and tasks of which are closely defined by Article 16. This board is headed by a chairperson with monocratic competences (Art. 16 para. 4).

Classes of the non-university sector in higher education (Fachhochschul-Studiengänge) must be formally recognized by the Council of the Non-university Sector in Higher Education (Fachhochschulrat) (Art. 6 para. 2 No. 1). The decisions on recognition require the approval of the Minister of Science and Traffic (Art. 6 para. 5). The members of this council are appointed by the Minister of Science and Traffic (Art. 7 para. 2), but, according to the constitutional provision of Article 7 paragraph 4 are not dependent on any directives. Institutes of the non-university sector in higher education (Fachhochschulen) are established by decree of the Minister of Science and Traffic in agreement with the Minister of Education and Cultural Affairs.

The autonomous right to adopt statutes of their own follows from the laws governing the organization of the respective holder. These laws, for example the Law on Associations,[36] rule on the necessary elements which the respective statutes must contain and on the relevant authorities of the State. Apart from this basic organizational structure of the holder and the board and chairperson of this board of an institute (Fachhochschulrat), which, however, also cannot be classified as an organ in the classical sense of the term,[37] the classes and institutes of the non-university sector in higher education are free of any structural prerequisites. Within the legal framework described above, it falls within the autonomy of the holder to decide on the internal structure of classes or institutes. Therefore, the autonomy of classes and institutes of the non-university sector in higher education is two-sided. It is broad concerning the relationship between the State and the holders of these institutions. On the other hand, it is supplemented by a guarantee of autonomy for the teaching

36 Vereinsgesetz 1951, Austrian Federal Law Gazette 1951/233, as amended by 1954/141, 1962/102, 1987/648, 1993/257.

37 So Berka (fn 3), p. 150.

staff and the persons responsible for the development of a class in the relationship with the holder of their class or institute. The existence of such an autonomy is a legal requirement for the recognition of a class and institute by the State (Art. 12 para. 2 No. 5, Art. 15 para. 2 No. 1).

2.2. *Independence in determining the recruitment and choice of personnel, etc.*

The majority of the personnel of Austrian universities is employed by the federal state of Austria. Therefore, the plan of posts authorized in the state budget is the decisive factor in determining the recruitment of personnel. The organs of the university are only entitled to make a proposal (Art. 17 para. 2 of the Austrian Act on the Organisation of Universities 1993).[38] The plan and the budgetary means attributed to a university in accordance with this plan define the recruitment of personnel. The state budget also prescribes the limit of financial means which are to be attributed to rooms, libraries and labaratories, other material, as well as capital goods at Austrian universities. The university is correspondingly free to decide only within the posts which are alloted according to the plan and which may actually be made. University decisions concerning the appointment of posts for university professors can be taken only under the right of veto of the Minister of Science and Traffic (Art. 22 para. 2).

The decision of which person to actually choose for an available post falls within the autonomy of the universities. This also applies to the decision on the appointment of a university professor, which is now made by the rector. The Act on the Organisation of Universities 1993 however, contains a detailed catalogue of necessary qualifications for the various categories of university personnel, which must be fulfilled for their recruitment (Arts 19–35). Universities are obliged to achieve a well-balanced relationship between the number of men and women employed (Art. 39 paras. 1 and 2).

A class of the non-university sector in higher education (Fachhochschul-Studiengang) must provide a minimum of four persons, who must hold specific qualifications, described by the respective Act.[39] An institute of the non-university sector in higher education (Fachhochschule) must provide at least two classes, which indirectly defines the minimum number of qualified personnel (Art. 15 para. 2 No. 1). Apart from these requirements, the holders of classes or institutes are free to determine the recruitment of their personnel, as well as to choose applicants with necessary qualifications. They are only bound by general labour law. Concerning the number of personnel, rooms and material equipment, Art. 12 para. 2 No. 9 of the Act on Classes of the Non-university Sector in Higher Education only asks for a 'necessary' number. The final

[38] See fn 1.

[39] See fn 4, Art. 12 para. 3.

assessment of this legal prerequisite is made by decision of the Council (Fachhochschulrat). Recognition as an institute (Fachhochschule) depends on the establishment of a plan for the development of the respective institution, whereby the achievement of a minimum number of 1000 places of studies within a period of five years can be substantiated (Art. 15 para. 2 No. 2). Indirectly, this requirement also defines the element of 'necessity'.

2.3. *Autonomy with respect to the fulfilment of the educational objective*

The autonomy of universities with respect to the educational objective is ruled by the Act on Studies at Universities.[40] This Act lays down general principles for the structure of studies and for the contents of study schemes, the adoption of which falls within the autonomy of the universities. The Act further defines the various categories of subjects and types of exams in an abstract manner. Concerning the contents of the studies, the law contains only provisions for their purpose, for their duration, and for the number of hours available per semester. Thus, the law is orientated at regulating necessary resources and procedural guarantees in order to safeguard the respect of the rule of law concerning the admission to universities and concerning exams.[41] Article 11 of the Act on Studies at Universities also provides for the conduct of central planning of the establishment and abolition of studies at individual Austrian universities.

Within this legal framework, the study commissions are free to take decisions on curricula. This refers to the structure of studies in two or three phases, their division into several branches, and the laying down of a catalogue of obligatory and non-obligatory subjects. This also applies to rules on exams which define the types and methods of exams. The supervisory power of the Minister of Science and Traffic does not relate to a material examination of the study schemes (Art. 15 para. 3). The realization of this broad legal autonomy concerning the fulfilment of the educational objective depends, however, on the available personnel and financial resources. This also limits the principal freedom of study commissions to decide on the number of students per class.

The legal framework concerning the fulfilment of the educational objective of classes and institutes of the non-university sector in higher education in Austria, is even more open than that for universities. The respective Act provides for a minimum duration of studies and a minimum of hours for studies which must be offered during this period. It requires a final exam and lays down its type and general structure. All other decisions are assigned to the autonomy of the respective institution, which must provide a study scheme

[40] See fn 25.

[41] See Berka (fn 3), p. 47.

and rules for exams.[42] The law trusts in experiments and in the development of respective standards by experience and in practice.[43]

2.4. *Autonomy of resources*

More than 98% of the financial resources of Austrian universities are covered by the state budget.[44] The influence of universities on the state budget is restricted to cost and need accounting, to applications concerning the university budget and to respective negotiations with the responsible Minister of Science and Traffic. The minister, however, makes the final political decision on how to deal with these applications, how to place them in the Governmental project for the annual federal budget law and how to allot the financial means definitively according to this law, as adopted by the Parliament. The annual allotment of financial means by the minister differentiates between property and posts for personnel, and equipment and expenditure (Art. 17 para. 4 Act on the Organsiation of Universities). The effective dimension of financial autonomy, thus, depends on how detailed these ministerial allocations are made. Universities are free to raise money through sponsoring and any other means in accordance with general laws. The extent of this money will not, however, replace the role of supplementing the state contribution to the university budget. Universities are not allowed to charge tuition fees.[45]

The holders of classes and institutes of the non-university sector in higher education (Fachhochschul-Studiengänge, Fachhochschulen) are not constrained in their financial autonomy by legal norms, apart from general laws. In practice, no class of this sector could exist in Austria without the considerable financial commitment of the State. The State can thus influence the development of the non-university sector in higher education in Austria in material, qualitative and quantitative regard without any legal determination,[46] just by using the instrument of their recognition. So far, this instrument has also been used by non-admitting classes and institutes to charge tuition fees.

[42] See fn 4, Art. 3 para. 2 Nos 2–6.

[43] See Berka (fn 3), p. 167.

[44] See Berka (fn 3), p. 50.

[45] See the rules concerning the admission of students, Arts 34–42 of the Act on Studies at Universities (fn 25)and Art. 1 of the Act on University Fees (Hochschul-Taxengesetz 1972), Austrian Federal Law Gazette 1972/76 as amended.

[46] See Berka (fn 3) pp. 146 f for further references.

2.5. *Defence of the autonomous sphere by legal means against the state or government*

According to Article 8 paragraph 5 of the Act on the Organisation of Universities,[47] the university organs have legal capacity in the supervisory procedure and the right to lodge a complaint against the final supervisory decision with the Austrian Supreme Administrative Court. Whether they are entitled to defend their autonomous sphere by other legal means depends on the acceptance of a legal personality under public law for universities.[48]

In the non-university sector in higher education in Austria, the Council (Fachhochschulrat) has legal capacity in the supervisory procedure and the right to lodge a complaint against the final decision with the Austrian Supreme Administrative Court.[49] The procedure concerning the recognition of classes of this sector and the withdrawal of a recognition is ruled by the General Administrative Procedural Law 1991[50] (Art. 17 para. 1).[51] No ordinary legal remedy exists against an adminstrative decision of the Council (Art. 17 para. 2). The applicants for the recognition of a class or the holders of such a class concerned by a withdrawal are thus restricted to lodging a complaint with the Austrian Supreme Administrative Court or the Austrian Constitutional Court, respectively, depending on the contents of the complaint and the general procedural rules for the access to these courts.

3. Individual autonomy

3.1. *Latitude of discretion for teachers/professors in educational matters*

By the constitutional guarantee of Article 17 paragraph 1 Basic Law on the General Rights of Nationals 1867,[52] persons who prove to be able and qualified for scientific teaching are free, with all regards to discretion, concerning the contents and methods of their teaching. The borders of the freedom of science lie in the general law. The freedom of scientific teaching is limited by prohibitions emanating from the Penal Code.[53] The guarantee covers teaching at universities, but – and this is still controversial – not at classes and institutes of the non-university sector in higher education (Fachhochschul-Studiengänge,

[47] See fn 1.

[48] See section 2.1 above.

[49] See Art. 11 para. 4 of the Act on Classes of the Non-university Sector of Higher Education (fn 4).

[50] Austrian Federal Law Gazette 1991/51.

[51] See fn 4.

[52] See fn 2.

[53] See e.g. Berka (fn 3), 56 for further references.

Fachhochschulen).[54] The guarantee aimed at the education of subjects by autonomous activity in freedom is therefore directed against interventions from outside, as well as from inside universities.[55] In consequence of this constitutional guarantee, neither the Act on the Organisation of Universities 1993,[56] nor the Act on the Studies at Universities[57] include any provisions which permit the issuing of directives concerning the contents and methods of scientific teaching. The study schemes are restricted to defining the contents of the subjects that must be taught in an abstract manner and to describing the types of lectures and seminars which must be used for this teaching. The legal competence of Article 43 paragraph 2 No. 2 of the Act on the Organisation of Universities 1993 permitting the Dean for Study-Affairs (Studiendekan) to issue directives does not refer to the contents and methods of teaching. His competence is restricted to the maintainance of the operation of the studies according to the study schemes.

Article 3 paragraph 2 No. 1 of the Act on Classes of the Non-university Sector in Higher Education[58] recognizes the plurality of scientific opinions in teaching and of scientific methods, as well as the principle of freedom of teaching, as principles which must be observed in structuring classes in this sector. The freedom of teaching also refers to the conduct of courses. This provision, although not providing a constitutional guarantee, binds the Council of Institutes of the Non-university Sector in Higher Education (Fachhochschulrat) and Minister of Science and Traffic in their decisions concerning the recognition of classes and institutes, and also the holders of such classes and institutes in the relationships with persons developing these classes or forming the teaching staff. The persons developing classes need, or even must not obey directives given by the holder, which infringe their freedom of teaching.

Article 3 paragraph 2 No. 1 of the Act mentioned above does not, however, serve as a legal basis for an individual right of a member of the teaching staff of a class or institute (Fachhochschul Studiengang, Fachhochschule) on freedom from directives comparable to the constitutional guarantee of Article 17 paragraph 1 of the Basic Law on General Rights of Nationals 1867. The individual autonomy of a teacher/professor at such a class or institute is confined to the contents and methods of their teaching within the framework

[54] See section 1.2 above.

[55] See Berka (fn 3) pp. 24 f for further references and W. Frühauf, 'Wissenschaftsfreiheit und UOG (Freedom of Science and Act on the Organisation of Universities), in: R. Strasser (ed.), *Aktuelle Probleme des Universitätsrechts* (Actual Problems of the Law of Universities). Vienna 1982, pp. 19–32 (pp, 21 f).

[56] See fn 1.

[57] See fn 25.

[58] See fn 4.

of the teaching task of the class or institute. The law does not deal with this teaching task in an explicit manner. Therefore, it is not prohibited that the concept of a class may define the teaching task in a precise and detailed way. From this it must be concluded that no individual freedom from directives exists for the members of a teaching staff at classes and institutes. Nevertheless, directives by the responsible authorities must respect the individual pedagogical freedom of the members of the teaching staff concerning the contents and methods of their teaching.[59] In case of any conflict, the position of such a teacher/professor must be considered to be rather weak. In practice, he or she is threatened by the termination of his/her employment contract.

3.2. *Issue of instructions in professional matters to the teaching staff*

Apart from the limits described in section 3.1 above, the superiors within the structure of a university are legally entitled to issue instructions to the teaching staff, depending on the legal status of the respective category of persons to which the actual member of staff belongs, and depending on the superior's sphere of competence.[60] These instructions are restricted to professional matters. This authority follows from the general concept of the law on state officials which, in principle, is also applied to most members of the teaching staff at universities.[61]

The same goes for the teaching staff at classes and institutes of the non-university sector in higher education (Fachhochschul-Studiengänge, Fachhochschulen) and is defined by the legal structure the respective holder has chosen for the organization. The barriers for the contents of instructions given by the holder, the head of the teaching staff,[62] or the head of the Board of Institute of the Non-university Sector in Higher Education (Fachhochschulkollegium)[63] are considerably less restrictive than in the university sector, as has been pointed out in 3.1 above.

3.3. *Participation of teachers/professors in the universities' or classes'/institutes' self-governing bodies*

The structure of the universities, according to the Act on the Organisation of Universities 1993,[64] can be characterized as installing a two-fold system of monocratic and collegial organs. At all levels of the university structure a

[59] See Berka (fn 3), pp. 152–156.

[60] Compare e.g. Arts 29 and 30 of the Act on the Organisation of Universities 1993 (fn 1).

[61] See e.g. Art. 9 para. 6, Arts 37, 38 of the Act on the Organisation of Universities 1993.

[62] See Art. 13 para. 4 No. 2 of the Act on Classes of the Non-university Sector in Higher Education (fn 4).

[63] See Art. 16 para. 4 (fn 4).

[64] See fn 1.

proportionate number of representatives of the various categories of members of the teaching staff is included by means of elections to the respective collegial organ.[65] Members of the teaching staff – sometimes a limited number[66] – may stand for election to all monocratic organs.

At classes of the non-university sector in higher education (Fachhochschul-Studiengänge), due to the wide field of organizational discretion for the respective holder, apart from the grouping of persons within a teaching staff, a self-governing body embracing all or some members of the teaching staff is not required by law.[67] The establishment of such a body falls within the autonomy of the respective holder. In case of an institute of the non-university sector in higher education (Fachhochschule), the Act on Classes of the Non-university Sector in Higher Education provides for the establishment of a board (Fachhochschulkollegium).[68] This board includes eight representatives of the teaching staff, up to four of them elected by the teaching staff. At least four members, who have been entrusted with the development of each class at the respective institute, are members of the board by law for a period of three years. Members of the teaching staff may offer themselves as candidates for the position of chairperson of the board.

4. Consequences of autonomy

4.1. *Guarantee of general aims or values*

The Act on the Organisation of Universities 1993[69] provides for two major instruments in order to guarantee the achievement of general aims or values such as, for example, the quality and unity of Austrian education at universities. One instrument must be seen as the creation of a mechanism for cooperation between Austrian universities, the other lies within the supervisory function of the Minister of Science and Traffic.

The most intense form of cooperation is ruled by Chapter XII of the Act on the Organisation of Universities 1993. This Chapter provides for the potential of creating inter-university institutions. Such institutions are based on corresponding decisions of the senates of the respective universities and are

65 For departments see Art. 45, for faculties see Art. 48, for the senate and the university assembly (Universitätsversammlung) at the top of the universities see Arts 51 and 55 (58 and 60: universities not structured by faculties) of the Act on the Organisation of Universities 1993 (fn 1).

66 See e.g. the functions of the rector or dean, Art. 53 para. 5, Art. 49 para. 3 (fn 1).

67 See Art. 12 para. 3 of the Act on Classes of the Non-university Sector in Higher Education (fn 4) and section 2.1 above.

68 Art. 16 (fn 4).

69 See fn 1.

established by the Minister of Science and Traffic (Art. 79). The Act provides for joint organs (e.g. inter-university commissions).

The Advisory Council of Universities (Universitätenkuratorium), which consists of four recognized experts from inside the universities and four from outside, both groups appointed by the Minister of Science and Traffic, is established to advise the minister in his decisions with regard to Austrian universities (Art. 83). Thus, it has primarily a coordinating function, which relates to quality as well as budgetary matters restricted, however, to an advisory power. Similarly, the activities of the rectors, vice-rectors, and chairpersons of the supreme collegial organs of universities are coordinated by the Conference of Rectors (Art. 84). This conference gives opinions on all university matters and projects of laws and ministerial decrees referring to these matters. It consists of the rectors and their deputies and is also restricted to an advisory function. The Act further provides for the creation of conferences representing the various categories of the members of the teaching staff at universities in order to coordinate the activities of their representatives (Art. 85). The powers of these conferences are also limited to advice and expert opinion.

The power to supervise Austrian universities is in the hands of the Minister of Science and Traffic. According to Article 8 paragraph 1 of the Act on the Organisation of Universities, this power extends to the control of the observance of laws and decrees, as well as the fulfilment of the tasks of the university. The power includes the right of information on all university matters, but also the duty of universities to submit to ministerial inquiries. The supervisory power is linked to sanctions on the overruling of university decisions or refusal of the minister's approval, where such an approval is provided by law (Art. 8 para. 3). Apart from this, the Act on the Organisation of Universities 1993 provides for annual reports of the university organs concerning the fulfilment of the tasks of the universities on all university levels (Art. 18). The minister is entitled specifically to evaluate universities or studies and their developement and may rule by decree on the evaluation of achievements at the universities (Art. 18 paras 6–8).

Concerning classes of the non-university sector in higher education (Fachhochschul-Studiengänge) the coordination regarding the achievement of general aims or values takes place by means of the policy of recognition or withdrawal of recognition by the Council of Institutes of the Non-university Sector in Higher Education (Fachhochschulrat), the decisions of which are subject to approval by the Minister of Science and Traffic.[70] The Council's powers are comparable to the supervisory power of the Minister of Science and Traffic (Art. 11). Concerning institutes of this sector (Fachhochschulen), the co-ordinating policy is exercised directly by the Minister of Science and

[70] See Arts 6 and 12 of the Act on Classes of the Non-university Sector in Higher Education (fn 4).

Traffic in agreement with the Minister of Education and Cultural Affairs, combining decision-making and supervision (Art. 15).

4.2. *Necessary linkage of autonomy with a supervisory power*

According to the existing legal situation concerning universities and classes or institutes of the non-university sector in higher education (Fachhochschul-Studiengänge, Fachhochschulen) autonomy is necessarily linked with a supervisory power.[71]

4.3. *Relations between autonomy, responsibility, and accountability*

Both the Act on the Organisation of Universities 1993,[72] and the Act on Classes of the Non-university Sector in Higher Education[73] provide for quality control within the respective institutions. Universities are obliged by Article 7 paragraph 2 No. 13 of the Act on the Organisation of Universities 1993 to include guidelines concerning the conducting of evaluation measures in teaching and research in their basic statutes. Similarly, Article 12 paragraph 2 No. 8 of the Act on Classes of the Non-university Sector in Higher Education requires a scientific evaluation of the respective class as a precondition for its recognition by the council and minister. As the decision on recognition as an institute of this sector (Fachhochschule) on the existence of at least two classes, this requirement also extends to such institutes (Art. 15 para. 2 No. 1).

Concerning responsibility and accountability the institutions of both sectors fall under the supervisory power of the Minister of Science and Traffic and under the control of the audit office of the Austrian Parliament (Rechnungshof).[74]

4.4. *Tendencies in Austria towards enlargement of autonomy in the university and non-university sectors in higher education*

A comparison of the Act on the Organisation of Universities 1993 with its predecessor, which had been adopted in 1975, clearly shows a tendency in Austrian policy towards enlargement of autonomy of universities. This tendency has been considerably strengthened by the adoption of the Act on Studies at

[71] See secitons 1.4, 2, and 4.1 above.

[72] See fn 1.

[73] See fn 4.

[74] For the supervisory power of the minister see section 4.1 above. For the control of the audit office of the Parliament (Rechnungshof) see Art. 17 para. 10 of the Act on the Organisation of Universities 1993 (fn 1) and Art. 11 para. 1 of the Act on Classes of the Non-university Sector in Higher Education (fn 4).

Universities.[75] This direction of the state policy concerning university autonomy is motivated partly by deliberations of efficiency, partly by deliberations concerning how to administer a constantly growing stringency of financial means contributed to the educational sector by the State. In times when many Austrian universities have changed to mass universities, autonomy has been recognized as a means to strengthen the responsibility and accountability of universities, to activate their innovative potential and to reduce a contraproductive bureaucratization. Thus, last but not least, the political parties recognized that the quality of the fulfilment of the tasks of universities can be improved by strengthening university autonomy.[76] On the other hand, since the 1970s, the direct administration of scarce financial means by the Minister of Science and Traffic has turned into an ever-growing political problem moving the politically responsible minister into the centre of conflicting demands and interests. The autonomous administration of scarce financial means by universities themselves led to a transfer of the decision concerning conflicting demands and interests to inter-university forces. The minister does not take part in these conflicts and restricts himself to settling inter-university rivalries for a bigger proportion of the resources contributed by the State to individual universities. Thus, by strengthening the autonomy of universities the minister could also improve his field of manoeuvre. Plans exist entitling universities to found their own companies.

Concerning the non-university sector in higher education, no legal basis existed until the adoption of the respective Act in 1993. This Act signals a remarkable change in the orientation of Austrian policy concerning the tertiary sector in education. A whole complex of education has been established quite far from state engagement and has been transfefred to experimental development in practice. The social autonomy of this new non-university sector in Austrian higher education serves as an innovative pool for developing new models and manners of interaction between the State and private subjects in educational matters. This refers to the financial basis, as well as to the contents and methods of fulfilling educational tasks. It can be considered as a sign of deep confidence of the Austrian state in the creative force of autonomy.

[75] See fn 25.

[76] See Berka (fn 3), pp. 61–65.

BRECHT STEEN

Autonomy in Education in the Flemish Community of Belgium

BELGIAN REPORT

Introductory remarks

Because they influence the terminology of the report, I want to start with two remarks: one on the constitutional framework of Belgium, another on the structure of the educational system in Flanders.

This report only focuses on the question of autonomy in education in the Flemish Community (*Vlaamse Gemeenschap*) of Belgium. Since 1988, Belgium has been a federal state where the Communities are responsible for education. As a consequence, the three Communities (Flemish Community, French Community and German Speaking Community) have developed their own education policy and education law. In principle, the elements which are described here only apply to the Flemish Community, though some of them, especially the constitutional principles, can probably be applied to the other communities. An act of the community legislator (Flemish Parliament and the government together) is called *decreet* (decree). The word law is used as a general term or to indicate a federal Act.

In Flanders, primary and secondary educational institutions are divided up into three 'networks' (*netten*). On the one hand, we have the free (subsidized) educational institutions (*vrij gesubsidieerd onderwijs*). These schools are set up by private persons or institutions, mainly the Catholic church, and subsidized by the Community.[1] On the other hand, there is the official education, which can be divided into Community education (*Gemeenschapsonderwijs*) and the official subsidized education (*officieel gesubsidieerd onderwijs*). The Community

[1] There are also some private institutions, founded by private persons but not subsidized by the government. They do not fall under the scope of this report.

Walter Berka, Jan de Groof and Hilde Penneman (eds.), Autonomy in Education, 295–321.

education is the former state education which is completely funded by the Community. The official subsidized education is founded by the local authorities, i.e. the provinces (*provincies*) and the municipalities (*gemeenten*), but subsidized by the Community. A similar division exists in the non-university higher education (see further).

In the text, we used Dutch terms several times and the Dutch abbreviated names of laws and decrees. The first time we use such a term or name, there is a translation in brackets. At the end of the report there is a list with details of the most important laws and decrees.

1. *Constitutional legal basis of autonomy in education*

1.1. *Autonomy constitutionally guaranteed?*

Article 24 of the Constitution, which deals with the rights and liberties with regard to education, does not guarantee autonomy 'as such'.

Article 24 § 1 of the Constitution establishes the 'freedom of education'. Legal doctrine and also the Court of Arbitration (*Arbitragehof*), the (semi-)constitutional court in Belgium, interpret this paragraph as follows. The freedom of education means that everyone has the right to organize education and to establish educational institutions without any interference, not even preventive measures, by the government. To put this freedom into practice, private founders have a right to subsidies.[2] Or, in other words, the Community has a duty to subsidize free initiative. The Community only does so under certain conditions, which implies a certain rate of intervention and control. So, the right to subsidies of private founders in a way creates a 'right' of the government to 'interfere'. However, the freedom of education protects the free educational institutions against excessive intervention by the government. So, in an indirect way, autonomy is guaranteed.

Article 24 § 2 of the Constitution gives the Communities the opportunity to create an 'autonomous' body which will organize, independently from the government, the education of the Community. The Community legislator can do so by special decree, accepted with a two-thirds majority. Up to now, only the Flemish Community has used this opportunity (see further).

Articles 41 and 162 of the Constitution guarantee that the law will organize the municipal and provincial institutions in accordance with some principles laid down in Art. 162 of the Constitution. Legal doctrine says that these principles guarantee the autonomy of the local authorities. If municipalities or provinces organize education, they do so on the basis of their autonomy.

The conclusion is that the word 'autonomy' only appears in Art. 24 § 2 of

[2] e.g. Court of Arbitration, no. 25/92, 2 April 1992, *Belgisch Staatsblad – Moniteur Belge*, 10 June 1992; Court of Arbitration, no. 18/93, 4 March 1993, *Belgisch Staatsblad – Moniteur Belge*, 24 March 1993.

the Constitution. This provision creates the possibility of organizing an autonomous Community education. On the other hand the Constitution guarantees in an indirect way that free education and education organized by the local authorities can act relatively autonomously in relation to the government.

1.2. *Teacher's educational freedom and academic freedom*
The Constitution does not literally guarantee any form of academic freedom or freedom to teach.

However, there is a tradition of academic freedom in the universities. The specific laws which founded and organized the universities established by the Community recognize the academic freedom of their teaching staff, but there is no general legal basis for all universities.

More recently, at the other educational levels, some authors recognize the freedom to teach as an element of pedagogical freedom.[3] The basis of both freedoms are to be found in Art. 24 § 1 of the Constitution in combination with Art. 19 of the Constitution, which guarantees the freedom of speech. Even in 1830, some members of the National Congress defended this interpretation.

Anyway, it is not clear if there exists something such as the freedom to teach. And if it exists, it seems more like a negative freedom or a latitude of discretion (see further).

1.3. *The underlying notion of autonomy*
The ability to create an autonomous Community education has been created to relieve the Minister of Education of his double and confusing role in educational matters. On the one hand he was responsible for the general education policy. On the other hand he organized and supervised the state education. During the 1980s, the opinion gained ground that this double role prevented an objective and modern education policy. A second reason for giving autonomy was the feeling that there was a need for decentralization of the state education.

The freedom of education established in 1830, was a reaction to the large involvement of the French and Dutch governments in educational matters during the first decades of the 19th century (1794–1830). It ensured the right of the Catholic Church to organize education and to found educational institutions following its own principles, so that Catholic families could send their

[3] e.g. J. De Groof, 'The Legal Status of Teachers – The Global Framework – An Introduction', in J. De Groof (ed.), *The Legal Status of Teachers in Europe*, Louvain, 1995, p. 15; J. De Groof, 'On Pedagogical Freedom – Some Legal and Policy Considerations', in J. De Groof and J. Fiers (eds), *The Legal Status of Minorities in Education*, Louvain, 1996, pp. 235–236; J. De Groof, 'The Freedom of Teachers – Some Notes', in J. De Groof and E.F.J. Malherbe (eds), *Human Rights in South African Education*, Louvain, 1997, pp. 295–296.

children to Catholic schools. More recently, this freedom covers the freedom of private persons (or associations) to found educational institutions, to organize their structures and to fill in their pedagogical project (ideological, methodological, etc.).

Autonomy is given to the local governing bodies because the founding fathers of Belgium were afraid of a strong centralized state. So the law had to provide some constitutional principles in order to imply a certain degree of autonomy.

1.4. *Legal bases for autonomy*

As a preliminary remark, it can be mentioned that some observers suggest that the principle of legality of Art. 24 § 5 of the Constitution, which says that the organization, the recognition and the subsidization of education has to be regulated by the formal legislator (by decree in the Community), makes it quite difficult to ensure autonomy for educational institutions.[4] Anyway, a movement towards autonomy can be discerned on two fronts: Community education and education in general.

First, in the *ARGO-decreet* of 1988 (see further), the special decretal legislator has created an autonomous body, which organizes the education of the Community. So the Minister of Education no longer stands in a hierarchical relation to Community education. Undoubtedly, the Flemish Community education can act far more autonomously from the Flemish government than before. The recent *Decreet Gemeenschapsonderwijs* (see further), will strengthen this autonomy in the future.

Secondly, since 1988, the government and the decretal legislator have made a lot of effort to give more autonomy to all types of educational institutions (free, official subsidised, Community) at all levels. However, nowhere is an explicit strict legal basis for autonomy in education set forth. In the *Decreet Basisonderwijs* (Decree on primary education, 1997), the *Decreet Maatregelen Secundair Onderwijs* (Decree on measures in secondary education, 1998), the *Universiteitendecreet* (Decree on the universities, 1991) and the *Hogescholendecreet* (Decree on the non university higher educational institutions, 1994), the degree of autonomy appears implicit from the general conception of the decrees. Autonomy can be derived from the Articles which regulate the personnel policy, the internal organization of the school, the curriculum, the financial management, etc. We can add that the reports of the parliamentary discussions themselves prove that one of the aims of each of the said decrees was to increase the autonomy of the institutions. Recent modifications of these decrees (in 1999) aim at further increasing the autonomy of the institutions.

4 e.g. J. De Groof, 'The Legal Status of Teachers', in J. De Groof (ed.), *The Legal Status of Teachers in Europe*, p. 12.

2. *Autonomy of educational institutions*

2.1. *Organisational autonomy of educational institutions*

2.1.1. *Primary and secondary education*

(a) *Free education*
The freedom of education grants the free subsidized educational institutions the theoretical right to organize themselves freely. The *Schoolpactwet* (Law on school peace (1959), which still governs secondary education) and the *Decreet Basisonderwijs* set up the existence of an organizing body (*inrichtende macht*) or school board (*schoolbestuur*) as a condition for subsidies. This body is either a natural person or a legal person. In fact, almost all organizing bodies of free subsidized educational institutions have private legal personality. Thus, it is this body (which can group one or more schools) and not necessarily the school itself which is endowed with legal personality. The education legislation does not formulate any condition with regard to the form or contents of the legal personality. So, almost all organizing bodies have adopted the form of a *V.Z.W.* (non-profit association). This form of association is governed by the *V.Z.W.-wet* (Law on non-profit associations). This law ordains the members of the association to work out a constitution (*statuten*) and to create specific organs, but the law does not say much about the contents of the constitution and the composition and competences of the organs of the association. So, with respect to the legal personality, the members of the organizing body or school board are relatively free. However, some specific education legislation interferes with this autonomy of organization (see 2.6.).

(b) *Community education*
As stated, in 1989 the Flemish legislator set up an autonomous body to organize the Community education, the *ARGO* (*Autonome Raad voor het Gemeenschapsonderwijs* – Autonomous Council for the Community education) using Art. 24 § 2 of the Constitution as a basis. This body had legal personality in public law. The ARGO had two policy levels, a central level, *ARGO-centraal* (Central Council) and a local level, the *LORGOs* (Local Councils). Neither the schools nor the *LORGOs* had legal personality. The *ARGO-decreet* organized the whole structure of the Community education, in a rather detailed way. The basic competences (including some regulatory power) were assigned to the central level. Minor competences, e.g. local administration, were allotted to the *LORGOs*. *ARGO-centraal* had supervisory power over the local level (e.g. it could annul decisions of a *LORGO*).

The *Decreet Gemeenschapsonderwijs* (Decree on Community education) of 14 July 1998 redraws the whole structure of Community education. The scope of the reform was to realize a further decentralization of the Community education and make it more efficient. The decree creates a new body, the

Gemeenschapsonderwijs (Community education) which organizes the Flemish Community education and lays down the new basic organizational rules of the Community education. The Community education will be organized at three levels: the central level, the intermediary level or *Scholengroepen* (groups of schools) and the local level or *Scholen* (Schools). Every level has its own competences and organs.[5] More than before, the central, intermediate and local level can adopt their own organizational rules within the framework of the decree. The hierarchic structure has almost disappeared (the central level and the *Sholengroepen* each have their own exclusive competences). The central level has a limited supervisory power on the *Scholengroepen* and has become more a supporting body (e.g. it will organize the quality control of the Community education). Just as in the former system, only one body has been granted full legal personality, i.e. the *Gemeenschapsonderwijs*. However, the organs of each level have those aspects of legal personality which are necessary to execute their competences (e.g. the legal responsibility for their acts, representing the *Gemeenschapsonderwijs* in court, etc.). From 1 April 1999 until 1 January 2003 the old system will be gradually transferred into the new one.

(c) *Official subsidized education*
The schools which are organized by the provinces and the municipalities do not have legal personality. The province or municipality itself is responsible for education and is the legal person who organizes it. The schools are part of the administration of the local governments. Within the framework of the *Nieuwe gemeentewet* (new law on municipalities) and the *Provinciewet* (law on provinces) the political organs of these authorities can organize their educational institutions. In order to grant more autonomy to the institutions and to limit the role of these political organs, there is undoubtedly a tendency to search creatively for an alternative way of organizing official subsidized education but the framework of the legislation is an obstacle here. Very recently, a federal regulation anticipates that the municipal and provincial Council can establish an autonomous municipal or provincial undertaking (*autonoom gemeente- of provinciebedrijf*) to manage some elements of their education. How the authorities will use this innovation is yet to be assessed in reality.

(d) *Scholengemeenschappen* (communities of schools)
A recent innovation for all types of education on the secondary level are the so-called *scholengemeenschappen*. School boards can voluntarily create such a community of schools (or join it) in order to rationalize the educational offer. If school boards choose this type of cooperation, the structure and competences of it are laid down in the *Decreet Maatregelen Secundair onderwijs*. The school

[5] V. Rotsaert, 'The Flemish Community of Belgium', *EJELP* 1999, no. 1, not yet published.

boards can decide whether or not this community of schools is granted with legal personality.

2.1.2. *Higher education*

(a) *Non-university higher educational institutions*
The non-university higher educational institutions (*hogescholen*) are nominatively recognized by law in the *Hogescholendecreet*. The organizational framework for the *hogescholen* is laid down in the Articles 254–304 *bis* of this decree.

Legal personality in private law is a subsidy condition for the free *hogescholen*. The free *hogescholen* are all organized like a *V.Z.W.* What has been said above on the *V.Z.W.* and its constitution also applies here. The rules in the *Hogescholendecreet* on the administration organs for subsidized (free and official) *hogescholen* are rather vague. The decree only requires the creation of departments, the appointment of a head of the department and allows the potential for delegation of powers, e.g. towards the departments. The decree stipulates some rules on the participation organs (see further 2.6.).

The same provisions of the *Hogescholendecreet* apply on the official subsidized institutions, with the exception of legal personality. What has been said above on legal personality and on the organization of official subsidized institutions on secondary level also applies here.

The non-university higher education of the Community is organized by several independent legal persons of public law, the *Vlaamse Autonome Hogescholen* (Flemish autonomous non-university higher educational institutions). In 1995, the ARGO had to transfer its institutions of non-university higher education to these *Autonome hogescholen.* These *hogescholen* each have their own legal personality and their own school board. In contrast to the subsidized *hogescholen*, the Articles 254–283 of the *Hogescholendecreet* establish in detail the rules on the organization of the *Autonome hogescholen*. The relationship between the Community and these *hogescholen* is established in the *Autonome Hogescholendecreet* (Decree on Flemish autonomous non-university higher educational institutions).

Since 1994, the government has stimulated cooperation between the *hogescholen*. As a consequence, almost all *hogescholen* organized by the local authorities have disappeared (only two are left) and transferred to the *Autonome hogescholen*.

(b) *Universities*
The universities are nominatively recognized by law in the *Universiteitendecreet*. They all have legal personality. On the one hand there are the free universities founded on private initiative. On the other hand, there are universities established by law. Two of them are universities of the Community. In 1991 they took over the organization power of the Community by a special decree on

the basis of Art. 24 § 2 of the Constitution. Two others, the so-called pluralistic universities, are established by law and have a specific status, but they do not form part of the higher education of the Community. The public institutions have legal personality in public law established by law. The free institutions have legal personality in private law.[6] The *Universiteitendecreet* offers just the global framework for universities but provides few rules on the internal organization of the universities. So the free universities have their own basic constitutions and regulations. The universities founded by the Community are governed by specific laws. The organs and powers of these organs are established in these laws in quite a detailed way. However, these rules are less centralistic than before 1991.

2.2. *Autonomy and recruitment of personnel*

2.2.1. *Introduction*

The recruitment of personnel is determined by two premises. First, the organizing bodies or school boards of the free educational institutions at all levels have the right in principle to freely recruit their personnel. This right is based on Art. 24 of the constitution. The organizing bodies are private legal persons and relations with their personnel are governed by a private (labour) contract. The freedom of education and the freedom of contract guarantee that these bodies can demand ideological commitment of their personnel.

Secondly, the personnel of the official subsidized and the Community education are (a special category of) civil servants. This means that the organising bodies (ARGO, provinces, municipalities) have to respect some rules which also apply to the recruitment of civil servants in general (equality, capacity conditions, nationality conditions, etc.).

2.2.2. *Primary and secondary education*

(a) *Free education*

Over the years the freedom of personnel recruitment of the free school boards has been limited by several provisions of the education legislation. The *Rechtspositiedecreet gesubsidieerd onderwijs* (Decree on the legal status of teachers of subsidised education) provides some general conditions for the recruitment of new teachers (e.g. nationality of an EU-Member State, civil and political rights, language, qualification, health conditions). However, within these limits, the school board is still free to decide if and who it recruits and on which

[6] It is remarkable that the legal personality of the Catholic University of Louvain and the Free University of Brussels is also established by law. The reason is that in 1912 legal personality had to be recognized individually by the legislator, because there was no general law on the private legal capacity of non-profit organizations.

(additional) criteria. Moreover, the constitutional right to recruit on an ideological basis is reaffirmed in Article 15 of the *Rechtspositiedecreet gesubsidieerd onderwijs* and also recognized by the Court of Arbitration.[7] Organizing bodies with a denominational orientation may expect a certain loyalty of applicants and personnel with regard to the so-called pedagogical project. It means for instance that Catholic schools may expect that their personnel profess the Catholic religion. So, the core of the freedom of recruitment is still present.

Once recruited, the relationship between the personnel and the school board of a free institution is still that of a private contract. But the freedom to formulate this contract is limited among other things by the legal status of teachers of free schools laid down in the *Rechtspositiedecreet gesubsidieerd onderwijs*. The school board is bound by this decree. This decree establishes the rights and duties of the personnel, the conditions of promotion, some qualification conditions, the disciplinary status, etc. A characteristic of this limitation is that the private contract relationship shows more and more public law aspects. Nevertheless, recent judgments of the highest Belgian courts have shown that these public law aspects do not take away the private law nature of the contract.[8] As a consequence, the contract parties have little space left to negotiate the written contract; and if there is some space, it is usually occupied by collective bargaining.

There is also other legislation which limits the contents of the relationship between the teachers and the school board. Moreover, these provisions strengthen the public law aspects of the contract. The salaries of teachers are based on the so-called salary scales. If a teacher is appointed in a function, he or she has to be paid in accordance with the salary scale of that function. Traditionally, the school board could not freely decide the number and type of personnel it recruited. The government provided elaborate rules on the personnel establishment (*personeelsformatie*). Since 1998, in primary education the government subsidizes a number of functions in relation to the number of pupils. The school board itself can work out the personnel establishment.

(b) *Community education and official subsidised education*

The personnel of the Community education and the official subsidized education are (a special type of) civil servants under a specific statute. The personnel of the institutions of the local authorities are recruited by the executive college. This recruitment has to be ratified by the provincial or municipal council. In

[7] Court of Arbitration, no. 34/98, 1 April 1998, *Belgisch Staatsblad – Moniteur Belge*, 1 May 1998; see also Court of Arbitration, no. 18/93, 4 March 1993, *Belgisch Staatsblad – Moniteur Belge*, 24 March 1993.

[8] e.g. Court of Cassation, 18 December 1997, (Joye and Gees), *Rechtskundig Weekblad*, 1998–99, p. 86, note W. Rauws and note R. Verstegen; Court of Arbitration, no. /99, June 1999, not yet published.

the new system, the personnel of the Community education will be recruited by the head of the school. The status of teachers of the official subsidized schools is also governed by the *Decreet rechtspositieregeling gesubsidieerd onderwijs*. The status of teachers of the Community education is laid down in the *Decreet rechtspositieregeling Gemeenschapsonderwijs* (Decree on the legal status of teachers of Community education). This statute is similar to the statute for members of personnel of the subsidized education. The three statutes are very similar, and this shows again the public law aspects of the statute of teachers of free schools. What was stated above with regard to free education (recruitment limitations, salary scales, collective bargaining and personnel establishment) also applies here. Moreover, the personnel of the Community education have to sign the *neutraliteitsverklaring* (declaration of neutrality), worked out by the ARGO. This is to guarantee that personnel are loyal to the constitutional duty to provide ideological neutral education.

(c) *scholengemeenschappen*
When a school is member of a *scholengemeenschap*, the board of this community of schools is responsible for the criteria of personnel recruitment.

2.2.3. *Higher education*
The freedom of recruitment of the boards of the *hogescholen* is limited by some provisions of the *Hogescholendecreet*. This decree provides one statute for the personnel of all types of *hogescholen*. Notwithstanding this identical regulation with a lot of public law elements, the relationship between school board and staff is contractual in the free institutions and statutory in the autonomous and official institutions. On recruitment, the decree contains some rules on the permitted number of teaching staff, on job specifications and there is a fixed maximum proportion of some functions. The school board itself has power to make some rules, for instance on the procedure on making vacancies public (they have an obligation to announce free functions). Within these limits, school boards can choose their personnel. They also have to take into account the rules of collective bargaining. There is also a financial limitation: the *Hogescholendecreet* establishes salary scales and provides that the cost for personnel cannot exceed 80% of the global envelope.

The *Universiteitendecreet* contains few rules on the status of the teaching staff. The university board itself has to draft a statute, including rules relating to the recruitment of personnel. The decree contains some general provisions, as was the case for the *hogescholen* in the *Hogescholendecreet*: staff numbers, job specifications, obligation to work out a procedure of making vacancies public, etc. Within this framework the university board can act. For the universities of the Community, the decree ensures a broad range of autonomy, because before 1991 the statute and the rules of recruitment were regulated in detail by the legislator and the teaching staff was directly appointed by the government.

Now, it is the university board which regulates the recruitment procedure and autonomously appoints its staff. The salary scales of the teaching staff of all universities are fixed by the government, but *Onderwijsdecreet X* gives more opportunity for the university board to differ between several scales according to the merits and reputation of the teaching staff.

There are no explicit decretal provisions which allow the boards of free universities and *hogescholen* to recruit on an ideological basis, but undoubtedly, one can rely on Article 24 of the Constitution.

2.3. *Choice among applicants with necessary qualifications*

2.3.1. *Primary and secondary education*

As mentioned in 2.2. the statute governing the personnel of the free educational institutions presents more and more public law characteristics. One of the consequences is that the choice among applicants with the same qualifications is limited. The limitations in the free education are more or less the same in the official subsidized and the Community education.[9]

In all types of education or networks (the so-called *netten* (see introduction) and only within the network), a system of priority exists. Certain groups of teachers have a better position because they have built up more seniority (*anciënniteit*). A second limitation is the so-called system of '*reaffectatie en terbeschikkingstelling*'. It means that a school board first has to appoint existing teachers who have no actual job before they can recruit a new young one. A third limitation is that existing teachers who request a transfer also have priority over new ones. A recent decretal initiative (*Onderwijsdecreet XI* (Decree on education XI)) tries to initiate some new emphases: end of the right to transfer, periodical evaluation, no longer tenured but mandated heads of school, etc.

Only if there is no teacher with priority or no exisitng teacher who has a right in that function, is the school board free to choose among equally qualified applicants.[10] The free school boards are totally free and do not even have to explain why they have chosen someone. Provincial and municipal councils, as organizers of official schools, or the heads of a school of the Community education (new system) have a duty to justify their choice.

For the Community education, every year in January, a call for new personnel is published in the *Belgisch Staatsblad*, the official journal of the Belgian

9 See M. Verbruggen, 'The Legal Status of Teachers in Belgium: The Flemish Community', in J. De Groof (ed.), *The Legal Status of Teachers in Europe*, Louvain, 1995, p. 257.

10 Remarks that there is a difference between sufficient and required quilifications. As long there is an applicant with required qualifications, he or she has to be appointed. For more details, see M. Verbruggen, 'The Legal Status of Teachers in Belgium: The Flemisch Community', p. 256.

State. This formality does not apply to the subsidized education. They have to communicate vacancies to the Flemish and Brussels Service for Labour Mediation and Vocational Training.

2.3.2. *Higher education*
In both types of higher education, the institution boards are fairly free to choose between qualified applicants within the sketched framework. They have to work out a procedure which they must respect. In any event, the institution boards (also the free ones, in contrast with secondary and primary education) have a decretal duty to justify why someone is appointed. As far as recruitment is concerned, the general principles of good administration (*algemene beginselen van behoorlijk bestuur*) as a whole seems to be relevant.

2.4. *Autonomy and educational objective of the school*

2.4.1. *In general*
Each educational institution, including those of the higher education level, can or even have to establish the goals of its education. A lot of goals can be pursued: raising pupils and students as critical and responsible citizens, making pupils and students 'self-working', promoting the multicultural society, teaching the Christian values, attacking social inequality, etc. Sometimes, the goal can only be realized on an ideological, denominational or methodological basis. The goals and the way to realize them, are part of the pedagogical project. Every school has such a project, at least in an implicit way. It is the core of the educational job. But these goals and the way to reach them can only be chosen and pursued within the framework of the educational legislation as described further. Article 24 § 3 of the Constitution imposes one limit: every education has to respect the human rights and liberties.

2.4.2. *Primary and secondary education*
Until 1991, free schools had to use the curriculum (*leerplan*) of the state schools as a model. Inspection controlled in detail if the institutions respected the curriculum. Diplomas were only valid after homologation by the *homologatie-commissie* (commission of homologation).

This concept, however, has totally changed. Not the educational process, but the output of education is important. For this reason, the Community sets forth a set of *eindtermen* and *ontwikkelingsdoelen* (basic competences and development goals) which has to be reached by a certain group of pupils after a certain educational period. No goals exist for religious courses. The inspection controls the *results* of the educational process overall, no longer the process itself. The *eindtermen* and *ontwikkelingsdoelen* are worked out within the administration by educational specialists, determined by the government and ratified by the Flemish Parliament. The schools now have to work out a curriculum by themselves in relation to the *eindtermen* en *ontwikkelingsdoelen*. This curriculum has to be approved by the government. The schools also have to work out a school action plan (*schoolwerkplan*), which reflects among other things the pedagogical project. Schools organized on a certain methodological or ideological basis which cannot act within this system, may ask for exemption from the *eindtermen* and *ontwikkelingsdoelen*. They then have to set their own goals. These are subject to approval by the Flemish government and ratification by the Flemish Parliament. The *eindtermen*-project is realized in the primary education level, but is still in the implementation phase in the secondary education level (only the goals for the first two cycles are realized).

In order to ensure the quality and a certain unity of the provided education, the curriculum of primary schools has to offer certain 'instruction fields' (*leergebieden*). Secondary schools have to respect a minimum time table (*lessenrooster*).

A recognized school which respects the described conditions (*eindtermen*, recognized *leerplan*, *schoolwerkplan*, etc.), can award diplomas autonomously. The *klassenraad* (class council) decide autonomously if a pupil is passed.

The government fixes the duration of holiday periods and how long a school day lasts (e.g. 28 lesson times in primary education, etc.). The number of pupils per class is not explicitly laid down in any rule. But since the number of pupils per class depends on the number of teachers and the number of (funded) teachers depends on time equivalents (*lestijden*) calculated in relation to the total number of pupils of the school, the government indirectly influences the number of pupils per class.

The government also determine the structure of education (global structure: general secondary/technical/vocational education, year structure, cycles, etc.), especially in secondary education. On the one hand, since the 1970s, funding existing and new educational institutions by the Community (and before 1988 the State) was subject to strict conditions (number of students, number of schools of that network in a certain area, etc.). This process is called *rationalisatie en programmatie* (rationalization and programmation). On the other hand, since the 1970s the government wanted to redraw the global structure in order to realize a better 'orientation' of the students. The recent *Decreet Maatregelen secundair onderwijs* crowns this tendency and sets an important step towards further scaling up. The decree wants to reduce the number of programmes that can be offered to the students. Therefore, the decree introduces (geographical) *onderwijszones* (educational areas) in which schools and *scholengemeenschappen* will operate. School boards can join *scholengemeenschappen* and will receive additional financial support on condition that the *scholengemeenschap* organizes a 'multisectoral educational offer' (*multisectoraal onderwijsaanbod*) or, in other words, a well-defined combination of programmes. For that, the decree introduces a lot of new terminology and instruments: *studiegebieden* (study fields) which encompass a whole set of *structuuronderdelen* (parts of a structure), *basisopties* (basic options), *modules, opleidingsprofielen*, etc. The whole system is too complicated to explain in this report. In any event, this system certainly curtails the pedagogical autonomy of the institutions.

2.4.3. *Higher education*

Until the beginning of the 1990s, the goals and curricula of the higher education programmes established by the government were quite detailed. The universities, since 1991, and the *hogescholen*, since 1994, are free in principle to work out the curricula of their study programmes. However, there are still some limits. The institution board is bound by the *Hogescholendecreet* and the *Universiteitendecreet* which describe the global study structure and the *studiegebieden* (study fields) and fix the *onderwijsbevoegdheid* (educational competence) of each institution. The board also has to respect the system of *studiepunten* (study points), which specifies total study time. In the future, further rationalization and re-arrangement of the offer of higher education can be expected. A government commissioner is preparing this evolution. On the other hand, the institutions cannot neglect the (federal) legislation on the entrance regulations of several professions (e.g. public health professions).

The institutions of higher education award diplomas autonomously. Quality control is guaranteed by a system of external visiting commissions which report periodically on the quality of the offered programmes. The educational legislation sets forth the duration of the academic year but remains silent on the number of student per class, etc.

2.5. *Autonomy of raising and expending resources*

2.5.1. *Introduction*

The theoretical premises of the 19th century can be described as follows: the free institutions had their own private resources, decided freely how to expend this resources and could ask tuition fees. The official educational institutions were funded by the central or local authorities and had to expend these resources in the way the authority wanted and had to ensure education was free of charge.

Things have changed a lot, on primary and secondary level as well as on higher education level. Now all institutions receive money from the Community in relation to the number of pupils or students. Article 24 § 4 of the Constitution guarantees that every institution will be treated on an equal basis. Unequal treatment is only allowed when objective differences exist, so it is reasonable that Community education receives more money because it has a larger (constitutional) duty towards society.

2.5.2. *Primary and Secondary education*

The resources of free institutions consist for a large part of community subsidies. The school boards mostly have their own private patrimony and some private benefits. But they are normally organized as non-profit associations and have to respect the *V.Z.W.-wet* when they generate private resources. Official subsidized institutions receive subsidies from the Community. The local authorities own and manage the infrastructure of their schools. They can also give them additional support. However, they cannot grant their schools additional social benefits (*sociale voordelen*) because on this point the law requires the local authorities to treat all educational institutions (including the free ones) in their territory equally. Community education is funded exclusively by the Community.

Schools receive three types of financial support from the government: for personnel, for administration and for investments. Typical of the Flemish system, however, is that there is a juridical link between the school board and the personnel, the Community pays the subsidies for the salaries of personnel not to the school but directly to the teacher. The school is obliged to expend the other subsidies for the goal for which they have received them. Though, within the category of working funds, they are fairly free to expend them.

Competition is inevitable in a system of funding based on the number of pupils, so it is forbidden to undertake acts of unfair competition. In principle, it is also forbidden for primary institutions to undertake some and for secondary institutions to undertake any commercial activities within the school (Article 41 *Schoolpactwet*; Article 51 *Decreet Basisonderwijs*). It is not clear if sponsoring is lawful under these provisions of the educational legislation. Recently there have been several complaints by parents and profit organisations. Maybe the Flemish government can clarify this problem in the future.

Article 24 § 3 of the Constitution guarantees that the entrance to education is free until the end of compulsory education, so tuition fees in all types of primary and secondary education are not permitted.

2.5.3. *Higher education*

Until 1994, the *hogescholen* were ruled by the *Schoolpactwet*. The system of raising and expending resources was just as it is now in secondary and primary education. As far as raising resources is concerned, since 1994 the boards of the *hogescholen* receive a 'global envelope'. This means that they receive a certain amount of money for personnel and administration together. In other words they are funded on a lump-sum basis. Investments do not form part of the envelope. In some way the *hogescholen* are free to expend their money, but they must stay within the boundaries of the envelope, and only 80% of the envelope can be spent on personnel. Though the envelope includes subsidies for salaries, it is remarkable that the salaries are still paid to the teaching staff direct by the government and not by the board of the *hogeschool*. To a large extent, universities are funded by the Community. They are free to expend these resources. Salaries are paid by the university board. Even the free universities hardly have any resources of their own. The amount of resources is mainly fixed in relation to the number of students.

Universities and *hogescholen* can receive money from the government or private companies for research and societal service on the basis of a contract. They can also participate in profit and non-profit associations. But these two alternative ways of funding are bound by stringent decretal conditions. This way of earning money is gaining ground (especially funds for research projects), but is still a subsidiary way of funding. The *hogescholen* can undertake commercial activities but unfair competition is forbidden. A recent decree (*Onderwijsdecreet X* (Decree on education X)) charges the universities and the *hogescholen*, to work out together a code of conduct concerning unfair competition.[11]

Universities and *hogescholen* are entitled to ask tuition fees, but the Court of Arbitration pointed out that the maximum amount of these fees has to be established by decree.[12] However, in comparison with some other countries, this maximum is fixed rather low. Within these limits, the institution board can determine the amount of the tuition fee.

2.6. *Autonomy of organisation*

2.6.1. *Primary and secondary education*

(a) *Free education*

The basic organizational rules of free educational institutions are sketched in 2.1. Nevertheless the principle right on free organization, the educational legislation permanently threatens or at least curtails this freedom of organization.

The educational legislation interferes with the internal organization of the institutions. For instance, it requiress all free subsidised institutions to have some participation organs in which parents, teachers, local community, etc. are represented. The Court of Arbitration declared that the imposition of certain conditions of organization could violate the freedom of education. So the obligation to erect participation organs is not an attack on the freedom of education so long as these organs do not take any decisions.[13] That is why the manner of implementing this obligation is a matter for the institution itself. The most important participation organ is the *participatieraad* (council of participation). It has advisory and consultative competences. There is also an *onderhandelingscomité*, a committee in which social matters are discussed by the representatives of the school board and the representatives of the personnel.

[11] V. Rotsaert, *op. cit.*

[12] e.g. Court of Arbitration, no. 33/92, 7 May 1992, *Belgisch Staatsblad – Moniteur Belge*, 4 June 1992; Court of Arbitration, no. 30/96, 15 May 1996, *Belgisch Staatsblad – Moniteur Belge*, 6 June 1996, *Tijdschrift voor Onderwijsrecht en Onderwijsbeleid*, 1996–97, note R. Verstegen.

[13] Court of Arbitration, no. 85/95, 14 December 1995, *Belgisch Staatsblad – Moniteur Belge*, 4 January 1996.

However, in social matters the school board itself takes the final decision. Another recent example of curtailing the freedom of internal organization can be found in the legislation on primary education. In personnel policy the *Decreet basisonderwijs* introduced a redistribution of powers between the school board and the head of the school. The Court of Arbitration accepted this limitation on the freedom of organization.[14]

The legislation on secondary education gives an example of a limitation of the external organization. Under the scope of budgetary implications, the government tried to rationalize the structure of the education. At a certain moment, the Minister of Education even considered the imposition of mergers of free (and other) educational institutions, first at the higher education level (see further), later at the secondary level. But the Council of State pointed out that this was unreconcilable with the freedom of education.[15] Now the *Decreet Maatregelen secundair onderwijs* provides for financial stimuli for educational institutions which merge voluntarily or which voluntarily set up or join a *scholengemeenschap* (community of schools). So in an indirect way, the freedom of organization of free institutions, or the autonomy of organization of all institutions is curtailed.

(b) *Community education*

We described the general structure of the Community education in 2.1.

In the regulation of 1988, the basic policy competences (general policy, personnel policy, regulatory power, financial management, etc.) were attributed to the central level. Minor competences, e.g. local administration, were appointed to the *LORGOs*. The central level had supervisory power over the *LORGOs*. One or several Community school(s) were managed by such a *LORGO* (*lokale schoolraad* – local school council). This council grouped one or more schools. The school heads, parents, students, teaching staff and members of the local community were represented in the *LORGOs* and could participate in the decision-making process. The *ARGO-decreet* attribute no real competences to the head of the school.

As stated, the *Decreet Gemeenschapsonderwijs* redraws the whole structure of Community education. The major competences are attributed to the intermediary level or *scholengroepen*, but at the local level the schools also received important competences (pedagogical organization, the offered programmes, management of the local infrastructure, local personnel policy, etc.). The organs of a school are the head of the school (*directeur*) and the school council (*schoolraad*). The head of the school is responsible for the administration and

[14] Court of Arbitration, no. 19/99, 17 February 1999, *Belgisch Staatsblad – Moniteur Belge*, 17 March 1999.

[15] Advice of the Council of State, legislative section, 24 November 1993, *Tijdschrift voor Onderwijsrecht en Onderwijsbeleid*, 1993–94, p. 198.

exercises the competences of the local level (e.g. he or she works out a school regulation and a school action plan, recruits new teachers, etc.). The school council in which parents, personnel and members of the local community are represented only has advisory and consultative competences. Two members of the *schoolraad* are represented in the general assembly (*algemene vergadering*) of a *scholengroep*.

(c) *Official subsidized education*
In principle, the political organs of the local authorities determine how their schools will be managed. However, the rules on participation which apply to the free subsidized institutions also apply to official subsidized education. The *participatieraad* only has advisory and consultative competences. Here, not the freedom of education but the autonomy of the local authorities is at stake.

(d) *Scholengemeenschappen* (communities of schools)
Schools of all networks can voluntarily join a *scholengemeenschap*, but if they do so they are bound by the rules of the *Decreet Maatregelen secundair onderwijs*. The decree defines certain competences which have to be transferred from the school board to the *scholengemeenschap* (agreements on personnel policy, choice of offered programmes, use of time equivalents, etc.). The school boards can decide to attribute additional competences to the *scholengroep* in a written contract.

2.6.2. *Higher education*
As stated in 2.1.2., the *Hogescholendecreet* regulates the participation organs (Academic Council, Department Council, Student Council and *onderhandelingscomite*). This regulation is rather detailed, but the participation organs only have advisory and consultative competences, no decision-making power. The decree imposes the installation of these organs and lays down the basic principles, but within this framework the institution itself has to regulate organization of these organs. Thus, the freedom of education and the 'autonomy' of the local authorities is respected.[16]

As stated, the *Universiteitendecreet* is silent on the organization and the participation organs of the universities. The universities established by law are governed by some specific laws. In these laws their organization and their participation organs are regulated quite substantially. In practice the organization of the free universities is similar to that of the universities of 'public law'.

16 Court of Arbitration, no. 85/95, 14 December 1995, *Belgisch Staatsblad – Moniteur Belge*, 4 January 1996.

2.7. *Opportunities for educational institutions to take juridical actions against the government*

Juridical action against the government is possible only if education is organized by a body which is independent from the central government. This has always been the case for the free and official subsidized institutions. Since 1989, this has also been the case for Community education (see above).

An Act of the legislative power – the Flemish (or federal) Parliament – which violates the rights and freedoms with regard to education or the principle of equality can be annulled by the Court of Arbitration. If an Act of the government or the executive power in general is unlawful, every interested party, including a school board or the competent organ of the *Gemeenschapsonderwijs* can request the Council of State to suspend and annul it. The law can also organize an administrative procedure. Sometimes this procedure has to be followed before appeal can be made to the Council of State.

If an Act of the executive violates a subjective right (e.g. the right to financial support), a free school board can go to the civil courts and tribunals. Sometimes, simultaneous procedures in the Council of State and the courts are possible.

3. *Individual autonomy*

3.1. *Latitude of discretion of teachers/professors in educational matters*

3.1.1. *Primary and secondary education*

As described in 1.3., neither the Constitution nor any education law explicitly guarantee the freedom to teach; however, some authors accept the existence of this kind of freedom. This freedom should be an aspect of pedagogical freedom, i.e. on micro-level. These authors even assume that this freedom is necessary to accomplish the teaching activity.

With regard to pedagogical and methodological matters, it is questionable if there is a real legally enforceable freedom of the teacher. I think it is better to talk about a latitude of discretion. The educational legislation (*eindtermen*, informatisation project, duties of the teacher, statute of the pupils, etc.) and the model curricula and the directives of the educational 'umbrella organizations' (the ARGO, the Flemish secretary of Catholic education) curtail the freedom of the teacher. Moreover, the teacher is a member of a pedagogical team, which further reduces his or her freedom. This team works out a pedagogical project and pursues a local school policy. In the bosom of this team, school board and teachers will make, at least informal agreements on the means to realize their project and their policy (handbooks, didactical materials, etc.) (see further 3.2.). The room left is the margin where the teacher can act fairly autonomously. He or she is qualified and should decide how to educate concretely his pupils (method, punishment, evaluation of pupils, etc.). But the degree of latitude will vary in each educational situation and is difficult to measure. It seems not so much a juridical, but more a pedagogical question and that is certainly not within the scope of this report.

3.1.2. *Higher education*

What is stated above also applies to the teaching staff of the *hogescholen*. However, as a consequence of the specific task of the *hogeschool*, the latitude of discretion of the teacher will be much larger. In some institutions it will even reflect the situation at the universities.

In the universities academic freedom is, even without any explicit legal basis, an attainment. Under the responsibility of the institution, the professor decides on the contents of the course, the method of teaching and evaluation, etc. However, there is undoubtedly a tendency towards less freedom (see further 3.2.). The institutions themselves also seem to show more interest in educational and methodological matters by introducing educational plans and promoting some (new) educational methods.

3.2. *Relationship between head of the institution and teaching staff in professional matters*

3.2.1. *Primary and secondary education*

The organizing body or the school board are responsible for education. The head of the institution is their representative. He or she has to supervise the realization of the pedagogical project and the quality of the education. The decrees on the legal status of teachers set forth that teachers must be loyal to the institution and have to accomplish their tasks, among others those charged by the school board (e.g. in the contract). So, the headteacher has the right to give some orders on professional matters (principally concerning methodology, but also additional tasks such as surveillance in the playground).

New decretal initiatives can clarify even more the relationship between the headteacher and the teachers. First, the headteacher has to draft a function description (*functiebeschrijving*) for each teacher. This description establishes (in detail) all tasks of the teacher. The government has devised models of function descriptions. Secondly, on the basis of the function description there will be a triennial evaluation of the teacher. So, the way he or she fulfils their tasks and use their pedagogical autonomy can be controlled.

3.2.2. *Higher education*

The relationship between teachers and professors and the head of the institution is similar to the relationship in primary and secondary education in the realization that this relationship is more decentralized on the level of the faculties (in the universities) and the departments (in the *hogescholen*). Moreover, the academic freedom and the fact that members of the teaching staff participate more in the institutions' policy (see 3.3.) create a less-hierarchical relationship.

Here also, the decretal legislator initiated an evaluation procedure for both types of higher education. The system is not yet operational because the boards of the universities and *hogescholen* have to work out the procedure by themselves. This is because of the freedom or autonomy of the institution.

3.3. *Participation of teaching-staff in school policy and self-governing bodies*

3.3.1. *Primary and secondary education*

In principle, school policy is a matter of the organizing body or the school board and not of the teaching staff. As stated, the head of the institution is a representative of the school board and executes the policy of the board.

Teachers of subsidized schools are represented in the participation council (*participatieraad*) of the school. As described above, these organs have no real decision-making power. Teachers also are represented in the *onderhandelingscomité* in which social conditions are discussed. Sometimes a teacher is a member of the school board itself, but this is not the general rule.

Teachers in Community schools are represented in the school council. They may represent the school, if they are elected, in the general assembly (*algemene vergadering*) of the group of schools.

3.3.2. *Higher education*

In the universities and their faculties it is a tradition that the staff are involved in the policy of the institutions. The educational legislation does not impose any conditions. The way in which the universities founded by the community are managed and the teaching staff are elected is regulated by decree.

Since the *hogescholen* have a similar tradition to secondary schools, the cooperation of teachers in the institutions' policy is not a tradition. The teachers are represented in the academic council (*academische raad*) and the departmental council. As stated, these organs have only advisory and consultative powers. In these institutions, there is also an *onderhandelingscomité*. Maybe one can expect that the involvement of the teaching staff in the institutions' policy will increase in the future.

4. *Consequences of autonomy*

4.1. *Autonomy, quality and unity*

4.1.1. *Primary and secondary education*

The regulation on *eindtermen* en *ontwikkelingsdoelen* has been sketched in 2.4. This system suits a new approach on the quality of education; but quality does not mean unity. Diversity is a valuable resource for education. Indeed, there are some minimum standards of knowledge and skills every pupil must reach. These minimum standards are laid down in the *eindtermen* and *ontwikkelingsdoelen*. As stated, the central government establishes these *eindtermen* and the school itself works out a curriculum, which reflects these *eindtermen* and the means to reach them. This curriculum has to be approved by the government on the advice of the inspectorate, in order to ensure the (quality) level of the education. The school also has to work out a *schoolwerkplan*, that reflects the pedagogical project and the educational organization. Secondary schools also have to respect a minimum timetable (*lessenrooster*).

The inspectorate oversees whether the institution realizes the curriculum and succeeds in bringing pupils to the *eindtermen* and *ontwikkelingsdoelen*. It seems as if the inspectorate is less interested in a detailed control of the educational process than in the overall quality approach of each institution. If the pupils of a certain school do not reach the goals, and after a warning there is no improvement, the Community can stop or reduce funding or subsidizing this school. Note that the inspectorate does not control the pedagogical methods.

4.1.2. *Higher education*

As stated above, the higher educational institutions are free to determine the curricula of the programmes they offer. The limitation of educational competence is a constructive way to guarantee the quality of the programmes. Since the reform of higher education, monitoring the substantive quality of the offered programmes is an explicit responsibility of the institutions (Article 122 *Universiteitendecreet*; Article 58 *Hogescholendecreet*). Internally, they required to constantly evaluate the quality of the education; externally, the institutions of each sector of the higher education level have to jointly organize a periodical evaluation of the global quality of similar programmes (every five years for the *hogescholen*; every eight years for the universities). This global examination is executed by the so-called Commissions of Visitation in the universities (*visitatie-commissies*) and Commissions of Evaluation (*doorlichtingscommissies*) in the *hogescholen*. The commissions are composed of Flemish and foreign specialists in the field of these programmes. The examination is comparative and the institutions must give effect to the recommendations of the commissions. This kind of evaluation will undoubtedly encourage institutions to increase their quality and strengthen competition between the institutions, as the reports of these commissions are published.

So, the government just oversees that there is adequate evaluation and observes how the institutions deal with the results of this evaluation. If the quality of a certain programme is constantly insufficient, the students who end this programme still obtain a valid diploma, but the government can proscribe the number of students of that programme when fixing the working-funds of the institution.

4.2. *Autonomy and supervisory power*

If supervisory power means that the government can impose its view if an institution misuses its autonomy by means of annulling decisions or obliging them direct to take some decisions, there is no real supervisory power. On the contrary, autonomy for the institutions of Community education means precisely the end of supervisory power by the government. Since 1988, the autonomous body itself stands under limited supervisory power of the Flemish government, and with the recent reform of Community education, this supervisory power seems to have disappeared. Since the free and official subsidized institutions are legally independent of the Community there has never been a real supervisory power, though, official subsidized institutions are supervised by the organs of the local authorities. Community education schools are supervised by the central level of the *Gemeenschapsonderwijs* (the former ARGO), but as stated, the recent reform of Community education has also reduced this supervisory power.

This does not mean that there is no supervision by the Community government. There is an inspectorate which operates in the core of the administration. This inspectorate inspects the quality of primary and secondary education, ensures that the institutions respect the educational legislation and advises on the recognition and funding of schools. There is also a financial audit of the educational institutions. As far as Community education is concerned, the Flemish government will examine annually the reports of a commission of accountants on financial matters and the annual report of the head of the *Gemeenschapsonderwijs* on educational matters. At the higher educational institutions, there is a government commissioner who ensures that the institutions do not infringe the law or endanger the financial balance of the institution. On the basis of the reports of these services (inspectorate, commission of accountants, government commissioner), the government can impose administrative (financial) sanctions on the institutions of Community education, but the institution or school boards can appeal against these sanctions at the Council of State or the regular courts.

4.3. *Relations between autonomy, responsibility and accountability*

This is a difficult topic since the 'relation' between autonomy, responsibility and accountability does not exist. Moreover, this relationship seems to differ from domain to domain (educational quality, financial management, personnel policy, etc.). Only a personal global appreciation can be given about it.

Autonomy seems necessarily linked with responsibility. This is most clear in the field of financial autonomy. The institutions receives a budget and has to manage it. The institution is responsible for policy choices made and will be sanctioned if it infringes the law. As far as personnel policy is concerned, the rate of autonomy varies from level to level. In higher education, within the financial framework, the institution is responsible for personnel policy. In primary and secondary education, this responsibility is much more limited because the statutes relating to the teaching staff already fix the rules. In the field of quality control, the institutions are also responsible for the results of their pupils and students. If an institution does not reach the quality goals, it can be subject to financial sanctions. However, it can still award a valid diploma. As a result, graduate students will have a poor position in the labour market and it is not impossible that the institutions will be responsible for this under civil law (Art. 1382 Civil Code) and will have to pay damages.[17] Autonomy does not mean that there is no accountability for the institutions. However, it seems that this accountability has another 'outlook'. Whereas in the old days every decision had to be justified if demanded, now, the government has opted for supervision on the basis of general reports (e.g. annual reports of universities and *hogescholen*, annual report of the *Gemeenschapsonderwijs*). On the other hand, there is a tendency towards accountability, not only to the government but to the Flemish Parliament and society as a whole (e.g. the reports of the quality control in higher education).

At first sight, autonomy is linked with quality control within autonomous educational institutions, but if this link is necessarily, is not clear. In any event, the institutions play, more than before, an important role in the quality control. The higher educational institutions are even explicitly responsible for internal quality evaluation and it seems that in the future also primary and secondary schools, by means of their school action plans, will have to pay more attention to internal control. But an important part of quality control is still external. In Flanders, it seems that autonomy is necessarily linked with at least a less active role by the government in controlling educational quality.

4.4. *Recent trends with respect to autonomy of educational institutions*

There is indefinitely a trend to more autonomy at all educational levels on 'meso-level', or in other words for the educational institutions. This was one of the goals of every recent educational reform. Autonomy is present in certain domains such as financial management, personnel policy and quality control. Maybe this operation has not yet succeeded at secondary level. Anyway, on the higher education level the operation is most successful, but there was a tradition of autonomy at the universities.

On the other hand there are also movements in the other direction: first at all levels there is a tendency of rationalizing the number of offered programmes which reduces the autonomy of institutions to choose which programmes they may offer and how to fill the curricula of the programmes. Secondly, strengthening the autonomy of the institution seems to decrease the autonomy of the individual teacher, by introducing function descriptions and evaluation procedures. Thirdly, however, from a juridical viewpoint the autonomy of organization has been saved, the government threatens this autonomy in an indirect way, by giving financial incentives to those institutions who step into the

[17] R. Verstegen, 'De regeling van het hoger onderwijs in Vlaanderen', in L. Van Hoestenberghe (ed.), *Studentenrecht. Juridische en sociale gids voor de student hoger onderwijs*, Louvain, 1999, p. 26.

structure promoted by the government. Finally, it is not clear which role the 'umbrella organizations' play in supporing autonomous institutions. It is not impossible that the supervision of the government is replaced by the supervision of these organizations.

So, in conclusion, it seems not always clear if autonomy is an ideological term in the language of educationalists and politicians or if it is something which is (or can be) effectively realized in the field. Although a lot of efforts are made to increase financial and administrative autonomy, to deregulate these matters and to limit supervision, in other domains (e.g. the structure of the education, etc.), interference by the government, especially by means of detailed regulation, is increased.

List of laws and decrees

Schoolpactwet, Wet van 29 mei 1959 tot wijziging van sommige bepalingen van de onderwijswetgeving (Law on School peace, Law of 29 May 1959, on changing some provisions of the educational legislation), *Belgisch Staatsblad – Moniteur Belge*, 19 June 1959, and in De Groof, J., *De Schoolpactwetgeving. Coördinatie en annotatie*, Antwerp, 1996, 191 pp.

ARGO-decreet, Bijzonder decreet van 19 december 1988 betreffende de Autonome Raad voor het Gemeenschapsonderwijs (Special decree of 19 December 1988, on the Autonomous Council of the Community education), *Belgisch Staatsblad – Moniteur Belge*, 29 December 1988.

Rechtspositiedecreet gesubsidieerd onderwijs, Decreet van 27 maart 1991 betreffende de rechtspositie van sommige personeelsleden van het gesubsidieerd onderwijs en de gesubsidieerde psycho-medisch-sociale centra (Decree of 27 March 1991, on the legal status of certain members of the personnel of the subsidised education and the subsidised psycho-medical-social centra), *Belgisch Staatsblad – Moniteur Belge*, 15 May 1991.

Rechtspositiedecreet Gemeenschapsonderwijs, Decreet van 27 maart 1991 betreffende de rechtspositie van bepaalde personeelsleden van het Gemeenschapsonderwijs (Decree of 27 March 1991, on the legal status of certain members of the personnel of the Community education), *Belgisch Staatsblad – Moniteur Belge*, 25 May 1991.

Universiteitendecreet, Decreet van 12 juni 1991 betreffende de universiteiten in de Vlaamse Gemeenschap (Decree of 12 June 1991, on the universities in the Flemish Community), *Belgisch Staatsblad – Moniteur Belge*, 4 July 1991.

Hogescholendecreet, Decreet van 13 juli 1994 betreffende de hogescholen in de Vlaamse Gemeenschap (Decree of 13 July 1994, on the non-university higher educational institutions in the Flemish Community), *Belgisch Staatsblad – Moniteur Belge*, 31 August 1994.

Decreet Basisonderwijs, Decreet van 25 februari 1997, basisonderwijs, (Decreet of 25 February 1997, on primary education), *Belgisch Staatsblad – Moniteur Belge*, 17 April 1997.

Decreet Gemeenschapsonderwijs, Bijzonder decreet van 14 juli 1998 betreffende het Gemeenschapsonderwijs (Special Decree of 14 July 1998 on the Community education), *Belgisch Staatsblad – Moniteur Belge*, 30 September 1998.

Decreet Maatregelen secundair onderwijs, Decreet van 14 juli 1998 houdende diverse maatregelen met betrekking tot het secundair onderwijs en tot wijziging van het decreet van 25 februari 1997 betreffende het basisonderwijs (Decree of 14 July 1998 containing several measures on secondary education and on modification of the decree of 25 February 1997, on primary education), *Belgisch Staatsblad – Moniteur Belge*, 29 August 1998.

LITERATURE

De Groof, J., 'Academisch personeelsbeleid: vrijheid in gebondenheid. Juridische en beleidsmatige overwegingen over de relatie universiteit-overheid', in De Groof, J. (ed.), *Personeelsbeleid aan de Vlaamse universiteiten. Cahiers voor onderwijsrecht en onderwijsbeleid, Volume I*, Antwerp, 1995, pp. 1–52.

De Groof, J., 'The legal status of Teachers – The Global Framework – An introduction', in De Groof, J. (ed.), *The Legal Status of Teachers in Europe. Mobility and education*, Louvain, 1995, pp. 11–37.

De Groof, J., 'On pedagogical freedom – some legal and policy considerations', in De Groof, J. and Fiers, J. (eds.), *The Legal Status of Minorities in Education*, Louvain, 1996, pp. 235–258.

De Groof, J., 'The Freedom of Teachers – Some Notes', in De Groof, J. and Malherbe, E.F.J. (eds), *Human Rights in South African Education. From the Constitutional Drawing Board to the Chalkboard*, Louvain, 1997, pp. 295–314.

De Groof, J., 'Verzelfstandiging. Autonomie versus "centralisatie" in het hoger onderwijs van de Vlaamse Gemeenschap?', in De Groof,J. and Van Loon, F., *Optimalisering van beleidsbeslissingen in het hoger onderwijs. Cahiers voor onderwijsrecht en onderwijsbeleid, Volume IV*, Antwerp, 1998, pp. 1–39; translated and revised as 'Gaining independence: "Autonomy" versus "Centralisation" in the Higher Education of the Flemish Community?' in *Autonomy in education. Syllabus of the 6th ELA-Conference, Salzburg 17–19th December 1998*, 16 pp.

Ministry of the Flemish Community – Department of Education, *Higher Education in Flanders (Belgium)*, Brussels, 1998, 30 pp.

Rotsaert, V., 'Country Report – The Flemish Community of Belgium', *European Journal of Education Law and Policy*, 1999, No. 1, not yet published.

Verbruggen, M., 'The legal status of teachers in Belgium: the Flemish Community', in De Groof, J. (ed.), *The Legal Status of Teachers in Europe. Mobility and education*, Louvain, 1995, pp. 255–260.

Verstegen, R., 'De regeling van het hoger onderwijs in Vlaanderen (The regulation of higher education in Flanders)', in Van Hoestenberghe, L. (ed.), *Studentenrecht. Juridische en sociale gids voor de student hoger onderwijs* (*Student and Law. Juridical an social guide for the higher education student*), Louvain, 1999, pp.15-73.

THOMAS ROED JAKOBSEN[1]

Autonomy in the Education System

DANISH REPORT

Choice of method

The answers given in the following report will try as far as possible to follow the arrangement of the questionnaire, but please note that in some instances, the author has felt it neccesary to deviate from this principle. In general it must be noted that the Danish education system is quite complex. An all-encompassing presentation should thus not be expected. The overall aim will be to provide insight into the general notion of autonomy in the Danish education system, frequently illustrated by examples.

1. *Constitutional legal basis*

1.1. *Is autonomy of the educational system or some of its parts constitutionally guaranteed?*

1.2. *Does the constitution guarantee teacher's educational freedom or the liberty of scientific teaching (academic freedom)?*

1.3. *If autonomy is constitutionally granted: which notion of autonomy underlies the constitution?*

1.4. *Are there strict legal bases and describe it.*

The constitutional act of Denmark – *Grundloven* – only has one provision related to education:

> *Article 76.*
> *All children of school age shall be entitled to free instruction in primary*

[1] The views presented here are the authors' own.

Walter Berka, Jan de Groof and Hilde Penneman (eds.), Autonomy in Education, 323–339.

> *schools. Parents or guardians making their own arrangements for their children or wards to receive instruction equivalent to the general primary school standard shall not be obliged to have their children or wards taught in a publicly provided school.*

Several notions can be derived from the wording.

The provision grants a right and duty to receive education to all children of school age, but the term 'school age' is left to be defined in an ordinary Act.

In a perspective of autonomy it can be seen that parents or guardians wishing to make their own arrangements for instruction of their children and wards can do so. The method is left open, so long as the output is the same – children taught outside the public school system must be given '*instruction equivalent to the general primary school standard*'. This is indeed autonomy at its best – and worst, some would say.

To ensure that this principle of free choice of school type is real, the state provides subsidies – roughly 80% of the cost, for various types of private schools – provided that they are, amongst other things, independent.

The notion of 'independence' is aimed at the *organizational* independence of the individual school, and there is no requirement for *pedagogical independence*, so naturally different private schools can follow the same pedagogical theory.

The school age is set in the Act on the *folkeskole* (public school). Thus, Article 34 reads:

> *34. (1) Compulsory education shall commence on 1 August of the calendar year of the child's 7th birthday, and it shall terminate on 31 July, when the child has received regular instruction for 9 years (not including the pre-school class). The compulsory education requirement shall however terminate on 31 July of the calendar year of the child's 17th birthday at the latest or when he has completed basic school or equivalent education, cf. section 33(2)–(4).*

Any education offered after termination of the compulsory education requirement is consequently not covered by the constitution, and rules pertaining to youth education and higher education are set out in ordinary Acts. Even though not formally covered by the constitution, the regulation of these areas is a reflection of the general state of society, namely the spirit expressed in the constitution.

The constitution contains no requirements for standards of academic freedom. Any restrictions will therefore be set out in ordinary Acts, but as we shall see, Denmark has a tradition of a large degree of autonomy for educational institutions, operating within overall frameworks, adopted for each educational area by the Parliament.

2. *Autonomy of educational institutions*

2.1. Is autonomy granted with respect to the organisation of the educational institutions? Are schools or universities vested with a legal personality of their own? Have schools or universities individual constitutions of their own (basic statutes, basic charters)? Are these autonomously set up by the educational institutions or conferred onto them by the state government?

As the current report is to provide an insight into the Danish educational institutions, a graphical overview of the Danish education system is annexed. This will hopefully help the understanding of references to the various types of educational institutions.

Where appropriate, the full text of acts and/or ministerial orders will be given, to provide a more genuine feel of how closely or loosely an area is regulated.

In general one can distinguish between two groups of institutions:

'Basic institutions' are institutions that provide publicly approved tuition and education, and that, in accordance with the respective laws, form part of a coherent national educational planning.

'Alternative institutions' are institutions that are not established with a view to fulfilling a public obligation to provide sufficient educational opportunities nationwide.

In general, the latter will enjoy greater autonomy than the former.

To illustrate, some youth education institutions must be deemed to form part of a suitable national educational planning, in order to be approved. Similarly, if an educational institution falls within this category, the minister will have power to withdraw approval of the institution if the need for the institution is no longer there, while the approval of an alternative institution will only be withdrawn if certain specific criteria are not met – i.e. if an institution is not found to be independent.

Determining which category an institution falls within can only be made upon individual assessment.

The actual organization of a given institution is usually regulated more closely, to ensure a proper balancing of interests.

In general, the Danish education system operates with a large degree of financial support. Often the funds will be given to a 'private self-governing institution', that is an institution not part of the public hierachy.

Not surprisingly, such a private self-governing institution must fulfil certain criteria in order to benefit financially, such as that their statutes will be subject to approval by a public authority.

It is not possible to provide an exact list of the differences between private and public institutions, as it is possible through legislation to transfer large amounts of powers to public institutions, thereby limiting the powers of intervention of central government.

Conversely self-governing private institutions can be regulated in such a way, that their functioning is close to that of the public institutions.

Legal personality

An educational institution may well be vested with a legal personality of its own. However the relevant distinction can only be made after an indivudual assessment of the relevant legislation. The exercise of this distinction has given rise to some doubt.

Common theory assumes that a specially intensive and actual control must be present, before an educational institution is considered to be part of the public administration. The mere fact that a given institution is granted financial resources and operates within a general framework relating to, for example, admission requirements, educational content and exams is not in itself enough to consider an educational instituion to be part of the public system.[2]

Statutes

For private self-governing institutions, the statutes are often subject to approval by the Ministry of Education. In general, minor changes to a statute must be presented to the ministry, while more fundamental changes, i.e. regarding the aim and purpose of the institution, must be presented to a special authority in charge of administration regarding foundations, as private self-governing institutions are covered by rules regarding foundations.

2.1.1. *Primary and lower secondary education (ISCED 1 and 2)*

Non-public schools

As for the various types of private schools and private independent boarding schools, their approval by the Ministry of Education is quite closely regulated. To illustrate this, in order to be approved, they have to meet special criteria, i.e. to be organizationally independent. Their regulations are subject to approval by the ministry, and there are restrictions on the categories of persons who can be elected to the board of the school.

The folkeskole

In respect of public schools, the law provides a legal framework, within which the municipality must set out a statute:

> the statute for the administration of the municipal school system shall among other things contain provisions about the following:

[2] Hans Gammeltoft-Hansen, Jon Andersen Kaj Larsen and Karsten Loiborg, Forvaltningsret, 1. udgave 1994, p. 69.

(1) The number of parent representatives on the school board.
(2) Voting members on the school board, cf. section 42 (4).
(3) The appointment of a possible member of the municipal council to the school board, cf. section 42 (3).
(4) The procedure for the election of representatives to the school board.
(5) The composition of possible joint advisory bodies for the municipal school system, cf. section 40 (4).

(2) The statute shall furthermore contain a description of any powers that may be delegated to the school board in pursuance of section 40 (4).
(3) Decisions made by the municipal council regarding the school structure etc., cf. section 40 (2), items (3) to (6) shall be recorded in an annex to the statute.

In general, the area is covered by framework regulations which leave a large degree of everyday freedom to the municipalities and the schools.

2.1.2. *Youth education (ISCED 3)*

There are a multitude of different types of youth education, covering the following categories

- vocational education and training;
- specific types of vocational or semi-professional types of education and training, i.e. maritime education;
- general upper secondary education, covering public and private gymnasiums, alternative 2-year 'gymnasium programme', higher preparatory examination programme, higher commercial examination programme, higher technical examination programme; and
- 'alternative and untraditional' youth education and training programmes.

Hopefully this list will convey some impression of a very flexible youth education system, designed to meet the individual needs of a very large variety of students.

2.1.3. *Higher education (ISCED 5, 6 and 7)*

This category covers

- higher education at university level;
- medium-cycle higher education – non-university level; and
- short-cycle higher education.

Higher education at university level

The universities are administered by a framework Act and their individual statutes. The system is based on extensive self-government.

To illustrate, it is left to the highest collegiate body – 'the senate' – to approve the organization of the institution, including faculty and departmental structure, the budget of the institution and proposals for the statutes of the institution.

Medium-cycle higher education – non-university level

Giving a brief overview of this area is not easy: a majority of institutions are self-governing, private, state-financed institutions, others are state institutions, while yet others (nursing schools) are county institutions.

In general, these institutions do, however, share one common feature, namely that they have a board and a rector.

As regards the state institutions, the appointments of rector and institutional staff are made by the Ministry of Education.

Short-cycle higher education

Such education is offered at institutions which are governed by a ministerial framework, on recommendation of a committee composed of representatives from the various interest groups, i.e. representatives of the labour market, higher education and teachers and pupils from the relevant educational sector.

2.2. *How independently can they determine the recruitment of their personnel?*

2.2.1. *Primary and lower secondary education*

Non-public schools

Schools within this category are free to determine the recruitment of their personnel.

The folkeskole

With reference to the section above, the municipality has freedom to choose within the boundaries of Chapter 4 of the Act on the *folkeskole*. While the Act presupposes that as many powers as possible are delegated from the municipality to the local school, recruitment is one of the powers that cannot be delegated to the school, cf. Article 40, section (4).

> *Chapter 4 of the Act on the folkeskole*
> The Teachers
> Art. 28. (1) In order to be considered for a teaching post in the *basic school and the 10th form*, a candidate must have completed the Folkeskole teacher-training programme (cf. however subsections (2) and

(3)), or other teacher training approved by the Minister of Education in this respect. The approval may be made conditional upon the candidate passing a test at a college of education. The Minister of Education may in special cases deviate from the provision laid down in the first clause.

(2) Persons with special qualifications may be appointed to teach certain subjects.

(3) Pre-school teachers and infant school teachers, who have received training in pursuance of the regulations laid down to this effect, may teach at the 1st to 4th form levels as well as PE, textile design and home economics at the other form levels.

Art. 29. (1) In order to be considered for a teaching post in a *pre-school class*, a candidate must have completed the training course for educators or one of the training programmes mentioned in section 28 (3) or a similar programme approved by the Minister of Education in this respect. The approval may be made conditional upon the candidate passing a test at an educator training college. The Minister of Education may in special cases deviate from the provision laid down in the first clause.

....

Art. 30.a. (1) The Minister of Education may lay down more detailed provisions regarding the qualification requirements for persons, who are to assume special teaching tasks or tasks of a special nature in connection with the teaching.

The above framework should illustrate that the school can primarily choose among persons with teacher qualifications. While it also follows that persons with other relevant qualification can perform instruction, such persons can never be given a right to teach at all form levels in the primary and lower secondary school.

2.2.2. *Youth education*

Vocational schools

The board of the school hires teachers who must meet certain requirements laid down by the minister.

These requirements cover a range of qualifications, but to illustrate the lowest acceptable standard, a teacher who has no training in teaching methodology must complete a postgraduate teacher training course of around 500 hours' duration.

Private and public gymnasium and higher preparatory examination

The county council has the right to hire and dismiss teachers upon recommendation from the headteacher. The county council must seek the opinion of the minister before appointing the headteacher.

The actual choice of employee is made from amongst applicants who fulfil the general requirements stipulated by the minister, primarily a twofold demand that they must have both pedagogical and professional subject-related competence as further specified in the rules issued by the minister.

Higher commercial examination programme, higher technical examination programme

The minister issues rules regarding teacher qualifications. Hiring is made conditional upon the teacher passing a pedagogical test within two years of appointment.

As a very simplified rule of thumb one can say that an institution may choose amongst teachers who fulfil general qualifications stipulated by the minister, while the actual hiring and dismissal of teaching staff is left to a superior politically founded council, upon recommendation by the head of the institution.

2.2.3. *Higher education*

Higher education at university level

Rules regarding the awarding of doctoral degrees, appointment of professors and academic staff are covered by ministerial orders.

There are detalied procedural rules that must be followed. A review board composed of persons with the necessary professional subject insight gives a recommendation to the management of the institution, who then decide – or in some cases lay their recommendation before the ministry.

Other types of higher education

There are a large number of different schemes that apply, making it very difficult to provide a short overview. Some institutions have to lay their decisions regarding hiring and dismissal before the ministry, while others do not.

2.3. *Are schools or universities entitled to choose freely among applicants with necessary qualifications?*

2.3.1. *Primary and lower secondary education*

Non-public school

Yes.

The folkeskole

It follows from Article 40, section 2 of the Act on the *folkeskole*, that the municipality council decides on

> *(2) The appointment and dismissal of headteachers and teachers. Decisions regarding the appointment of headteachers and teachers shall be taken on the recommendation of the school board concerned, cf. section 44 (7).*

While the preparatory work on the Act on the folkeskole presupposes that a maximum of power is actually delegated from the municipal council to the individual school, certain powers cannot be delegated:

> *Article 40, section (4)*
> *The municipal council may – wholly or partly – delegate its powers in pursuance of this Act to the school boards, with the exception of the powers following from its competence as grant-awarding authority and employer.*

So the individual public school can never be awarded an independent right to appoint headteachers or teachers.

2.3.2. *Youth education*

Please refer to the answers given in 2.2.2.

2.3.3. *Higher education*

Please refer to the answers given for question 2.2.3.

2.4. *Is autonomy granted with respect to the fulfilment of the educational objective? Can schools or universities independently organise their curricula, decide autonomously on the number of students per class etc.?*

2.4.1. *Primary and lower secondary education*

Non-public school

In respect of private schools it is clear that their pedagogical foundations do not have to be approved by the ministry, presupposing that the foundation is not contrary to other existing law.

The folkeskole

For a public school, a ministerial order defines 'central knowledge and proficiency areas' (CKP) for each individual topic. At present these can best be described as frameworks. They do not specify at what grade level a student must possess certain abilities, rather they formulate sub-topics and overall methods of teaching that must be included in the instruction of the given subject. To provide some illustration, the CKP for English as a foreign language states under the heading of 'Language learning' that

They (the pupils) shall therefore work with:

- varied working and cooperation methods;
- different media, including electronic media, among other things for word processing, information retrieval and communication.

There is, however, ample space for a teacher to choose how the actual instruction is to take place, which allows an almost free choice of method.

Similarly the Act on the folkeskole is a framework act, that does set some boundries, such as the minimum and maximum number of lessons and maximum number of pupils per class, but the municipalities and schools retain a large degree of autonomy.

2.4.2. *Youth education*

Youth education in general is also governed by framework regulations laid out by Parliament, which lay down the overall targets and framework for the various types of general upper secondary education, including aims, subjects and examination forms. The minister then specifies the aim of each subject, the contents and the number of lessons.

In everyday life, these regulations leave ample room for the pedagogical choices of the individual teacher.

The ministry holds responsibility for the control of the quality of the education. This is mainly done through various quality development projects and the drawing-up of examination questions at central level.

In effect, this leaves the management of each institution with a large degree of autonomy.

2.4.3. *Higher education*

Overall orders about the structure, general content, general admission requirements and examinations are laid down by the Ministry of Education for the higher education programmes.

Within the long-cycle programmes, the actual number of study places in the different programmes, the contents of the programmes, and the special admission criteria are made by the collegiate bodies of each institution.

Through the use of advisory boards, a certain measure of coherence is aimed at for the various types of higher education.

2.5. *Autonomy of resources: Are schools/universities free to determine the raising and expenditure of financial resources? Do they have facilities to raise money through sponsoring or through other means, etc. Are they able to charge tuition fees?*

Tuition fees

Almost all types of public education in Denmark are free, indicating that a tuition fee will very seldom be charged, in some cases, cannot be charged. This principle is stated in the constitution as regards the public school system, and also covers teaching materials.

Conversely at *gymnasium*, students may be asked to fund certain tools, e.g. a special calculator. At university, only instruction is free.

For institutions which offer alternatives to the public system, there will often be a user-charge to supplement the state subsidies.

Raising money

It is presupposed that in general an educational institution must operate within the boundaries which are created by their aim – to provide education. In other words, it is not their aim to accumulate profits by acting like other profit-seeking bodies in the economic market.

This general statement does not preclude universities acting somewhat like a profit-seeking body and using any profits that may come from their research, as this will be a result of their core task – education and research.

Similarly, other basic educational institutions are not excluded from performing income-generating activities, but these must have a close link with the normal activities of the institution, which must be very careful that the activities do not lead to unfair competition.

Ordinary financial framework

2.5.1. *Primary and lower secondary education*

A public school is granted money by the municipality, and this power cannot be delegated to the school, as referred to above.

The municipality is given a total grant which it may use as it sees fit. Thus, a municipality may give an individual school a lump sum of money to be used according to principles set out by the school board and headteacher in close cooperation, but the municipality can also provide a detailed specification, indicating how much money must be spent on, for example structures, instruction, etc.

Public schools may receive private sponsoring, but parents are not allowed to provide extra funds for teachers' pay, in order to increase the number of lessons offered to the children.

Any sponsoring does not relieve the municipality of its obligation to provide sufficient funds for the schools within the municipality.

2.5.2. *Youth education*

A somewhat similar structure is characteristic for the youth education system, one primary difference being that it is often the counties which hold overall responsibility, and not the municipalities, as for the public primary and lower secondary school.

Where applicable, the county council sets out a financial framework within which the individual institution can act. It is then left to the school board to decide on the distribution of the framework budget adopted by the county council on the recommendation of the headteacher.

2.5.3. *Higher education*

All institutions, whether, state or private self-governing institutions, are financed by the State, and no tuition fees can be charged.

Some institutions are awarded finances on the basis of a cash-per-student grant, and will accordingly enjoy elaborate freedom when spending the money – provided that it is spent on the educational activities concerned.

By offering for example special courses selling know-how, or by concluding research contracts with external partners, the institutions will be able to raise extra funds.

2.6. *Autonomy of organisation for schools?*

2.6.1. *Primary and lower secondary education*

There is a framework governing management whilst ensuring parent participation through school boards, with very detailed compositions. These boards must not be thought of in the sense of a normal business board; rather their function is to set principles for the school's work.

2.6.2. *Youth education*

With reference to the sections above, schools are able to organize themselves within a framework laid down by the minister.

2.6.3. *Higher education*

Like the system described for the previous educational institutions, the higher educational institutions can organize themselves quite freely, excluding the obligation to establish various types of boards, with a broad representation of interest groups.

2.7. *Are schools or universities entitled to defend their autonomous sphere by legal means against the state or government? Do schools have the legal capacity to appeal against acts of supervisory authority?*

Any educational institution which can be defined as a self-governing private institution, will be regarded as being a separate legal person from the State, and will consequently be able to defend its legal sphere against the State.

As mentioned earlier however, the educational system does not contain a clear-cut easily expressed rule. A private school being deprived of its state funds could be an example of an educational institution which can appeal acts of a supervisory body, in this case the Ministry of Education.

Educational institutions which are not defined as self-governing, form part of the hierarchical structure of the State, and thus have to abide by the decisions made by a superior body. (See the answers given for question 2.1 and the distinction between public and private institutions.)

The general idea of framework regulation does not promote an ongoing process of real acts of supervisory authority.

3. *Individual autonomy*

3.1. *How much latitude of discretion is granted to teachers/professors in educational matters (content of education and methodological decisions)?*

Please refer to the answers given for question 2.3, which also covers the academic freedom of each teacher.

3.2. *Is the head of a school (university) or any of its bodies entitled to issue instructions in professional matters to teaching staff?*

3.2.1. *Primary and lower secondary education*

The school board has the right – in co-operation with the headteacher – to lay down principles, but the Act on the *folkeskole* confers a number of obligations on the headteacher.

> Art. 45. (1) A head teacher shall be appointed at each independent school. The head teacher of a school shall be responsible for the administrative and educational management of the school and for the activities of the school *vis-à-vis* the school board and the municipal council.
> (2) The head teacher shall be responsible for the supervision of and distribution of work tasks between the staff of the school, and he shall take all concrete decisions regarding the pupils of the school.
> (3) The head teacher shall draw up proposals for the school board regarding the principles for the activities etc. of the school, cf. section 44 (2), and proposals for the budget of the school, cf. section 44 (3)

within the financial framework laid down by the municipal council, cf. section 40 (2), item 1.
(4) The head teacher shall carry on his activities in co-operation with the staff.

3.2.2. *Youth education*

A very similar system applies for the youth education system where the head-teacher is in charge of everyday management in questions related to instruction. There is, however, no specified right to intervene in the methodological choice of the individual teacher.

3.2.3. *Higher education*

While the head of an 'institution', in this context the smallest subject-oriented formation of persons, has the power to instruct an academic employee to perform a specific task, he or she must do so having regard to the employee's free choice of scientific and/or pedagogical methods.

3.3. *Do the teachers/professors participate in the universities or schools self governing bodies?*

3.3.1. *Primary and lower secondary education*

Yes. two representatives of the teachers and other staff elected by and from among the staff of the school must participate. If they are given voting power, the number of parent representatives is increased from 5 to 7. When speaking of a 'self-governing body' it must be remembered that the school board must act within the framework set by the municipality, which has to respect the framework set up by the law.

3.3.2. *Youth education*

A general idea of representation of academic staff is often expressed in the Danish education system's governance structures and thus, academic staff also participate in the various types of boards that have been set up for youth education. However, the staff do not always hold voting power, but are observers.

3.3.3. *Higher education*

Yes. In line with the earlier remarks, academic personnel are also a part of the 'governing' bodies.

As a general rule of thumb one can say that academic staff never represent the majority of a board, and will usually amount to around 20% of a given board.

4. *Consequences of autonomy*

4.1. *If educational institutions can act autonomously, how are general aims or values like quality and unity of the education guaranteed?*

4.1.1. *Primary and lower secondary education*

Various types of evaluation, such as participation in international tests from OECD and other international organizations, will produce real effects in society. In this, the press plays a major role, focusing heavily on international tests if Danish students perform poorly, compared to other relevant countries. Furthermore, local democracy plays a key role as guarantor for a keen interest in quality development, for example the participation of parents.

A tool such as the specification of the obligatory contents of subjects in the *folkeskole* (the previously mentioned *central knowledge and proficiency areas*), is a potentially powerful tool to – theoretically – ensure unity.

Furthermore, a *Centre for Quality Assurance and Evaluation of Higher Education* was established in 1992 as an independent institution under the auspices of the Ministry of Education, with the task of contributing to quality assurance of higher education programmes in Denmark by:

- effecting systematic evaluation of higher education programmes
- developing methods for programme evaluation and quality assurance; and
- inspiring and counselling institutions of higher education in questions regarding evaluation and quality, accumulating national and international know-how in programme evaluation and quality assurance.

4.2. *Is autonomy necessarily linked with a supervisory power?*

This answer is best read in conjunction with the answer for question 4.3.

This is a political question since the answer can be both yes and no. One could argue that if the input into a given educational activity is allowed to be free, one would have to look at the output instead. If, on the other hand, the input is very specified, one could argue that the requirements for output control could be relaxed somewhat proportionally. It is the classical question of how much quality you want at what cost.

Incidentally, one could add that the word 'quality' in itself contains no value-judgement, i.e. one would have to speak of good, bad, or medium quality to provide actual guidance as to the understanding of a given quality. To argue that of course we all want 'the best quality' is to ignore the subjectivity of the cost/benefit approaches that – hopefully – encompass all human activity.

4.3. *What are the relations between autonomy, responsibility and accountability? Is autonomy necessarily connected with quality control within autonomous educational institutions?*

This question is of a more philosophical nature, and I will thus answer it accordingly. Any responsible leader of an educational institution should be able – within a reasonable time – to provide evidence that the basic educational targets of the given subject are met for a large majority of the students.

There would seem to be an inverse relationship between the two factors, quality control and autonomy. It seems harder to establish whether or not the relationship is directly inverse, as this is will be a cost/benefit-based answer.

4.4. *Is there a tendency towards enlargement of autonomy or towards more government control? Why is it so?*

There is a very clear tendency in Denmark aimed at quality measures which have a clear potential for *reducing autonomy*, encompassing all levels of education.

Looking back, one could say that the establishment of an evaluation centre for higher education as mentioned above, was a first indication of this.

Evaluation, the launching of various – voluntary – quality-improvement projects and tightening of central knowledge and proficiency areas for public schools, are all indicators of a potiential reduction of autonomy.

Recent initiatives for quality development

At the time of writing, a bill on a National Centre of Evaluation for all areas of the education system is being prepared.

Self-evaluation through development and availability of quality measurement tools, including both tools for the process itself and the actual measurement, have been, and still are, very much used, but the new bill goes further than this, proposing – with some variation – a right for the minister to order an institution to act according to the results of an evaluation.

However, a large degree of autonomy continues to exist in the education system. A newly launched quality project for municipal schools provides a total system, containing methods and tools for overall quality development. Use of the system is not obligatory. The system is available on demand through the Internet, and the general tools and questionnaires can be customized to fit the specific needs of each individual school. As work proceeds, the individual school can log on through the use of a password, to access and continue with earlier work.

Reasons

The government's overall ambition to present Denmark as a frontrunner country has a large say, as the aim is to make the Danish education system one of the best in the world.

Furthermore the coming years are expected to bring a shortage of labour. According to many this has brought forward labour market policy-guided proposals, which have an overall goal of reducing total study time, by getting students through the education system faster, reducing their 'waste-time' in education, and improving the possibilities of transfer of credits.

Sources

Notwithstanding individual footnotes, the following sources have been used for the writing of this report:

Administration of the folkeskole, Ministry of Education, 1997
Education in Denmark, The Education System, Ministry of Education 1998
Skolebestyrelsen, hæfte 1–8, Minstry of Education, 1998
Selvejende undervisingsinstitutioner, Ministry of Education 1995

PAUL MEREDITH

Autonomy in Education in England and Wales

ENGLISH AND WELSH REPORTS

1. Constitutional legal basis

1.1–1.3. As is well known, there is an absence of any entrenched constitutional guarantees of rights within the UK constitution or legal system. The UK constitution is an unwritten one with no hierarchically superior norms with which ordinary Acts of the UK Parliament must conform. The ground rule of the UK constitution is that the Westminster Parliament is supreme in the sense (a) that it is free to enact legislation on any subject matter it sees fit; (b) as a logical consequence of (a), it has no capacity to bind itself or its successors by enacting any entrenched provisions; and (c) no court of law can challenge the constitutional legitimacy or legal validity of a duly enacted statute – one which has gone through all the required Parliamentary stages, which has received the Royal Assent, and which is valid on its face. Although these fundamental principles must be qualified by many practical political constraints upon the freedom of the UK Parliament to legislate as it pleases, and by the very important qualification of the supremacy accorded to EC law over the domestic law of Member States, it remains none the less true that there is an absence of entrenched guarantees of rights within the UK constitution and legal system, and such 'rights' as are protected by the ordinary law promulgated by statutes are vulnerable to repeal by the normal legislative process.

It should be emphasized that the incorporation of the European Convention on Human Rights into domestic law, effected by the Human Rights Act 1998 (which is not due to come into force late 2000) will *not* be entrenched as hierarchically superior law within the UK and will *not* confer upon the UK courts any capacity to strike down legislation on the basis of incompatibility with Convention rights. The fundamental principle of the Sovereignty of the UK Parliament will therefore be preserved.

Walter Berka, Jan de Groof and Hilde Penneman (eds.), Autonomy in Education, 341–347.

The consequence of adherence to the basic principle of Parliamentary omnicompetence as the ground rule of the UK constitution for education law is that there are in UK law NO constitutional guarantees of rights in the sphere of education, either for the individual child, parent, teacher or researcher, or for the governing bodies of schools, colleges or Universities. Such rights as are enjoyed by individuals or by institutions in the UK in the context of education are created by ordinary statutes or subordinate legislation, vulnerable to amendment or repeal by the ordinary legislative process; or by the common law by virtue of the judicial decision-making process.

1.4. The principal statutory source for the law governing the provision of school education in England and Wales is now the Education Act 1996, a consolidation Act re-enacting in a single statute most of the extant statutory provisions relating to school education previously to be found in a wide range of earlier statutes starting with the Education Act 1944, which may be regarded as the foundation statute of the present school system in England and Wales. The Education Act 1996 repealed the last remaining extant provisions of the 1944 Act.

The statutory regime for school inspections and quality control in schools – of central importance in the context of school autonomy – is, however, to be found in the School Inspections Act 1996, another consolidating measure reenacting in one statute a range of measures previously contained in earlier statutes.

Since these two important consolidating measures in 1996, Parliament has enacted a range of education statutes, including the Education Act 1997, the Education (Schools) Act 1997, the School Standards and Framework Act 1998, and the Teaching and Higher Education Act 1998.

The Education Act 1997 was the last education statute to be passed by the Conservative government, and was enacted in diluted form just before the dissolution of Parliament. It deals with a miscellaneous range of matters, including school discipline, baseline assessment of primary school pupils, the Qualifications and Curriculum Authority and the Qualifications, Curriculum and Assessment Authority for Wales, and the inspection of local education authorities.

The Education (Schools) Act 1997 – the first education statute of the new Labour government – was a single-purpose measure meeting a politically significant electoral commitment to abolish the assisted places scheme – a scheme under which the State contributed towards the fees payable by selected pupils at independent schools. The School Standards and Framework Act 1998 is a very substantial Act embodying the government's wide-ranging proposals for raising standards in schools and amending the framework of maintained schools. It includes provisions relating to LEA Education Development Plans, Education Action Zones, intervention in schools giving cause for concern, school admissions, the selection of pupils, the relationship between schools and LEAs, the abolition of grant-maintained school status, and much else. The Teaching and Higher Education Act 1998 makes provision for the establishment of General Teaching Councils for England and for Wales with wide-ranging functions relating to the school teaching profession, for professional qualifications specifically for the headteachers of schools, and new arrangements for financial support for students and for the payment of fees at institutions of further and higher education.

For further and higher education, reference should be made principally to the Further and Higher Education Act 1992.

2. Autonomy of educational institutions

2.1. The governance of schools in the maintained sector is now provided for in the School Standards and Framework Act 1998, Part II, Chapter III. Every maintained school is required by virtue of section 36 to have a governing body, which is *body corporate* in English law, constituted in accordance with Schedule 9 of the Act. Schedule 10 provides for the general powers of the governing body, and Schedule 11 provides for its composition and proceedings. The formal constitution of the governing body is laid down in its Instrument of Government, promulgated in accordance with Schedule 12.

Universities fall into two main categories: (a) those founded *before* the Further and Higher Education Act 1992, which are generally governed in accordance with a Royal Charter; and (b) those founded *since* the enactment of the 1992 Act, whose governance is provided for in that Act. The majority of those in category (b) are former 'Polytechnics'.

2.2. The staffing of schools in the maintained sector is now provided for in Part II Chapter V of the School Standards and Framework Act 1998. The staffing of community, voluntary controlled and community special schools is provided for in Schedule 16; and the staffing of foundation, voluntary aided and foundation special schools is provided for in Schedule 17. These two Schedules make detailed provision for the appointment, discipline, suspension and dismissal of teachers (including headteachers). Within this highly prescriptive framework, however, school governing bodies do enjoy a significant element of autonomy and discretion in the process of appointing teaching and other staff.

2.3(a). In the maintained schools sector, teachers are required to hold qualified teacher status (see s. 218(2), Education Reform Act 1988), and must not be prohibited (by virtue, for example, of certain types of misconduct) from employment as a teacher as a result of a direction under section 218(6) of the 1988 Act. The new General Teaching Councils for England and for Wales will be charged with the maintenance of a Register of teachers (see Teaching and Higher Education Act 1998, ss 3 and 9).

An important innovation introduced under section 18 of the Teaching and Higher Education Act 1998 will be a requirement that headteachers hold a specific 'professional headship qualification'.

In addition to these requirements relating specifically to the employment of teachers, there is a mass of employment protection and anti-discrimination legislation, including the Sex Discrimination Act 1975 and the Race Relations Act 1976 which limits the discretion of appointing authorities. Additionally, many authorities have adopted equal opportunities policies which go beyond the strict limits of anti-discrimination legislation and prohibit discrimination on grounds such as marital status and sexual orientation.

In the University sector, there is generally no legal regulation of qualifications, although in certain subject areas – notably medicine, dentistry, veterinary surgery – the relevant professional bodies lay down requirements as to the qualifications of those employed in the clinical sector. Anti-discrimination legislation will apply to the University sector as it does in the schools sector. Virtually all Universities have also adopted anti-discrimination policies going beyond the strict requirements of the legislation.

2.3(b). In schools within the maintained sector, curricular autonomy has been relatively limited since the introduction of the national curriculum, initially under the Education Reform Act 1988. The national curriculum has been introduced in stages, and subsequently refined and developed, since 1988 by Order of the Secretary of State, the contents of programmes of study and assessment arrangements being spelled out in considerable detail in substantial documents for each subject within the national curriculum accompanying the relevant Orders.

The primary statutory provisions relating to the National Curriculum are now to be found in the Education Act 1996, Part V. This provides in section 351 that the school curriculum shall be 'balanced and broadly based'; that it should promote 'the spiritual, moral, cultural, mental and physical development of pupils at the school and of society'; and that it should prepare pupils for 'the opportunities, responsibilities and experiences of adult life'. It is provided, further, that the basic curriculum for every maintained school shall include religious education for all registered pupils (s. 352(1)(a)), subject to parental right of withdrawal; and, in the case of secondary schools, sex education (s. 352(1)(c)), again subject to a parental right of withdrawal. In primary schools, the governing body has a discretion as to whether sex education should be provided: if it does so decide, the parental power right of withdrawal again arises.

In Universities, there is no legal regulation of curricular content or aims. However, in certain subject areas – for instance, law, medicine, dentistry, veterinary surgery, engineering – the relevant professional bodies lay down certain requirements regarding curricular content and subject area coverage. In all areas of University teaching there is, however, increasingly detailed audit and inspection of the entire teaching and examination process by way of periodic 'teaching quality assessment' under the auspices of the Higher Education Funding Councils.

In the context of research conducted at Universities, many consider that the traditional concept of academic freedom has been significantly eroded in the past decade by virtue of a range of developments, including the abolition of the 'tenure' of established academic staff (see Education Reform Act 1988, sections 202–205); and selective funding based upon (arguably questionable) periodic assessments by the Higher Education Funding Councils of research quality in Universities. The abolition of tenure in the 1988 Act created a considerable furore at the time and prompted an important amendment to the Education Reform Bill during its passage through the House of Lords, tabled by Lord Jenkins of Hillhead (Chancellor of the University of Oxford and formerly, as Mr Roy Jenkins, President of the European Commission) to the effect that

> ... academic staff [shall] have freedom within the law to question and test received wisdom, and to put forward new ideas and controversial or unpopular opinions, without placing themselves in jeopardy of losing their jobs or privileges they may have at their institutions. (Education Reform Act 1988, s. 202(2)(a)).

2.4. Schools in the maintained sector are financed through their local education authority on the basis of a 'budget share' allocated to each school by the maintaining authority. The determination of each school's budget share is provided for in the School Standards and Framework Act 1998, Part II, Chapter IV, and Regulations issued by the Secretary of State.

Maintained schools are prohibited from charging fees, with limited exceptions provided for under sections 455–458, Education Act 1996. In practice, however, many schools do seek and obtain donations from parents and engage in a range of fund-raising activities.

Universities are funded through Higher Education Funding Council grants; tuition fees paid by students (see Teaching and Higher Education Act 1998, Part II Chapter I); through the Research Councils; through contracts with the private sector; and through the fruits of extensive fund-raising activities.

2.5. Generally the conduct, internal organization and running of a school are under the direction of the school's governing body (School Standards and Framework Act 1998, s. 38).

2.6. In principle it would be possible to defend any unlawful interference in the governance or conduct of a school by a local education authority or the

Secretary of State by way of an Application for Judicial Review in the High Court. In recent months, the conduct by the Office of Standards in Education (OFSTED) of school inspections has given rise to considerable dissatisfaction on the part of individual school governing bodies, and it may be possible to envisage legal challenge by way of judicial review in this context, although this is probably unlikely. A significant recent development in this context has been the appointment of an Adjudicator to adjudicate over such disputes between school governing bodies and OFSTED.

3. Individual autonomy

3.1. In maintained schools, the discretion enjoyed by teachers is limited by the constraints of the National Curriculum (see answer to 2.3(b), above). As initially promulgated following the Education Reform Act 1988, the national curriculum programmes of study were widely criticized for their excessive detail and high level of prescription. Following the recommendations of an important committee chaired by Sir Ron Dearing (now Lord Dearing) (see *The National Curriculum and its Assessment: Final Report*, School Curriculum and Assessment Authority, 1994), however, the National Curriculum has now been significantly modified and made considerably less prescriptive in content, thereby giving teachers rather more (though still limited) professional discretion.

In the University sector, teachers enjoy very substantial discretion in respect of course content, though every Department, Faculty and University will adopt rigorous mechanisms for the scrutiny of course content; and course delivery and the examination process are subject to detailed scrutiny through periodic teaching quality assessment exercises under the auspices of the Higher Education Funding Councils.

The issue of academic freedom in the context of research has already been addressed in paragraph 2.3(b), above.

3.2. At school level, the headteacher does have overall responsibility, subject to the governing body, for academic matters, and would have power to issue instructions to teaching staff. This would not apply in the case of the head of a University where academic control would normally be devolved to Faculty or Departmental level, subject to more general oversight by the University Senate (or equivalent body).

3.3. The composition of maintained school governing bodies is provided for in section 36 and Schedule 9 of the School Standards and Framework Act 1998. Normally there are either one or two teacher governors in addition to the headteacher and a representative of support staff. In Universities, members of academic staff actively participate in virtually all the University's committees, including the Senate, the Council and the Court (terminology varies from one university to another).

4. Consequences of autonomy

4.1. As already explained, the scope for autonomy at school level is limited by the (arguably too) prescriptive nature of the contents of the national curriculum programmes of study. None the less there is still scope for autonomy and professional expertise in many aspects of the delivery of the curriculum, and accountability and quality assurance are regarded as of the utmost importance. The key mechanism for quality assurance in schools is the periodic (approximately every 4–5 years) inspection of the school by OFSTED, carried out under the School Inspections Act 1996 and a detailed Code of Practice.

4.2–4.4. School autonomy in England and Wales may be traced to many possible origins, but delegated management and delegated budgetary responsibility initiated under the Education Reform Act 1988 is perhaps the most obvious starting point. School autonomy has since been developed and refined in many respects, but has been paralleled by significant supervisory and controlling trends on the part of LEAs and the central department. LEAs have powers under the School Standards and Framework Act 1998 to issue 'warning notices' to schools where they are concerned over the quality of educational provision; they may appoint further governors or may withdraw budgetary devolution; and the LEA is directly involved in the process of target-setting for each school under the School Standards and Framework Act. Similarly, the Secretary of State has important powers of intervention at individual school level under the same Act, and may ultimately direct the closure of a school which is severely failing. The Secretary of State also has a significant role to play in approving, modifying or rejecting LEA education development plans – a process which directly links the central department to the 'front line' at the level of the LEA and the individual school. All of this involves a significant element of monitoring and control from above: a central feature of this process of monitoring and control is OFSTED, through the conduct of the school inspection process – and, more recently, through the inspection of LEAs. OFSTED may, indeed, be viewed as the 'eyes and ears' of the Secretary of State at ground level. Under the School Standards and Framework Act 1998 in particular, there is a significant expansion of external and centralized control from the level of the central department down through the LEA to the level of each individual school. This Act may, indeed, be viewed as a major centralizing measure, which is arguably a most significant current trend in the governance and the delivery of education in England and Wales.

ANDRÉ LEGRAND

Réponse française au questionnaire sur l'autonomie dans l'éducation

FRENCH REPORT

1. Base constitutionnelle

1.1. L'autonomie du système éducatif n'est pas garantie constitutionnellement. Au contraire, le Préambule de la Constitution de 1946, repris par celui de la Constitution de 1958, fait de l'Etat le responsable du système éducatif et lui confère l'obligation d'organiser un enseignement public, laïque et gratuit.

1.2. Dans une décision du 20 janv. 1984[1], confirmée par la suite dans une autre décision du 29 mai 1992[2], le Conseil Constitutionnel fait de l'indépendance des professeurs de l'enseignement supérieur un principe fondamental reconnu par les lois de la République, qui a donc valeur constitutionnelle. Dans ses fonctions tant consultatives que contentieuses, le Conseil d'Etat a, par la suite, été amené à préciser les contours du principe, pour dire d'abord que celui-ci ne faisait pas obstacle à ce que les corps d'enseignants-chercheurs accueillent, par la voie d'un détachement organisé par des dispositions règlementaires, d'autres agents publics (avis n° 347–490 du 6 mars 1990), d'autre part qu'il ne bénéficie qu'aux professeurs au sens strict (les anciens titulaires de chaires), donc pas aux enseignants de rang inférieur, même s'ils enseignent dans une université (Cons. d'Et., 29 juil. 1994, Le Calvez, Rec. p. 977). En revanche, le fait d'inclure, pour l'élection à divers conseils universitaires, certains personnels de laboratoire ou

[1] A.J.D.A. 1984.163, note Boulouis; D. 1984.593, note F. Luchaire; G.P. 1984. 19.20 déc.1984, note Léo Hamon; Rev. Adm. 1984.261, note De Villiers; Rev. dr. pub. 1984.702, note Favoreu.

[2] Pet. Aff. 4 mars 1994, p. 4, note Mathieu et Verpeaux; Rev. Adm., 1993.443, note Etien; Rev. Fr. de Dt Const. 1993.381, note Philippe.

Walter Berka, Jan de Groof and Hilde Penneman (eds.), Autonomy in Education, 349–356.

des personnels scientifiques de bibliothèque dans le collège électoral des professeurs d'université porte atteinte au principe d'indépendance, «en privant ces derniers de la représentation propre et authentique nécessaire à l'exercice de leurs responsabilités particulières» (29 mai 1992, Association des professeurs du muséum d'histoire naturelle, Rec. p. 217; 9 juil. 1997, Picard, A.J.D.A., 1997.718). Par contre, le fait de prévoir par voie règlementaire l'organisation de procédures d'évaluation des enseignements supérieurs «faisant notamment appel à l'appréciation des étudiants» ne porte pas atteinte au principe, dans la meseure où cela ne comporte aucune incidence sur les prérogatives ou la carrière des enseignants (Cons. d'Et., 13 mars 1996, Gohin, A.J.D.A. 1996.659, note MEKHANTAR).

1.3. sans objet.

1.4. L'autonomie éventuelle des établissements est donc exclusivement consacrée par des textes législatifs. Son contenu et son étendue dépendent cependant de l'ordre d'enseignement concerné:

1.4.1. *Dans l'enseignement primaire public*, il n'y a pas d'établissement au sens strict du terme. Les écoles ne disposent donc ni de la personnalité juridique, ni de l'autonomie financière; elles ne constituent que de services non personnalisés assurant un service public d'Etat et fonctionnant dans des locaux propriétés communales. Elles n'ont pas de budget propre et leur administration matérielle incombe à la commune.

Malgré une tentative de réforme en 1987, qui visait à en faire un véritable chef d'établissement, mais qui fut vite abrogée suite au changement de majorité parlementaire, le directeur d'école appartient au même corps que les autres enseignants et il a surtout des compétences de coordination et d'animation. L'école est cependant dotée de deux conseils collégiaux, dont les attributions sont fixées par le décret n° 90–788, le conseil d'école qui dispose de véritables pouvoirs de décision, notamment sur le réglement intérieur de l'école, et le conseil des maîtres, qui a surtout des pouvoirs d'animation pédagogique.

1.4.2. *L'enseignement secondaire public* est au contraire traditionnellement assuré par des établissements publics. Les collèges et les lycées publics ont longtemps été des établissements publics nationaux, rattachés à l'Etat. Depuis la loi de décentralisation n° 83–663 du 29 juil. 1983, ils constituent des établissements publics locaux d'enseignement (E.P.L.E.), rattachés aux départements (collèges) ou aux régions (lycées). C'est donc de la loi qu les collèges et les lycées tirent leur caractère d'établissements publics, et donc l'existence de leur personnalité juridique et de leur autonomie financière; à ce titre, ils ont en particulier un conseil d'administration élu et un budget propre voté par ce conseil.

En revanche, le chef d'établissement, nommé par le ministère central, est à la fois le président du C.A. et le directeur de l'établissement. C'est le décret n° 85–924 du 30 août 1985, modifié à deux reprises[3], qui règle l'organisation des E.P.L.E. C'est en particulier dans l'article 2 de ce texte qu'est définie l'autonomie dont «dispose, en matière pédagogique et éducative,» l'établissement scolaire. Le contenu et l'étendue de son autonomie, qui s'exerce dans le respect des dispositions en vigueur, ainsi quedes objectifs pédagogiques et éducatifs fixés par le ministre et les autorités académiques, résultent donc largement de la compétence réglementaire (voir aussi 2.3 bis).

1.4.3. *Dans l'enseignement supérieur*, le changement essentiel a été apporté par la loi 68-978 du 12 nov. 1968, aujourd'hui remplacée par celle du 26 janv. 1984[4]. L'apport essentiel de cette loi a été de créer une nouvelle catégorie d'établissement public, l'établissement public à caractère scientifique, culturel et professionnel (E.P.S.C.P.). Toutes les universités sont des E.P.S.C.P.; en revanche, tous les E.P.S.C.P. ne sont pas des universités. Et par ailleurs, il existe des établissement d'enseignement supérieur qui ne sont pas des E.P.S.C.P.

La caractéristique essentielle de cette nouvelle catégorie est double: d'une part, les E.P.S.C.P. bénéficient de l'autonomie statutaire; ils ont donc (art. 22 de la loi de 1984) le pouvoir de déterminer «leurs statuts et leurs structures internes conformément aux dispositions de la ... loi». D'autre part, la désignation de leurs organes résulte exclusivement du principe de l'élection; en particulier, le président de l'E.P.S.C.P. est élu librement par les conseils qui existent au sein de l'établissement. Pour le reste, les E.P.S.C.P. répondent au régime juridique général des établissements publics (personnalité juridique et autonomie financière).

2. *Autonomie des institutions d'éducation*

2.1. Comme cela vient d'être indiqué, seules les universités ont l'autonomie statutaire qui leur permet de s'organiser librement et de voter leurs propres statuts. Encore faut-il rappeler que cette autonomie ne peut s'exercer que dans le cadre de la loi votée par le Parlement. Même s'ils disposent aussi de la personnalité juridique, les établissements secondaires n'ont pas cette autonomie statutaire et leur organisation est déterminée par décret, donc par décision du gouvernement, générale, commune à tous les établissements.

2.2. Aucune institution d'enseignement, à quelque niveau que ce soit, n'a le pouvoir de déterminer le nombre des emplois de personnels *titulaires* (enseignants ou non enseignants) dont elle peut disposer. Ses dotations en la matière (qui constituent la très grande majorité de leurs ressources en personnels) sont déterminées par le ministère central à partir du budget voté par le Parlement. En revanche, les Universités peuvent engager sur leurs budgets propres des

[3] par les décrets n° 90–978 du 31 oct. 1990 et 93–530 du 26 mars 1993.

[4] loi n° 84–52.

personnels vacataires ou contractuels dont elles ont la maîtrise du recrutement. Les textes leur fixent cependant certaines limites en matière de recrutement d'enseignants. (Ex: n'engager que des personnes ayant déjà une activité professionnelle principale). Cette possibilité n'est pas ouverte aux établissements secondaires publics.

Quant au choix des personnes, il y a des distinctions à opérer. Le principe général, dans l'enseignement supérieur, est le principe du choix du personnel enseignant par des conseils internes regroupant des représentants du grade au moins égal au personnel recruté. Absolu en matière de mutation, ce principe peut connaitre des atténuations en matière de première nomination, des personnels reçus à un concours de recrutement pouvant être affectés à un établissement universitaire par décision du ministère central.

En revanche, pour les autres ordres d'enseignement (primaire et secondaire), toutes les nominations de personnels résultent d'une décision individuelle des autorités de l'Etat.

2.3. L'affectation des élèves dans *les écoles* est en principe de la compétence du maire de la commune. Il agit en pareil cas en qualité d'agent de l'Etat et il délègue souvent l'exercice de cette compétence au directeur de l'école concernée. Dans *les établissements secondaires*, elle relève de la compétence des autorités déconcentrées de l'Etat, très généralement l'inspecteur d'académie au niveau du département. Cette affectation obéit à un principe de carte scolaire largement définie à partir du domicile des candidats. Le ministère a cependant atténué la rigueur du principe en instaurant, depuis une quinzaine d'années, des procédures de «sectorisation souple», qui permettent, sous la responsabilité de l'inspecteur d'académie, des dérogations au secteur.

Dans *les universités*, les principes sont posés par l'art. 14 de la loi de 1984. Il interdit toute sélection à l'entrée *en premier cycle*, sauf dans quelques disciplines (essentiellement celles du secteur santé et certaines formations technologiques. Plusieurs décisions jurisprudentielles ont rappelé ce principe (Cons. d'Et. 27 juil. 1990 Ardant et Langlois-Meurinne, A.J.D.A. 1990.). Les universités fixent une capacité d'accueil dans chacune de leurs formations et elles sont obligées d'inscrire tous les candidats qui se présentent, tant que cette capacitré n'est pas atteinte. Lorsqu'elle l'est, il appartient au recteur d'académie, autorité déconcentrée de l'Etat, de répartir les candidats en surnombre, en particulier en fonction de leur domicile, de leur situation de famille et des préférences qu'ils ont exprimé. *En troisième cycle*, la sélection est en revanche admise.

2.3 bis. Il faut distinguer la décision sur les curricula et les questions d'organisation interne. L'Etat dispose en France du monopole de collation des grades. En revanche, les établissements scolaires et universitaires disposent d'une autonomie qui s'est élargie en matière éducative et pédagogique.

Les Universités peuvent délivrer deux types de diplômes: des diplômes nationaux, (en particulier ceux qui correspondent aux «grades» dont l'Etat a le monopole de la collation, licence, maîtrise, doctorat) dont le cadre est largement réglementé par l'Etat[5]; c'est au nom de celui-ci qu'elles les délivrent et il leur accorde pour ce faire une habilitation pluriannuelle renouvelée périodiquement après examen d'un dossier destiné à vérifier le respect des exigences posées par les textes. Cela n'interdit cependant pas une certaine souplesse dans l'interprétation des contenus des enseignements dispensés, où la latitude laissée aux enseignants est coutumièrement très grande. Les Universités peuvent par ailleurs délivrer des diplômes d'université, dont elles déterminent alors librement le contenu et les conditions de validation. Mais les diplômes de cette seconde catégorie ne peuvent pas porter des noms qui permettraient une confusion avec les grades «protégés».

Les contenus des programmes de *l'enseignement secondaire* sont largement déterminés par des textes réglementaires et ils s'imposent non seulement aux établissements publics, mais aussi aux établissements privés qui, placés «sous contrat d'association», reçoivent des subventions de l'Etat.

En revanche, en matière d'organisation interne, les textes récents ont fortement élargi les possibilités ouvertes aux établissements. Ceci est évident pour les universités; mais ce l'est aussi pour les établissements secondaires. Le décret du 30 août 1985 modifié énumère, dans son art. 2, la liste des sujets sur lesquels porte leur autonomie en matière pédagogique et éducative: l'organisation de l'établissement en classes et les modalités de répartition des élèves; l'emploi des dotations en heures d'enseignement, (mais dans le respect des obligations résultant des horaires réglementaires); l'organisation du temps et de la vie scolaires; la préparation de l'orientation et de l'insertion; la définition des actions de formation complémentaire et continue; l'ouverture de l'établissement sur son environnement social, culturel, économique; la définition des compléments possibles aux programmes nationaux; les activités facultatives d'action éducative à destination des élèves.

2.4. A côté des dotations de fonctionnement attribuées par les collectivités publiques, les établissements scolaires et universitaires peuvent bénéficier d'autres types de ressources.

En raison du principe constitutionnel de gratuité de l'enseignement, ils ne peuvent décider librement de «taxer» les étudiants ou les élèves par des droits financiers. Le montant des droits d'inscription à percevoir par les universités est fixé par arrêté du ministre et la jurisprudence administrative a rappelé à plusieurs reprises que tout droit supplémentaire ne pouvait être que facultatif et devait en outre nécessairement correspondre à une prestation particulière sortant du cadre ordinaire de l'établissement. A plusieurs reprises aussi, des circulaires ministérielles ont rappelé aux établissements scolaires l'interdiction

5 Voir, comme dernier exemple, ce qu'on a appelé la réforme Bayrou, décidée par plusieurs arrêtés du 14 avril 1997.

de tout droit général ou spécifique (ex: droit de photocopie ou de constitution de documents polycopiés).

Cependant, *les établissements scolaires* peuvent bénéficier de ressources propres: taxe d'apprentissage versées par les entreprises, à un taux fixé par la loi, pour le financement des activités de formation technique ou professionnelle; ressources provenant des activités de formation continue des adultes ou de la vente d'objets confectionnés ... Par leur nature, nombre de ces ressources sont loin de concerner à un degré important tous les établissements.

Les universités peuvent disposer de ressources provenant de legs, dons, fondations, rémunérations de services rendus, fonds de concours, participation des employeurs par le biais de la taxe d'apprentissage (formations technologiques et professionnelles) et subventions diverses, en particulier des collectivités territoriales.

2.5. Voir réponse aux rubriques 1 et 2.1.

2.6. Les principes applicables à cette question sont ceux qui régissent, de façon générale, le problème de la tutelle. L'autorité de tutelle, qui peut être soit une autorité de l'Etat central, soit celle de la collectivité de rattachement (voir ci-dessous n° 4.2), ne peut pas exercer un pouvoir de sanction qui ne lui serait pas reconnu par un texte. En cas d'abus de sa part, l'établissement public peut saisir le juge administratif d'un recours contre la décision abusive.

3. *Autonomie individuelle*

3.1. Compte tenu de ce qui a été dit précédemment, le pouvoir des enseignants sur le contenu de l'enseignement secondaire est très limité sur le plan juridique. Il porte pour l'essentiel sur les compléments éventuels aux programmes: comme la lourdeur de ceux-ci est souvent dénoncée, cela indique la difficulté qu'il peut y avoir à les augmenter.

En revanche, le fonctionnement de l'enseignement français est caractérisé par une large application d'un principe de liberté pédagogique des enseignants qui donne à ceux-ci de grandes possibilités de choix des méthodes pédagogiques qu'ils appliquent; ceci se manifeste par exemple dans le pouvoir laissé à chaque établissement dans le choix des manuels scolaires.

3.2. C'est un grand sujet de débat, dans les établissements primaires ou secondaires, à propos d'une institution apparue au début des années 80: le projet d'école ou d'établissement ; comme à propos du souhait qui s'est aussi souvent exprimé de voir se développer la notion d'équipe pédagogique. Jusqu'ici, l'idée que la liberté pédagogique est un apanage ou un droit individuel des enseignants garde, malgré des développements intéressants en sens inverse, une force importante dans le fonctionnement du système. Comme reste très prégnant le refus, tant par les enseignants individuels que par leurs organisations syndicales, du développement de tout pouvoir pédagogique au profit du chef d'établissement. Ce refus va de pair avec la reconnaissance exclusive des compétences pédagogiques au profit des corps d'inspection, considérés comme indépendants de toute hiérarchie administrative.

3.3. Dans les Universités, les enseignants sont représentés dans les trois conseils créés par la loi: leur proportion en leur sein est fixée par les dispositions de la loi de 1984 (environ 40% dans le Conseil d'administration, qui est l'organe essentiel en matière de détermination de la politique générale de l'université et en matière budgétaire; plus de la majorité au conseil scientifique, qui détermine la politique de recherche de l'université). Dans les E.P.L.E., les enseignants constituent environ le tiers du Conseil d'administration.

4. *Conséquences de l'autonomie*

4.1. L'unité et la qualité de l'éducation sont garanties, *dans les établissements scolaires*, par l'existence de corps d'inspection existant au niveau national, régional ou local. Au niveau national, coexistent deux inspections générales, l'Inspection Générale de l'Education Nationale, chargée de l'évaluation de l'activité pédagogique et l'Inspection Générale de l'Administration de l'Education Nationale, chargée du contrôle administratif et financier.

Dans les secteur universitaire, il existe un Comité National d'Evaluation, créé par la loi du 26 janvier 1984, organisé par deux décrets du 21 février 1985 et 7 décembre 1988. Composé de dix-sept membres indépendants, choisis par la communauté scientifique, le Conseil d'Etat, la Cour des Comptes et le Conseil Economique et Social, il est chargé d'examiner et d'évaluer l'ensemble des activités des E.P.S.C.P. Ses rapports sont publics.

Il a par ailleurs existé au ministère une Direction de l'Evaluation et de la Prospective, créée en 1987, dont une partie des tâches ont été reprises en 1996 par la Direction de la Programmation et du Développement. Dans cette dernière direction, les tâches d'évaluation du système éducatif ont été fortement réduites.

4.2. Il existe une tutelle qui s'exerce sur les établissements publics. *Dans le second degré*, les règles sont différentes pour ce qui concerne l'action éducatrice et le reste de l'activité des établissements.

Dans l'action éducatrice, les délibérations des conseils d'administration et les décisions du chef d'établissement en sa qualité d'organe de l'établissement, sont transmises aux autorités académiques et ne sont exécutoires que quinze jours après réception. Dans l'intervalle, ils sont annulables pour illégalité ou atteinte au fonctionnement du service public.

Dans les autres domaines, les actes sont adressés à trois autorités: le préfet qui peut déférer au tribunal administratif celles qu'il estime illégales; la collectivité locale de rattachement et l'autorité académique qui peuvent en demander la révision. Le budget est également soumis à obligation de transmission et il ne devient exécutoire que par l'accord de l'autorité académique et de la collectivité locale de rattachement. Faute de cet accord, il sera arrêté par délibération de la Chambre Régionale des Comptes.

Dans les universités, les statuts doivent être transmis au ministre après leur adoption. Les décisions et délibérations réglementaires ne peuvent entrer en vigueur qu'après leur transmission au recteur d'académie, dont les services assistent aux réunions ordinaires des Conseils d'administration. Aucune approbation préalable n'est donc nécessaire. La connaissance des décisions ainsi acquise permet au recteur d'intenter, le cas échéant, les actions juridictionnelles qu'exigerait une éventuelle illégalité. Au cas où l'exécution de la mesure attaquée peut compromettre gravement le fonctionnement de l'établissement, le recteur peut en suspendre l'application pour une durée de trois mois. Enfin, le recteur a le pouvoir d'arrêter le budget au cas où il n'est pas voté en équilibre par le conseil d'administration.

4.3. Il n'existe pas d'organes internes d'évaluation au sein des établissements. Cependant, comme on l'a vu au 1.1, la réforme Jospin-Lang de 1982 autorise les universités à mettre en place en leur sein des procédures internes d'évaluation et ceci n'a pas été jugé incompatible avec le principe d'indépendance des professeurs de l'enseignement supérieur.

4.4. Le principe d'autonomie et le principe de subsidiarité se frayent progressivement, mais difficilement, un chemin dans l'organisation du système administratif français. On voit bien le développement important qu'ils ont connu depuis les mesures prises à partir du début des années 80. Mais on voit aussi la difficulté de leur conciliation avec les principes d'égalité qui caractérisent l'enseignement français

HANS-PETER FÜSSEL

Autonomy of the Educational Institutions – Actual Developments and Actual Discussions in Germany*

GERMAN REPORT

1. In Germany these days we have an intensive discussion about autonomy of schools. We can observe some very successful autonomous schools in Germany but nevertheless the general public and also scientific debate has – in my opinion! – come to a point where one may ask if the German development has now reached a kind of crossroads.

The answer to that question comes out of a very personal view – and it is focused on state schools because the conditions of the Higher Education Institutions are quite different for constitutional reasons.[1]

2. The question how far educational institutions should be free from state intervention is, at least in Germany, an old one: since the pedagogical discussions of the last century demanded freedom for the education process because of the personal relationship between the educator and the pupil, the question is how far the school as an institution requires its own freedom.[2]

But these discussions never became fruitful in the daily reality of the state schools in Germany. The reason for that is the perception of schools as state institutions; for example the term 'supervision of the entire school system' (Art. 7 para. 1 of the German Federal Constitution, the 'Basic Law') has always

* The many references given in this article may also give a kind of overview of the discussion in Germany.

1 Art. 5 para. 3 of the German Federal Constitution, the 'Basic Law', guarantees the freedom of science and research – and this also includes the freedom of the institutions of higher education (the Federal Constitutional Court, BVerfGE 68, 193, 267, and 75, 192, 196); a similar clause for schools is not included in the constitution.

2 Richter, *Bildungsverfassungsrecht* (1973), p. 241 ff.

Walter Berka, Jan de Groof and Hilde Penneman (eds.), Autonomy in Education, 357–362.

been understood in a very broad way as 'all rights of the state in direction of the schools including organizing, planning, leading and controlling'.[3]

During the last fifty years some efforts have been made to extend the autonomy of schools – but always accepting the State's responsibility for the school system.[4] All of these approaches had been unsuccessful – until the early 1990s.

The reason for this new acceptance of the concept of school autonomy seems to me on one hand the international developments[5] and on the other hand the understanding that an extensive 'supervision' of schools will not work any more (if it ever worked – nobody proved it in Germany but everybody believed in it!): schools became too different, so centralized regulations and systems of centralized steering could not fulfil their purpose any more.[6] The influence of a 'New Public Management'[7] also reached the school sector and the manner governing schools.[8]

So the development in Germany is similar to that in other European countries – one also has to add that inside Germany the situation is also different from *Land* to *Land* because of the constitutional principle of 'Cultural Sovereignty'[9] which includes the right of each of the 16 German *Länder* to regulate their school affairs themselves.

3. With different efforts and different intensity each *Land* made their way towards more autonomy for the school – Hesse,[10] Hamburg,[11] Brandenburg[12]

3 Since Anschütz, *Die Verfassungsurkunde für den Preußischen Staat* (1912), p. 417; now used also by the Federal Constitutional Court, f.e. BVerfGE 34, 165, 182.

4 Becker, *Die verwaltete Schule* (1954), reprinted in: *Recht der Jugend und des Bildungswesens* 1993, p. 130 ff.; Deutscher Bildungsrat, Empfehlungen der Bildungskommission, *Zur Reform von Organisation und Verwaltung im Bildungswesen,* Teil 1: *Verstärkte Selbständigkeit der Schule und Partizipation der Lehrer, Schüler und Eltern* (1973), p. A 19 ff.; Deutscher Juristentag (ed.) *Schule im Rechtsstaat, Band I – Entwurf für ein Landesschulgesetz* (1981), p. 334 ff.

5 See the reports in this volume; also Döbert and Geißler (eds), *Schulautonomie in Europa* (1997).

6 See Bericht Nr. 9/1996 der Kommunalen Gemeinschaftsstelle (KGSt): *Neue Steuerung im Schulbereich* (1996).

7 Buschor, 'Schulen in erweiterter Verantwortung – Die Schweizer Anstrengungen und Erfahrungen', in: Avenarius, Baumert, Döbert and Füssel (eds), *Schule in erweiterter Verantwortung* (1998), p. 67 ff.

8 Also Weiß, 'Schulautonomie im Licht mikroökonomischer Bildungsforschung', in: v. Weizsäcker, *Deregulierung und Finazierung des Bildungswesens* (1998), p. 20.

9 BVerfGE 6, 309, 346 f.

10 Hessisches Schulgesetz from 15 May 1997.

11 Hamburgisches Schulgesetz from 16 April 1997.

12 Brandenburgisches Schulgesetz from 17 December 1996/10 March 1998.

and Bremen[13] passed new School Acts and the schools in these *Länder* are obliged to produce their first school programmes[14] by 1999 or 2000.[15]

But this development in schools is not free from other 'influences' – and these 'influences' create some conflicts and dilemmas one should also mention.

The discussion about the conflicts concerning school autonomy is – as I see it – still under ground, not yet in the open although one can read and hear some hints.[16]

This is not meant to sound the funeral bell of school autonomy in Germany – but there are some signs which may raise uncertainty about future developments ...

(a) The *first* problem one may mention is the actual situation of schools in Germany.

The new development towards a more autonomous school had, at least in Germany, been developed not by the schools or by teachers but by the school adminstration. So this new approach came 'top down'[17] – which means for support from the 'bottom', the schools, the teachers and also the parents and the pupils, must be persuaded to take part in this process.[18]

Development of autonomy in schools as a process needs actors; these actors must become the driving forces. It may be a headmaster or headmistress of a school[19] – but the teachers are also a very important group for the success of that process.[20]

But for teachers this reform sometimes seems to be another project of school-reform imposed on them, not their own project. So politicians must promote this project and need support.

In the other direction, teachers in Germany do not feel much support from the politicians – and it is not important whether this feeling decribes the reality or not. However, if this feeling is wrong it may hinder any reform.

13 Bremisches Schulverwaltungsgesetz from 20 December 1994.

14 Risse (ed.), *Schulprogramm – Entwicklung und Evaluation* (1998).

15 Examples in Risse (ed.), *op. cit.*, p. 315 ff.

16 See e.g. Philipp, 'Konstruktiv mit Widerstand umgehen', in: Risse (ed.), *op. cit.*, p. 235 ff.

17 e.g. the Minister of Hesse Holzapfel, Schule 2000 (1996).

18 Seyler, 'Personalentwicklung an der selbstverwalteten Schule – Wie kommen Lehrerschaft und Schulprogramm zueinander?', in: Risse (ed.), *op. cit.*, p. 225 ff.; Allhoff, Herden and Müller, 'Ohne Schhlerinnen und Eltern geht es nicht – aus Schüler – und Elternsicht', in: Risse (ed.), *op. cit.*, p. 243 ff.

19 The headteacher as 'gatekeeper' (Fullan 1991), see Rolff, *Wandel durch Selbstorganisation* (1993), p. 175 ff.

20 Also Böttcher, 'Autonomie aus Lehrersicht', in: Daschner, Rolff and Stryck (eds), *Schulautonomie – Chancen und Grenzen* (1995), p. 55 ff.

The situation of teaching has became more difficult in Germany during the last few years.[21]

One problem is the increase in the percentage of older teachers. Because of the financial cuts of the last decade very few young teachers had been employed.[22] 'Our youngest colleague became fifty' – this is not only a cartoon of the teachers' union, it also describes the reality in many schools![23] A 'burn out-syndrome' of the older teachers is therefore not only a theoretical discussion but in many schools also a reality: the possibilities of part-time work because of age[24] is much more interesting for many of these older teachers than the discussion about the new school-programme!

The actual working conditions of most of the teachers has also become worse in the last few years:

- the number of lessons which had to be given by each teacher had been increased in the last two years in nearly all of the 'Länder';[25]
- the number of pupils per class had been increased;[26] and
- teachers also had to accept some financial cuts in salaries.[27]

Therefore teachers in Germany feel very little support from the politicians – especially since criticism of teachers has become a kind of political sport.[28] The circumstances for school reform and for active actors and supporters among the teachers are not as good as they should be – but for the development of the single school we need the support of all groups. Some doubts may be allowed in asking if teachers as a whole will be the first promoters of the new development or if they will try to undermine this process, directly or indirectly.

(b) A *second* point which could be added: the new development towards more

21 The main subject of the monthly journal 'Pädagogik' Nr. 12/1998 was about the boundaries of teaching ('Wenn Lehrerinnen an Grenzen kommen').

22 In 1996 the number of all teachers in Germany was 671 700; this year only 15 076 new teachers had obtained a post – and about the same number of teachers was unemployed.

23 Terhart, 'Neue empirische Untersuchungen zum Lehrerberuf', in: Böttcher (ed.), *Die Bildungsarbeiter* (1996), p. 186 ff.

24 Krauss, 'Teilzeitarbeit an deutschen Schulen: Chance oder Dilemma?', in: *Recht der Jugend und des Bildungswesens* 1996, p. 286 ff.

25 See Krauss, 'Lehrerarbeitszeit in der Retrospektive. Zur Entwicklung der Lehrerarbeitszeit in Deutschland', in: *Recht der Jugend und des Bildungswesens* 1996, p. 60 ff.

26 The average is about one pupil more per class since 1990 – and this development is continuing.

27 It should be noted that German teachers get quite high salaries compared with their colleagues in other European countries.

28 For example in 1998 the newly elected chancellor once described teachers as 'lazy buggers' – with applause from some people ...

autonomy of schools should also bring better results, in that it should increase the quality of schools.[29]

It has been said that quality of schools will be more than simply the results of the school examinations; the quality of the single school should be a criterion which emphasizes the quality of the communication structure of a school much more than any examination.[30]

But after the new 'Sputnik-Shock' in Germany, the publication of the knowledge of German pupils in mathematics and science ('Third International Mathematics and Science Study'/TIMSS[31]), only the outcome-orientated results of quality seems to be of any interest to the politicians. New systems of measuring the outcome are discussion in German, a nationwide testing in the main subjects is in preparation – and it seems that the former extensive approach of quality-assessment is being lost.

These new assessements also concentrate on the traditional main subjects of the school: German, mathematics and a foreign language. Also if schools are obliged to react to actual developments in society – the movement 'back to basics' is influencing the daily school life much more than every good step forward in other fields of school activities.

Parents – and pupils – also react to that: they demand better preparation in these fields; they do not care so much any more for social training or the social life of a school. The call to publish a ranking-list[32] of schools is also becoming more popular in Germany.

(c) A *third* problem influences the development in Germany towards more autonomy of the single school.

A new system of administering schools should be developed – that was one of the aims of the new direction. And this has to include a new description of the role and function of the school inspectors: they should – so the idea goes – become much more advisers of the schools, their control-function should become of less importance.

'External evaluation' should be part of the new system of controlling schools – but just one part, beside the much more important 'internal evaluation'.

But it seems that not all school inspectors have found their new role yet – schools often complain about the old way of acting of the school inspectors by only using the new terms. Whether this is a kind of obstruction or only an

[29] Weiß, *op. cit.*, p. 17.

[30] Rolff, 'Schulprogramm und externe Evaluation', in: Risse (ed.), *op. cit.*, p. 256 f.; Hannemann, 'Mit Schulprogrammen "Gute Schule" machen?', in: *Schul-management* vol. 5/1998, p. 14 ff.

[31] Baumert and Lehmann, *TIMMS – Mathematisch-naturwissenschaftlicher Unterricht im internationalen Vergleich* (1997).

[32] Like the English 'School-League-Tables', see Weiß, *op. cit.*, p. 30.

inability of the school inspectors who have not been trained for their new role – cannot yet be answered properly.

(d) At least a *fourth* problem should be added and mentioned here: it is a constitutional one and therefore it must be taken very seriously. It is the question of the borderline for autonomy in a system where the State's responsibility for schools still has to be retained.

The German Federal Constitutional Court decided that every decision of importance must be made by a representative of the State who is responsible for his or her actions.[33] This clause had been statedd by the Court very appositely – and we now discuss in Germany how far this rule has to be accepted in the different fields of 'New Public Management'.[34]

The discussion about the special conditions of educating and schooling and the influence of that on the new kind of autonomy must become clear before a new court decision may disturb the whole process. The good aim of doing will not convince a court of law.

4. The picture which has been painted may be seen as a pessimistic one – but that was not the aim.

I think that the development in Germany towards more autonomy of the single school must bear in mind all the problems which are connected with this project.

The politicians especially must recognize that for the success of this process one needs confidence and patience – and that with other kinds of influences the whole process may be disturbed, even stopped.

Therefore an appeal goes in the direction of the politicians and school administrators: they have begun this process for more autonomy of the single school – and because of the fact that this seems to be the right approach these persons are obliged to do everything not to disturb or interrupt this process.

Strong support is necessary and sometimes one may doubt if this is still given in the necessary way to the schools and the personnel of the schools. But this support is a must and without it the process may fail – and this should and must not happen.

33 BVerfGE 93, 37 ff.

34 Avenarius, 'Schulische Selbstverwaltung – Grenzen und Möglichkeiten', in: *Recht der Juhgend und des Bildungswesens* 1994, p. 256 ff.; Höfling, 'Die Bedingungen für eine Schule in erweiterter Verantwortung nach deutschem Verfassungsrecht', in: Avenarius, Baumert, Döbert and Füssel (eds), *op. cit.*, p. 51 ff.

DYMPNA GLENDENNING

Autonomy in Education
IRISH REPORT

Preliminary point

By contrast with other Member States of the EU where denominational education exists alongside a public system of education, Ireland's educational system is predominantly denominational. Few state schools exist. Informality has been a unique feature of the system which is still governed largely by departmental circular and regulations. However, the traditional system is on the cusp of change as the first substantive piece of legislation in the history of the State, *Education (No. 2) Bill 1997*, is currently passing through the Oireachtas (Parliament). Further educational legislation is planned.

1.

1.1. *Is autonomy of the educational system or of some of its parts constitutionally guaranteed?*

Yes, the family is recognized as the primary and natural educator of the child, a right which is subject only to the State's right, as guardian of the common good, to require that the children receive 'a certain minimum education, moral, intellectual and social'. While there is no express protection for denominational education, the majority of parents belong to the Roman Catholic faith and there is implicit protection for denominational education in the Constitution. Every religious denomination has the right to manage its own affairs, own and acquire property and maintain institutions for religious or charitable purposes, which include educational institutions. The property of any religious denomination or any educational institution may not be diverted except for necessary works of public utility and on payment of compensation.

Walter Berka, Jan de Groof and Hilde Penneman (eds.), Autonomy in Education, 363–367.

1.2. *Does the Constitution guarantee teachers' educational Freedom or the liberty of scientific teaching (academic freedom)?*

No, although there is a tradition of respect for this concept within certain parameters.

1.3. *If autonomy is constitutionally granted: which notion of autonomy underlies the Constitution?*

Family/parental autonomy.

1.4. *Are there strict legal bases and describe it?*

Yes, the State recognizes the family, as constituted in a valid marriage, as the natural, primary and fundamental unit group of society and as a moral institution possessing inalienable and imprescriptible rights antecedent to all positive law. Parents are free to educate their children in their homes, in private schools or in schools recognized or established by the State provided the constitutional minimum is met. The State may not oblige parents, in violation of their conscience and lawful preference, to send their children to any specific type of school, e.g. a State school or any school designated by the State.

2. Autonomy of educational institutions

2.1. *Is autonomy granted with respect to the organisation of educational institutions? Are schools or universities vested with a legal personality of their own. Have schools or universities individual constitutions of their own (basic statutes, basic charters)? Are these autonomously set up by the educational institutions or conferred on them by the State or government?*

A. *Schools*

Schools have been traditionally set up by the Patrons, usually the bishop of the diocese who took the initiative on behalf of parents. In recent years parental initiative has been responsible for the establishment of multi-denominational and *gaelscoileanna*, i.e. schools which conduct their entire educational enterprise through the medium of the Irish language. These latter schools receive full state support and more favourable funding than all other schools including officially designated 'disadvantaged schools'. Their growth has been quite dramatic.

Primary schools were not established by statute but as a result of an educational experiment which had its genesis in a letter written by the Chief Secretary for Ireland (Lord Stanley) in 1831. Later two Royal Charters conferred certain powers on the newly established voluntary board which administered the system. This informal structure has continued, with little change to the present day, although the *Education (No. 2) Bill 1997* proposes to establish a statutory framework for first and second level education.

Minimal statutory provision was made for secondary schools in the *Intermediate Education Acts 1878–1924.*

The Vocational Education Acts 1930–1970 provide a statutory basis for the vocational schools and community colleges.

B. *Universities*

The University of Dublin (Trinity College) was founded in 1591 as a Reformation foundation. It was established by Charter of Queen Elizabeth 1 in 1592 and was 'to endure forever'.

Maynooth College was set up in 1795 for the training of Catholic priests in Ireland as the French Revolution had resulted in the closure of the continental seminaries which were attended by most Irish priests. It was established by Act of Parliament.

The three Queen's Colleges opened amid controversy in 1849 in Belfast, Cork and Galway as a result of the *Colleges (Ireland) Act 1845*. They were to be state-funded and non-denominational, the staff to be appointed by the British sovereign.

In 1908, the Irish Universities Act 1908 gave birth to two new universities, which were *de jure* non-denominational; the National University of Ireland and Queen's University, Belfast. The former consisted of 3 constituent colleges, Cork, Galway and University College Dublin, which was to be *de facto* a university for Catholics, being closely associated with Cardinal Newman.

The newer universities such as Dublin City University and the University of Limerick Act are grounded in statute being established by the *Dublin City University Act 1989* and the *University of Limerick Act 1989.*

The *Universities Act 1997* is the first comprehensive university legislation since 1908. This much-amended Act:

- reconstitutes the three colleges of the National University of Ireland as full universities;
- provides for the updating of the universities' governing structures; and
- redefines the relationship between the State and the universities.

2.2. *Are schools or universities entitled to choose freely among applicants with necessary qualifications?*

Yes.

2.3. *Is autonomy granted with respect to the fulfilment of the educational objective? Can schools or universities independently organise their curricula, decide on the number of students per class etc.?*

In schools there is a national curriculum which must be followed. However, in 'disadvantaged schools' there is a wider discretion given to the schools to adjust the curriculum to the needs of students. There are recommended figures of enrolment for maximum and minimum numbers in class. The objects, functions and academic freedom accorded the universities is provided for in the much-amended *Universities Act 1997*.

2.4. *Autonomy of resources*

Some schools supplement the state funding with sponsored walks, cake sales, etc. A small minority of schools charge fees. University students no longer pay fees *per se*.

2.5. *Autonomy of organization for schools*

It is fair to say that there is a high degree of autonomy in the organization of schools especially in the voluntary secondary schools (60% of second-level schools).

2.6.

Yes, the process of Judicial Review of administrative action is available to schools and teachers. In at least one instance a teacher successfully judicially reviewed the action of the Minister for Education in relation to a post of responsibility.

3. Individual autonomy

3.1. A high degree of autonomy at university level and second level with lesser autonomy in primary schools.

3.2. All school principals have a role in the guidance and direction of the teachers in this sphere.

3.3. Teachers do not yet have a self-governing body although this is now being seriously explored and will, it appears, soon become a reality.

Consequences of autonomy

4.1. By school inspections at primary level; by State examinations at second level.

4.2. Yes.

4.3. I suppose the ideal is essentially striking a reasonable balance between autonomy and accountability.

4.4. There is a definite movement towards more government control at university level as illustrated in the *Universities Act 1997*. Furthermore, a body of legislation is planned for first- and second-level education.

LUCIO GUASTI

Autonomy in Education

ITALIAN REPORT

1. Constitutional legal basis

1.1. *Is autonomy of the educational system or some of its parts constitutionally granted?*

Primary and Secondary education
Yes.

Higher Education and University Education
Yes.

1.2. *Does the constitution guarantee teachers' educational freedom or the liberty of scientific teaching?*

Primary and Secondary education
Yes, it guarantees the teacher's educational freedom.

Higher Education and University Education
Yes, it guarantees the academic freedom.

1.3. *The constitutional notion of autonomy*

Primary and Secondary education
Freedom of education.

Higher Education and University Education
Freedom of education and scientific research.

1.4. *Strict legal basis*
Primary and Secondary education

Walter Berka, Jan de Groof and Hilde Penneman (eds.), Autonomy in Education, 369–373.

Constitution and ordinary legislation.

Higher Education and University Education
Constitution and ordinary legislation.

2. Autonomy of educational institutions

2.1. (a) *Legal personality*

Primary and Secondary education
Public legal personality: only schools with more than 500 pupils.

Higher Education and University Education
Public legal personality.

2.1. (b) *Individual constitutions*

Primary and Secondary education
No.

Higher Education and University Education
Yes.

2.2. *How independently can they determine the recruitment of their personnel?*

Primary and Secondary education
State schools: no.
Private schools: yes.

Higher Education and University Education
Competitive examinations, but within framework of regional laws.

2.3. *Are schools or universities entitled to choose freely among applicants with necessary qualifications?*

Primary and Secondary education
State schools: no.
Private schools: yes.

Higher Education and University Education
State universities: no.
Private universities: yes.

2.4. *Can schools or universities independently organise their curricula?*

Primary and Secondary education
No, national curriculum.

Higher Education and University Education
Yes, but within framework.

2.4. *Can schools-universities decide autonomously on the number of students per class ?*

Primary and Secondary education
State schools: no.
Private schools: yes.

Higher Education and University Education
Some state faculties: numerus clausus.
Private universities: yes.

2.5. *Free to determine the raising and expenditure of financial resources and tuition fees*

Primary and Secondary education
State schools: no.
Private schools: yes.

Higher Education and University Education
Yes.

2.6. *Autonomy of organisation for schools or universities*

Primary and Secondary education
Wide within framework

Higher Education and University Education
Very wide

2.7. *Schools or universities entitled to defend their autonomous sphere by legal means?*

Primary and Secondary education
Yes.

Higher Education and University Education
Yes.

3. Individual autonomy

3.1. *How much latitude of discretion is granted to teachers/professors in educational matters?*

Primary and Secondary education

State schools: no.
Private schools: yes.

Higher Education and University Education
Highest degree of discretion.

3.2. *Is the head of a school entitled to give instructions?*

Primary and Secondary education
State schools: no.
Private schools: yes.

Higher Education and University Education
No.

3.3. *Do teachers/professors participate in the universities or school governing bodies?*

Primary and Secondary education
Yes.

Higher Education and University Education
Yes.

4. Consequences of autonomy

4.1. *If educational institutions can act autonomously, how is quality and unity guaranteed?*

Primary and Secondary education
Education inspectorate and national assessment service (currently being set up).

Higher Education and University Education
Evaluation unit of the Ministry of Education.

4.2., 4.3. *Is autonomy necessarily linked with a supervisory power and with quality control?*

Primary and Secondary education
Yes.

Higher Education and University Education
No.

4.4. *Trends*

Primary and Secondary education
Autonomy +.

Higher Education and University Education
Autonomy +.

P.W.A. HUISMAN, B.P. VERMEULEN
and H.J.M. HOEFNAGEL

Autonomy in Education: The Netherlands

DUTCH REPORT

1. Constitutional legal basis

1.1. *Is autonomy of the educational system or of some of its parts constitutionally guaranteed?*

The autonomy of the educational system is guaranteed by Article 23 of the Dutch Constitution.[1]

Article 23 reads as follows:

(1) Education shall be the constant concern of the Government.
(2) All persons shall be free to provide education, without prejudice to the authorities' right of supervision and, with regard to forms of education designated by law, their right to examine the competence and moral integrity of the teachers, to be regulated by Act of Parliament.
(3) Education provided by public authorities shall be regulated by Act of Parliament, paying due respect to everyone's religion or belief.
(4) The authorities shall ensure that primary education is provided in a sufficient number of public-authority schools in every municipality. Deviations from this provision may be permitted under rules to be established by Act of Parliament on condition that there is opportunity to receive the said form of education.
(5) The standards required of schools financed either in part or in full from

[1] See on this subject also: A. Postma, 'Report from the Netherlands', in: *Comparative educational law*. Special issue of the Nederlands Tijdschrift voor Onderwijsrecht en Onderwijsbeleid, 1996 nr. 3, pp. 11 ff.

Walter Berka, Jan de Groof and Hilde Penneman (eds.), Autonomy in Education, 375–389.

public funds shall be regulated by Act of Parliament, with due regard, in the case of private schools, to the freedom to provide education according to religious or other belief.

(6) The requirements for primary education shall be such that the standards both of private schools fully financed from public funds and of public-authority schools are fully guaranteed. The relevant provisions shall respect in particular the freedom of private schools to choose their teaching aids and to appoint teachers as they see fit.

(7) Private primary schools that satisfy the conditions laid down by Act of Parliament shall be financed from public funds according to the same standards as public-authority schools. The conditions under which private secondary education and pre-university education shall receive contributions from public funds shall be laid down by Act of Parliament.

(8) The Government shall submit annual reports on the state of education to the States General.

The basic structure of the Dutch education system – as laid down in Article 23 of the Constitution – is dualistic or binary, in that it consists of two types of schools – public(-authority) schools and private schools – which are to a certain extent each others' opposites.[2]

Public(-authority) schools are generally governed by an organ of the State, mostly by the municipal executive (Article 23, paragraph 4). They do not enjoy autonomy understood as the freedom to ground their principles of education in a specific religion or belief. Education provided by these schools is regulated by law: it must be non-denominational, based on the principle of positive neutrality. Public schools are not allowed to select pupils and teachers on the basis of denominational criteria (Article 23, paragraph 3).

Private schools are run by corporate bodies under civil law, and enjoy autonomy – freedom of education (Article 23, paragraph 2). This freedom comprises the right to set up private schools, the right to organize them and to determine the teaching. It is a safeguard for parental choice, ensuring the possibility for parents to send their children to a school of the denomination of their choice. (See section 1.3 for more details.)

In order to receive state funding private schools have to meet certain conditions – a minimum number of students; quality standards; labour conditions, etc. However these conditions may not restrict the essence of the freedom to provide denominational education, nor may they restrict the right to admit and refuse pupils and select teachers on denominational grounds (Article 23, paragraphs 5 and 6).

[2] Cf. also H.J.M. Hoefnagel and B.P. Vermeulen, *European Journal for Education Law and Policy* 1997, nr. 1, 'Recent developments in Dutch legislation on education', pp. 155 ff.

Public-authority schools, being freely accessible to all pupils, have a certain primacy in that government has to guarantee that within a certain distance there is a public school for every pupil who wants to attend such a school (Article 23, paragraph 4: the *guarantee function of the public school*). Otherwise both sub-systems have an equal status. The public-authority schools and private schools that fulfil the conditions sketched above are funded according to the same criteria (Article 23, paragraphs 5 to 7).

It has to be stressed that the framers of Article 23 of the Constitution have written it primarily for primary and (partly) secondary education. However, many of the principles laid down in this article nowadays are also applied to other sectors (the entire sector of secondary education, vocational training and higher education). The precise status of the constitutional principles in these sectors is not entirely clear: must it be assumed nowadays that they are also covered by the text of the Constitution? Or is it the case that these principles as far as these sectors are concerned must be regarded as customary constitutional law? Or is it entirely up to the legislature to apply analogously these principles to these sectors?

At least it is clear that not all paragraphs of Article 23 – for instance the freedom to refuse students who do not subscribe to the denominational basis of the school – can unconditionally be applied to institutions of vocational training and higher education.

1.2. *Does the constitution guarantee teachers' educational freedom or the liberty of scientific teaching (academic freedom)?*

Article 23 paragraph 2 of the Constitution guarantees the freedom of education. This freedom also comprises the right of the individual to teach. For instance, a policeman is free to give driving lessons in his spare time, although his superior objects against it (even if he has reasonable objections).[3]

However, this individual right is at least partially given up when a person accepts an appointment as a teacher at a school. Then the collectivity – the school, or more precisely the school board – becomes the primary subject of this right (the freedom of education). Consequently according to constant case law, in denominational conflicts between the school board of a private school and a teacher, concerning the school board's interest to maintain the religious goal of the school the board's interest prevails.

Academic freedom (scientific teaching) is considered as being comprised in the said Article 23 paragraph 2. The liberty of scientific teaching is also protected by freedom of speech, guaranteed by Article 7 of the Dutch Constitution. However, it could be argued that by accepting an appointment

[3] Centrale Raad van Beroep 16 November 1989, NTOR 1990, pp. 97 ff (annotated by Verheij and Vermeulen).

as a teacher at a university one also accepts the authority of the board of the faculty or university with regard to the curriculum, the subjects to be taught, etc. Nevertheless, the position of a teacher at an institution of higher education is stronger than the position of teachers at primary and secondary schools and institutions for vocational training. According to Article 1.6 of the Higher Education Act (Wet op het Hoger wetenschappelijk onderwijs en Wetenschappelijk onderzoek, WHW) the institutions for higher education have to respect the 'academic freedom', which comprises the liberty of scientific teaching. This implies that the teacher is free – within the constraints set by the organization, the curriculum and scientific standards – to advance his own points of view and choose the teaching methods.[4]

1.3. *If autonomy is constitutionally granted: which notion of autonomy underlies the constitution?*

The autonomy of schools is not absolute. Schools can never be entirely independent from the State, because they fulfil a public task toward society. The State has a responsibility for the quality of all schools (Article 23 para. 1 of the Constitution). The State has a responsibility for the quality of education, and has laid down certain minimum standards with regard to the quality of teachers and the contents of the curriculum (Article 23 para. 2). More standards – e.g. concerning the minimum number of pupils; additional quality criteria; administrative regulations; conditions of employment, etc. – are applied to public-authority schools, and to private schools that are funded by the government (Article 23 paras. 5 and 6). Of course these standards form constraints of the freedom of education.

The freedom of education consists of three rights.

1. *The right to found a school, the 'vrijheid van stichting'.* This right only has practical meaning when it also comprises a right to funding by the government. In recent years funding conditions have been changed. Nowadays it is very difficult to show the prognosis one has to give in order to make plausible that the future school will be attended by sufficient pupils/students. The last four years but a few primary schools have been founded; and hardly any new secondary school has been established.
2. *The freedom of 'direction' (vrijheid van richting), the right to base the education in the school on a religion or other belief.* This is the core freedom of a private school; the state is incompetent in this matter. Article 23 paragraphs 5 and 6 of the Constitution guarantee that when the State issues quality standards (funding conditions for the private schools), this freedom of 'direction' must be respected, especially but not exclusively in relation to the choice of teaching materials and the right to appoint teachers.

[4] P.J.J. Zoontjens, Vrijheid van wetenschap, Zwolle 1993, p. 84.

3. *Finally there is the freedom of organization (vrijheid van inrichting).* This freedom includes the right to pedagogical choice, the freedom to determine the internal organizational structure of the school, including arrangements for participation by parents and teachers, the management of financial resources and the right to choose the services from institutions within the support structure. The freedom of organization is also, within legal boundaries, applicable to public schools.

The third freedom is not so well protected as the freedom of 'direction'. Thus, the State can very much interfere in pedagogical and organizational matters, based on the argument that measures are necessary because of the quality of education. There is some sort of a sliding scale: when the 'richting', the religion or philosophy of life of the school is concerned, the State has in principle no competence to interfere; when it comes to pedagogical concepts, the contents, the methods, the State has more grounds to interfere; and in the field of technical and financial matters the State is fairly free to regulate.

1.4. *Are there strict legal bases and describe it*

The legal bases are laid down for private schools in Article 23 paragraphs 2, 5 and 6 of the Constitution. The freedoms guaranteed in these paragraphs are further developed in the Education Acts. For instance the freedom of education with regard to the content of the subjects to be taught is codified in Article 9 of the Primary Education Act, which gives the school board the right to develop its own (equivalent) curriculum.

A freedom that is not protected by the Constitution but solely by an Act of Parliament is the liberty of scientific teaching, protected in Article 1.6 of the Higher Education Act.

2. Autonomy of educational institutions

2.1. *Is autonomy granted with respect to the organization of educational institutions? Are schools or universities vested with a legal personality of their own? Have schools or universities individual constitutions of their own (basic statutes, basic charters?) Are these autonomously set up by the educational institutions or conferred onto them by the state or government?*

The freedom of private schools and other educational institutions (universities, etc.) is constrained by funding conditions. One condition is that any private school must be maintained by a fully competent legal person; this corporate body must have as its aim to provide education, without profit-making motive. In general private schools are governed by foundations and associations. These legal persons have their base in the Civil law code book, which contains the main criteria concerning their status. However, these criteria are primarily of a technical nature, and leave the founders much room to incorporate their ideas and ideals in the statutes. Private schools and universities are therefore in principle entitled to autonomously set up there own statutes, within the civil law framework.

Most public primary and secondary schools are run by a municipal executive – burgomaster and aldermen – or a committee of governors under section 82 of the Local Government Act.

Since 1996 it is possible for public schools in primary and secondary education to be governed by a foundation. These foundations are not directly, but indirectly related to the municipality. They are responsible for their own finances but are bound by detailed criteria (with regard to the specific content of their statutes) laid down in the Primary Education Act and the Secondary Education Act. For instance, foundations for public education are controlled by the municipality; they cannot change their statutes without the consent of the municipality; their only goal may be to give public education, so they are not free (as the school boards of private schools are) to change their goals.

At the moment their are no public schools for vocational training.

The public institutions for higher education are administered by public legal persons, which are regulated in the Higher Education Act. The Minister of Education appoints the members of the board.

2.2. *How independently can they determine the recruitment of their personnel, etc.?*

Article 23 paragraph 6 of the Constitution explicitly gives the private schools and institutions the right of appointment of teachers. This provision should be interpreted broadly: it includes also the appointment of school managers and the non-teaching staff, and the right to dismiss. Private denominational schools can ask their employees to make a commitment towards the (religious) philosophy of the school.

Personnel at public schools are civil servants, which means that there must be equal access to the job opportunities (Article 3 of the Constitution). Therefore selection on the basis of denominational criteria is not allowed (Article 3 and Article 23 paragraph 3).

The government has the right to examine the competence and moral integrity of the teachers in the sectors designated by Act of Parliament (Article 23 paragraph 2). The Primary Education Act, The Secondary Education Act and the Act on Vocational Training require that to be appointed as a teacher one has to have certain degrees and certificates concerning competence and good conduct.

Apart from these criteria, the recruitment of personnel for schools and other educational institutions, public or private, is – in theory – an autonomous competence. Measures by the government to cut down on expenditure for unemployed teachers have, however, reduced the extent of this freedom. See the next section.

2.3. *Are schools or universities entitled to choose freely among applicants with necessary qualifications?*

In theory, school boards are free to choose among applicants. However, primary and secondary school boards are obliged to (re-)appoint persons who were formerly teaching at one of their schools and are at that moment receiving unemployment benefit. Only when such a person is not available are they free to choose. If they do not follow this procedure they will have to pay a fine.

Primary and secondary school boards are also restricted by rules regarding dismissal of teachers. Teachers are appointed by the board, and do not have a privileged position at one specific school. This means that they have to move from one school to the other, if for instance there is a shortage of teachers in one school and a surplus in another school administered by the same school board.

Schools for primary and secondary education are obliged to pay a sum to the so called 'participatiefonds'. This fund, which is set up by the organizations of workers and employers, controls the dismissal of personnel from schools. The central criterion is whether a school has dismissed the teacher because of 'its own policy' or because of an external, objective cause like a decrease in the number of pupils (government funding is linked to the number of pupils). In the latter case, the participation fund will pay the school the unemployment benefit for the dismissed teacher; if the dismissal is caused by 'its own policy' the school board itself must pay the unemployment benefit. Of course, the school board is formally free to follow its own educational standards, but because of the financial consequences it is in fact bound by the rules made by the participatiefonds. These rules demand a certain active role of the board in order to avoid the increase of unemployment benefits for unemployed teachers, such as the setting up of a policy of mobility of personnel, counseling, courses, etc.

The other eucational institutions have to pay (a part or 100% of) the unemployment benefits of teachers themselves. In fact the responsibility for the unemployment of their personnel is entirely theirs. Of course this provides them with an incentive to reappoint former, currently unemployed (ex-)personnel. Furthermore this restricts their freedom to dismiss, in that they will have to pay a part or 100% of the unemployment benefit resulting from dismissal.

2.3'. *Is autonomy granted with respect to the fulfillment of the educational objectives? Can schools or universities independently organize their curricula, decide autonomously on the numbers of students per class, etc.?*

Central government control may be exercised by imposing qualitative or quantitative standards for the educational process in schools and/or for the results they produce. The ministry of Education, Culture and Science lays down conditions, especially in primary and secondary education, relating to the types of schools that can exist, the length of the courses, compulsory and optional school subjects, the minimum and maximum number of lessons to be given, the norms of class division, the examination syllabus and national examinations.

The Primary Education Act contains an Article in which the general aim of this type of education is described: it should focus on emotional and mental development, on developing creativity and on gaining the necessary knowledge and social, cultural and physical skills. Furthermore it must be taken into account that pupils grow up in a multi-cultural society. There is also a provision prescribing that pupils with the need for extra care should have individual guidance. Registration of the progress of these pupils is obligatory.

As for attainment targets in primary schools, the Primary Education Targets Decree describes for every subject the level of knowledge, understanding and skills that pupils should have attained when they leave primary education. At the end of the primary school, instead of certificates or diplomas (there is no examination), pupils receive a school report showing their progress at school and their learning potential.

Schools for secondary education start with a period of basic secondary education (basisvorming). The duration varies from two to four years. The goal is to give pupils a broad, general education. Basic secondary education consists of no less than fifteen compulsory subjects, including technical subjects, information sciences and self-sufficiency (social and life skills). Attainment targets have been established for the basic secondary education subjects. These provide a description of minimum qualities in the areas of knowledge, understanding and skills.

The following phase in secondary education will be fundamentally changed in the near future (from 1999/2000 onwards). In the second phase of secondary education the pupils in schools for pre-university education (VWO) and senior general secondary education (HAVO) will have to make a choice between four 'profiles'. Each of these profiles comprises a coherent range of subjects consisting of the following three parts: (1) a common part which is similar for all profiles and is obligatory (about 45%); (2) a profile-part which is obligatory for the profile in question and which is especially important for transfer to further education (some 30%); (3) a free part (20–25%). These profiles are 'nature and technology', 'nature and health', economics and society' and 'culture and society'. This is connected to a new form of secondary education in the concept of 'learning to learn'. This project has been given the name of 'study house' (studiehuis) and allows schools to differentiate between classical lessons and time in which the pupils have to work by themselves. Half of the examination will be set by the school board; the other half will take place in a central state examination. The averages of the marks for the internal and the national exam constitute the final grades.

A more or less similar restructuring will take place in the second phase secondary education in schools for general secondary education (MAVO) and preparatory vocational education (VBO). These schools will have to offer 'learning routes': the theoretical route, the professionally-oriented learning route and the mixed learning route. The education offered in these routes is divided into four sectors, among which the pupil has to choose: technology, care and welfare, economics, and agriculture. In addition to these learning routes and sectors there are also new examination programmes which have been set up by the government and will be mandatory for pupils starting their first year of the second plase of MAVO or VBO in 1999.

Vocational education concentrates on theoretical and practical preparation for practising a profession, where a professional qualification is required or useful. Vocational education also advances the general education and personal development of participants, contributing to their functioning in society. Since 1996 (Act on Vocational Training and Education) the institutions themselves are responsible for examinations in the entire field of secondary vocational education, although examinations for the core subjects of the programme are performed under external supervision.

The Higher Education and Research Act encompasses a few general provisions, including the objectives of the institutions for higher education, and the general structure of education such as pre-educational requirements and the study load per year. Both universities and higher professional education institutions have central-entry systems. Because of capacity problems and labour-market considerations, branches of study to which intake restrictions apply are designated each year. In the event that the number of first year entrants is restricted to a maximum lots are drawn.

Otherwise, the institutions are fairly autonomous: they determine the curricula, and the examination procedures are entirely in their own hands.

2.4. *Autonomy of resources: Are schools/universities free to determine the raising and expenditure of financial resources? Do they have facilities to raise money through sponsoring or through other means, etc.? Are they able to charge tuition fees?*

According to the Primary Education Act the admittance of pupils may not depend on financial contributions of parents. Contracts in which parents are obliged to pay are void. Under specific conditions contracts can be set up for certain extra-curricular activities, as long as it is made clear that participation is voluntary. The same regime applies for the first years of secondary schools.

Pupils/students aged 16 and over must pay annual tuition fees, determined by law. Parents with lower incomes can apply for allowances.

Sponsoring in primary and secondary education is regulated through a central agreement between the organizations of school boards and the ministry.

All schools except the primary schools may do contract-activities on behalf of third parties, if that does not harm the regular interest of the educational activities. Universities can offer post-doctoral study programmes. These have not been regulated by law and are not paid for by the government. In principle, the costs are paid for by the students or their employers.

2.5. *Autonomy of organization for schools?*

Public schools are bound by the provisions laid down in regulations concerning governmental bodies such as municipalities. Private schools have freedom of organization when it comes to their internal affairs. The competent authority, in general the school board, assumes the responsibilities involved in running a school insofar as based on statutory provisions.

The daily management of primary and secondary schools may be mandated to the head teacher (the head of school/school management in primary and secondary schools; the central management in schools for vocational training). The ultimate responsibility still rests with the school board itself.

The tasks and responsibilities of the boards of public and private schools are very similar. The competent authority, as the law calls it, has decision-making power when it comes to the curriculum, the choice of teaching materials, the establishment of the school plan, the appointment and dismissal of head-teachers, teachers and non-teaching staff, the admission and expulsion of pupils, the use of the school-buildings, the management of financial resources and arrangements for their administration.

The freedom of organization applies to both public as well as the private schools, but to a different degree, in that the State cannot interfere in the sphere of private schools when it comes to denominational matters. When it comes to non-denominational matters the situation of both types of schools is more or less the same. In particular the State must be cautious in interfering with the pedagogical autonomy of private schools as well as public-authority schools.

2.6. *Are schools or universities entitled to defend their autonomous sphere by legal means against the state or government? Do schools have the legal capacity to appeal against acts of a supervisory authority?*

The Minister of Education, Culture and Sciences supervises the educational system. The actual supervision is done by the Education Inspectorate under the authority of the minister. The tasks of the inspectorate are defined in the Education Acts, which also establish that the competent authorities and staff of schools and institutions must always allow the inspectorate access and are obliged to provide all information requested.

The school boards and the university boards are (organs of) legal persons which can defend their autonomous sphere by legal means, against the inspectorate, the minister and other governmental agencies. However, laws which are adopted by government and the first and second chamber (parliament) – Acts of Parliament – cannot be declared unconstitutional by the courts. In so far as acts of the inspectorate, the minister, etc., flow directly from an Act of Parliament, they cannot be submitted to judicial review. Otherwise, every action of the minister or the inspectorate which has legal effect can be challenged in an administrative court.

3. Individual autonomy

3.1. *How much latitude of discretion is granted to teachers/professors in educational matters (content of education and methodological decisions)?*

In general, the teacher is considered as a professional. Given the minimum requirements set by law, such as diplomas, he or she is fairly autonomous in pedagogical matters. This does not mean that he or she is entirely free. He or she has to work within the criteria set by law and the instructions given by the school board.

In as far as the principles of the school are concerned, the teacher is not free, in that it can be demanded that he or she upholds the positive neutrality of the public school (Article 23 paragraph 3 of the Constitution) or the religion or philosophy of the private denominational school (Article 23 paragraph 6 of the Constitution).

3.2. *Is the head of a school (university) or any of its bodies entitled to issue instructions in professional matters to the teaching staff?*

Article 23 paragraph 2 of the Constitution guarantees the freedom of education. This freedom also comprises the right of the individual to teach. However, the individual right is given up (partially) when a person accepts an appointment as a teacher at a school. Then the collectivity – the school, or more precisely the school board – becomes the primary subject of this right (the freedom of education). Nevertheless in practice the teacher enjoys a considerable amount of pedagogic freedom. However, this does not preclude the school board from issuing instructions to the teacher. In practice this competence is delegated or mandated by the board to the head of the school or the school management.

As discussed before (section 1.2) the position of a teacher at an institution of higher education is better guaranteed than the position of teachers at primary and secondary schools and institutions for vocational training. According to Article 1.6 of the Higher Education and Scientific Research Act the institutions for higher education have to respect 'academic freedom', which comprises the liberty of scientific teaching. This implies that the teacher is free – within the constraints set by the organization, the curriculum and scientific standards – to advance his or her own points of view and choose the teaching methods.

3.3. *Do the teachers/professors participate in the universities or schools self-governing bodies?*

Under the Education Participation Act of 1992 (WMO 1992) every primary, secondary and school for vocational and adult education, and under the Higher Education and Scientific Research Act (WHW) every institution for higher vocational education is legally required to set up a participation council. This comprises an equal number of elected staff members and parents/pupils-students. The participation council has a number of general competencies: the right to give advice or consent and the ability to make proposals. Universities can choose between two regimes: a regime which is more or less similar to that for the other sectors (employees and students participating in the University council and the faculty council); and a regime with separate organs, one for employees and one for students.

4. Consequences of autonomy

4.1. *If educational institutions can act autonomously, how are general aims or values like quality and unity of the education guaranteed?*

There are different instruments to guarantee educational quality. The Education Acts contain certain provisions that set minimum standards of quality. These provisions contain general aims of education, such as the already mentioned attainment targets, as well as requirements concerning exams. Recently new developments in establishing quality within primary and secondary schools have occurred. The law now contains specific Articles concerning quality control by the school boards themselves. This means at least that the board will live up to its school plan, the central document of the school's education philosophy, in which the board explains how it wants to achieve the standards set by law and how to realize its own pedagogical aims. Furthermore, school boards are obliged to bring out a school guide, in which they explain to parents/pupils what their aims are and how they are going to achieve them. Furthermore, the parents/pupils will have a right to file complaints before a mandatory complaint commission, attached to the school. Thus, by enhancing the role of the 'consumer' the idea is that the quality of the 'producer' and his 'products' will increase.

The unity of the system is guaranteed by laying down minimum standards, by procedures prescribed by law, by the formulation of attainment targets and by the Education Inspectorate (section 4.2).

4.2. *Is autonomy necessarily linked with a supervisory power?*

School autonomy does not imply that schools can operate totally independently. For reasons of quality, equality and cohesion within the system, supervision and/or control is necessary. This is primarily the task of the Education Inspectorate.

The Education Inspectorate has the following tasks:

- to ensure compliance with statutory regulations (supervision);
- to remain conversant with the current state of education, for example, by visiting and inspecting schools (evaluation);
- to promote the development of education through consultation with competent authorities, school staffs and regional or local government (promotion); and
- to report to and advise the Minister, either at his request or on its own initiative (reporting).

The supervision and evaluation is done by the Inpectorate itself with regard to primary and secondary schools, and by the institutions of vocational and higher education themselves in the form of examination institutes or so-called 'visitation' committees. See also the next section.

4.3. *What are the relations between autonomy, responsibility and accountability? Is autonomy necessarily connected with quality control within autonomous educational institutions?*

Strengthening autonomy of educational institutions can be realized on different levels:

- autonomy in financial matters;
- autonomy in organization, the way the institution is governed, and how the participants have a say;
- autonomy in a moral sense, the choice of and implementation of the religious and pedagogical values;
- autonomy in labour issues; and
- educational autonomy, which involved both the process of education and the output (the product) of education.

More autonomy implies that the school(board)s are more responsible for their results. Internal as well as external quality control is necessary. The concept of quality implies that there is an ongoing process of planning – implementation, (self)-evaluation – adjustment, to be guaranteed by procedures and quality standards. For a sketch of these procedures and standards for primary and secondary schools see section 4.1.

In vocational education a quality assurance system has been introduced. Institutions have to pursue quality improvement objectives and to produce progress reports every two years. A second element in quality assurance is the external validation of examinations. The basic principle is that the examinations for at least 51% of the qualifications required to obtain a full diploma will be administered under the aegis of some body external to the educational institution itself ('external legitimization'). Another important development (at least in theory) is the strengthening of the position of the participants: the students. Through an education-contract the rights and obligations of both parties – institution and student – for the duration of the enrolment are being set out.

With regard to institutions of higher education quality control is both a responsibility of the Minister of Education/Education Inspectorate as well as of the so-called 'visitation committees'. The committees do regular research on the quality of the study programmes; the task of the Education Inspectorate is limited to controlling the procedures followed by these committees (meta-evaluation).

4.4. *If there are recent trends in your country with respect to autonomy of educational institutions: Is there a tendency towards enlargement of autonomy or towards more government control? Why is it so?*

Until recently the national government in general employed and applied centrally formulated legal rules and funding conditions, primarily in the form of criteria concerning the input. In the last decade the notion has grown that many objectives could better be attained by delegating competencies to lower levels of decision-making. School(board)s have been made more responsible for the quality of primary educational processes, and municipalities for local coordination between education and other social sectors. The State still has a general responsibility for the functioning of the system, but the educational institutions themselves together with local government are held responsible for their achievements.

Increasingly parents, pupils and students are stimulated to act as quality controllers, adopting the role of the 'critical consumer'. School plans, school guides, complaint procedures, education contracts, reports of visitation committees, etc., are introduced to give substance to this role.

Furthermore a policy has been introduced to publish the comparative results of secondary schools and institutions, quality guides that give a 'ranking'. Especially with regard to secondary schools the quality guide gives a distorted view, while only the output, and not also the input (level of incoming pupils) is sufficiently taken into account.

It should be stressed that schools have primarily gained autonomy in the field of financial matters. All educational institutions except primary schools now are financed on a lump-sum basis. The government assumes that schools will operate more efficiently if they are 'master' of their own money. School(board)s can and have to develop their own policy regarding the spending of the lump sum.

This development has led to a greater scale (more institutions under one school board). Only when they have a certain scale are they able to carry the risks involved in lump-sum funding; and only then are they able to create a strong school management.

Nevertheless this autonomy is threatened by other developments.

(1) Local authorities have been given new responsibilities and competences in the field of education such as the housing of schools. Decentralization and school autonomy is not always compatible. Lump-sum funding presumes the school has a fair budget, with which it can make integral decisions concerning all aspects of the school's policy. When the decision-making power concerning school building, however, is in the hands of the municipality, it is obvious that this decreases the possibilities of making such an integral decision. Furthermore, the lump-sum budget is tight; there is no real autonomy, no room for real choices.
(2) Also, in the field of labour relations, primary and secondary school(board)s are more or less bound by rules imposed by external bodies like the participation fund, and by central agreements between labour unions and employers' organizations.

At the same time pedagogical autonomy for primary and secondary schools is decreasing. Schools are nowadays perceived as essential instruments for the promotion of social cohesion. To guarantee this goal, the State imposes all kinds of additional obligations to schools with regard to the aims of education, the output to be achieved, the role of participants (strengthening the role of the 'clients') and the duty to cooperate with municipalities and other school(board)s.

The policy directed towards financial autonomy leads to greater organizations with more schools, often with different denominations, and even comprising private and public schools. It is difficult for a school to maintain its philosophy or religion within such a pluralistic conglomerate.

ARLINDO AZEVEDO and LUIS GUIMARAES DE CARVALHO

Higher Education Autonomy

PORTUGUESE REPORT

1. Historical and political approach

The concept of educational autonomy has never been very familiar to Portuguese Governments until very recently, in particular between 1926 and 1974 one can say that the word was not part of the official Portuguese vocabulary.

Although the Republican regime had recognized the autonomy of universities, in practice no real steps were taken to strengthen it and during the authoritarian regime which was established in 1926 state intervention in the universities was present in everyday life.

The public power was virtually in the hands of one person – António de Oliveira Salazar, Prime Minister from 1932 until 1969 – and even academic freedom had been in jeopardy due to his fear that university professors might spread 'subversive ideas' among the students. Many professors were fired due to their political ideas and some of them even had to go abroad to escape political imprisonment. The so-called administrative autonomy given to universities and Schools of Higher Education was closely controlled by the Government in such a way that even to spend money in some particular items permission had to be obtained from the Minister of Education. Hiring teachers was also restricted and also had to be authorized by the minister following the 'good' opinion of the political police. On the other hand curricula of study programmes were centrally defined and were the same for all universities. This homogeneity was possible due to the small number of universities[1] and the relatively small number of students.

[1] University of Coimbra, University of Lisboa, University of Porto and Technical University of Lisboa. In 1971 the Portuguese Catholic University was allowed to begin its activities (Decree-law 307/71, published on 15 July).

Walter Berka, Jan de Groof and Hilde Penneman (eds.), Autonomy in Education, 391–400.

In 1969 the then Prime Minister suffered an accident and was replaced by the former Rector of the University of Lisbon – Marcelo Caetano – who had resigned from that position in 1962 in disagreement with the way the Government and the police dealt with some riots and political demonstrations inside the University campus. Despite being a supporter of the dictatorial regime Marcelo Caetano was brought some hope for the modernization of the Higher Education system. He appointed a well-known liberal Professor – José Veiga Simão as Minister of Education and, as a result, education as a whole has undergone some positive developments. A new framework law[2] was then published, allowing the creation of new types of Higher Education Institutions, namely Polytechnic Institutes.[3] As a result, three new universities, one University Institute[4] and six Polytechnic Institutes were created.[5] Professors who had been fired were allowed to return and reintegrated into their jobs and new legislation regarding the University teachers' profession[6] and doctoral degrees[7] was published implying at that time more university centralism than any other before. One can say that state intervention has gradually changed to state control although it continued to exist.

2. The pathways to autonomy

2.1. *The trends of the 1970s*

The political reforms of the Minister of Education could not be really tested since in 1974 the regime was overthrown by a military *coup d'état* – the April Revolution. It must be said that some important basic legislation published during the time José Veiga Simão was minister guided the education system for a long time.

The April Revolution introduced many changes in the Portuguese higher education system. The newly created universities and some of the polytechnics were called to participate strongly in the democratization of the system in the

2 Law 5/73, published in 25 July 1973.

3 Teaching in these institutions is more professionally and technically oriented than in universities. They are also more connected to the problems and needs of the region where they are situated.

4 Independent Public University Schools or Institutes existed before 1973 and new ones were created later. Most of them are now integrated in Universities and only one remains with the same status: Instituto de Ciências do Trabalho e da Empresa.

5 Decree-law 402/73, published 11 August 1973.

6 Decree-law 132/70, published in 30 March 1970.

7 Decree-law 388/70, published in 18 August 1970.

late 1970s and new Polytechnic Institutions or Schools were founded.[8] Two Polytechnic Institutes created in 1973 were transformed into University Institutes.[9] Later some University Institutes became universities.[10] Four new universities were also created between 1974 and 1990. The management of higher education institutions changed in order to allow participation of students and non-academic staff.[11]

However the real power of decision-making remained in the hands of the minister for some time.

The number of students presenting as candidates for higher education increased sharply and the 'traditional' Public Institutions were unable to accept them all while some social tensions were visible and felt by the Government. Unrestricted availability of Higher Education was new to the country and it was not easy to deal with it. Public Institutions were not prepared to receive such a large number of students and a *numerus clausus* mechanism was introduced; the Central Administration was unable to cope with this new situation and the private sector[12] was prepared to take its share in the new 'market'. The conditions to increase autonomy of the Institutions were created and the option of the authorities was to move slowly in that direction.

2.2. *The first steps towards autonomy*

The first real sign proving that the State was prepared to give autonomy to the Universities was the approval of the Portuguese Constitution of 1976. In this fundamental Law there was, and still remains, an Article recognizing that Universities hold statutory, scientific, pedagogic, administrative and financial autonomy according to the law.

The autonomy defined by the Constitution may be regarded as having two dimensions: a personal one, granting to the academic community the right to teach and create knowledge; and an institutional one that grants the university itself the fundamental right to autonomy. Whereas the first is an easy dimension since it may be regarded as part of the fundamental rights of the individuals concerning the intellectual and teaching creation, the second raises the problem of knowing the nature of the rights of a 'public collective person'. This important

[8] Decree-law 513–T/79, published 26 December 1979 and Law 29/80, published 28 July 1980.

[9] Law 49/79 published 14 September 1979 and Law 44/79 published in 11 September 1979.

[10] Decree-law 482/79, published 14 December 1979, Decree-law 60/86, published in 22 March 1986 and Decree-law 78–B/86, published in 30 April 1986.

[11] Decree-law 781–A/76, published 28 October 1976.

[12] Universities, University Schools or Institutes, Polytechnic Institutes and Polytechnic Schools.

Article of the Constitution demanded a framework law that would define the limits and the nature of the autonomy as well as the limits of the interference of the State. It was only approved in 1988! In the meantime some steps have been taken.

The very first steps towards autonomy of the universities were taken at the end of the 1970s. The minister initiated a procedure which would continue for some years and still exists today to a lesser extent: the delegation of powers in the Director General for Higher Education and possible sub-delegation in the rectors of the Universities. This procedure devolved some power to the institutions but has proved very cumbersome since it had to be repeated every time there was a change of minister.

We will now mention the main legislation that has contributed during these last years to the real increase of the autonomy of the universities. As was said above, it was a slow process.

In 1979 the Government approved new legislation on teaching careers, increasing the role of the universities on the choice and appointment of teachers.[13] Although the final decisions still belonged to the minister, the real decisions were taken by the universities.

In 1980 the credit system was introduced[14] as an opportunity to organize the study programmes of the Portuguese universities. Although the approval of the credits of each scientific area continued to be a competence of the Minister, the disciplines attributed to those credits were defined by the universities.

In addition in 1980 the rectors of the universities were given the power to hire teaching assistants and other teaching personnel for the first time. The legislation was a breakthrough but still had some limitations: the minister continued to hold the power to appoint professors and it was his/her role to prescribe the number of teachers the rectors could hire.

Rectors were chosen and appointed by the minister. By the beginning of the 1980s the attitude had changed. In 1982 the University of Coimbra elected the rector, the minister accepted the result and appointed him. Since then and until the Law of Autonomy[15] was published no other rector was appointed before being elected.[16] This attitude is not the result of any new legislation but is worth being mentioned to demonstrate the evolution of mental attitudes towards autonomy.

Equivalence and recognition of foreign degrees were tasks of the Ministry

[13] Decree-law 448/79, published 13 November 1979 and amended by Law 19/80, published 16 July 1980.

[14] Decree-law 173/80, published 29 May 1980.

[15] Law 108/88, published 24 September 1988.

[16] Only after the publication of the Law of Autonomy are the Ministers compelled to appoint the elected rectors.

of Education until 1983. New legislation[17] has given the universities the capacity to perform those tasks instead of the ministry.

It was only in October 1984 that the Government recognized the absurdity of repeating the same delegations of powers every time a minister changed. At that time everybody was aware that there was no way back in the delegation of powers. Any change could only be in the direction of delegating more and more. Thus the Government published legislation enlarging the powers of the rectors mainly in matters concerning administrative issues.[18]

2.3. *A difficult transition*

However despite all these important changes the model of state control was still very much in the minds of the Central Administration. Financially the degrees of freedom of the Universities were virtually non-existent. The control was performed in different ways: the budget was earmarked, any change during the year having to be approved by the Ministers of Education and Finance; money not spent by the end of the financial year could not be carried over to the next year; it was virtually impossible to transfer money for personnel to other expenses. Investment was, and still is, a tool used by the ministry to control the universities. Administration was less ponderous, but many decisions had still to be taken by the Ministry of Education and the general laws of Public Administration were also applicable to universities, regardless of their specificity. Pedagogic autonomy was only partly assured. Study programmes still had to be approved by the minister, any major changes in those study programmes needed his/her approval. Scientific areas in which universities could award degrees or titles had also to be approved by the minister.

These examples do not constitute the whole list of constraints. They are just paradigmatic examples.

2.4. *The Law of Autonomy*

The publication in 1988 of the Law of Autonomy[19] was very much welcomed by scholars. According to the Law, Universities have statutory, administrative, financial, scientific, pedagogic, disciplinary and patrimonial autonomy. It is not within the scope of this presentation to go into detail and describe the meaning of each item. Therefore we will try to emphasize the aspects that are important without being concerned with the details.

This autonomy means that some of the constraints have disappeared. In particular it means that:

[17] Decree-law 283/83, published 5 June 1983.

[18] Decree-law 323/84, published 9 October 1984.

[19] Law 108/88 referred to in fn. 15.

- The universities have the right to organise themselves by creating their own statutes. However the law imposes some limitations, mainly regarding the representation of teachers and students in collegial boards (Senate and Assembly).
- The Senate has powers regarding the approval of the budget and accounts, the approval of the university development plans, the creation, extinction and changes of study programmes, the definition of scientific areas in which the university can award degrees and titles, the creation, extinction or merging of faculties and inter-disciplinary departments.
- The Assembly elects and dismisses the Rector and has the power to approve or change the statutes of the university.
- The Rector has all the powers that are not attributed to other university bodies.
- Universities can extinguish permanent positions and in their place create new ones without increasing the total number of positions.
- Universities are free to use their income according to their needs and interests.
- Universities can hire people by using their private income *according to the existing legislation.*
- Universities hire their own teachers according to relevant legislation without the interference of the Government.
- Universities can carry over the money not spent during a particular year.
- Universities have a patrimony consisting of the buildings given to them by the State or by someone else to pursue their objectives and those bought by them.

But:

- Universities do not have the right to increase the number of permanent positions (academic or non-academic).
- Universities do not have the right to decide freely about their investments.

The Law defines the limits of intervention of the State in the universities. Those limits are mainly related to the selling or renting of patrimony, to the right to ask for bank loans and to the right of universities to set the number of new students accepted each year. It is important here to underline that, due to the low number of places available in Public Higher Education Institutions, universities do not have the right to choose their students recognized in this Law.

It also determines that other laws should be published, namely one regarding performance and evaluation.

One could say that this Law would give universities a great degree of freedom providing they follow the national defined policies for higher education. It is indeed a very liberal law.

We will now briefly refer to the private sector since the Law of Autonomy is only applicable to public universities. Private universities and university schools are ruled by special legislation[20] and their autonomy is much less than the autonomy of the public institutions, as far as approval of programmes, permission to function and conferring of degrees are concerned. Much controversy has been present since the first private university was allowed to function. Thus some mistrust permanently surround those institutions, a reason which may explain the existence of special legislation that, many times, has not been put into practice, allowing institutions of doubtful quality to function. However, due to the nature of the private sector, their autonomy of organization, of using their funds and of hiring their teachers is much higher than the autonomy of public universities. Some of them used that autonomy to hire teachers who were members of public universities without any permission of the latter; this fact created a great deal of tension between the two sub-sectors (public universities claim it is illegal) and led the Government to publish legislation[21] which prescribes the advertisement of teaching posts for all higher education institutions. All of these cases must be further clarified. Many problems still exist and the wounds can only be healed with time and the future performance of private institutions.

Therefore when we mention autonomy throughout this work we will be referring only to public universities.

2.5. *Constraints on the application of the Law*

Deliberately or not the legislator has forgotten one important point which would be the centre of a permanent dispute between the institutions and the public powers: the general laws published later applicable to Public Administration were also applied to universities. Some of the provisions of the Law of Autonomy became meaningless. Once again we are not going to describe in detail all of the problems arising from this new legislation. However we will mention some of them.

The National Budget Law, approved every year by Parliament, introduces financial and human resources constraints to the Public Administration. Thus, for instance, the universities could carry over the money not spent in one year to the following year, but had to use it for personnel! That was against the Law of Autonomy approved unanimously by the same Parliament! The general Law freezes the admission of personnel in Public Administration. Therefore universities cannot hire additional staff, except those who already have a link with the State. Once again the general Law is contradicting the Law of Autonomy. The patrimony of the universities was never given to them despite

[20] Decree-law 271/89, published 19 August 1989 and Decree-law 16/94 published 22 January 1994.

[21] Decree-law 15/96, published 6 March 1996.

what the Law of Autonomy prescribes. However universities had to spend their money to maintain the buildings.

On the other hand the funding of Portuguese universities was low and not transparent. Public Universities (through the Portuguese Rectors' Conference, composed of Rectors of Public Universities and the Rector of the Portuguese Catholic University) were able to convince the Government that the financing system was not appropriate, in all senses. The result was that, as far as Public Institutions were concerned, a funding formula was negotiated. This negotiated funding formula is mainly based on the number of attending students, taking also into account staff/student ratios according to the scientific disciplines. The formula does not take properly into account the research activities of the institutions (it merely accepts that 6% of the budget should be allocated to research, but even that is not clearly followed by the government) and the main funding source of research is the Ministry of Science and Technology. It is however worth mentioning that the necessary transparency regarding funding of Public Institutions is now accepted (despite some reservations claimed by some teachers and some students, mainly due to some staff/student ratios that are not suitable to some scientific areas).

Another constraint worth mentioning is the complete withdrawal by the Ministry of Education in respect of scientific research, remitting full responsibility in this field to the Ministry of Science and Technology. This aggravates the risk of universities being turned into 'factories' merely producing graduates, without the necessary care dedicated to one of their basic elements. As a matter of fact, the University's Budget does not allow for a meaningful item for scientific research (excepting the aforementioned 6% of the total amount that is absorbed by educational activities).[22]

State intervention is still felt at other levels, one of them of utmost importance to the quality of the institutions. The Statute of the University Teaching Profession,[23] a law of indisputable importance and relevance at the time of its publication (1979) is nowadays looked upon as obsolete, for several reasons, according to the source of its critics. No doubt certain matters are the subject of common reflections, notwithstanding the point of view advocated: (a) academic competition procedures for the teaching staff have proved to be inadequate (they allow for scientific production of the applicants, but discount their pedagogical performance as well as other teaching staff activities. These academic contests are, on the other hand, written contests, thus preventing an exaggerated assertion on the part of the applicants and precluding jury-based decisions to genuinely evaluate applicants); (b) the recurrent 'evaluation' of teachers is restricted to the periodical presentation of a report on academic

[22] CRE Auto-evaluation Report, University of Lisbon, 1996.

[23] Decree-law 448/79, published 13 November 1989 and amended by Law 19/80, published 16 July 1980.

activities with no practical equivalent; (c) universities are not free to invite highly skilled professors as members of the faculty teaching staff; (d) there are several doubts as to the improvement in the field of automatic graduation from assistant to assistant professor by simply obtaining a doctor's degree; and (e) current procedures do not allow for enhancing and awarding excellence.[24]

Finally we will mention another problem introduced by the Law of Autonomy. This Law includes some restrictions on the freedom of organization which prevent, in certain cases, an improved efficiency regarding institutional management, two of which can easily be identified: (a) the requisites for the representation of several bodies; and (b) the mandatory participation of Faculty bodies lacking adequate fitness.[25]

3. Recent trends

The mistrust between the State and universities has been a permanent issue and had to be solved. Accountability was something that was at stake in the beginning of the 1990s. Universities decided without any pressure from the Government to begin a process of evaluation of the study programmes in 1992. This later led to a formal negotiation with the Government of a new Law on Evaluation of Higher Education Institutions to be proposed to the Parliament. It was approved in 1994.[26]

In the meantime (1993) the mentioned funding formula was also negotiated between the Government and the universities in spite of the non-existence of legislation to support the final decision. Since then universities have never applied for more funds after the approval of the budget of each year. This position was clearly assumed by the rectors to show their good faith in the negotiations. However it must be said that the amount calculated by the use of the formula is frequently above the approved funding.

In 1996 the Ministers of Education and Finance finally agreed to face the problems posed by legislation approved against the Law of Autonomy. The main issues were the flexibility in the management of human resources, the guarantee of freedom to use the money carried over from previous years, the freedom to hire non-permanent staff by using private money and the transfer of patrimony.

It was agreed that every year the Minister of Education, based on student/staff ratios and academic staff/non-academic staff ratios, should publish the number of staff universities can hire with state funding. It was also agreed that the minister should define the criteria to fix the number of permanent

[24] See fn. 23.

[25] See fn. 23.

[26] Law 37/94, published 11 November 1994.

positions and that that number could be changed every two years at the demand of the universities. It was still agreed that universities could hire non-permanent staff to carry on with their projects by using their private funds. Finally the two parts reached a compromise regarding patrimony. The possession of the buildings and real estate should be transferred to the universities (except some buildings of public interest). If the university wished to sell any part of the patrimony 50% of the revenue would belong to the State and the other 50% would belong to the university and could only be used in investment. The universities accepted a requirement to perform external audits every two years and to send their results to the two ministries.

The legislation was published in 1997[27] and had a special Article which clearly defined it as special legislation prevailing over other general legislation that may be in conflict with the present one.

It can be said, in conclusion, that autonomy of Portuguese universities is increasing; the State has now taken a more supervisory role and accountability is now a part of the 'game'. It must, however, be clear that some of the existing legislation still prevents good management, as we have mentioned before.

Some other important laws and decree-laws regarding higher education were published but they are not mentioned here because they did not strongly affect the autonomy of the universities. A law dealing with financing higher education[28] was published in 1997. It may well affect its autonomy in the near future; however it is still unknown if the effect will be negative or positive. Nevertheless one negative effect is already obvious: the state funding has decreased by the same amount as the fees paid by the students, meaning that the introduction of fees did not have a direct positive effect for the institutions.

[27] Decree-law 252/97, published 26 September 1997.

[28] Law 115/97, published 19 September 1997.

HANS VISSER and ELMENE BRAY

Autonomy in Education
SOUTH AFRICAN REPORT

Note: The answers to many of the questions depend on a value judgement and there may obviously be differences of opinion regarding certain issues.

1. Constitutional legal basis

1.1. No. The constitutional principles regarding cooperative government (Chapter 3 of the Constitution) have produced a system of self-government and shared rule in education generally. Independent schools and other private educational institutions seem to enjoy relatively more 'autonomy'.

1.2. Yes (see section 16(1)(d) of the Constitution which provides for academic freedom and freedom of scientific research as part of the right to freedom of expression).

1.3. Academic freedom is granted to 'everyone". The purpose of such freedom is not expressly or directly dealt with in the Constitution and is thus a matter of interpretation. The limits to academic freedom are provided in terms of section 36 dealing with the general limitations to all fundamental rights.

1.4. The 'strict' legal basis in respect of the right to academic freedom is presumably section 16(1)(d) of the Constitution.

2. Autonomy of educational institutions

2.1. Some measure of autonomy is granted to educational institutions in general. Schools and universities are juristic persons. A public schools does not have a statute or a basic charter. However, the governing body must adopt a constitution for itself, develop the mission statement of the school and adopt other policies (dealing with inter alia language, religion and admission). The

Walter Berka, Jan de Groof and Hilde Penneman (eds.), Autonomy in Education, 401–403.

governing body must also develop a code of conduct for learners at the school. There are restrictions on the powers of the governing bodies in regard to all this. Universities are based on their own private statutes. These statutes must conform to the Higher Education Act, 101 of 1997.

2.2. *Public schools*: The state plays a major role but the governing body may make binding recommendations as to appointments. A school may also, through its governing body, and subject to certain limitations, establish and fill posts financed by the school itself. *Universities*: They generally enjoy more freedom but are subject to legislation dealing with employment equity and section 195(1)(i) of the Constitution which provides that the 'public administration' must be broadly representative of the SA population.

2.3. There is obviously not complete freedom.

Universities: They obviously have more freedom. There are, however, general standards in regard to professional degrees.

Schools: The governing body of a public school determines only the extra mural curriculum. The rest is determined by the state education authorities. The number of learners per class is also determined by the appropriate state authorities.

2.4. There is relative freedom to determine the raising and spending of financial resources. Schools' use of the school fund is restricted by policy rules of the education authorities. Governing bodies of public schools are encouraged to raise funds. They may charge tuition fees if certain conditions are met (e.g. parental approval, reasonable conditions of exemption, etc.). Universities may and do raise funds and enjoy relative freedom in the use of all their financial resources.

2.5. The question is not clearly understood. Schools are, in terms of the South African Schools Act, 1996 organized into two main categories: public schools and independent schools. Within a public school the state-appointed principal is in charge of the professional management and administration of the school (subject to the directives of the head of the education department; the governing body governs the school in non-professional fields (such as general school policy)).

2.6. Generally 'yes'. Provision is usually made for an administrative appeal to a higher level of authority. A right of review lies to the High Court in certain limited circumstances.

3. Individual autonomy

3.1. A reasonable measure of discretion is allowed subject to educational policies.

3.2. Yes, subject to the directions of the head of the education department (in the case of schools).

3.3. Yes. There is teacher representation on school governing bodies. Professors serve on the senate of a university.

4. Consequences of autonomy

4.1. In so far as autonomy exists, there are in any event policies and minimum standards that must be met (also in private education and home education).

4.2. The question is not clearly understood. The concept of autonomy does not mean 'total independence'. Therefore, there is always some form of supervision from within and/or outside the institution.

4.3. The Constitution and education legislation provide the framework for democratic government in educational institutions – obviously including principles such as participation, responsibility and accountability. There is quality control in various forms.

4.4. The situation is complex. There may be a considerable de facto autonomy in some instances and areas. The SA education system is still in a transitional stage and the government policies aimed at the eradication of the consequences of apartheid and sexism tend to limit too much autonomy generally. The relative inexperience of many school governing bodies also limit autonomy at these schools. There will probably in the foreseeable future be a move to greater autonomy once education management development programmes and capacity building programmes have produced positive results. There has in fact been a recommendation that schools be placed at the core of education management development, rather than at the bottom of a hierarchical and bureaucratic management pyramid.

JUAN MANUEL DEL VALLE PASCUAL
and FERNANDO GURREA CASAMAYOR

Autonomy in Education

SPANISH REPORT

1. Constitutional legal basis.

1.1. *Is autonomy of the educational system or of some of its parts constitutionally guaranteed?*

The principle of autonomy in the Spanish educational system is constitutionally guaranteed with the characteristics that are set out below. The 1978 Spanish Constitution (SC) recognizes, in Art. 27.1, the *liberty of education*, which in principle means that there cannot be a state monopoly in education, and therefore allows private enterprise to be involved. But the liberty of education also covers the position of the teacher, specifically under Art. 20.1.c, academic liberty, and this will be analysed elsewhere.

Liberty of education needs to be seen as a supra-concept, adopting the modality of *freedom of creation of educational centres* (SC Art. 27.6) if it is intended to set up an educational centre for official education, and the modality of *academic freedom* if a teacher is going to exercise his profession in a centre, be it public or private. Finally, liberty of education enables any citizen, outside an educational centre or system, to carry out an educational activity. This concept of educational freedom in the SC also serves to distinguish the freedom of creation of educational centres from the freedom of enterprise. The difference lies in the possibility of endowing the various levels of teaching with a specific ideological trend which may be manifest in a syllabus, an educational ideology or a specific nature, always within the framework of certain legal conditions.

The structure of the exercising of this freedom of creation of educational centres, which the SC guarantees to individuals and corporations, within the framework of constitutional principles, is regulated by ongoing legislation, with

Walter Berka, Jan de Groof and Hilde Penneman (eds.), Autonomy in Education, 405–426.

the SC establishing only the important general principles, which may be summarized as follows:

(a) The freedom to establish a particular ideology or nature, which while not appearing specifically in Art. 27 of the SC, is recognized by the Constitutional Tribunal (CT) in its judgment of 13th February 1981 (appeal against the Schools' Regulatory Act (LOECE)) and in Constitutional Tribunal Judgment (CTJ) 77/1985 of 27th June 1985, concerning the LODE (Regulatory Right to Education Act). The existence of an ideology is not a constitutional imposition, but a resource which may be used by the owners of educational centres and which manifests its main complexity in relation to the rights of other individuals involved in education – pupils, parents and teachers – and in relation to the general principles of the legal system. Any conflict arising between the ideology and other individuals' rights has to be settled by the courts.

(b) *The right of the owner to manage the centre as they see fit*, which, again, while not specifically regulated by the SC, is nevertheless a necessary consequence of the freedom of creation of educational centres, and this has been recognized by CTJ 77/1985 of 27 June. However, the freedom of management is limited by other rights, such as the one recognized in Art. 27.7 of the SC on the involvement of parents, teachers and students, if applicable, in the administration of state-subsidized centres. The LODE grants a series of powers to the *School Councils* which act in conjunction with the centre owner and, in some cases, this provides for a certain involvement by the Administration. The scheme is apparently designed to try and achieve a bringing together of interests in the daily running of the centre, starting with the initiative of the owner, without forgetting the important role assigned to the School Councils in the appointment of the Director, the hiring and firing of the teaching staff or the exercise of discipline on the students.

(c) *The possibility of public funding of private centres* does have, however, a direct link with the SC. Article 27.9 of the SC states that: '*the Administration will help educational centres to fulfil the requirements established by law*'. The interpretation of this clause – as a result of certain precedents – was definitively established by CTJ 86/1985 of 10 July 1985. The CT declared that Art. 27.9 of the SC does not impose subjective rights on funding which might give rise to jurisdictional challenges. This is a mandate to the legislator and, therefore, the legal conditions governing these pretensions originate from the law. This law cannot act against the rights and public liberties inherent in the educational system; neither can it violate the principle of equality and must respect the constitutional clauses governing public expenditure and the services of the Administration.

In the university field it should be emphasized that Art. 27.10 of the SC establishes clearly that: '*University autonomy is recognized, in the terms established by Law*'. For the content, scope and boundaries of university autonomy in Spain, we refer *in toto* to the paper to be presented at this Conference by Professor A. Embid Irujo, (see p.**) using some of his data in this report. University autonomy is a basic constitutional concept for the configuration of the regular legal system governing universities. The CT has made, and is still making, numerous pronouncements on this question, one of the most important being CTJ 26/1987 of 27 February 1987, delivered as a result of an unconstitutionality appeal lodged by the Basque Government against the LORU (University Reform Act). In this CTJ, the legal concept of university autonomy was defined as a fundamental right, which implies recognizing a subjective right for university communities making up each institution.

Article 3 of the LORU states that: '*Universities are incorporated bodies and carry out their functions on the basis of autonomy and co-ordination between them all*'. The autonomy of the universities is demonstrated in their self-government, which includes the drawing up of their statutes and other regulations, in their academic autonomy (syllabus), in their financial or administrative autonomy, including the management of their resources, and finally, in their power to select and promote their teaching staff and non-academic personnel, always respecting the principles of merit and ability, advertizing and non-discrimination which all Spanish public bodies are bound by. Restrictions on university autonomy are those arising from: (a) those imposed by other fundamental rights (e.g. equality of access to education, teaching and research), (b) the existence of a national university system which requires coordinative measures, and (c) those that are a result of the concept of higher education and university being a public service.

1.2. *Does the constitution guarantee teachers' educational freedom or the liberty of scentific teaching (academic freedom)?*

Article 20.1.c of the SC establishes the recognition and protection of : '*The right to academic freedom*'. The recognition of this right appears in a clause devoted entirely to regulating the forms of freedom of expression. As mentioned in the previous section, this is the affirmation of each teacher's *educational freedom*, whatever his/her category or level taught (CTJ 5/1981 of 13 February). Therefore the characteristics of its content and restrictions will be explained in detail in section 3.1 of this report, devoted to *Individual autonomy*.

1.3. *If autonomy is constitutionally granted: which notion of autonomy underlies the constitution?*

In addition to what is expressly regulated by the Constitution, the following international treaties and agreements have been ratified by Spain:

- European Community Establishment Treaty, Arts. 2, 3.n and q, 149 and 150.
- Universal Declaration of Human Rights, of 10 December 1948, Arts. 18 and 26.
- Convention for the Protection of Human Rights and Fundamental Liberties, of 4 November 1950 (BOE No. 243 10 October 1979), Art. 9.
- Additional clause to the Convention for the Protection of Human Rights and Fundamental Liberties, of 20 March 1952 (BOE No. 11 12 January 1991), Art. 2.
- Convention relating to the Fight against Discrimination in the Educational Field, adopted 14 December 1960 by the UNESCO General Conference (BOE No. 262 1 November 1969).
- International Agreement for Civil and Political Rights of 19 December 1966 (BOE No. 103 30 April 1977), Art. 18.
- International Agreement for Economic, Social and Cultural Rights of 19 December 1966 (BOE No. 103 30 April 1977), Art. 13, and
- Ratification Document of 4 December 1979 of the Agreement of 3 January 1979 between the Spanish State and the Holy See on Education and Cultural Agreements (BOE No. 300 15 December 1979).

The basic laws of the Spanish educational system which ratify the clauses in the Constitution are as follows:

- Act 8/1985 of 3 July 1985, regulating the right to education (BOE No. 159 4 July)
- Act 1/1990 of 3 October 1990, General Legislation of the Educational System (BOE No. 238 4 October).
- Act 9/1995 of 20 November 1995 concerning the participation, evaluation and administration of schools (BOE No. 278 21 November), which partly modifies the LODE and some clauses of the LOGSE (General Educational System Act). This reform overhauls the clauses in the Acts referring to participation, and completes the organization and functions of the administrative councils in schools funded with public money, safeguarding the autonomy of educational establishments and reaffirming with absolute guarantees the right to an education for all, without discrimination.
- Act 12/1987 of 2 July 1987, concerning the absence of charge for Bachillerato, Vocational Training and applied Arts and artistic trades in State schools and the autonomy of financial management in non-university State educational centres (BOE No. 167 13 July).
- Act 11/1983 of 25 August 1983 concerning University Reform (BOE No. 209 1 September).

1.4. *Are there strict legal bases and describe it.*

The tenor of the SC's clauses mentioned in this report, together with notes and comments on their legal reference, is as follows:

Art. 20.1. The following rights are recognized and protected ... (c) academic freedom. This is ratified in Art. 2 of the LORU and will be analysed further on.

Art. 27.1. All citizens have the right to an education. Educational freedom is recognised. Legal protection of these rights is regulated for in Art. 53.2 of the SC. Their protection is covered by the special procedure in Act 62/1978 of 26 December 1978 concerning legal protection of the individual's fundamental rights (BOE 3 January 1979). The rights recognized in this Article are ratified in Arts. 1 to 8 of the LODE.

2. The aim of education is the full development of the human character in consideration of democratic principles of coexistence and fundamental rights and freedoms.

The rights of students are ratified in Art. 6 of the LODE and RD No. 732/1995 of 5 May 1995.

3. The authorities guarantee the right held by parents for their children to receive moral and religious training in accordance with their own beliefs.

In addition to other regulations, the teaching of Religion is specifically legislated for in RD No. 2,438 of 16 December.

4. A basic education is compulsory and free.The concept of basic education is defined in Art. 5 of the LOGSE, with the age group being 6 to 16.

5. The authorities guarantee the right of all citizens to education, through a general syllabus, with the effective participation of all sectors involved and the creation of educational centres.

The general educational syllabus is legislated for in Arts. 27 *et seq.* of the LODE which, among other measures, set up a State Education Council, an advisory body of the Administration. RD No. 2,378/1985 of 18 December 1985 was responsible for regulating its workings. The Autonomous Communities have also set up and regulated Education Councils in their territories (Art. 34 LODE).

The Universities establish in their own statutes the mechanisms for participation of all sectors making up the university community in their self-government, including the drawing up of syllabuses, within the general guidelines established for each degree or title.

6. The liberty for individuals and entities to set up educational establishments, within the framework of constitutional principles, is recognized.

The creation of private non-university educational centres is legislated for in the LODE and RD No. 332/1992 of 3 April 1992, and the creation of private universities in Arts. 57 to 59 of the LORU.

7. Teachers, parents and, where applicable, pupils shall be involved in the management and administration of all educational centres funded with public money, within the guidelines established by law.

The right to participation in educational centres' governing boards has been ratified in Art. 6.1.e) of the LODE and in the LOPEG (Public Participation, Evaluation and Administration of Educational Centres Act). The exercise of this right is restricted by the provisions of Art. 12 of the LOPEG, which differentiates the degree of participation depending on the age of the pupil. Involvement in state educational establishments is legislated for in Art. 8 *et seq.* of the LOPEG, and for direct grant schools, in Arts. 54 *et seq.* of the LODE, some of these Articles being modifications of Articles from the LOPEG. Parents' associations are legislated for in RD No. 1,533 of 11 July, and Pupils' associations in RD No. 1,532 of 11 July.

In the University sector, each University's statutes are responsible for establishing and guaranteeing the representation of the teaching staff, students and non-academic staff on the governing and administrative board, Art. 27.4 of the LORU.

8. The Administration shall inspect and standardise the educational system with the object of guaranteeing compliance with the law.

Various RD's have set up Senior State Inspection Services for education and they operate for non-university education. Other services have as their remit the inspection of the granting of academic qualifications in the education sector covered by the LOGSE, the standardization and validation of foreign non-university qualifications and the establishment of Diplomas in Spanish as a foreign language. RD No. 928/1993 of 18 June 1993 legislates for the National Quality and Assessment Institute.

In the University sector there is the Universities Council, a national body, which functions as an active body within the Administration (Art. 23 LORU), as well as performing other advisory duties. Some ACs (Autonomous Communities) have set up similar bodies within their regions. Various RDs (Royal Decrees) legislate for the acquisition, granting and standardization of Spanish university awards, those granted by EU Member States and by other EEA Agreement states, and the validation of foreign higher education qualifications. Since 1995 there has been a National Quality Assessment Plan for universities.

9. The public authorities will help educational centres to fulfil the requirements established by law.

Articles 49 *et seq.* of the LODE set up *educational accords*, ratified by RD No. 366/1997 of 14 March 1997 and by various MO (Ministerial Orders). These educational accords are bilateral legal instruments whose content is predetermined by the regulations. The Administration's part of the agreement is to provide funds which will ensure the provision of an education without charge (including the salaries of the teaching and administrative staff, maintenance, renovations, etc.). The management of the educational centre is obliged to provide the education laid down in the accord without charge, in line with the syllabus in force, without receiving any financial consideration for this activity. It is bound by the organizational rules of the centre established by the LODE, and the authorization of extra-curricular activities and services which, without exception, are open to all pupils.

10. University autonomy, within the framework established by law, is recognized.

The LORU ratifies what Constitutional case-law, especially CTJs 26/1987 of 27 1987 February and 55/1989 of 23 February 1989, has pronounced as a fundamental right, with a collective as well as individual aspect, and as an institutional guarantee, which is in accord with its identification as a constitutional principle.

Art. 44.2. The public authorities shall promote learning and scientific and technical research for the benefit of all.

This precept is ratified by Act 13/1986 of 14 April 1986, concerning the Promotion and General Coordination of Scientific and Technical Research (BOE No. 93 18 April).

Art. 148. The Autonomous Communities shall have the right to be responsible for the following:

(15) Museums, libraries and Music Conservatories of interest to the Autonomous Community.

(17) The promotion of its culture, research and, where applicable, its language.

Art. 149.1. The State shall assume exclusive responsibility for the following:

(15) The promotion and general co-ordination of scientific and technical research.

(30) The regulation of the conditions for the acquisition, granting and standardisation of academic and professional qualifications and the basic precepts for the development of article 27 of the Constitution, with the object of guaranteeing the observance of the public authorities' obligations in this matter.

2. Autonomy of Educational Institutions

2.1. Is autonomy granted with respect to the organisation of educational institutions? Are schools or universities vested with a legal personality of their own? Have schools or universities individual constitutions of their own (basic statutes, basic charters)? Are these autonomously set up by the educational institutes or conferred on them by the State or government?

State educational institutions are those owned by a public authority (Art. 10.1 of the LODE). They are under the control of either Central Government or the ACs, or in some cases, local government. Responsibility for higher education not corresponding to the State has been entirely transferred to the ACs, a process completed in 1995. At present Spain is witnessing the transfer of responsibility for non-university education to the other nine ACs which as yet do not possess this competence, and so within the next few months the principles of political decentralization required by the SC and its ratifying Acts will have been completed as far as education is concerned.

State educational institutions are set up by the Government or, if applicable, by the Governing Council of the AC (Art. 17 LODE). They are bound by constitutional principles and the guarantee of *ideological neutrality* (Art. 18 LODE) as well as the respect for religious and moral options referred to in Art. 27.3 of the SC. This neutrality has been defined by CT case law, especially in the CTJ of 13 February 1981. They are not individual legal entities, and their regulations, depending on the type of education provided – infants, primary or secondary – are approved by the Administration that controls them: either central government or the ACs. They have pedagogic, financial and administrative autonomy (Art. 58.2 of the LOGSE and Art. 5 of the LOPEG).

Direct grant educational establishments are under private ownership and individual legal entities which have signed an educational accord establishing rights and obligations on both sides. This accord incorporates the institution into the state education network, offering its services to the general education programme. The institution's organization and configuration, admission of pupils, etc. is similar in many aspects to the state institutions, although it has the right to establish its own ideology and style.

Private educational institutions are owned by either an individual or legal entity and the type of ownership must figure in the MEC's (Ministry of Education and Culture) public register of institutions. They have their own legal title and autonomy to establish their own regulations, select their teaching staff in accordance with the qualifications required by legislation in force, determine the admission process for pupils, establish their disciplinary code and define their financial administration (Art. 25 LODE). They require official authorization to start operating as an establishment (Art. 23 LODE) if they provide general or special education, but this is subject to the observance of only certain requirements such as: the qualifications of the teaching staff, teacher–pupil ratio, teaching and sporting facilities and number of places available.

Public universities have their make-up defined in the LORU (Art. 3) and in their own statutes as Public Entities, Corporations or Institutions, as a public service, with their own legal title and capital, independent of the State and other public entities. They provide, within the framework of their competence, the public service of higher education and have autonomy in accordance with the SC and the law. They are established by Act of national or autonomous Parliament. The statutes of the universities, as established by CTJ 55/1989, although authorized by the LORU are not actually rules dictated by its ratification; they are autonomous regulations where the university's power of self-regulation is given substance in terms permitted by the law. They are approved by the governments of the ACs (Art. 12.1 LORU) and can only be controlled for their legality, not for their appropriateness.

Private universities enjoy autonomy, with one or two differences to that enjoyed by public universities, and are *recognized* by Act of national or autonomous Parliament. Their statutes are approved by the owner and the university community is involved in their drafting. Within the private university sector, special mention should be made of the Catholic Church universities and the appearance of a possible *tertium genus* in Spain, public universities under a private mantle, as is the case with the appearance of universities which are, legally speaking, private but where the AC government is the majority trustee in the foundation.

2.2. *How independently can they determine the recruiment of their personnel, etc?*

Non-university teachers in *state education institutions* have civil servant status. Their legal system is shaped by the general regulations of the Civil Service and by specific precepts for state teachers. In addition, the ACs may intervene in this sector, ratifying the basic state legislation (Art. 149.1.18 of the SC), and may carry out recruitment, transfers, appointments, grant licences etc. AP No. 9 of the LOGSE defines as the basic nucleus that derived from the Civil Service Act, plus certain rules belonging to the LOGSE such as admission, mobility, acquisition of head of department status, rearranging of departments and salary scales, the assigning of posts through competitive examinations on a national scale and any ratification of these matters that may be carried out. Access to the non-university state teaching service is by competitive examination under the auspices of the competent educational Authorities, in the same way as the assigning of posts.

The selection of non-university teaching staff in *direct-grant schools* is governed by the principles appearing in Art. 60 of the LODE: (a) public advertizing of vacancies; (b) the establishing of selection criteria by the School Council, with the agreement of the owner, governed basically by the principles of merit and ability; and (c) the owner, together with the Head, will then select staff in accordance with the selection criteria established by the School Council, to whom they are accountable for the assignment of the posts. In *private schools*, the selection of teaching staff is free, the only requirement being that the applicant possesses the qualifications required by the legislation in force.

In *public universities*, the teaching staff is regulated by the LORU (Arts. 33–48) and its modifications, in particular RD No. 898/1985 of 30 April 1985, concerning the status of university teaching staff, and RD No. 1,888/1984 of 26 September 1984, which regulates the competitive examinations for vacancies in the university teaching service. Also important is the part played by the University statutes which are empowered to set rules for situations not regulated by the LORU, such as in the non-permanent teaching staff sector. Teaching is carried out fundamentally by career civil servants belonging to the four Bodies established by Art. 33.1 of the LORU: University Professors, University

Lecturers, Training College Professors and Training College Lecturers. They are selected by competitive examination on a national scale. The examining Committees are formed by five members who are teachers of the subject in question, of whom two are chosen by the university offering the post, and the remaining three members are appointed by lot by the Universities Council. The members will belong to the body for which the application is being made.

However, the LORU as well as other Acts allow for the appointment of other categories of teaching staff with fixed-term contracts. Thus, in the same section dealing with the university teaching Bodies in the LORU, subsection 3 allows for appointment by the universities of: (a) *associate* lecturers, (b) *visiting* lecturers; (c) Art. 34 of the same Act allows for the appointment of *assistants* for Universities as well as Training Colleges; (d) to this list the figure of the *emeritus* professor must be added, a figure established by AP No. 7 of Act 30/1984 of 2 August 1984, concerning measures for the reform of the Civil Service. The selection procedures for these types of teaching staff are internal, and must comply with qualifications, requirements and principles of public diffusion, equality, merit and ability. Non-academic staff are appointed by each university in accordance with AC Civil Service rules and basic State Civil Service and labour legislation.

The selection of teaching staff for *private universities* is governed by each university's own procedure, although there are some minimum requirements as far as academic qualifications are concerned, such as the percentage of the staff who must hold doctorates.

2.3. *Are schools or universities entitled to choose freely among applicants with necessary qualifications?*

Access to educational centres is an essential component of the right to education. If the availability of places is lower than the demand, at *non-university level* there are some common principles valid for state schools and direct grant schools (Arts. 20 and 53 LODE), ratified by RD No. 366/1997 of 14 March 1997. These principles consist of establishing priority criteria such as annual household income, proximity of home or work-place of one of the parents and the presence of brothers or sisters on the school roll. In addition, there are other complementary criteria, such as the size of the family, registered disability and other circumstances freely applied by the school in accordance with objective criteria notified prior to the admission procedure. Each school's Council has the final word on admission of pupils (Arts. 42.1.c and 57.c of the LODE).

The LORU refers: (a) to the Act, for the regulation of access to universities (Art. 25); (b) to Central Government – *viz.* The Universities Council – for the setting of admission procedures to universities (Art. 26.2) and (c) the Board of each university, following the Universities Council report, for the rules governing students' staying at university (Art. 27.2). Act 30/1974 of 24 July 1974 regulates the entry exams for Faculties, Advanced Technical Colleges, Training Colleges and Training Schools and the text of this Act is ratified by regulations. It must be remembered that this was a pre-Constitutional Act, in force today as a regulation (FP No. 4 of the LOGSE), and therefore it would seem that a new regulation is needed to bring this entrance exam system in line with today's educational system in Spain.

RD No. 1,005/1991 of 14 June 1991 regulates admission procedure for university centres, with access being limited, basically, by the number of places available. The RD defines a system consisting of preference being given to those who have passed the entrance exam in the area where the university is located, the phases of granting of places (priority being given to those who pass the exam in June over those who do so in September), different criteria for administering admission, basically with reference to the grades obtained, with a portion of places being reserved for: those coming from another catchment area; those who already have university qualifications; foreign students; those with vocational training qualifications; certain disabilities and top-grade sports-men and women.

2.4. *Is autonomy granted with respect to the fulfilment of the educational objective? Can schools or univesities independently organise their curricula, decide autonomously on the numbers of students per class, etc.?*

The drawing up and approval of study and research syllabuses is another essential component of *university autonomy* (Art. 3.2.f of the LORU). This approval is not entirely free; it is limited by the State's power to establish basic legislation in the matter of education (Art. 149.1.30 SC). The Government, at the suggestion of the Universities Council, approves the general guidelines of syllabuses to be followed in order to obtain official academic qualifications, as well as their standardization (Art. 28 LORU). The universities, following these guidelines, draw up and approve the syllabuses, stating which subjects are compulsory and which optional, the number of hours (theory and assignments) for each subject, etc. These syllabuses are standardized by the Universities Council, which means an *a posteriori* control, but the Council may not interfere in the universities' discretionary rights. Those universities which foresee demand for places exceeding supply request the Universities Council to impose an entry limit.

For *non-university general education*, the existence of various educational authorities requires mutual co-operation in the question of objectives, content, methodology and assessment criteria, all coming under the heading of 'curriculum' in Art. 4.1 of the LOGSE. Central government is responsible for establishing the basic aspects of this curriculum in order to guarantee standard training for all students and the validity of qualifications. Fifty five per cent of class-time in ACs whose official language is not Spanish, and 65% in the other ACs is devoted to basic content established by Central government. The ACs with educational authority may then supplement these basic aspects in the class-time available beyond the percentage ceiling established by law. Thus, infant, primary, secondary, *bachillerato*, vocational training and special education each have their own curriculum establishing basic aspects and the way these aspects are supplemented by each AC with non-university educational authority. Similarly, other educational categories – the arts (music and dance, theatre, fine arts and design) and languages have their respective curricula.

2.5. *Autonomy of resources: Are schools/universities free to determine the raising and expenditure of financial resources? Do they have facilities to raise money through sponsoring or through other means, etc.? Are they able to charge tuition fees?*

Autonomy of resources in non-university *state schools*, recognized in Art. 58.2 of the LOGSE, Act 12/1987, the LOPEG and other legislative instruments, allows them to freely assign income obtained for services other than those raized by taxation, legacies, donations, sale of assets etc., to their running expenses. Their accountability is made more flexible by substituting the furnishing of detailed receipts with vouchers issued by the School Council. Any surplus available does not have to be handed over to the Authority, besides other aspects which fall within the parameters of autonomy and responsibility. Educational authorities may delegate powers to the state schools' management to purchase equipment, contract building work, services and supplies, all within the limits established by the pertinent regulations. The autonomy exercized by schools in administering these resources is subject to stipulations regulating the contracting, purchasing and justification of expenses process for the educational authority under whose jurisdiction they fall (Art. 7 LOPEG). Each school's Council has the power to approve its budget and subsequent administration. *Private schools* are run according to the type of legal entity they are, be they companies, educational trusts, educational co-operatives or any other type of legal entity recognized by law as competent to impart education.

Universities enjoy economic and financial autonomy within the framework established by the LORU. They draw up and approve their budget following the budgetary criteria of public authorities. Public universities' income comes from the annual subsidy established by the ACs – this being the highest proportion of their income: approximately 70% of the budget – tuition and other fees, subsidies, legacies or donations, income deriving from capital and other financial operations, income from research activities, and so on (Art. 54.3 LORU). They are subject to financial control by the Management Council, the body that approves the budget and settlement account, and, of course, by the courts of justice and auditors, or similar bodies, in the ACs that have them.

2.6. *Autonomy of organization for schools?*

In non-university education, *state schools* have autonomy to decide on their mode of *organizational management* (Art. 5 LOPEG). They set up and approve an *educational project* which defines the objectives, priorities and procedure, following the School Council's guidelines. When drawing up the guidelines the School Council has to take into account the characteristics of the school environment and the specific educational needs of its pupils, taking into consideration proposals made by the teaching staff. The organization of the school, as far as management, composition, powers and appointment procedures are concerned, is governed by the LOPEG: School Council, Teaching Staff, Head, Director of Studies, Secretary and, if applicable, Bursar. *Direct grant schools* may endow their educational project with their own style and their organization, as far as management bodies are concerned, is governed by Arts. 54 to 63 of the LODE, with the composition, powers and appointment procedures stipulated therein: Head, School Council, Teaching Staff. Other managerial departments, if applicable, are determined by each school's administrative system.

Article 4 of the LORU, from the point of view of *university organization*, states that this must be such that the representation of the various sectors of the university community is assured, in accordance with the functions corresponding to each one (Art. 1.2 LORU), as well as participation by representatives of social interests. This representative principle influences the making up of the university management and administrative bodies and the election of their members. Established as collegiate bodies are: the Management Council, the Academic Staff, The Board of Management, the Board of Faculties, Higher Technical Schools and Training Schools, and Councils of Departments and University Institutes. Individuals are: the Rector, Vice-rectors, the General Secretary, Deans of Faculties, Heads of Training Schools, Departments and University Institutes (Art. 13 LORU). The election process, powers and legal basis of these bodies are always, without exception, decided by the university statutes which nevertheless are required to comply with minimum requisites imposed by the LORU.

2.7. *Are schools or universites entitled to defend their autonomous sphere by legal means against the state or government? Do schools have the legal capacity to appeal against acts of a supervisory authority?*

It must be remembered that *the right to education* is regulated in the SC as one of the 'fundamental rights' requiring ratification by Act of Parliament – which needs a qualified majority for its approval – and possessing widespread protection, including the power to use summary proceedings for the re-establishment of the right when it is violated and even to apply to the CT.

This means that this subjective and fundamental right is held simply because it is subject to the protection of the Constitution, and possession of this right enables one to make claims against the public authorities and also against individuals (e.g. the owner of a private school). This is a right held by all Spaniards and foreign residents, not only students enrolled in educational centres.

This very wide protection afforded by our legal system for the defence of the right to education is modified when referring to the defence of educational centres' autonomy against educational authorities. Thus, *non-university state schools* under a public authority are not, in principle, regarded as institutions with power to contest directly agreements taken by the educational authority they are under, since, in line with the principle of administrative hierarchy, they would not have the legal capacity to do so. Nevertheless, they may contest these decisions indirectly through the holders of the right, if this right appears to have been violated. *Direct grant schools*, in the case of disagreements with the educational authority, are subject, in the first place, to the complaints procedure regulated by the LODE, Arts. 61 *et seq*. This procedure consists of a Reconciliation Committee, made up of a representative from the pertinent Educational authority, the owner of the school and a representative from the School Council elected by an overall majority of the Council among teachers or parents who are members thereof. If there is no agreement, the way is open for the courts to decide. *Private schools* can apply direct to the Courts provided they have complied with procedural rules.

The shared and convergent powers that exist in the university sector between Central Government, the ACs and the universities themselves give rise to tension and conflict. Universities may contest actions and decisions which do not enjoy legal status made by the ACs and Central Government. Protection may be obtained not only by regular judicial means, but also through preferential and summary proceedings before the regular courts and by means of an appeal for legal protection before the CT (Art. 53.2 SC). It must be remembered that the holder of the right to university autonomy, and therefore, the holder of entitlement, is the university community. Decisions made by Central Government and the ACs which do enjoy legal status cannot be contested directly by the universities, but they can be contested indirectly through the action of application of these decisions.

3. Individual Autonomy

3.1. *How much latitude of discretion is granted to teachers/professors in educational matters (content of education and methodological decisions)?*

The margin of *discretion* enjoyed by teachers in the matter of education is constitutionally guaranteed, in the present Spanish system, by the *fundamental right of academic freedom*, recognized by Art. 20.1.c of the SC. Following its historical evolution, this principle needed to be recognized constitutionally in order to give rise to a freedom of learning, somewhat in line with the evolution of the fundamental right of the *liberty of education*, which appears in Art. 27.1 of the SC, which complements the previously-mentioned right.

CTJ No. 5/1981 of 13 February 1981 states that academic freedom is a freedom before the State, or, in more general terms, before the public authorities, and its content is of necessity shaped by the specific nature of the post or chair whose possession gives rise to the exercise of this freedom: a combination of the status, public or private, of the educational centre in the first place, and the educational level of the post in question. This is, in substance, *freedom of expression*, with a uniform negative content, in that it enables the teacher to resist any order to give his teaching a particular ideological orientation, in other words, any orientation which involves a particular focus on natural, historical or social reality within the broad framework afforded by constitutional principles. This is a notion incompatible with the existence of official knowledge or doctrine, and it is worth noting that it has a broad positive content which was not analysed at the time. Academic freedom has to co-exist with the educational centre's own ideology or character.

3.2. *Is the head of a school (university) or any of its bodies entitled to issue instructions in professional matters to the teaching staff?*

The public authorities are obliged to guarantee the effective exercising of the right to education through an *overall education programme*, with the effective involvement of all sectors, which will adequately meet educational needs and the creation of educational centres, as stated in Art. 27 of the LODE. The Teaching Staff of *state schools* are responsible for the programming of teaching activities, the establishing and coordination of criteria for assessment and re-assessment of the students, as well as the coordination of orientation and tutoring of the students (Art. 45). *Direct grant schools* have the right to define their own character, but teaching must be imparted with full respect for the freedom of conscience (Art. 52) with teachers, parents and students being involved in the control and running of these centres, through the School Council (Art. 55) which participates in the application of the pedagogical scheme of the centre, and approves and evaluates the overall programming drawn up annually by the management team (Art. 57). *Private schools*, in other words, those that are not grant-maintained, may set up in their in-house regulations educational committees, with the involvement of teachers, parents and, if applicable, students, very similar to those described previously.

In the university sector, regulated by the LORU, the fundamental right of university autonomy is developed, recognized by Art. 27.10 of the SC, based on the principle of *academic liberty*, shown by the *freedoms of academic activity, research and study* (Art. 2.1), which, according to CTJ 26/1987 of 27 February, simultaneously includes an institutional guarantee and a fundamental right, containing an individual as well as collective aspect, the latter applying to the university community, made up of the teaching, student and non-academic staff sectors, in accordance with the functions corresponding to each sector, but guaranteeing that all are involved in the running of the university (Art. 4). All sectors are involved in the drawing up and approval of the study and research syllabuses (Art. 3.2.f). The verification of students' knowledge is the responsibility of the university as a legal entity (Art. 27.1) and not the right of individual teachers, according to CTJ 217/1992 of 1 December 1992. The syllabuses are drawn up by each university, detailing the subjects to be studied, whether compulsory or optional, for the granting of each academic qualification, and the time devoted to theory and assignments (Art. 29.1), although these syllabuses are standardized by the Universities Council.

The organization and development of research and teaching of each area of learning in one or several Faculties, Higher Technical Schools, Training Schools and other institutions, is the responsibility of the University Departments (Art. 8.1), in their role as coordinators of teaching and other activities (Art. 8.3). The Faculties, Higher Technical Schools and Training Schools manage and administer all university teaching leading to the granting of academic qualifications (Art. 9.1 LORU).

Therefore, subjectively, the central bodies, Departments and Faculties, Higher Technical Schools and Training Schools guarantee the fulfilment of the functions of the teachers. Materially, the syllabuses, the programmes determined by each department and the specifications corresponding to each teacher make up the content of the teaching imparted to university students, in a ratio that accepts various alternatives but which can in no way violate the individual teacher's freedom of academic expression. The level of autonomy enjoyed by the teaching profession is governed by the level of education imparted, whether in the infant, primary, secondary, *bachillerato*, vocational training or university sectors, categories fixed by the LOGSE.

3.3. *Do the teachers/professors participate in the universities or schools self-governing bodies?*

Teachers are involved in the self-government of the universities, and this principle is part of the right of university autonomy (Art. 4 LORU), by participating through universal, free, equal and secret vote in the election of all university management bodies, and especially in the election of the Rector by the University Senate (Art. 18.1). The Management Council is the body involved in the management of the university; it approves the budget and long-term planning, the supervision of the university's financial activities and return on its services (Art. 14.2). Two-fifths of the Council represents the Board of Management, among whose members the Rector, the General Secretary and the Manager must be counted, and the remaining three-fifths is nominated externally by an Act passed by the AC in question (Art. 14). The Council may not take decisions on academic matters (CTJ 26/1987).

The management bodies of non-university *state schools* are regulated by the LODE. The Head is elected from among the teachers by the School Council. The School Council is composed of academic bodies from the school, representatives of the City or Town Council, and a certain number of parents, students and teachers. The School Council decides on the admission of students, resolves conflicts and imposes disciplinary sanctions; it approves the school's budget, its overall syllabus, guidelines for extra-curricular activities, criteria for the school's involvement in cultural, sporting and recreational activities; the establishing of ties with other schools and the approval of the internal regulations of the school, among other things (Art. 42).

4. Consequences of autonomy

4.1. *If educational institutions can act autonomously, how are general aims or values like quality and unity of the education guaranteed?*

Educational institutions function with a high degree of autonomy in the university system, compatible with a coordination and planning by the State which is the responsibility of the MEC, with advisory input from the Universities Council made up of those in charge of university teaching, the Cabinets of the ACs, the Rectors of the public universities and fifteen members nominated from among people of recognized prestige or specialists in the various sectors of university teaching and research, designated equally by the Congress of Deputies, the Senate and the Government (Arts. 23 and 24 LORU). On a regional level, political coordination is carried out by the Minister of Education and Culture of that AC. The AC Parliaments exercise political control, which at a state level is exercized by the Spanish Parliament.

Non-university education is subject to control by those responsible for education in the respective Central and AC Governments (Art. 27 LODE), with the aid of the State Education Council, a national body for the involvement of all sectors affected in the general education programme and with an advisory capacity with respect to regulatory functions (Art. 30), with components representing all sectors of education.

4.2. *Is autonomy necessarily linked with a supervisory power?*

The aforementioned bodies also have powers of supervision, reinforced by the educational inspection system of each administration (Art. 61 LOGSE), complemented by the general assessment of the system carried out by the National

Quality Assessment Institute, a national body in which the respective educational administrations are involved (Art. 62).

The universities are subject to summary supervision by the various university bodies, and particularly by the Management Council (Art. 14.2 LORU). At AC level, the respective Parliaments have in many cases approved the setting up of university coordination bodies, on which the corresponding public and university authorities are represented.

4.3. *What are the relations between autonomy, responsibility and accountability? Is autonomy necessarily connected with quality control within autonomous educational institutions?*

The relationship between autonomy and responsibility in universities and the rest of the educational institutions is highly diverse. Particularly noteworthy is the degree of awareness shown by society towards its university, especially with more recently opened universities and in single-province ACs where regional government members tend to be part of the university, thus somewhat duplicating university government through instruments of control. Within the university, a certain effect of take-over of the educational functions of the university has tended to come about, as a sign of a weakness of social responsibility concerning university structures.

The system has shown more inflexibility in non-university sectors, since their degree of autonomy is lower and a greater power is exercized by Regional ministers with educational responsibility, and this greater responsibility reduces the framework of autonomy of the individual centres.

4.4. *If there are recent trends in your country with respect to autonomy of educational institutions: Is there a tendency towards enlargement of autonomy or towards more government control? Why is it so? (examples).*

The older universities have a more consolidated system of autonomy, which has been maintained with a certain level of self-sufficiency even in times when the legislation allowed for lesser powers of autonomy during the pre-democratic regime; a regime that could not suppress the autonomous vitality of the student and teaching collective, who at that time assumed a certain political responsibility tending towards social reform and claims for public liberties, including those beyond the purely educational scope.

Non-university centres have traditionally enjoyed lesser autonomy, as they are very heavily under the power of politicians. It has practically only been since the mid-1980s that a change has started to come about, albeit only in its initial stages and far from consolidation or actual format. This situation is marked by its heavy dependence on the educational authorities, and its very scant financial and decision-making autonomy. The negative birth-rate means having to re-format the structure of non-university centres, and this, together with the high cost of implementation of the new LOGSE educational system, at a time when there are restrictions on public expenditure, is hampering the attainment of genuine autonomy which the regulations have decreed, but which the present situation is hindering.

Literature

Arias Rordíguez, A.: *El régimen económico y financiero de las universidades*, Estudios Complutenses, Editorial Complutense, Madrid, 1997.

Bintanel Gracia, B.; Gurrea Casamayor, F., y, Madrigal de Torres, J.: *Sistema de garantías en los procedimientos de selección del profesorado no permanente en las universitades públicas. Órganos encargados de esta función, II Seminario sobre aspectos jurídicos de la gestión universitaria,* Universidad de Murcia, Murcia, 1996.

Bintanel Gracia, B.; Gurrea Casamayor, F.; Martínez Ballarín, A.; Santos Ortega, M., y, Solchaga Loitegui, J.: *Regulación del acceso a la universidad y de los procedimientos para el ingreso en los centros universitarios, en III Seminario sobre aspectos jurídicos de la Gestión universitaria,* Universidad de Zaragoza-Lex Nova-Ibercaja, Valladolid, 1998.

Chaves García, J.R.: *La universidad pública española: configuración actual y régimen jurídico de su profesorado*, Universidad de Oviedo, Oviedo, 1991.

– *Organización y Gestión de las Universidades Públicas,* PPU, Barcelona, 1993.

Chaves García, J.R., y, del Valle Pascual, J.M.: *Un enfoque jurídico sobre la investigación universitaria, en III Seminario sobre aspectos jurídicos de la Gestión universitaria,* Universidad de Zaragoza-Lex Nova-Ibercaja, Valladolid, 1998.

De Groof, J.: *Aspectos comparados en Europa en relación con la educación superior, en III Seminario sobre aspectos jurídicos de la Gestión universitaria,* Universidad de Zaragoza-Lex Nova-Ibercaja, Valladolid, 1998.

Del Valle Pascual, J.M.: *El profesorado universitario y la carrera docente,* «Actualidad Administrativa», 12, 1993.

– *Libertad de cátedra, I Seminario sobre aspectos jurídicos de la gestión universitaria,* Universidad de Castilla-La Mancha, Ciudad Real, 1995.

– *La función pública docente universitaria: diferencias entre catedráticos y profesores titulares,* «Revista española de Derecho administrativo», 87, 1995.

Del Valle PascualL, J.M., y, López Quevedo, M.: *Los Consejos sociales en el marco autonómico, II Seminario sobre aspectos jurídicos de la gestión universitaria,* Universidad de Murcia, Murcia, 1996.

Embid Irujo, A.: *El Tribunal Constitucional y la protección de la libertades públicas en el ámbito privado, El Tribunal Constitucional,* IEF, Madrid, 1981.

– *El contenido del derecho a la educación,* «Revista española de derecho administrativo», 31, 1981.

– *Las libertades en la enseñanza,* Tecnos, Madrid, 1983.

– *Derecho a la educación y derecho educativo paterno,* «Revista española de derecho constitucional», 7, 1983.

- *La jurisprudencia del Tribunal Constitucional sobre la enseñanza,* «Revista española de derecho constitucional», 15, 1985.

- *Los principios de la jurisprudencia ordinaria sobre la enseñanza tras la Sentencia del TC sobre la Lode, en X Jornadas de estudio de la Dirección General del Servicio Jurídico del Estado (Introducción a los derechos fundamentales),* vol. III, Madrid, 1988, y en «Revista de Administración Pública», 116, 1988.

- *La ampliación de competencias educativas,* «Revista Jurídica de Navarra», 7, 1989.

- *La autonomía universitaria: límites y posibilidades a través de la reciente jurisprudencia constitucional y ordinaria,* «Autonomíes», 17, 1993.

- *La transferencia de competencias a las CC.AA. en materia de enseñanza,* «Revista Jurídica de Castilla-La Mancha», 21, 1994.

- voces: *Administración educativa, alumno, autonomía universitaria, beca, catedrático, centro docente concertado, centro docente privado, centro docente público, concierto educativo, Consejo de universidades, Consejo escolar, Consejo escolar del Estado, Consejo Social, Departamento universitario, Derecho a la Educación, Disciplina escolar y académica, doctorado, educación compensatoria, enseñanza de régimen especial, enseñanza de régimen general, Estatutos de las universidades, evaluación, Instituto universitario, Investigación científica y técnica, lengua y enseñanza, plan de estudios, profesor asociado, profesor de enseñanzas no universitaria, profesor de enseñanza universitaria, profesor emérito, profesor titular, Rector, religión en la enseñanza, Título académico y profesional, y universidad,* en *Enciclopedia Jurídica Básica,* ed. Cívitas, Madrid, 1995.

- *El Consejo Escolar del Estado ante el final del proceso de transferencias educativas. Funciones, composición, expectativas,* «Revista española de Derecho administrativo», 90, 1996.

- *La enseñanza privada en España: consideraciones sobre su problemática actual en el marco de la política europea sobre educación,* «Revista española de Administración Pública», 142, 1997.

- *Informe sobre la conveniencia de promulgar una Ley Orgánica Reguladora de la Organización en régimen de autonomía de las Enseñanzas superiores artísticas en España,* Salamanca, Asociación española de centros superiores de enseñanzas artísticas, 1997.

- *La autonomía universitaria y la autonomía de las CC.AA.,* «Revista de Administración Pública», 146, 1998.

- *Las universidades privadas: régimen jurídico, III Seminario sobre aspectos jurídicos de la gestión universitaria,* Universidad de Zaragoza-Lex Nova-Ibercaja, Valladolid, 1998.

- *Legislación sobre enseñanza. Normativa básica y enseñanzas de régimen general,* vol 1, 2» ed. Tecnos, Madrid, 1998.

- *Legislación sobre enseñanza. Enseñanzas de régimen especial (Artísticas y de idiomas),* vol. 2, Tecnos, Madrid, 1995.

- *Legislación sobre enseñanza. Profesorado,* vol.3, Tecnos, Madrid, 1995.

Embid Irujo, A. y Gurrea Casamayor, F.: *Legislación universitaria. Normativa general y autonómica*, 6» ed., Madrid, Tecnos, 1997.

Gurrea Casamayor, F., *Políticas retributivas universitarias: complementos del profesorado*, «Revista Aragonesa de Administración Pública», 10, 1997.

Michavila, F. y Calvo, B.: *La Universidad española hoy. Propuestas para una política universitaria,* Síntesis, Madrid, 1998, p. 213.

MEC. Secretaría General Técnica: *Historia de la educación en España. Textos y documentos*, V tomos, MEC, Madrid, 1985-1990.

Muñoz Machado, S.: *La intervención del Gobierno en la delimitación de la autonomía universitaria, Tercer curso sobre régimen jurídico de las Universidades públicas*, Universidad Politécnica de Madrid, Madrid, 1995.

Souvirón Morinello, J.M.: *La Universidad española. Claves de su definición y régimen jurídico institucional,* Valladolid, Secretariado de Publicaciones de la Universidad de Valladolid, 1988.

Tardío Pato, J.A.: *El Derecho de las Universidades públicas españolas*, 2 vol., Barcelona, PPU, 1994.

FRANK NORDBERG

Autonomy in Education

SWEDISH REPORT

Ad.1.1. *Universities and University Colleges*
There are no guarantees in the constitution; however the Higher Education Act contains a directive about research which provides that problems shall be chosen freely, methods shall be freely developed and results shall be published freely.
Schools
Yes. The Swedish Education Act states that each individual municipality is free to decide how its schools should be run.

Ad.1.2. *Universities and University Colleges*
See answer above. The Higher Education Act also provides that as well as knowledge and skills education shall also give the students ability to exercise independent and critical judgement, ability to solve problems independently and ability to follow the development of knowledge in the area of chosen education.
Schools
No. The constitution guarantees teachers' educational freedom indirectly. There are no regulations in this field, and the government cannot intervene in education without an explicit regulation.

Ad.2.1. *Universities and University Colleges*
In Sweden the majority of Universities and University Colleges are state institutions. Their conditions are regulated by the Higher Education Act, which is issued by the Parliament, and the Higher Education Ordinance, which is issued by the Government. Inside those frameworks they have freedom to set up their own constitutions. The non-state Universities have a wider autonomy, since they are not subject to the Higher Education Ordinance and are only in limited dimension subject to the Higher Education Act.

Walter Berka, Jan de Groof and Hilde Penneman (eds.), Autonomy in Education, 427–431.

Schools
The municipalities are granted autonomy by the Education Act in this respect. The board of the schools in each municipality is to be looked upon as a legal personality. Each independent school (approved by the National Agency for Education) also has a legal personality. It is rare that schools have individual constitutions of their own, but they are free to set them up if they like, within the framework of the Education Act.

Ad.2.2. *Universities and University Colleges*
The recruitment of professors and other teachers is regulated in the Higher Education Ordinance, according to which those who have proven scientific and pedagogical skills are accredited to apply for the position. Further there is also a requirement of administrative skills and other skills needed relating to the subject content which the institution decides; and a referee's assessment of the applicants from one or two outside experts – depending on the kind of position – is also demanded. Anyone who has applied for but not obtained the position has a right to appeal against the appointment decision to the Appellation Board of Higher Education. Independent Universities and University Colleges are free to recruit their personnel, and their decisions are not subject to appeal.
Schools
For public schools there are regulations in the Educational Act about necessary qualifications for teachers. Independent schools are free to recruit their personnel.

Ad.2.3. See answers under 2.2.

Ad.2.3.b *Universities and University Colleges*
Every institution is given a block grant for undergraduate education, which is to cover all costs. For each institution the government also specifies every special activity. If the institution does not award the expected number of degrees their grant is reduced.
Schools
The Swedish Parliament and the Swedish government have defined the framework for the educational objective by national curriculum for both primary schools and secondary schools. They have also fixed syllabuses and timetables for public schools. Independent schools shall give education on a similar level as the public schools. There are no regulations relating to the numbers of students per class.

Ad.2.4. *Universities and University Colleges*
Tuition fees are expressly forbidden. They can raise funds by gifts,

research grants and contract teaching. That means that a corporation can make an agreement with the institution to educate their employees.

Schools

The municipalities are given financial resources for their tasks in general (they are not restricted to specific objects). Independent schools are entitled to financial support by the municipalities. All schools are free to raise money through sponsoring. Tuition is free in both public schools and independent schools. Neither pupils nor their parents usually incur any costs for teaching materials, school meals, health care, school transport, etc.

Ad.2.5. All schools are free to build up their organization.

Ad.2.6. *Universities and University Colleges*

State institutions cannot of course defend themselves by legal means against the government, since the State can not undertake legal activities against itself.

An independent institution can, of course, legally defend itself against the State, for example if the State is violating their mutual contract. State institutions are also under the supervision of the National Agency of Higher Education.

Schools

All schools are under the supervision of the National Agency for Education. Independent schools can appeal against negative decisions by the Agency. For public schools, the Agency can make critical remarks but not any binding decisions.

Ad.3.1. *Universities and University Colleges*

See answer under 1.12.

Schools

This is not regulated in the Education Act. It is a question for discussion within the profession.

Ad.3.2. *Universities and University Colleges*

The head of the department can decide about a teacher's presence at the department, the extent of the teaching load within the limits of the collective agreement, the allocation of time in the teaching load and which courses the teacher should teach. The individual teacher has the freedom to choose methods but is bound by the syllabus.

Schools

Yes. The headteacher of the school is pedagogical leader of the teaching and has the task of drawing up a local working plan based on the curricula, national objectives and the education plan. This must take place in consultation with teachers and other staff.

Ad.3.3. *Universities and University Colleges*
The teachers are entitled to appoint three out of of thirteen members of the board. The rector is also a member of the board. The rest of the members are appointed by the government.
Schools
For public schools there is a local board of education (municipal politicians). As a pilot scheme it is possible to form a board of Parents/Pupils and school staff. The final responsibility lies with the local board of education in those cases even.

Ad.4.1. *Universities and University Colleges*
The institution are under the supervision of the National Agency of Higher Education. The Agency makes quality audits, quality assessments of different education, supervises how the institutions adapt to legal demands, supporting pedagogical development activities, gather statistics and make investigations at the request of the Government.
Schools
The quality and unity of education is guaranteed by the national curriculum, syllabuses and time schedules. The Education Act has rules for necessary qualifications for headmasters and teachers.

Ad.4.2. *Universities and University Colleges*
See answer under 4.1.
Schools
Yes. The National Agency for Education has a supervisory duty to ensure that the provisions of the Education Act are complied with and that the rights of individual pupils are respected.

Ad.4.3. *Universities and University Colleges*
Yes. Quality controls are conducted by the institutions themselves but also by the agency.
Schools
The National Agency for Education has the task of developing, evaluating, following up and supervising schooling in Sweden. The Agency also makes survey controls by Educational Inspectors.

Ad.4.4. *Universities and University Colleges*
During the period 1990–1994 there was a strong development towards autonomy. During the years 1995–1998 there was a reverse action towards strong governmental control. The situation has now been stabilized and it is difficult to trace any definite tendency.

Schools

There is a tendency towards support for increased autonomy. The government has recently set up a committee with the task of overseeing the Education Act based on strong autonomy and self-determination

CHARLES GLENN

Autonomy in Education: United States

1.1. *Is autonomy of the educational system or some of its parts constitutionally guaranteed?*

Yes and no. The United States Constitution makes no mention of education; the state constitutions, in different ways, require state governments to promote education and, in many cases, give state government oversight responsibilities. Local public school systems are creatures of the state and, at least in theory, may be established, modified, or abolished at will be the state legislature.

There is important constitutional and statutory jurisprudence which protects non-public schools from excessive government regulation that would prevent them from expressing their distinctive character. The distinction between publicly-funded schools, operated in almost all cases by local government or by special government entities set up for the purpose, and non-public schools, which do not receive public funds (except for certain ancillary purposes in some cases), is much sharper in the United States than in most of Europe. An OECD study found that US public schools had *less* individual autonomy than those of comparable European systems, while US private schools have much *more* autonomy than those in Europe.

1.2. *Do the state and federal constitutions guarantee teachers' educational freedom or the liberty of scientific teaching (academic freedom)?*

No. The First Amendment to the US Constitution guarantees 'freedom of speech' in general, but teachers, in their capacity as employees and representatives of the schools that employ them, may be placed under reasonable limitations of what they may say to their pupils. Teachers in public schools may not use the classroom to promote their religious or political views, though it is by no means simple to draw the line between discussion of controversial matters

Walter Berka, Jan de Groof and Hilde Penneman (eds.), Autonomy in Education, 433–443.

and advocacy of a position. Similarly, the tendency of teachers to draw examples from their personal experience – including their sexual orientation – may in some cases cause offense on the part of pupils and their parents. As a result, there is an ever-growing jurisprudence around teacher freedom of speech, with some cases decided in favor of the teachers but most upholding the right of school officials to determine what is and what is not appropriate teacher classroom speech.

The controversy over this issue reflects not just the litigious nature of American society but also the system of local-government monopoly of the right to provide publicly-funded schooling in a particular area. Teachers and parents do not commonly find it easy to transfer to another school reflecting a different viewpoint on what is appropriate in the classroom.

By contrast, the freedom of non-public schools to select staff and pupils enables them to express and to enforce a distinctive ethos, and teachers and parents are less likely to engage in conflict over what teachers say or the assignments that they give. Nevertheless, there have been a few highly-visible cases of litigation arising from the determination of non-public school officials to discipline teachers whose teaching or personal behavior conflicted with the ethos of the school; generally, the courts have upheld the school's right to do so.

Instructors in higher education enjoy nearly-total freedom of speech, though in a recent celebrated case an African-American professor was deprived of his department chairmanship (though not of his teaching position) for teaching as fact views unsupported by historical evidence as well as anti-Semitic and racist. Faculties who express traditional religious views at élite institutions may experience collegial or occasional official disapproval, as is true of faculties who express radical political views at non-élite institutions. Evangelical and (to a lesser extent) Catholic colleges expect their faculties to refrain from criticizing beliefs and norms central to the institutional mission, though often they make a point of employing non-believers.

2.1. *Is autonomy granted with respect to the organization of educational institutions? Are schools or universities vested with a legal personality of their own?*

Public schools (with an exception to be noted) do not 'exist' as separate legal entities; it is the local school system which has a legal personality accorded to it by state law, and only the school system may execute contracts, be sued, expend public funds, and so forth, though of course it may delegate certain of its responsibilities to its agents at the school level. Local school systems may operate a single school or more than a thousand (New York City); there are more than 15,000 in the United States.

The exceptions are 'charter schools', an innovation of the 1990s. These are individual schools which have been granted charters by state government (or, in some states, by a public university or local school system) to operate as an independent public school under the supervision and control of a board – typically made up of parents and teachers – specified in the charter.

Non-public schools are operated under various auspices with a legal status regulated by state law. The states vary widely in their requirements for approval of non-public schools and thus for pupils who attend those schools to satisfy compulsory school attendance laws. Parents may also educate their children at home, and the statutes and jurisprudence regulating such home schooling also vary widely and are in constant change.

Public universities are agents of the state; non-public universities and post-secondary colleges are chartered by the state as independent legal entities. A special feature of the American university system in contrast with those of Europe is that, for historical reasons, both public and non-public universities and colleges are generally governed by boards of trustees made up of lay people (typically successful businessmen, distinguished citizens, and alumni representatives) rather than by government officials or their faculties. This sometimes causes tensions around questions of academic freedom, but it also contributes to their autonomy.

2.2. *How independently can educational institutions determine the recruitment of their personnel, etc.?*

There are essentially no legal restrictions upon what a public school system, a non-public school, or a university can do to recruit applicants, though most make special efforts to identify and encourage qualified applicants who are members of minority groups.

2.3. *Are schools or universities entitled to choose freely among applicants with necessary qualifications?*

Public school systems must in most cases comply with state law and regulations requiring that they employ only state-certified teachers, other professional staff, and administrators. Preliminary state certification is typically granted upon evidence of successful completion of a state-approved university-based academic program, including a period of practical experience under supervision. Permanent state certification typically requires several years of successful employment.

Public school systems may not discriminate in hiring on the basis of race, sex, religion, or other characteristics irrelevant to the position. In some states, 'sexual orientation' is also a protected category. Employment discrimination on the basis of handicap is forbidden if the school system can make a reasonable accommodation to permit the applicant to do the work effectively.

Non-public schools are in most states not required to employ state-certified teachers, though many make a practice of doing so. Those schools (and higher education institutions) with a distinctively religious character may make employment decisions on the basis of religious identity, under a provision of federal law designed to protect that distinctive character, but many do not, and this exemption does not apply to those schools whose religious identity has become residual or nominal. They may not discriminate on the basis of race or sex.

Both public and non-public higher education institutions may choose freely among applicants for employment on the basis of qualifications, but may not discriminate on the basis of race, etc., except in the case of those which are distinctively religious.

2.3. *Is autonomy granted with respect to fulfilment of educational objectives? Can schools or universities independently organize their curricula, decide autonomously on the number of students per class, etc.?*

Public school systems are subject to state laws and regulations; in some cases these specify detailed curricula and in other cases these do not. Some states have recently mandated limits on class size, but most do not. Choice of textbooks and other materials is left up to the school systems (which sometimes delegate the decision to each school), but in some states these books must be selected from a state-approved list. In general, states mandate the number of days of school, and sometimes state that in terms of number of minutes of instruction.

Collective bargaining agreements between public school systems and the local teacher and other unions frequently specify class sizes and many other elements of teaching conditions. These agreements are negotiated locally, though the two large teacher unions (the National Education Association and the American Federation of Teachers) exercise a powerful and sometimes predominant influence on legislative and administrative decisions at the state and federal levels.

Non-public schools have wide latitude in deciding how to fulfil their educational objectives, though they are expected to be generally comparable to local public schools. Their teachers are seldom organized in unions. States have exercised jurisdiction over non-public schools in many ways, even though many do not receive or seek public funds.

> The state can mandate that the instructional language be English (*Meyer*). The state can require private schools to provide an education that is 'basic', 'equivalent [to public education]' (*Yoder*, 406 US at 213), or an 'adequate education' (*Wolman v. Walter*, 433 US 229, 240 (1977)) that meets 'minimal educational standards' (*Yoder*, 406 US at 239). The state can regulate the 'quality and nature' (*Board of Education v. Allen*.

> 392 US 236, 245 (1968)) of the curriculum consisting of 'elemental skills' (*Wolman v. Essex*, 342 F.Supp. 399, 411, aff'd., 409 US 808 (1972)) and 'prescribed subjects of instruction' (*Allen*, 392 US at 246 (1968)) 'necessary for a productive and valuable life' (*Wolman* 342 F.Supp. at 411). The state may also set the standards requiring 'minimum' hours of instruction (*Allen*, 392 US at 246). Teachers may also be examined to ensure that they have received 'specified training' (*Allen*, 392 US at 246). The state may also inspect schools to ensure that they are in compliance with 'fire inspections ... building and zoning regulations' (*Lemon v. Kurtzman*, 403 US 602, 614 (1971)) and 'safety standards' (*Wolman*).[1]

In fact, however, the states generally exercise little effective oversight over non-public schools.

Public universities and other post-secondary institutions are subject to much less regulation than are public schools; control and influence are exercised primarily through the budgetary process.

Non-public universities and other post-secondary institutions, while more independent than their public counterparts, are subject to more government oversight, in general, than are non-public schools. For example, those institutions which prepare candidates for teacher and administrator certification must obtain approval from the state of the courses which will be provided. Since students attending non-public (including religious) higher education institutions are eligible for state and federal government grants and guaranteed loans, as pupils in non-public schools are not, there is a certain amount of reporting and oversight to ensure that these funds are provided for legitimate educational programs.

In general, however, the primary guarantor of the quality of higher education institutions, both public and non-public, and of non-public and public secondary schools, is some form of accreditation process carried out by associations of which the schools or colleges/universities are members. This 'peer accreditation' is based upon stated criteria of quality and periodic on-site reviews. How effectively this system works is a subject of considerable disagreement, and no doubt there is great variation in the nature and rigor of the standards employed.

2.4. *Autonomy of resources, fund-raising, tuition, etc.*

Public schools may not generally charge tuition, though pupils who do not live in the geographical area of a school district may be charged to attend its schools. In some cases, parents pay tuition to send their children to out-of-district schools, and in other cases school systems provide the tuition for pupils

[1] E. Vance Randall, *Private schools and public power: a case for pluralism*, New York: Teachers College Press, 1994, 75.

who seek an educational program (such as a language or vocational program) which is not available locally. Public schools may charge fees for supplementary activities such as instrumental music lessons. They may solicit funds from the public, from parents, and from alumni for various enrichment purposes; since public schools are not legally autonomous, such donated funds must be deposited in a municipal account and expended by special appropriation, unless a private foundation has been established for that purpose.

Non-public schools are in most cases supported primarily by tuition charges, though in some cases these are subsidized by endowments or by sponsoring churches. They can charge as much tuition as the market will bear, and raise funds in other ways.

Public universities and other post-secondary institutions in most cases charge tuition, though the level of tuition and other fees is often set by the state and not by the individual institution. Much of the income of these institutions is provided directly by state appropriation. Some – most notably the University of Texas – have substantial endowments as well.

Non-public universities and other post-secondary institutions charge tuition which they set themselves with an eye to the competition; they often have substantial endowments donated by alumni and other well-wishers.

Very substantial income from research projects in the sciences and social sciences, from federal government and business sources, is shared among a relatively small number of universities, both public and non-public.

2.5. *Autonomy of organization for schools?*

In general, both public school systems and non-public schools are free to determine their grade-structure (for example, whether the transition from elementary to intermediate school occurs at the sixth or the seventh grade, or whether the intermediate school is simply incorporated as the upper grades of the elementary school, through the eighth grade) and administrative staffing, departmental organization, and so forth.

2.6. *Are schools or universities entitled to defend their autonomous sphere by legal means against the state or government? Do schools have the legal capacity to appeal against acts of a supervisory authority?*

Individual public schools are the creatures of local public school systems and have no legal recourse against decisions of the district school board and administration (though well-mobilized parents may give them considerable political recourse and not-infrequently reverse unpopular decisions). In most cases they are highly constrained by collective bargaining agreements negotiated by their school systems with teacher and other unions.

Non-public schools have – and use – full access to legal resistance to decisions by government. The freedom from close government supervision enjoyed by non-public schools in the United States is not simply a reflection of neglect of institutions which do not receive public funding; it is also based upon several important decisions by the Supreme Court. In *Pierce v. Society of Sisters* (268 US 510 (1925)), the court struck down an Oregon law requiring all children to attend public schools until completion of the eighth grade, finding that this unjustly threatened the rights of private corporations (schools) to carry out their business and that it interfered with the right of parents to direct the education of their children:

> the fundamental theory of liberty upon which all governments in this Union repose excludes any general power of the state to standardize its children by forcing them to accept instruction from public teachers only. The child is not the mere creature of the state; those who nurture him and direct his destiny have the right, coupled with the high duty, to recognize and prepare him for additional obligations.

Subsequent decisions by lower courts have frequently invoked this decision to uphold the right of non-public schools to maintain their distinctive character against intrusive state regulation. In an important state-court case in 1976, the Ohio Supreme Court ruled that the state-mandated

> standards are so pervasive and all-encompassing that total compliance with each and every standard by a non-public school would effectively eradicate the distinction between public and non-public education, and thereby deprive these appellants of their traditional interest as parents to direct the upbringing and education of their children (*The State of Ohio v. Whisner*, 351 N.E.2d 750, at 768).

Nor may government, under the American Constitution, seek to make non-public schools or social agencies its instruments in imposing particular viewpoints.

3.1. *How much latitude of discretion is granted to teachers/professors in educational matters (content of education and methodological decisions)?*

It depends. The national government has no authority at all over what or how teachers teach. Some states have adopted specific curriculum guidelines, but in general it is at the local school system level that curriculum decisions are made.

Legally, there are few limits on the detailed specification of what and how teachers must teach. In fact, they have substantial – often very substantial – discretion. Public school teachers are subject to the instructions of and supervision by both the school principal and the school-system curriculum specialists. Non-public school teachers generally have to reckon only with their principal. On a scale from 0 ('no influence or control') to 5 ('a great deal of influence or complete control'), public school teachers nationwide replied to a government survey in 1993–94 as follows: discipline 2.7, curriculum 2.7, technique 4.3, grading 4.4, discipline 3.8. In each case, the ratings by non-public teachers were higher: 3.5, 3.4, 4.5, 4.5, 4.2, respectively.

In theory, states could seek (as commonly in Europe) to impose requirements upon non-public schools comparable to those they impose upon public schools, consistent with the *Pierce* decision of the Supreme Court, cited above, affirming

> the power of the state reasonably to regulate all schools, to inspect, supervise, and examine them, their teachers and pupils; to require that all children of proper age attend some school, that teachers shall be of good moral character and patriotic disposition, that certain studies plainly essential to good citizenship must be taught, and that nothing be taught which is manifestly inimical to the public welfare.

'Reasonably' is the key word here, and each state has had to work out its own balance between intrusiveness and respect for the autonomy of schools which it does not operate or (except in limited and indirect fashion) support. Must non-public school teachers be state-certified? How can government ensure that non-public schools are academically equivalent to public schools? Should the state somehow intervene if a non-public school is teaching racist doctrines? In most cases, the regulatory impact of government has been quite limited, but if we move toward more extensive public funding for non-public schools, on the model of most other Western democracies, these questions are sure to recur in acute form, as they have in other countries.

Professors in higher education have very substantial discretion in determining the content and method of their courses, subject to some process of peer review and, in the case of courses required for state professional certification, subject to state review. Except in unusual instances, both forms of review are perfunctory.

3.2. *Is the head of a school (university) entitled to issue instructions in professional matters to the teaching staff?*

In the case of schools, yes, both theoretically and practically. In the case of universities and colleges, theoretically yes but practically no. Faculties, especially in the research-level universities, defend their academic freedom vigorously. The most notable exceptions in recent years have involved individual faculty members who are accused – rightly or wrongly – of insensitivity on issues of race, sex, or sexual orientation; they may come under considerable pressures and receive little support from colleagues. The pejorative term 'political correctness' is commonly applied to such situations.

3.3. *Do the teachers/professors participate in the universities' or schools' self-governing bodies?*

It depends upon the arrangements made in each case, state-by-state and even district-by-district. Public schools (except for charter schools) are not self-governing, but many have parent-teacher boards which advise or even make decisions on certain matters. In Chicago (an exceptional case), these boards have very extensive powers. Most charter schools include teachers as members of their decision-making boards. Non-public schools do as they choose.

Professors participate in many levels of decision-making at colleges and universities, and sometimes have one or more seats on the board of trustees.

4.1. *If educational institutions can act autonomously, how are general aims or values like quality and unity of the education guaranteed?*

This is the most controversial issue in American education. The state governors and President Bush agreed upon a short list of national educational goals, but translating them into specific standards at the federal or state level and determining how to hold schools accountable to these standards has proved extremely difficult. No short answer is possible; this deserves to be the topic of the 1999 ELA Conference.

4.2. *Is autonomy necessarily linked with a supervisory power?*

To reiterate, individual public schools (except for charter schools) are closely supervised by the school systems to which they belong, and the latter in turn function within a framework established by state and to a lesser extent by federal laws, regulations and court decisions. The states differ greatly in how closely they regulate school systems.

Non-public schools – even Catholic schools which are part of diocesan systems – operate under much less outside supervision.

Public universities are under generally loose state government supervision, exercised primarily through the budgetary process. Non-public universities are largely autonomous.

While the federal government does not possess direct authority over schools or higher education institutions, it exerts considerable influence verging on control in some respects. The mechanisms of federal influence are threefold: (1) under the federal Constitution and various statutes, the federal government has the responsibility of enforcing civil rights protections, which in turn entails the authority to require submission of extensive data and to undergo reviews, either routinely or in response to a complaint; these can in turn lead to enforcement actions and to the withholding of federal funding; (2) federal funding represents only a small part of the budget (nationwide, less than 7 per cent) of public school systems, but the requirements attached to these funds frequently affect local decisions; higher education institutions are similarly influenced by federal research and facilities grants, while guaranteed student loans and tuition grants are an essential part of their budgets, especially in the case of private institutions which charge higher tuition; and (3) data-collection, reports, and federally-sponsored research have a considerable influence upon decisions made in states, school systems, and universities, and upon public perceptions of these decisions.

4.3. *What are the relations between autonomy, responsibility and accountability? Is autonomy necessarily connected with quality control within educational institutions?*

These are general, even philosophical questions, not easily answered within this format. The lack of decision-making autonomy and of accountability for results has allowed public school staff to be fundamentally irresponsible. Those – perhaps the majority – who do their best and who seek ways of serving their pupils better do so largely out of personal conviction and professional values, and not because the system is set up to reward and require such behavior. It is common for teachers and administrators to attribute poor results on the frequent standardized state or national tests upon the social class background of the pupils whom they serve.

Staff of non-public schools perceive themselves as having more control over their work, and are more directly accountable to satisfy the parents who pay to enroll their children. External testing plays a much small role for non-public schools, but the rate of graduates who go on to the most selective universities is watched closely.

How to make higher education institutions accountable for educational quality is a matter of intense debate at present, and some states – New York, for example – are moving to put quality control measures in place. There is nothing like agreement on how these can function.

4.4. *If there are recent trends with respect to autonomy of educational institutions, is the tendency toward enlargement of autonomy or towards more government control?*

There are clear trends, but they go in both directions. On the one hand, the development of hundreds of public 'charter' schools and the growing support for education vouchers, together with measures within local school systems to delegate more management responsibilities to the school level, have increased school autonomy. The development of national and state educational standards and associated testing, and higher qualifications for becoming a teacher, are vehicles for greater government control of schooling.

Trends are less marked within higher education. While there is considerable discussion of adopting quality standards for higher education, little progress has been made apart from some career-training programs.

RAINER FANKHAUSER

Development of Education Law in Austria

AUSTRIAN REPORT

In the first half of 1999 the most important Acts relating to school legislation were the adoption of the *Akademien-Studiengesetz* and of two amendments concerning the laws on school organization and instruction at schools.

Akademien-Studiengesetz 1999

In contrast to non-compulsory school teachers who must acquire a university degree, the initial training of compulsory school teachers is organized at *Pädagogische Akademien* or *Berufspädagogische Akademien.* While teachers for primary and lower secondary education receive their training at the first institution the second one is reserved for those who give instruction at technical and vocational schools (*Berufsschulen*) or teach vocational subjects at Medium or Higher-level Secondary Technical and Vocational Colleges.

In-service training is the responsibility of *Pädagogische Institute*. They are not only in charge of the compulsory sector of education but provide courses and programmes for all categories of teachers.

The organizational structure of all these institutions for the training of teachers is governed by specific chapters of the School Organisation Act (*Schulorganisationsgesetz*), a law that marks the beginning of school legislation in Austria, the first version of which dates from 1962. Concerning their inner functioning, however, no adequate legal basis has been established since then. Without the Parliament being involved they have been operating on ministerial decrees, a rather questionable procedure with respect to Article 18/1 of the Federal Constitutional Act, stipulating that the entire public administration shall be based on law.

The *Akademien-Studiengesetz* changes this situation. Applicable to all teacher-training institutions (including those in the field of agriculture and

Walter Berka, Jan de Groof and Hilde Penneman (eds.), Autonomy in Education, 445–448.

forestry) which are now summarized under the term *Akademien*, the law constitutes a framework with regard to study matters (enactment of curricula and examination regulations; admission and enrolment; crediting of examinations and periods of study; completion of studies; certificates; exclusion from studies), describes the competences directors, heads of departments, lecturers and curricular committees are endowed with and lays down the status of students including their rights and duties.

Among the law's guiding principles there is the obligation of the *Akademie* to provide a classroom-orientated training on a high level, solidly based on the results of educational science. The organization of instruction has to take into account the variety of pedagogical methods and theories and shall encourage mutual exchange between research and practical teaching. It ought to be aware of a European dimension in education. It has to respect the freedom of instruction and the institution's autonomy as stipulated by Acts of Parliament. Finally, the organization of instruction shall be tied to the principles of equal treatment of men and women and of equality of opportunities.

Based on a framework-ordinance issued by the Minister of Education and Cultural Affairs the curricular committee (*Studienkommission*) of the *Akademie* develops a specific curriculum for each of the programmes. According to the *Akademie-Studiengesetz* a curriculum must distinguish between required and non-required courses which must be categorized into lectures, seminars, exercises and block courses. It has to set the course contents, decides on the number of courses, prescribes the minimum hours of enrolment and assigns the required subjects to the respective stages of study. Furthermore, a curriculum must provide regulations concerning examinations.

In order to maintain a high quality of training the *Akademien-Studiengesetz* obliges the curricular committees to have a regular evaluation of study programmes, courses and examinations. The results obtained must be used on the spot for quality-development and in-service training.

For every type of *Akademie* management conferences (*Leitungskonferenzen*) will be established at federal level and at the level of each *Land*. The *Akademien* will usually be represented by their directors. Promoting and encouraging cooperation between the *Akademien* and designing a credit system for studies completed at universities constitute the main tasks of management conferences. Apart from these responsibilities they may also nominate members for the research board (*Forschungsbeirat*) established at the Ministry of Education and Cultural Affairs. The board not only advises the *Akademien* in developing focuses of research and in matters concerning evaluation but also proposes projects for educational research.

The *Akademien-Studiengesetz* has not changed the legal status of institutions in which compulsory school teachers are trained. These institutions are still considered as schools. However, the new legislation obliges the federal administration to create a new system (*Hochschule fürr Pädagogische Berufe*) within the following eight years. A system which shall incorporate adult education as well as other sectors belonging to education provided that they have not yet been reserved for universities. The *Hochschulen für Pädagogische Berufe* foreseen by the *Akademien-Studiengesetz* shall be entitled to award academic degrees. In order to enter as quickly as possible into the conceptual phase an evaluation of the existing system is going to take place. It will be carried out by an Evaluation and Planning Committee established at the Ministry of Education and Cultural Affairs. Based on the committee's work the Minister of Education and Cultural Affairs must prepare a report to the Parliament every year, informing it about the kind of progress that has been made in connection with the implementation of the new system.

School Organisation Act (*Schulorganisationsgesetz*)

To some extent the latest amendment to the School Organisation Act was caused by the Akademien-Studiengesetz. The amendment re-structures responsibilities in the field of teacher training, assigning initial training and postgraduate study programmes to Pädagogische or Berufspädagogische Akademien and in-service training to Pädagogische Institute. The latter are also involved in programmes concerning the probationary year for non-compulsory school teachers and may participate in some well-defined areas of initial training.

In connection with the final examination at the Pädagogische and Berufspädagogische Akademien the term 'Teaching Examination' will be replaced by 'Diploma Examination for the Teaching Profession'.

School Instruction Act (*Schulunterrichtsgesetz*)

The introduction of a single legal scope applicable to all school leaving examinations was the main reason for amending the School Instruction Act. The scope applies to all examinations on upper secondary level, including professional qualification examinations, matriculation examinations and the relatively new school-leaving examinations at Medium-level Technical and Vocational Colleges.

The regulation contains a framework regarding the organization of examinations and outlines the examination procedure It dwells on matters concerning the structure of examinations (written and/or oral), the composition of examination boards (the number of members has generally been reduced) and the role of the chairmen, examination dates, admission to examination, subjects of examination, decision-making on examination tasks, certificates, repetition of examinations and supplementary examinations. More detailed provisions will be contained in ordinances (*Verordnungen*) of the Minister of Education and Cultural Affairs. Within the constitutional system of Austria ordinances are regarded as subordinate legislation issued by the administration. Ministers are part of the administration. They or the government do not form a separate state function. In making use of its competence to issue acts of subordinate legislation the administration must respect the framework set by law. Ordinances that do not pay attention to this framework are considered an abuse of discretionary power which renders them unconstitutional.

With regard to the details of the amendment only the new provision on the repetition of examinations shall be mentioned. According to previous regulations a certain period of time had to expire before a student who had failed in one or more examination subjects would be entitled to do them a second time. The length of the period depended on the number of subjects that had been rated 'insufficient'. The maximum period could amount to one year. The provision introduced by the latest amendment has abolished all kinds of probationary periods. Instead, it fixes a time scope of three years in which the entire examination must be completed, leaving the matter of examination dates up to the students.

In order to guarantee compatibility in connection with examinations the School Instruction Act for Working Adults (*Schulunterrichtsgesetz für Berufstätige*) has been amended along the same lines.

List of Authors

JAN DE GROOF is Commissioner for Universities in Belgium (Flemish community) and professor at the University of Ghent. He is head of the European Association for Education Law and Policy (ELA). He has published several books and articles in the sphere of Public Law. He was head of the cabinet of the Minister of Education and Vocational Training.

HILDE PENNEMAN is scientific researcher at the 'Interuniversitair Centrum voor Onderwijsrecht' (ICOR) in Belgium.

CHARLES GLENN is Professor of Educational Policy at Boston University (USA), where he is Chairman of the Department of Administration, Training and Policy Studies. He is author of several books and articles on educational policy and practice. He has worked recently with Russian and Chinese education officials on comprehensive legislation.

MICHAEL GEISTLINGER is Associate Professor of International and Comparative Constitutional Law at the University of Salzburg (Austria).

NEVILLE HARRIS is Professor of Law at the School of Law, Social Work and Social Policy at John Moores University in Liverpool (UK).

ANDRÉ LEGRAND est professeur à l'Université de Paris X – Nanterre (France).

PAUL MEREDITH is Senior Lecturer at the University of Southampton (UK). He is joint editor of *Education and the Law* (Longman). He has been visiting professor at the Universities of Hamburg, South Carolina, Hanover and Groningen. He has published extensively in the field of Education Law.

DYMPNA GLENDENNING is a Barrister and was formerly a school principal (Dublin, Ireland).

THOMAS ROED JACOBSEN is Head of Section of the Department of Primary and Lower Secondary Education at the Ministry of Education in Denmark.

WALTER BERKA is Professor of Constitutional and Administrative Law at the University of Salzburg (Austria).

ROGER STANDAERT is Director of the Department of Educational Development at the Ministry of Education in Belgium (Flemish Community).

Walter Berka, Jan de Groof and Hilde Penneman (eds.), Autonomy in Education, 449–451.

WOLFGANG MANTL is Professor at the Institute of Public Law, Political Science and Administration at the University of Graz (Austria).

ELSA HACKL has a Doctor's degree (politics) and a Master's degree (Law). She is working at the Federal Ministry of Science and Higher Education in Vienna (Austria).

ANTONIO EMBID IRUJO is professor of Administrative Law at the University of Zaragoza and Chairman of the Spanish Association for the Study of Education Law and Policy (Spain).

BÄRBEL DORBECK-JUNG is Associate Professor of Jurisprudence at the Faculty of Public Administration of the University of Twente, Netherlands. She is the author of several publications on higher education legislation and Comparative Law.

CESARE ONESTINI is official at the European Commission, Directorate General XXII, Education, Training and Youth in Brussels (Belgium).

ANTONIO PEDRO BARBAS HOMEM is Assistant Professor at Faculdade de Direito de Lisboa and Invited Professor at Universidade Internacional (Lisboa), in the History of Law and History of Political Ideas.

ANTONIO ABREU is Counsellor for Education at Lisbon City Hall (Portugal).

HANS VISSER is Professor at the Department of Private Law at the University of Pretoria (South Africa).

ELMENE BRAY is Associate Professor at the Department of Constitutional and Public International Law at the University of South Africa. She also lectures part-time in education law in the Faculty of Education at the same university. She is a Deputy Director Inter-university Centre for Education Law and Education Policy of South Africa (CELP). She has published several articles on Public Law and Education Law.

BRECHT STEEN is assistant at the Institute for Education Law at the Catholic University of Leuven (KU Leuven, Belgium).

HANS PETER FÜSSEL is Professor of Administrative Law at the Hochschule für Öffentliche Verwaltung in Bremen (Germany). He has been active co-editor and author of a number of books and articles in the field of Education Law.

LUCIO GUASTI is a scholar. He is working at the Biblioteca di Documentazione Pedagogica in Firenze (Italy).

P.W.A. HUISMAN is a Lecturer at the Faculty of Law (Education Law section) at the Catholic University of Nijmegen (The Netherlands).

B.P. VERMEULEN is Professor at the Faculty of Law at the Catholic University of Nijmegen (The Netherlands).

H.J.M. HOEFNAGEL is General Secretary of the Education Council in The Hague (The Netherlands).

ARLINDO AZEVEDO is a Legal Adviser of the Rector at the Lisbon University (Portugal).

LUIS GUIMARAES DE CARVALHO is working at the International University of Lisbon (Portugal).

JUAN MANUEL DEL VALLE PASCUAL is Head of the Legal Department at the University Polytechnic of Madrid (Spain). He is also Vice-Chairman of the Spanish Association for the Study of Education Law and Policy.

FERNANDO GURREA CASAMAYOR is Head of the Legal Department and Lecturer in Administrative Law at the University of Zaragoza (Spain). He is Secratary of the Spanish Association for the Study of Education Law and Policy.

FRANK NORDBERG is Chief Legal Service at the National Agency for Higher Education in Stockholm (Sweden).

RAINER FANKHAUSER has a Doctor's degree. He is working at the Ministry of Education and Cultural Affairs in Vienna (Austria).

Yearbook of the European Association for Education Law and Policy

1. J. De Groof and H. Penneman (eds.): *The Legal Status of Pupils in Europe.* (1996). 1998 ISBN 90-411-0521-2
2. P. Akkermans, J. De Groof and H. Penneman (eds.): *Education Law and Policy in an Urban Society.* (1997). 1999 ISBN 90-411-1146-8
3. W. Berka, J. De Groof and H. Penneman (eds.): *Autonomy in Education.* 2000 ISBN 90-411-1311-8

KLUWER LAW INTERNATIONAL – THE HAGUE / LONDON / BOSTON

GPSR Compliance

The European Union's (EU) General Product Safety Regulation (GPSR) is a set of rules that requires consumer products to be safe and our obligations to ensure this.

If you have any concerns about our products, you can contact us on ProductSafety@springernature.com

In case Publisher is established outside the EU, the EU authorized representative is:

Springer Nature Customer Service Center GmbH
Europaplatz 3
69115 Heidelberg, Germany

Batch number: 10755284

Printed by Printforce, the Netherlands